THE **NATURE** OF

D1290319

INTERSECTIONS IN ENVIRONMENTAL JUSTICE

THE **NATURE** OF **HOPE**

Grassroots Organizing, Environmental Justice,
and Political Change

edited by
Char Miller and **Jeff Crane**

UTAH STATE UNIVERSITY PRESS | UNIVERSITY PRESS OF COLORADO

Published by University Press of Colorado
245 Century Circle, Suite 202
Louisville, Colorado 80027

 The University Press of Colorado is a proud member of
the Association of University Presses.

The University Press of Colorado is a cooperative publishing enterprise supported, in part, by Adams State University, Colorado State University, Fort Lewis College, Metropolitan State University of Denver, University of Colorado, University of Northern Colorado, Utah State University, and Western State Colorado University.

∞ This paper meets the requirements of the ANSI/NISO Z39.48-1992 (Permanence of Paper).

ISBN: 978-1-60732-847-6 (cloth)
ISBN: 978-1-60732-907-7 (paper)
ISBN: 978-1-60732-848-3 (ebook)
DOI: https://doi.org/10.5876/9781607328483

Library of Congress Cataloging-in-Publication Data

Names: Miller, Char, 1951– editor. | Crane, Jeff, editor.
Title: The nature of hope : grassroots organizing, environmental justice, and political change / edited by Char Miller and Jeffrey Crane.
Description: Louisville : University Press of Colorado, [2018] | Includes bibliographical references and index.
Identifiers: LCCN 2018041476 | ISBN 9781607328476 (cloth) | ISBN 9781607329077 (pbk) | ISBN 9781607328483 (ebook)
Subjects: LCSH: Environmentalism—United States. | Community organization—United States. | Political participation—United States. | Environmental justice—United States.
Classification: LCC GE195 .N42 2018 | DDC 363.7—dc23
LC record available at https://lccn.loc.gov/2018041476

The University Press of Colorado gratefully acknowledges the generous support of Saint Martin's University toward the publication of this book.

Cover photograph, "Native Nations Rise march in Washington D.C., March 2017," by S L O W K I N G. https://www.gnu.org/licenses/old-licenses/fdl-1.2.html.

Contents

Healthy Politics

Challenging Resources

Acknowledgments

The editing of a collection is a challenging and rewarding process. We owe a great deal to the contributors to *The Nature of Hope*: they wrote intriguing essays, hit every deadline, and believe in the project as much as we do. We also owe considerable thanks to Jessica d'Arbonne, formerly of the University Press of Colorado, who was with us every step of the way (and then some); she and her colleagues have been a joy to work with throughout the various stages of production. Char Miller is also indebted to co-editor Jeff Crane—naturally! A special dedicatory shout-out to his students and colleagues in the Environmental Analysis Program in the Claremont Consortium: for more than a decade, they have been raising incisive questions about the fundamental principles of US environmentalism and its oft-hesitant embrace of issues of access, justice, and equity. We have framed *The Nature of Hope* in part to advance these claims on the movement and, by extension, the larger society.

Jeff Crane thanks Char Miller, first and foremost. It has been a deep pleasure working with a top-notch environmental historian he studied in graduate school. As always, Jennine, Ella, and Chloe Crane have supported his work and endured the time apart as he wrote and edited others' work. Michael Egan helped conceive this book originally and is an inspiration in his commitment to helping ensure that environmental history remains relevant to the issues we face today. Andrew Lopenzina has been a steady and supporting voice, encouraging Jeff to maintain his commitment to scholarship. Similarly, Andrew Orr has been a wonderful companion in sharing ideas about scholarship and publishing. Sonalini Sapra has welcomed Jeff into her classroom to discuss food justice and community farming and generously edited a rough draft of his chapter. Finally, Jeff thanks the crew at the University of the Incarnate Word who supported community farming and challenged Jeff to become better at community engagement, more patient as an organizer, and positive in the efforts to create change. Monica Cruz, Denise Krohn, Michelle Wilk, Stephen Lucke, Jessica Thompson, Robert Langston, Chris Edelman, David Pryor, Barbara Aranda-Naranjo, Carlos Garcia, and Kathi Light, thank you for everything. He dedicates his efforts to the memory of Jim Crane and Bob Connelly.

THE NATURE OF HOPE

Introduction

CHAR MILLER AND JEFF CRANE

Hope. For poet Emily Dickinson, it is the "thing with feathers," a fearless lit-tle bird that "sings the tune without the words / And never stops at all." The fact that its voice can be heard even above gale-force winds is only part of its embodied power, metaphorical and galvanic. Another strength is reflected in its plumage. Individually, feathers are lightweight, immaterial. Yet when hooked together—hollow shafts inserted in skin—they provide insulation and uplift, warmth and flight.[1]

Hope. For novelist Barbara Kingsolver, it comes in the fragile form of the endangered and voiceless monarch butterfly, a central figure in her novel *Flight Behavior* (2012). A fictional homage to Dickinson's poetic insights, *Flight Behavior* also carries a political charge. In it, hope becomes a potent force for social change. Not to be confused with its smiley-faced analog, optimism, that oft-uncritical expectation that things will get better because they always get better, hope is made of sterner stuff. Securing its potential—fictively and factually—requires agency, intention, and action: lift. Hope is, Kingsolver observes tellingly in an interview about her novel, a "mode of survival" and

DOI: 10.5876/9781607328483.c000

a form of resistance. It is "how a cancer patient endures painful treatments. Hope is how people on a picket line keep showing up. If you look at hope that way, it's not a state of mind but something we actually do with our hearts and our hands, to navigate ourselves through the difficult passages."[2]

Navigators need charts to see and prepare for the shoals that lie ahead. *The Nature of Hope* offers one such mapping of the past as a guide, however complicated and fraught, to those who would act in and on the present and who seek a way forward to a more sustainable, just, and humane future. This book focuses on the dynamics of environmental activism and does so through an examination of the environmental and political cultures that have emerged in response to such contentious issues as mining in national parks, mitigation and adaption to the challenges climate change poses, and the dilemmas some South Texas communities have faced as their wealth and woes spiked with the advent of the hydraulic-fracturing boom. It probes as well the significance of urban farmers pursuing food justice, those confronted with toxic chemicals in the air and water, and others rallying to defeat a proposed expansion of a US air base in Japan. It also taps into the energy animating housing and worker-rights activists and those challenging the militarization of the US-Mexico border. Collectively, these chapters are also reflective of the drive for greater democracy, a politics of hope on the most fundamental of levels—human and ecological health—within communities large and small.

The stories these chapters interrogate demonstrate equally that local activism is as important and meaningful to the preservation of democracy as the protection of the environment, broadly defined. National environmental organizations such as the Sierra Club, the Nature Conservancy, and the Wilderness Society have grown into the hegemons of American environmentalism, exerting considerable influence in defining environmental issues at the national level and thus on the flow of money and political support to them and the issues they define as important. These organizations' dominance, for all their legislative success, has overshadowed the many community-based environmental battles that have profoundly shaped US environmental culture. These latter movements and moments are the focus of *The Nature of Hope*. In chapters framed around the fights over the wilderness areas in the Northern Cascades and the Stringfellow Acid Pits in Riverside County, California; brawls over flood control in San Antonio, Texas; battles to shutter coal-fired energy plants in North Carolina, and a host of other underreported struggles, this anthology illuminates the unsung and unstinting efforts of those fighting to protect the environments they inhabit. These activists—women and men, the poor and dispossessed, the young and old, those more vulnerable, others not—have pursued this work in the face of the failure of state and federal governments to adequately deal with the resulting degradation of air, water, and soil, food, infrastructure, and community life. In an age of environmental crisis, apathy, and deep-seated cynicism—to say nothing of a distressingly polarized political landscape—these engagements suggest how a politics of hope can offer an intersectional and compelling model of resistance, resilience, and regeneration.

Another objective of this book is to complicate assumptions about the paradigms that define the environmental movement in the United States—whether that involves certain celebrated, male leaders (think naturalist John Muir, the presidents Roosevelt, or activist David Brower); particular organizations such as Greenpeace; thematic orientations (such as conservationism, utilitarianism, and preservationism); or the human construction of nature and Nature viewed through an anthropocentric, romantic, or biocentric lens. There is nothing wrong with these varied classifications, but if we strictly or solely adhere to them, we will continue to overlook the powerful role of intersectionality in shaping the on-the-ground dynamics of popular protest and social change.

As the essays in *The Nature of Hope* make clear, new styles of leadership have emerged, which Bill McKibben likens to distributive energy production. The new structures of organizing are thus more horizontal and local than hierarchical and central. This shift is one reason why academics and activists need to pay closer attention to some of the critical implications that emerge from these stories about ecological activism so we can better understand why protecting the environment has been and remains so critical to sustaining the health of civil society (and vice versa). Consider, for example, the role the nation's wealth of nature has played in its development. Yet that development has always come at a cost, contested by those who disproportionately bear its burdens. Across time, Americans have organized in opposition to forms of ecological change and environmental degradation that have undercut their social status, community strength, and economic opportunities. Many of these principled efforts to protect or improve the environment have resulted in democratization at all levels of government: every campaign to preserve green space, limit pesticide poisoning, obtain environmental justice, or slow climate change has resulted in corresponding alterations—some limited, some not—in the political process. These include greater access to government documents and information, expanded participation by traditionally marginalized constituencies, and the creation of broad-based, intersecting political coalitions. The ongoing efforts of Americans—wherever they were born—to confront and resolve environmental issues has regenerated our politics while managing the core problems that affect everyone: clean air and water, disrupted climates, species protection, and the production of and access to healthy food.

To help identify some of these changes and their manifold ramifications, we have structured this anthology around a set of themes. The first, "Building Agency," lays out the theoretical terrain and ideological insights that set the stage for subsequent chapters. The title of Bill McKibben's essay—Movements without Leaders—speaks volumes (and directly to one of this volume's organizing motifs): that new models of leadership must guide the global effort to respond to climate change and its imperiling of all species. Indeed, he advocates what he calls a new "planetary architecture" of leadership that builds off the diligent work of innumerable local organizations and interest groups and charts an intersectional relationship between them. The result is a new kind of movement: "We may not need capital-L Leaders, but we certainly need small-l leaders by the tens of thousands. You could say that instead of a leaderless movement, we need a leader-full one."

Brinda Sarathy underscores and expands this compelling claim in her close analysis of the academic literature on environmental justice, as concept and praxis. At the heart of her project is how the theoretical and the applied intersect: "The concept of environmental justice is not only composed of discrete types (such as environmental racism, sexism, and classism)," she observes, but "these varying dimensions often interact together in important ways." The nature of these interactions matters "not just for the manifestation of environmental harm within a community but also for the shape of social movement activity in response to those harms." Sarathy's insight is then tested and revealed in Cody Ferguson and Paul Hirt's analysis of the degree to which environmental issues are debated, negotiated, and adjudicated on local, state, and federal levels. One of their focuses is on Save Our

Cumberland Mountains (SOCM), a grassroots organization in rural eastern and central Tennessee that in the 1970s emerged in opposition to landfills and strip mining. But these site-specific issues were also global in their reach: SOCM's members "were concerned about water and air pollution and the health of their families and communities; their understanding of environmental issues was tightly woven into ideals of good government and the notion that citizens ought to have a right to participate in decisions that affect their lives." These local activists discovered, as Bill McKibben would forty years later, that creating a more accountable, participatory, and transparent nation requires a long view, an enduring vigilance, and a deep commitment to the power of individual and collective agency—and a multitude of leaders. Such "can only happen with a spread-out and yet thoroughly interconnected movement, a new kind of engaged citizenry," McKibben writes. "Rooftop by rooftop, we're aiming for a different world, one that runs on the renewable power that people produce themselves in their communities in small but significant batches. The movement that will get us to such a new world must run on that kind of power too."

Identifying the physical environment in which such change has occurred and can occur is the subject of the second section, "Spatial Dynamics." Each of its chapters explores particular locations—Portland, San Antonio, Tachikawa, and the US-Mexico borderlands—and sets their specific environmental-justice challenges in their unique historical contexts. For African Americans whose neighborhoods abutted the Columbia Slough in Portland, World War II brought new work and housing; but as Ellen Stroud explores these glimmering opportunities, she also uncovers the racial segregation and social injustice embedded in a low-lying landscape wracked by floods, disease, and death. These social forces and health stressors circumscribed residents' life chances: "Throughout the second half of the twentieth century, the land near the Columbia Slough appeared on the cognitive map of many Portlanders as a throwaway place, an area best suited to industry and waste. That perception, which has a multiplicity of origins, was as much a cause as an effect of the environmental disaster at the slough."

Many of these same pressures confronted those living in San Antonio's flood-prone and dense west-side barrios. Char Miller probes how Communities Organized for Public Services, a Hispanic organization that emerged in the early 1970s to combat flooding in these impoverished neighborhoods, achieved its goals only after it undercut Anglo domination of that city's government and thereby gained access to local, state, and federal financial resources to develop flood-control projects that protected these oft-inundated communities. Political change was also the result of intense protests in the mid-1950s over the expansion of the US air base in Tachikawa, Japan. Its markers are embodied, Adam Tompkins and Charles Laurier argue, as much in the composition of the cross-sector, mass movement of farmers and urban residents taking on the US Air Force as in the final, striking result of their actions: the military base became a park, concrete turned into grass.

Those activists protesting the construction of the infamous border wall separating the United States and Mexico, just south of San Diego, have also pushed for a more sustainable, life-affirming solution. Under directives from the George W. Bush administration, in 2007 contractors began to erect a triple-layer structure that bisected Friendship Park and cut off access to that once open space, part of a 700-mile-long project designed to halt the undocumented from crossing into a post-9/11 America. Over the next three years, activists held weekly prayer vigils just off-site as well as routine meetings with US Border Patrol officials. Their engagement bore fruit in two directions—a binational grassroots movement emerged, stronger than either segment alone could have been; and for a time the Border Patrol conceded some ground such that families trapped on either side of the wall would be able to see one another. Still, as Jill M. Holslin points out, not all victories endure. Indeed, in 2018, the Trump administration, after further militarizing the border and criminalizing those seeking asylum in the United States, then tore immigrant children from their parents. The right to a salubrious environment proves to be an equally contested and polarizing issue in American society. This concept constitutes the heart of this volume's third section, "Healthy Politics." The right to a healthy environment emerged in the 1950s and 1960s. Then, families—especially mothers—found that they needed to question the impact of global military conflict on their children's bodies. Jeffrey C. Sanders analyzes a series of women-led peace groups and their activist rhetoric that fused protection of their progeny's health in the Atomic Age with a call to break the silence Cold War anti-communism inflicted on Americans because of the damage it was inflicting on American bodies. The "bones, blood, and thyroids of children living in the United States moved to the center of the political debate over nuclear testing," Sanders indicates, "and inspired a movement." Part of what made it so inspiring—and catalyzing—was how the activists developed and disseminated new knowledge about the life-threatening effects of radioactivity in defiance of corporate, state, and federal scientists. The pressing need to develop citizen science emerged anew in the 1980s. In response to the Reagan administration's concerted effort to block citizens' access to scientific expertise, argues Michael Egan, a pair of grassroots organizations galvanized "policy for their protection by doing the work they felt government agencies were not." Their struggles to examine the carcinogenic impact of industrial pollution in Woburn, Massachusetts, and the consequences of spraying daminozide on apple orchards ran up against stonewalling corporations and agencies. As a result, these groups were compelled to produce their own "reliable environmental information as a means of evaluating social risks," a popular epidemiology that became an "important strategy in confronting toxic fear"; this strategy remains a vital part of an American environmentalism worried about toxins in the air, soil, and water.

A related anxiety that has also generated new forms of local knowledge and an uptick in political engagement revolves around food production itself. In response to scientific evidence detailing the residual impact of spraying pesticides on crops, spikes in obesity and related health problems linked to ubiquitous fast-food restaurants, and the existence of food deserts in many poor neighborhoods, an urban agricultural movement sprang up in the last decades of the twentieth century. In tracking its historical development and policy implications, Jeff Crane asserts that community farming is an identifiable form of environmental protest that, among other things, can reclaim lost knowledge, restore human health, regenerate brown fields, and rebuild communal solidarity. Yet who is involved in these community deliberations and progressive outcomes and whose needs they are projected to meet are integral to these projects' success. Anna J. Kim and Sophia Cheng confirm that expanding the range of people directly engaged on such issues is necessary to create sustainable communities. Doing so requires that we recognize "the interconnectedness of the urban and rural, the human and environmental, the social and the natural." It is just as essential to "identify the links between paradigms" and to recognize the inequalities embedded "within them as symptoms of problems of the ecosystem." In a case study of this intertwining, Kim and Cheng assess the labor conditions of contemporary workers in Los Angeles and the layered injustices they endure. In this manner, exposure to toxins in the workplace, like wage theft, food insecurity, and environmental inequality, are parts of a larger whole, militating against human sustainability.

The effort to sustain communities became a good deal more complicated with the advent of the Trump presidency. In a spate of late January 2017 Executive Orders, the new president undercut the Patient Protection and Affordable Care Act (ACA) and froze the US Environmental Protection Agency's budget and hiring (while his political appointees to that agency wiped clean its hitherto robust data on climate change). He asserted that the border wall separating the United States and Mexico would be completed and he approved construction of the controversial Dakota Access Pipeline and the Keystone XL Pipeline. The latter is a signal of his administration's commitment to ramping up oil, gas, and mineral extraction while further delaying climate-change action—a point it hammered home when it pulled out of the Paris Climate Accord and radically undermined domestic environmental protections. These and other declarations, along with like-minded policies, immediately generated an array of grassroots protests and legal challenges, an oppositional strategy that has a lengthy history dating back to the early twentieth century. Those earlier confrontations did not always succeed, and the same mixed outcome surely awaits those who have resisted the latest efforts to put profits before people, to elevate the privileged few even farther above those who struggle to get by, to degrade America the Beautiful because they can. Yet however partial previous campaigns to build a more resilient society and healthier environments may have been, they are a vivid reminder of the need for and capacity of local activism to assert its claims in the public arena, to fuse its calls for enhanced environmental protections and social justice with demands for a more open, accessible, and activist democracy.

Tracking these related concerns are the chapters included in the fourth section of *The Nature of Hope*—"Challenging Resources." In his essay on the lengthy fight to stop Kennecott Cooper Corporation from extracting ore from within the Glacier Peak Wilderness Area in the Northern Cascades of Washington State, Adam Sowards sifts through public documents and private correspondence to recreate the tools activists employed to derail the project. However beautiful the landscape, however hopeful opponents were that its aesthetic qualities would change the corporation's mind, their real success—and hope—lay in the political arena: in "the constitutional system and citizen action—as well as a moral sense of right." This potent combination, Sowards writes, was "cause for resounding optimism." There were other factors: "Maybe the combination of copper prices, changing costs, and differing priorities tipped the balance." Yet as the historical record also makes clear, "grassroots action made a difference to that place and that place made a difference to the grassroots," a reciprocal process that is evident as well in Hugh Fitzsimmons's analysis of the politics of fracking in South Texas in the first decades of the twenty-first century. A rancher who reintroduced bison to its original range, Fitzsimmons has a personal stake in the damage to local water quantity and quality that hydraulic fracking in the Eagle Ford play has brought to his county, and this stake propelled him into the political arena: "It was time for me to stop complaining and start campaigning." He won a seat on the local groundwater conservation district and was immediately drawn into a series of fights over serious aquifer draw-downs, contamination of once potable-water wells, and resulting threats to public health. His learning curve was steep, as was that of the larger community, and for all their shared activism and negotiations with industry to slow its vast uptake of local water supplies, the ultimate collapse of this energy boom may have been the real savior.

Salvation was harder to find in North Carolina, a state Duke Energy dominates—a dominance that a broad-based, multiply led, anti-coal movement has fought to check. Monica Mariko Embrey contributed to the development of this statewide coalition opposing the Charlotte-based utility's dependence on fossil fuel, and her chapter therefore brings an insider's perspective to community organizing. It also contains an academic understanding of how this environmental-justice group's principles shaped its diverse, cross-generational, and deeply intersectional mission and objectives. This coalition's political potency is a direct result of its ideological commitments: "Building alignment between historically diverging environmental and environmental-justice movements," she notes, has enabled energy-justice activists to tackle "the most formidable fossil-fuel industry and utility adversaries," which in turn made it possible to address "the growing climate crisis."

Keeping fossil fuels in the ground and expanding a network of like-minded and intersecting alliances to disrupt the development and use of the nation's energy infrastructure have similarly informed protests surrounding the

Keystone XL and Dakota Access Pipelines. Bill McKibben's opening essay in this volume addresses Keystone; bookending it is the final contribution, Kyle Powys Whyte's analysis of how the Standing Rock Sioux, other Native peoples of the northern Plains, and non-tribal allies, beginning in 2012, battled the construction of the Dakota Access Pipeline (DAPL). Arguing that the project was one more expression of a settler colonialism that had long determined US and tribal relations and that its completion would degrade local water quality and inflict considerable harm on the cultural heritage of the Dakota and Lakota people (and had already destroyed ancestral burial sites), the tribes put their bodies in front of bulldozers. Knowing that direct action and personal sacrifice would raise national consciousness but would also need legal backing, their attorneys went to court. A mass movement around the call for sacred justice sprang up over the summer and fall of 2016. So forceful was the collective pushback that President Barack Obama, in the waning days of his administration, called for a delay in the pipeline's construction until completion of a full environmental impact statement. The fact that his successor, through a January 2017 Executive Resolution, green-lit the project only underscores the thrust of LaDonna Brave Bull Allard's argument about this struggle's enduring significance: "We must remember we are part of a larger story. We are still here. We are still fighting for our lives on our own land."

Sill here, still fighting. Unbending and unrepentant. Persistent and vigilant: hope.

Notes

1. Emily Dickinson, "'Hope' Is the Thing with Feathers," in *The Poems of Emily Dickinson*, ed. R. W. Franklin (Cambridge MA: Harvard University Press, 1999), 182.

2. Interview with Barbara Kingsolver appended in "p.s.," *Flight Behavior* (New York: HarperCollins, 2012), 7.

Building Agency

1

Movements without Leaders

How to Make Change on an Overheating Planet

BILL McKIBBEN

The history we grow up with shapes our sense of reality—it's hard to shake. If you were young during the fight against Nazism, war seems a different, more virtuous animal than if you came of age during Vietnam. I was born in 1960, and so the first great political character of my life was Martin Luther King Jr. I had a shadowy, child's sense of him when he was still alive and then a mythic one as his legend grew; after all, he had a national holiday. As a result, I think, I imagined that he set the template for how great movements worked. They had a Leader, capital L.

As time went on, I learned enough about the civil rights movement to know it was much more than Dr. King. There were other great figures, from Ella Baker and Medgar Evers to Bob Moses, Fannie Lou Hamer, and Malcolm X; and there were tens of thousands more whom history doesn't remember but who deserve great credit. And yet one's early sense is hard to dislodge: the civil rights movement had his face on it. Gandhi carried the fight against empire; Susan B. Anthony, the battle for suffrage.

DOI: 10.5876/9781607328483.c001

That is why it is a little disconcerting to look around and realize that most of the movements of the moment—even highly successful ones like the fight for gay marriage or immigrant's rights—don't really have easily discernible leaders. I know that there are highly capable people who have worked overtime for decades to make these movements succeed and that they are well-known to those within the struggle, but there aren't particular people the public at large identifies as the face of the fight. The world has changed in this way, and for the better.

It's true, too, in the battle where I've spent most of my life: the fight to slow climate change and hence give the planet some margin for survival. We had a charismatic leader in Al Gore, but he was almost the exception that proved the rule. For one thing, a politician makes a problematic leader for a grassroots movement because boldness is hard when you still envision higher office; for another, even as he won the Nobel Prize for his remarkable work in spreading climate science, the other side used every trick and every dollar at its disposal to bring him down. He remains a vital figure in the rest of the world (partly because there he is perceived less as a politician than as a prophet), but at home his power to shape the fight has been diminished.

This doesn't mean, however, that the movement is diminished. In fact, it's never been stronger. In the last few years, it has blocked the construction of dozens of coal-fired power plants, fought the oil industry to a draw on the Keystone Pipeline, convinced a wide swathe of American institutions to divest themselves of their fossil-fuel stocks, and challenged practices like mountaintop-removal coal mining and fracking for natural gas. It may not be winning the way gay marriage has won, but the movement itself continues to grow quickly, and it's starting to claim some victories. That's not despite its lack of clearly identifiable leaders, I think. It's because of it.

A Movement for a New Planet

We live in a different world from that of the civil rights movement. Save perhaps for the spectacle of presidential elections, there's no way for individual human beings to draw the same kind of focused and sustained attention they did back then. At the moment, you could make the three evening newscasts and the cover of *Time* (not *Newsweek*, alas) and still not connect with most people. Our focus is fragmented and segmented, which may be a boon or a problem, but mostly it's just a fact. Our attention is dispersed.

When we started 350.org in 2008, we dimly recognized this new planetary architecture. Instead of trying to draw everyone to a central place—the Mall in Washington, DC—for a protest, we staged twenty-four hours of rallies around the planet: 5,200 demonstrations in 181 countries, what CNN called "the most widespread day of political action in the planet's history." And we've gone on to do more of the same—about 20,000 demonstrations in every country but North Korea.

Part of me, though, continued to imagine that a real movement looked like the ones I'd grown up watching—or maybe some part of me wanted the glory of being a leader. In any event, I've spent the last few years in constant motion around the country and the Earth. I'd come to think of myself as a "leader," and indeed my book, *Oil and Honey: The Education of an Unlikely Activist*, reflects on that growing sense of identity. However—and it's the curse of an author that sometimes you change your mind after your book is in type—I've come to like the idea of capital L leaders less and less. It seems to me to miss the particular promise of this moment: that we could conceive of and pursue movements in new ways.

For environmentalists, we have a useful analogy close at hand. We're struggling to replace a brittle, top-heavy energy system, in which a few huge power plants provide our electricity, with a dispersed and lightweight grid, where 10 million solar arrays on 10 million rooftops are linked together. The engineers call this distributed generation, and it comes with myriad benefits. It's not as prone to catastrophic failure, for one. It can make use of dispersed energy instead of relying on a few pools of concentrated fuel. The same principle, it seems to me, applies to movements. This idea was behind the 2014 nationwide series of rallies called Summerheat. We didn't organize them ourselves. We knew great environmental-justice groups all over the country, and we knew we could highlight their work while making links between, say, standing up to a toxic Chevron refinery in Richmond, California, and standing up to the challenge of climate change.

From the shores of Lake Huron and Lake Michigan, where a tar-sands pipeline is proposed, to the Columbia River at Vancouver, Washington, where a big oil port is planned; from Utah's Colorado Plateau, where the first US tar-sands mine has been proposed, to the coal-fired power plant at

Brayton Point on the Massachusetts coast and the fracking wells of rural Ohio—Summerheat demonstrated the local depth and global reach of this emerging fossil-fuel resistance. I've had the pleasure of going to talk at all these places and more besides, but I wasn't crucial to any of them. I was, at best, a pollinator, not a queen bee.

Or, consider a slightly older fight. In 2012 the *Boston Globe* magazine put a picture of me on its cover under the headline "The Man Who Crushed the Keystone Pipeline." I've got an all-too-healthy ego, but even I knew that it was over the top. I'd played a role in the fight, writing the letter that asked people to come to Washington to resist the pipeline, but it was effective because I'd gotten a dozen friends to sign it with me. And I'd been one of 1,253 people who went to jail in what was the largest civil disobedience action in this country in years. It was their combined witness that got the ball rolling. And once it was rolling, the Keystone campaign became the exact model for the sort of loosely linked well-distributed power system I've been describing.

The big environmental groups played key roles, supplying lots of data and information while keeping track of straying members of Congress. Among them were the Natural Resources Defense Council, Friends of the Earth, the League of Conservation Voters, and the National Wildlife Federation—none spending time looking for credit, all pitching in. The Sierra Club played a crucial role in pulling together the biggest climate rally yet, the February 2013 convergence on the Mall in Washington.

Organizations and individuals on the ground were no less crucial: the indigenous groups in Alberta and elsewhere that started the fight against the pipeline that was to bring Canadian tar sands to the US Gulf Coast graciously welcomed the rest of us without complaining about how late we were. Then there were the ranchers and farmers of Nebraska, who roused a whole stadium of football fans at a Cornhuskers game to boo a pipeline commercial, the scientists who wrote letters, the religious leaders who conducted prayer vigils. And don't forget the bloggers who helped make sense of it all for us. One upstart website, InsideClimate News, won a Pulitzer Prize for its coverage of the struggle.

Non-experts quickly educated themselves on the subject, becoming specialists in the corruption of the US Department of State process that was to okay the building of that pipeline or in the chemical composition of the bitumen that would flow through it. CREDO (half an activist organization, half a cell phone company), as well as Rainforest Action Network and The Other

98%, signed up 75,000 people pledged to civil disobedience if the pipeline were to get presidential approval.

And then there was the Hip Hop Caucus, whose head, Lennox Yearwood, has roused one big crowd after another, and the labor unions—nurses and transit workers, for instance—who have had the courage to stand up to the pipeline workers' union that would benefit from the small number of jobs to be created if Keystone were built. Then there are groups of Kids against KXL and a recent grandparents' march from Camp David to the White House. Some of the most effective resistance has come from groups like Rising Tide and the Tarsands Blockade in Texas, which organized epic tree-sitting protests to slow construction of the southern portion of the pipeline.

The Indigenous Environmental Network has been every bit as effective in demonstrating to banks the folly of investing in Albertan tar-sands production. First Nations people and British Columbians have blocked a proposed pipeline that would take those same tar sands to the Pacific Ocean for shipping to Asia, just as inspired activists have kept the particularly carbon-dirty oil out of the European Union. We don't know if we'll win the northern half of the Keystone fight or not, but so far it's still tied up in knots. President Trump has granted federal approval, but great local activists in Nebraska and the Dakotas have forestalled state approvals. At a decade and counting, the pipeline company has already spent billions in extra carrying costs. However, it's already clear that this kind of full-spectrum resistance has the ability to take on the huge bundles of cash that are the energy industry's sole argument.

What the Elders Said

This sprawling campaign exemplifies the only kind of movement that will be able to stand up to the power of the energy giants, the richest industry the planet has ever known. In fact, any movement that hopes to head off the worst future depredations of climate change will have to get much, much larger, incorporating among other obvious allies those in the human rights and social-justice arenas.

The cause couldn't be more compelling. There's never been a clearer threat to survival or to justice than the rapid rise in the planet's temperature caused by and for the profit of a microscopic percentage of its citizens. Conversely, there can be no real answer to our climate woes that doesn't address the insane inequalities and concentrations of power that are helping to drive us toward this disaster.

That's why it's such good news when people like Naomi Klein and Desmond Tutu join the climate struggle. When they take part, it becomes ever clearer that what's under way is not, in the end, an environmental battle at all but an all-encompassing fight over power, hunger, and the future of humanity on this planet. Expansion by geography is similarly a must for this movement. Recently, in Istanbul, 350.org and its allies trained 500 young people from 135 countries as climate-change organizers, and each of them is now organizing conferences and campaigns in their home countries.

This sort of planet-wide expansion suggests that the value of particular national leaders is going to be limited at best. That doesn't mean, of course, that some people won't have more purchase than others in such a movement. Sometimes such standing comes from living in the communities most immediately and directly affected by climate change or fossil-fuel depredation. When, for instance, the big climate rally finally occurred on the Washington, DC, Mall in February 2013, the 50,000 in attendance may have been most affected by the words of Crystal Lameman, a young member of the Beaver Lake Cree Nation whose traditional territory has been poisoned by tar-sands mining.

Sometimes it comes from charisma: Van Jones may be the most engaging environmental advocate ever. Sometimes it comes from getting things right for a long time: Jim Hansen, the greatest climate scientist, gets respect even from those who disagree with him about, say, nuclear power. Sometimes it comes from organizing ability: Jane Kleeb, who did such work in the hard soil of Nebraska, or Clayton Thomas-Muller, who has indefatigably (though no one is beyond fatigue) organized Native North America. Sometimes it comes from sacrifice: Tim DeChristopher went to jail for two years for civil disobedience, and so most of us are going to listen to what he might have to say.

Sometimes it comes from dogged work on solutions: Wahleah Johns and Billy Parish figured out how to build solar farms on Navajo land and to crowdfund solar panels on community centers. Sometimes truly unlikely figures emerge: investor Jeremy Grantham and Tom Steyer, a Forbes 400 billionaire who quit his job running a giant hedge fund, sold his fossil-fuel stocks, and put his money and connections to work effectively fighting Keystone and bedeviling climate-denying politicians (even Democrats!). We have organizational leaders like Mike Brune of the Sierra Club and Frances Beinecke of the National Resources Defense Council or folks like Kenny Bruno and Tzeporah Berman, who have helped knit together large coalitions; religious leaders like Jim Antal, who led the drive to convince the United Church of Christ to divest from fossil fuels; and regional leaders like Mike Tidwell in the Chesapeake and Cherri Foytlin in the Gulf and K. C. Golden in Puget Sound.

Yet figures like these aren't exactly "leaders" in the way we've normally imagined. They are not charting *the* path for the movement to take. To use an analogy from the internet age, it's more as if they were well-regarded critics on Amazon.com review pages or, to use a more traditional image, as if they were elders, even if not in a strictly chronological sense. Elders don't tell you what you must do, they say what they must say. A few of these elders are, like me, writers; many of them have a gift for condensing and crystallizing the complex. When Jim Hansen calls the Alberta tar sands the "biggest carbon bomb on the continent," it resonates.

When you have that standing, you don't end up leading a movement, but you do end up with people giving your ideas a special hearing, people who already assume that you're not going to waste their energy on a pointless task. So when Naomi Klein and I hatched a plan for a fossil-fuel divestment campaign last year, people paid serious attention, especially when Desmond Tutu lent his sonorous voice to the cause.

These elders-of-all-ages also play a sorting-out role in backing the ideas of others or downplaying those that seem less useful. There are days when I feel like the most useful work I've done is to spread a few good Kickstarter proposals via Twitter or write a blurb for a fine new book. Conversely, in 2013 I spoke in Washington to a group of grandparents who had just finished a seven-day climate march from Camp David. A young man demanded to know why I wasn't backing the sabotage of oil company equipment, which he insisted was the only way the industry could be damaged by our movement. I explained that I believed in nonviolent action, that we were doing genuine financial damage to the pipeline companies by slowing their construction schedules and inflating their carrying costs, and that in my estimation wrecking bulldozers would play into their hands.

But maybe he was right. I don't actually know, which is why it's a good thing that no one, myself included, is the boss of the movement. Remember those solar panels: the power to change these days is remarkably well distributed, leaving plenty of room for serendipity and revitalization. In fact, many movements had breakthroughs when they decided that their elders were simply wrong. Dr. King didn't like the idea of the 1964 Freedom Summer campaign at first, yet it proved powerfully decisive.

The Coming of the Leaderless Movement

We may not need capital-L Leaders, but we certainly need small-l leaders by the tens of thousands. You could say that instead of a leaderless movement, we need a leader-full one. We see such leaders regularly at 350.org. When I wrote earlier that *we* "staged" 5,200 rallies around the globe, I wasn't completely accurate. It was more like throwing a potluck dinner. We set the date and the theme, but everywhere other people figured out what dishes to bring. The thousands of images that accumulated in the Flickr account of that day's events were astonishing. Most of the people doing the work didn't look like environmentalists were supposed to. They were largely poor, black, brown, Asian, and young because that's what the world mostly is.

Often, the best insights are going to come from below: from people, that is, whose life experience means they understand how power works, not because they exercise it but because they are subjected to it. That's why frontline communities in places where global warming's devastation is already increasingly obvious often produce such powerful ideas and initiatives. We need to stop thinking of them as on the margins, since they are quite literally on the cutting edge.

We live in an age in which creative ideas can spring up just about anywhere and then, thanks to new forms of communication, spread remarkably quickly. This is in itself nothing new. In the civil rights era, for instance, largely spontaneous sit-in campaigns by southern college students in 1960 reshuffled the deck locally and nationally, spreading like wildfire in the course of days and opening up new opportunities. More recently, in 2012, during that year's immigration rights campaign, it was four "Dreamers" walking from Florida to Washington, DC, who helped reopen a stale, deadlocked debate. When Lieutenant Dan Choi chained himself to the White House fence, that helped usher the gay rights movement into a new phase. But Dan Choi doesn't have to be Dan Choi forever, and Tim DeChristopher doesn't have to keep going to jail over government oil and gas leases. There are plenty of others who will arise in new moments, which is a good thing, since the physics of climate change means the movement has to win some critical victories in the next few years but also last for generations. Think of each of these "leaders" as the equivalent of a pace line for a bike race: one moment someone is out front breaking the wind, only to peel away to the back of the line to rest for a while. In movement terms, when that happens you not only prevent burnout, you also get regular infusions of new ideas.

The ultimate in leaderlessness was, of course, the Occupy movement that swept the United States (and other areas of the world) in 2011–12. It, in turn, took cues from the Arab Spring, which absorbed some of its tricks from the Serbian organizers at Otpor, who exported many of the features of their campaign against Slobodan Milosevic in the 1990s around the planet. Occupy was exciting, in part because of its deep sense of democracy and democratic practice. Those of us who are used to New England town meetings recognized its Athenian flavor. But town meetings usually occur one day a year. Not that many people had the stomach for the endless discussions of the Occupy movement, and in many cases the crowds began to dwindle even without police repression—only to surge back when there was a clear and present task (Occupy Sandy, say, in the months after that superstorm hit the East Coast). All around the Occupy movement, smart people have been grappling with the problem of democracy in action. As the occupations wore on, its many leaders were often engaged as facilitators, trying to create a space that was both radically democratic and dramatically effective. It proved a hard balancing act, even if a remarkably necessary one.

How to Save the Earth

Communities (and a movement is a community) will probably always have some kind of hierarchy, even if it is an informal and shifting one. But the promise of this moment is a radically flattened version of hierarchy, with far more room for people to pop up and propose, encourage, support, drift for a while, then plunge back into the flow. That kind of trajectory catches what we'll need in a time of increased climate stress—communities that place a premium on resiliency and adaptability, dramatically decentralized but deeply linked.

And it's already happening. The Summerheat campaign ended in Richmond, California, where Chevron runs a refinery with casual disregard for local residents. When a section of it exploded last year, authorities sent a text message essentially requesting that people not breathe. As a result, a coalition of local environmental-justice activists has waged an increasingly spirited fight against the plant. Like the other oil giants, Chevron shows the same casual disregard for people around the world. The company is, typically enough, suing journalists in an attempt to continue to cover up the horrors it's responsible for in an oil patch of jungle in Ecuador. And of course, Chevron and the other big oil companies have shown a similar recklessness when it comes to our home planet. Their reserves of oil and gas are already so large that, by themselves, they could take us several percent of the way past the 2°C temperature rise the world has pledged to prevent, which would bring on the worst depredations of global warming—and yet the companies are now on the hunt in a major way for the next round of "unconventional" fossil fuels to burn.

In addition, as the 2012 election campaign was winding down, Chevron gave the largest corporate campaign donation in the post–Citizens United era. It came two weeks before the last election and was clearly meant to ensure that the US House of Representatives would stay in the hands of climate deniers and that nothing would shake the status quo. And so our movement—global, national, and most of all local. Released from a paddy wagon after the Richmond protest, standing in a long line of handcuffees waiting to be booked, I saw lots of elders, doubtless focused on different parts of the Chevron equation. Among them were Gopal Dayaneni of the Movement Generation Justice and Freedom Project, who dreams of frontline communities leading in the construction of a just new world, and Bay area Native activist Pennie Opal Plant, who has spent her whole life in Richmond and dreams, I suspect, of kids who can breathe more easily in far less polluted air.

I continue to hope for local, national, and global action and for things like a carbon tax-and-dividend scheme that would play a role in making just transitions easier. Such differing, overlapping dreams are anything but at odds. They all make up part of the same larger story, complementary and complimentary to it. These are people I trust and follow; we have visions that point in the same general direction, and we have exactly the same enemies who have no vision at all, save profiting from the suffering of the planet.

I'm sure much of this thinking is old news to people who have been building movements for years. I haven't. I found myself, or maybe stuck myself, at the front of a movement almost by happenstance, and these thoughts reflect that experience. What I do sense, however, is that it's our job to rally a movement in the coming years big enough to stand up to all that money, to profits of a sort never before seen on this planet. Such a movement will need to stretch from California to Ecuador—to, in fact, every place with a thermometer; it will need to engage not just Chevron but every other fossil-fuel company; it will need to prevent pipelines from being built and encourage windmills to be built in their place; it needs to remake the world in record time.

That won't happen thanks to a paramount leader or even dozens of them. It can happen only with a spread-out and yet thoroughly interconnected movement, a new kind of engaged citizenry. Rooftop by rooftop, we're aiming for a different world, one that runs on the renewable power that people produce themselves in their communities in small but significant batches. The movement that will get us to such a new world must run on that kind of power too.

2

An Intersectional Reappraisal of the Environmental-Justice Movement

BRINDA SARATHY

For scholars engaged in the theory and practice of environmental justice (EJ) in the United States, the case of Warren County, North Carolina, looms large. Most consider the community mobilization against toxics in the county to be a foundational moment in the history of environmental-justice activism in the United States.[1] In 1982, Governor Jim Hunt of North Carolina approved the siting of a landfill in the small town of Afton, which was to receive 6,000 truckloads of soil illegally contaminated with polychlorinated biphenyl, or PCB. Although studies suggested that Warren County was not an ideal location for a landfill (because of a high water table and porous soils), Environmental Protection Agency (EPA) officials claimed that superior technologies would ensure that it would be "state-of-the-art, Cadillac, dry-tomb" and zero percent discharge.[2] Warren County was also rural, predominantly African American, and among the poorest counties in the state.

The state government expected little resistance, especially because it framed the landfill as a source of economic development. Yet the Hunt administration ended up fighting a protracted battle against a handful of

DOI: 10.5876/9781607328483.c002

residents organized as Citizens Concerned. Between 1979 and 1982, this group led a multilayered strategy, using due process to criticize EPA regulations and the state's biased science, as well as litigation. More important, Citizens Concerned successfully forged connections with non-local leaders in the black church, who connected them with experienced civil rights organizers. Although the residents of Afton eventually lost their fight against the landfill, the Warren County protests and ensuing arrests indelibly linked concerns about environmental justice to struggles for racial justice.

Through most of the 1980s and 1990s, scholars, activists, and government officials viewed issues of environmental justice in the United States of America primarily through the lens of environmental racism. While the work of more contemporary scholars and activists has moved beyond this simplistic framework, environmental justice–as–environmental racism still predominates in policy circles and thinking within government agencies. It is thus worth revisiting how this approach is lacking in at least two important respects. It is theoretically lacking because it privileges attention to one particular dimension of power and injustice (race and racism) and does not sufficiently consider the ways other dimensions of inequality may mitigate or exacerbate these injustices. It is also descriptively lacking because it limits the kinds of cases that were—and are still—viewed as seminal to the environmental-justice movement. This is evident not only in the selective reading of movement events such as Warren County, North Carolina, that are central to the articulation of environmental justice–as–environmental racism but also in the outright exclusion of several important cases of community mobilization from the dominant narrative of the environmental-justice movement in the United States.

In this chapter I analyze the development of environmental-justice scholarship through the 1990s and its predominant focus on environmental racism. Particular sites of environmental harm and particular narratives about those sites became an integral part of the environmental-justice movement's origin story. I then discuss how more contemporary scholarship has pushed the bounds of environmental-justice literature by incorporating multiple axes of inequality, critical race theory, and studies of spatiality. In spite of their incisiveness and importance, initial attempts to complicate the terrain of environmental justice remained largely conceptual and theoretical, while earlier, "first-generation" works continue to wield the most influence among outside players (agencies, the public, policy circles) and shape "common sense" about environmental justice. In the past decade, however, scholarship in environmental justice has become more multivalent in orientation and, as scholar David Pellow recently noted, is situated at "the intersections of eco-feminism, Indigenous studies, American studies, and ethnic studies."[3] The intersectional framework implicit in more recent EJ scholarship (which I return to at the end of this chapter) provides greater nuance through which to understand the varied processes leading to environmental injustice and both embodies and amplifies much of what I call for herein.

Through revisiting particular case studies of environmental injustice, I argue for a fuller and broader conceptual mapping of the environmental-justice terrain, extending Pellow's framework on environmental inequality by devoting more attention to understanding why the more general concept of environmental justice has been conflated and reduced to a particular subtype: environmental racism.[4] In building on Pellow's framework, I draw on theories of intersectionality to show not only that the concept of environmental justice is composed of discrete types (such as environmental racism, sexism, and classism) but that these varying dimensions often interact together in important ways. And these interactions matter, not just for the manifestation of environmental harm within a community but also for the shape of social movement activity in response to those harms. An expansive and intersectional approach to environmental justice can help us better understand the varying ways environmental harm affects different communities and also acknowledge the role of multi-racial and cross-class alliances in struggles for justice. Thankfully, a newer generation of EJ scholars and activists has assumed just such a mantle.

A Movement's Narrative: Environmental Justice as Environmental Racism

The rise of "environmental justice" in scholarship may be understood in part as a reaction to the oversights of mainstream environmentalism. Critics have long noted the race, class, and gender biases of the mainstream environmental movement in the United States, with its substantive focus on the conservation or preservation of non-human nature and the predominantly white, male, middle-class constituency of its membership and leadership.[5] Moreover, despite the historical specificity of particular environmental concerns, both "first-wave" environmentalism, which revolved around peo-ple's concerns about pollution and population growth wrought in the years after the Industrial Revolution, and "second-wave" environmentalism, which followed in the wake of World War II, have tended to present a universalistic conception of humans and their relationship to the natural world.[6] Thus, for example, the concerns of nineteenth-century preservationists to secure open spaces for communion with nature and post–World War II alarms about the deleterious effects of pesticides (or climate change today) reference an ostensibly uniform and homogeneous population without acknowledging or accounting for disparities in effects by race, class, gender, and other mark-ers of difference. Historical narratives about US environmentalism have also typically ignored the mobilization of minorities and working-class people to address concerns about public health in urban areas, thus perpetuating par-ticular notions of "the environment" and "environmental activism" that are inherently classed, gendered, and raced.[7] In contesting such narratives, schol-ars like Dorceta Taylor have argued that women and working-class people have engaged with urban environmental issues for well over a century and shown the emergence of struggles for environmental justice well before the civil rights movement.[8]

Yet the rise of environmental-justice scholarship is more than just a reaction to mainstream environmentalism's exclusions. It has also been a response on the part of scholar-activists to document and make sense of environmen-tal struggles in communities of color and forge alternative visions of what constitutes "the environment." The first self-defined scholarship on "envi-ronmental justice" in the United States was motivated by a handful of anti-toxics protests in predominantly black communities in the Deep South that connected the struggle for healthy environments with strategies and actors from the civil rights movement. Numerous scholars, policy-makers, and nonprofit organizations consistently reference several key events surround-ing the "birth" of the environmental-justice movement, including mass pro-tests by African Americans against the siting of a PCB dump in Afton, North Carolina (1982); the publication of a US General Accounting Office report that found three quarters of toxic waste facilities in eight southeastern states to be located in primarily poor and minority communities (1983); the publi-cation of the United Church of Christ's seminal study, *Toxic Wastes and Race in the United States*, which noted that race was the single most important determinant in the siting of toxic waste facilities (1987); and the gathering of activists from across the nation at the First National People of Color Environmental Leadership Summit in Washington, DC (1991). These events culminated in the government's recognition (some would say co-optation) of the environmental-justice movement with President Bill Clinton's passage of Executive Order 12898 (1994), which required federal agencies to account for environmental justice in their projects. Although these milestones are sometimes presented as discrete, often within a time-line format, they are integrally connected.

Participation in the Warren County protests in particular had a deep and lasting impact on many black organizers who had been active in the civil rights movement. Several of these individuals went on to spearhead a national environmental-justice agenda, and their actions proved integral in cementing the concept of environmental justice with environmental racism. In 1982, Walter Fauntroy, District of Columbia congressional delegate and chair of the Congressional Black Caucus, was arrested in Afton, making him the first member of the US Congress to be taken into custody for protesting. After returning to Washington, Fauntroy used his high-profile position to ask the General Accounting Office (GAO) to "investigate the demographic characteristics of communities near commercial hazardous waste facilities."[9] The resulting 1983 GAO report (which focused only on the southern states in EPA Region 4) found that three of four waste facilities in the South that required EPA permits had majority black populations and were below the poverty level. Although the report could not produce statistically significant correlations between siting and communities with a majority of people of color, organizers and activists nevertheless saw it as a foundational study that suggested that poor, minority communities were bearing a disproportionate share of environmental burdens.[10]

Ben Chavis was another civil rights organizer whose participation in Afton proved seminal for his emergence as a key player in the national EJ movement. In his eventual appointment as executive director of the United Church of Christ's (UCC) Commission for Racial Justice, Chavis allied with Warren County activists Ken Ferruccio and the Reverend Leon White to leverage funds for a large-scale study focused on substantiating claims about the disproportionate impact of environmental harms in low-income communities of color. The statistical findings of the UCC study, *Toxic Wastes and*

Race in the United States, became landmark and demonstrated that "the disproportionate number of racial and ethnic persons residing in communities with commercial hazardous waste facilities is not a random occurrence, but rather a consistent pattern."[11] The UCC report is one of the most cited works in environmental-justice scholarship and has spawned an entire literature of spatial analysis to evaluate the claim of racism in facility siting and community demographics. Even studies that have contested the report's conclusions have reinforced the hegemonic position of the environmental racism subconcept in understandings of environmental justice by keeping the primary focus on race.[12] The 2007 follow-up study, *Toxic Wastes and Race at Twenty*, reinforced these findings and noted that not much had changed since the original UCC report.[13]

Perhaps most significant to sealing the connection between environmental injustice and racism, however, was the public way in which Ben Chavis presented the findings of the UCC report as proof of "environmental racism" at the National Press Club in the nation's capital. Although Afton organizers had used this term openly in the past, it gained considerable traction in the post–civil rights context where government officials had to address charges of racism backed by substantive evidence.[14] The framing of "environmental racism" thus resonated with a larger public given the ongoing legacies of Jim Crow and persistent racial discrimination and segregation. And the charge fundamentally shaped the way agencies could respond moving forward.

Sociologist Robert Bullard, who many consider the "father of environmental justice," has also played a central role in constructing a narrative of environmental justice predominantly associated with environmental racism. Bullard is the most cited scholar in the environmental-justice literature, and his leadership in both academic and policy circles has set a research agenda focused largely on the proliferation of case studies about environmental racism.[15] Along with other prominent environmental-justice scholars and activists, Bullard was integral to organizing the First National People of Color Environmental Leadership Summit held in Washington, DC, in 1991. The summit sought to connect activists from communities of color who were fighting environmental harms, foster leadership of racial and ethnic minorities, and officially put forth the vision of the environmental-justice movement as embodied in the "Principles of Environmental Justice" (https://www.e

jnet.org/ej/principles.html). In his remarks at the 1991 summit, Bullard did not mince words when he urged delegates to accept that environmental justice should be first and foremost about race: "We can clearly document that the environmental problems that confront our communities cannot be reduced solely to class; it is not just a poverty thing. Middle class African American communities are just as affected by environmental racism as poor poverty-stricken urban ghettos and rural poverty pockets in the Deep South. It is not a class thing. Racism cuts across class. And we have to understand that and drive that point home every time some white media person tries to spin it into 'it's a class thing.'"[16]

Bullard's points about race versus class are certainly legitimate, and his intent was to keep the focus on institutional racism and the historic marginalization of people of color from environmental policy- and decision-making in the United States. Yet this prioritization of race potentially belies a tension with other stated principles of the environmental-justice movement, including the goal of building cross-class and multi-racial coalitions for justice.

Environmental-justice scholar Dorceta Taylor has broadened the argument by noting that although the concept of environmental justice acknowledges the ramifications and inequalities perpetuated by colonialism, genocide, and racism, it also moves *beyond* focusing only on the most oppressed to invoke the need for larger social movements across class and race lines.[17] Most generally, the concept of environmental justice strives to mobilize a movement for healthy and sustainable relationships with the natural world and the liberation of communities from all forms of oppression.[18] Given that such lofty ideals may only be achieved through the coming together of multiple coalitions, environmental-justice scholarship would do well to seriously engage with the role of multi-racial and cross-class alliances in particular struggles and more broadly consider the manifestation of environmental harm in a variety of communities. The issue of how gender intersects with race and class to produce varying degrees of injustice also merits greater scrutiny. Although contemporary scholarship in environmental justice does not explicitly deny the importance of such thematic areas, it nevertheless constructs a more rigid concept of environmental justice by simply overlooking such formations.

Overall, the Warren County demonstrations merged civil rights and environmental concerns in the minds of many influential black male participants, and these individuals went on to investigate those linkages through channels in government, the nonprofit world, and academia. In this sense, the scholarly genealogy of EJ has been constituted as much by particular intellectuals as by the events they participated in and wrote about. While none of this may be surprising, it is important to acknowledge the formation of an EJ epistemic community. And like epistemic communities in other disciplines and fields, EJ scholars have understandably—given the racism and white privilege in mainstream environmentalism and academia—emphasized certain issues, events, and players to construct a particular conception of environmental justice–as–environmental racism.

The Environmental Racism Frame

The predominant concept of "environmental justice-as-environmental racism" has been deployed by traditionally marginalized groups to make claims on the state and the private sector for compensation, relocation, and site remediation, as well as to solicit resources for grassroots organizing and to gain broader public support.[19] An environmental justice–as–environmental racism discourse has also increased mainstream awareness about the nature of environmental atrocities that impact specific regions and groups in addition to raising the profile of some community activists so they may bring their message to larger arenas. Environmental-justice scholars and activists have also succeeded in getting policies such as Executive Order 12898 (also known as the Environmental Justice Order) passed, thus providing an institutional framework for addressing claims of environmental racism. While the language of the Executive Order has been rightly criticized for its lack of enforcement authority and while individual federal agencies often have few resources with which to implement or evaluate EJ concerns, the policy still makes avenues available to communities challenging environmental burdens.[20] Indeed, even when litigation brought forth on the basis of EO 12898 has not in and of itself demonstrated a disproportionate impact, the litigious route has resulted in waste-disposal facilities locating elsewhere.[21] Thus, there is moral (if not always legal) traction to the claim of environmental racism, and it is has garnered results for various groups in the struggle for justice.

Expanding the Environmental Racism Frame in Scholarship

Over the past fifteen years, a new crop of theoretical literature and qualitative empirical studies has expanded the analysis of environmental justice.[22] Laura Pulido was among the first to theorize how injustice itself came about as a result of historical white privilege shaping the spatial configuration of particular places and peoples in relation to salubrious or insalubrious sites.[23] Implicit in her analysis was an expansion of environmental justice beyond environmental *racism*, to account for processes of *racialization*. Others such as sociologist David Pellow have articulated the concept of "environmental inequality formation," which considers the dynamic and varied intersections of environmental quality and social hierarchies/axes of difference. Pellow's concept might be further enriched with theories of intersectionality and critical spatial politics. For feminist scholars of color, intersectionality captures the complex interaction of social forces that produce particular women and men as members of specific races, classes, ethnicities, nationalities, and so forth.[24] Intersectionality also suggests that processes of racialization and gendering, while distinct, are interrelated and that particular identities or groups are mutually constituted through multiple dimensions of social relationships and subject formations.[25] An intersectional analysis thus demands an examination of the relational processes that produce social difference. Applied to cases of environmental injustice, an intersectional analysis demands paying attention to how specific subjects are constituted in relation to others, while spatiality (the relationship between social space and society) allows us to see how particular places are formed in relation to others.[26]

An intersectional analysis also shifts the question from whether a particular case does or does not "count" as an instance of environmental justice to how injustice plays out differentially for various groups to produce greater or lesser degrees of social inequality over time and space. Today, for example, many prominent environmental-justice scholars acknowledge the role of the anti-toxics movement in raising the salience of hazardous waste as a national problem. Yet these scholars also regard the larger anti-toxics movement as distinct from struggles for environmental justice (which is viewed as involving cases with a disproportionate burden on communities of color).[27] While scholars are right to assert that the anti-toxics struggles of working-class white communities are distinct from those of communities of color, does this mean that the former group's fights are not still cases of "environmental justice"? Theories of intersectionality and spatiality can help reframe this conundrum by showing that, while indisputable, both differences between anti-toxics struggles spearheaded by working-class whites and struggles against environmental racism in communities of color are ultimately rooted in processes of racialization and gendering rooted in place and the historical operation of white privilege itself.[28] Put another way, it is necessary to see how groups and places are continually formed in relation to each other within the socio-spatial context of race/gender/class privilege.

Thus, from a conceptual and theoretical standpoint, environmental justice needs to more actively account for injustices in numerous types of communities in addition to focusing on how racism impacts minority communities. If it does not do so, then the concept of environmental justice risks reinforcing the idea of race as skin color rather than examining how racialization has manifested and continues to manifest as a process. As scholar Evelyn Brooks Higginbotham notes: "The totalizing tendency of race precludes recognition and acknowledgement of intragroup social relations as relations of power. With its implicit understandings, shared cultural codes, inchoate sense of a common heritage and destiny, the metalanguage of race resounds over and above a plethora of conflicting voices. But it cannot silence them."[29]

In the realm of environmental-justice research and policy, the metalanguage of race is seen through a sustained focus on environmental racism perpetuated by policies, practices, or directives that "differentially impact or disadvantage [whether intended or unintended] individuals, groups, or communities based on race or color."[30] This conflation of environmental justice–as–environmental racism is in part a response to the elisions of the mainstream environmental movement and may be seen as an intentional and conscious move on the part of scholars to create a particular environmental-justice narrative that avoids the trap of minimizing or drawing attention away from institutional racism. This framing may also encourage whites (in roles as government policy-makers and nonprofit employees) to "suspend their awareness of persistent racialized distributions of privilege and to look only for expressions of racialized disadvantage."[31]

Cases of Intersectionality and Environmental Justice

Because Warren County played such a formative role in the lives of environmental-justice leaders and takes center stage in historical accounts of the environmental-justice movement, it is instructive to also examine what gets left out of the story of Afton, North Carolina, and note how strategic exclusions (which have also had benefits) help maintain a narrow conception of environmental justice-as-environmental racism. A closer look at the Warren County struggle reveals that local organizers worked in a fragile but necessary multi-racial coalition, initially mobilized by white residents but soon expanding to partner with outsiders including leaders in the black church, black politicians, and experienced civil rights organizers. Incidentally, Lois Gibbs's fledgling organization, Citizens Clearinghouse for Hazardous Wastes, allied with Warren County protesters and shared its experiences around fighting against toxics in Love Canal. This connection to other anti-toxics struggles, especially those spearheaded by working-class whites, is rarely mentioned in the telling of Warren County. Residents Ken and Deborah Ferruccio, who initially spearheaded the predominantly white group Concerned Citizens, were connected through black parishioners to the Reverend Luther Brown of Coley Springs Baptist Church. Given his standing as a black pastor, Brown was able to introduce Concerned Citizens to the politically active minister Reverend Leon White of the United Church of Christ (and a member of the UCC's Commission for Racial Justice) and the broader community of civil rights leaders.

In her detailed account of Warren County, Eileen McGurty notes that the relationship between the predominantly white Concerned Citizens and the UCC worked both ways. While Concerned Citizens needed to broaden its base of support, the commission also courted the group to politicize blacks and increase voter turnout in the county.[32] The Warren County multi-racial coalition, while certainly concerned about the disproportionate impact of harm on minorities, was also about poverty and the marginalization of rural residents more generally. None of this complexity is apparent in most environmental-justice narratives that reference Afton.[33]

Partly through an incomplete rendition of events at Warren County, numerous scholars and activists have constructed environmental justice as a concept that emphasizes environmental racism. While this may be strategic and understandable, it has also led to lost opportunities to explore and learn from experiences of multi-racial organizing more generally. In Warren County, for example, tensions arose when white residents opposed the appointment of a black member to an oversight committee on the grounds that he was a biased state official. While black members of Concerned Citizens also actively opposed the state, they were conflicted about vocally opposing a black representative (given the larger context of racism and black exclusion from politics). Similar tensions surfaced over the need to foster black leadership while at the same time resisting token politics. The point here is not to go into these issues in detail but rather to highlight how a narrow construction of environmental justice potentially forecloses examinations of the need for, and simultaneous challenges of, multi-racial coalitions in fighting injustice.

Love Canal and Environmental Justice

Although Love Canal is internationally known for its prominent role in launching the anti-toxics movement in the United States, it is not generally considered within the pantheon of environmental-justice scholarship.[34] Yet this case holds important lessons about coalitional politics.

Between 1920 and 1953, Hooker Chemical, a subsidiary of Occidental Petroleum, dumped chemical and municipal waste in Love Canal and subsequently sold the land to the Niagara Board of Education. The board then built an elementary school on the site of the former dump, and by 1978 there were approximately 800 private single-family homes (owned mostly by working-class whites) and 240 low-income apartments (housing mostly black and single-parent renters) built around the canal. The elementary school was located near the center of the landfill. Although area residents periodically complained of noxious odors or substances oozing up out of the ground, Love Canal only began to make national headlines in 1978, when a New York State Department of Health (NYSDOH) study found an increase in reproductive health problems among residents living on the canal's perimeter and elevated levels of chemical contaminants in the air and soil. This study was conducted in response to the persistent activism of the Love Canal Homeowners Association (LCHA), an organization formed by working-class area residents because of growing concerns about toxic contamination, human health, and plunging home values. During the crisis, media attention focused largely on the LCHA and white mother-turned-community-leader Lois Gibbs. Ultimately, the NYSDOH issued an emergency health order recommending the closure of the 99th Street School, evacuation of pregnant women and children, and limited time in basements. A couple of days later, the state agreed to purchase all 239 homes in the first two rings of homes closest to the canal. In 1980, President Jimmy Carter ordered a total evacuation of the site and announced that the government would purchase homes at fair market value. This much of the Love Canal saga is fairly well-known.

Yet Love Canal is also a story about primarily black female renters in Griffon Manor, a low-income federal housing project adjacent to the canal. Elizabeth Blum has recently shown that Griffon Manor residents not only faced racism from city officials who resisted the relocation of blacks to white neighborhoods in Niagara Falls but that renters also had to fight perceptions about welfare recipients being able to "simply pick up and leave" and being undeserving of monetary compensation because they had no property at stake.[35] Interestingly, black media did little to highlight the plight of black renters at Love Canal and did not portray their crisis in terms of civil rights. In response, renters formed the Concerned Love Canal Renters Association (CLCRA) and worked closely with the local NAACP and the primarily white, middle-class Ecumenical Task Force (ETF).

Part of the story of black marginalization is the dynamic of renters generally having less political recognition and power than homeowners. ETF members in particular played a critical role in leveraging their race and class privilege to keep the Love Canal Area Revitalization Agency (LCARA) accountable for the relocation and compensation of *all* renters, and CLCRA eventually maintained a less tense relationship with the LCHA, in part because women in both groups were insistent on a more inclusive solution to the Love Canal relocation. Yet any "victory" for Love Canal residents was fundamentally structured through intersections of racial and class difference. When the federal government agreed to assist the state of New York in purchasing homes and relocating residents in 1980, LCARA "allocated $500,000 for renters and $17.5 million for homeowners. LCARA began to purchase Love Canal homes well before the issue of how to deal with Griffon Manor, or even what benefits the renters would receive, had been settled."[36] At the same time, LCARA's allocation of funds for relocation expenses and monetary compensation for the least privileged—black renters—was largely the result of anti-racist, cross-class, and multi-racial organizing that pushed for achieving an albeit limited environmental justice. If it hadn't been for "outsiders" like the NAACP issuing legal threats and ETF members keeping in touch with Griffon Manor residents *after* the passage of Superfund legislation, it is possible that renters would have received no compensation at all.

At the same time, gender and class biases were also an important part of the story. For example, exposure to toxic waste posed particular harm to pregnant mothers. Given their central role in the social production and reproduction of labor, mothers also bore the disproportionate burden of caring for schoolchildren made ill from toxic exposure. More important, race, gender, and class intersect to produce different outcomes in terms of how working-class mothers contextualized their demands for safer homes and communities. In expressing outrage at and disenchantment with government scientists and policy-makers for their initial lack of response to the Love Canal crisis, for example, Lois Gibbs reveals her race privilege: "I grew up in a blue-collar community, it was very patriotic, into democracy . . . I believed in government . . . I believed that if you had a complaint, you went to the right person in the government. If there was a way to solve the problem, they would be glad to do it."[37]

In contrast, the mostly single black mothers of Griffin Manor never held impressions of a government invested in their community. Embedded within their class disadvantage is a history of racial housing covenants and discrimination by realtors and lenders. In the post–World War II context, moreover, images of black women as either aggressive matriarchs or lazy welfare recipients further fueled racial stereotypes about "bad black mothers" and provided ideological (and policy) justifications for interlocking systems of race, gender, and class oppression.[38] In the case of Love Canal, government officials may have unconsciously mobilized such class and gender stereotypes to blame black mothers for their own victimization and thus impede an already slow response to their relocation and compensation.[39] Given lived experiences of disproportionate marginalization and harm, black women played a significant role in bringing the concerns of renters to the larger movement.

Finally, the environmental harm in Love Canal also had a disproportionate class impact. While the majority of those affected were homeowners, these were individuals of modest means, low education, and limited connection to avenues of political power.[40] These disadvantages were apparent throughout the struggle to get government attention, relocation, and compensation. For instance, residents and advocates pressed the state government to conduct studies of soil and groundwater contamination and the impacts on public health. The NYSDOH resisted these calls and consented only after residents initiated their own community-based studies and went to the press. Here, the race privilege of white women such as Lois Gibbs was attenuated by their lesser gender and class privilege, relative to state health experts. Yet once they were in the media spotlight, Gibbs's and her counterparts' white privilege likely helped keep Love Canal salient for federal policy-makers who moved to take action. Social movement organization and relative valences in race, class, and gender privilege thus all played a role in the ability of Love Canal residents to overcome their political and educational disadvantages and advocate for redress against environmental injustice.

Glen Avon and Environmental Justice

The case of the Stringfellow Acid Pits in Glen Avon, California, holds some important lessons about the role of community anti-toxics mobilization in laying the groundwork for future organizing for environmental and social justice. It demonstrates, for example, that organizing against environmental burdens by working-class whites can sow seeds for later multi-racial alliances against environmental racism. In the canyon above the town of Glen Avon sat the Stringfellow Acid Pits (SAP), one of the largest chemical dumping operations in the country. Between 1956 and 1972, hundreds of companies emptied toxic wastes into unlined pits, erroneously assuming that the bedrock below would prevent the migration of toxins into groundwater.[41] In 1972, unwilling and financially unable to comply with stricter environmental regulations, the dump's owner, James B. Stringfellow, declared bankruptcy and foreclosed on the property, which then passed to the state of California. Between 1969 and 1980, heavy rains coupled with poor site management led to several *intentional* releases of toxic waters into the surrounding area of Glen Avon. Particularly heavy flooding in 1978 resulted in the release of over 1 million gallons of toxic effluent from the SAP. This waste flowed through Glen Avon for five days, but government officials did little to warn residents about the hazards of contamination and human exposure. These threats and hazards included mutagenic effects; irritation to skin, eyes, and mucous membranes; nausea; headaches; respiratory problems; and cancer.[42]

At the time of the Stringfellow disaster, the Glen Avon area was a predominantly white, working-class community, although US Census statistics show that Latinos made up 14 percent of the population in 1980. Many of these residents had moved to Glen Avon from Los Angeles and other areas further west in pursuit of cheaper land and a rural lifestyle in which to raise families. In 1979, a handful of white, working-class women from Glen Avon formed Concerned Neighbors in Action (CNA) and began to draw sustained attention to the SPA and demand comprehensive remediation.

Partly as a result of CNA's mobilizing efforts, the state of California designated the SAP its top-priority site for the Superfund National Priority List, thus beginning the drawn-out process of site cleanup. In November 1984, CNA also filed a lawsuit against more than 250 corporate dumpers, the state of California, and Riverside County. At the time, the case was the largest toxic tort in the nation, with personal injury and damage claims made on behalf of 5,000 plaintiffs.[43]

Although the majority of Glen Avon plaintiffs were white, they still included a diverse constituency, reflective of the numerous individuals affected by Stringfellow and included Anglo and Latino residents as well as renters and homeowners. Indeed, CNA activists consciously organized across the dividing lines of race and property ownership and envisioned their community including *everyone* who had been exposed to toxins. CNA also strived to make the litigation process as accessible and transparent as possible to community members. Plaintiffs thus agreed to set up a Plaintiffs' Steering Committee that would serve as a liaison between them and their attorneys.

In 1995, the lawsuit was finally settled for over $114 million. By this time, CNA had expanded to form the Center for Community Action and Environmental Justice (CCAEJ) and began identifying a broader range of environmental injustices in San Bernardino and Riverside Counties. This institutionalization of community activism not only facilitated continued monitoring of the Superfund cleanup but also enabled locals to address other issues related to social inequality and environmental justice in the region, from campaigns focused on air and water quality to immigrant rights and Latino voter mobilization. CCAEJ also collaborates with a number of other coalitions throughout the state and actively participates in legislation to limit pollution and other harms. In this sense, CCAEJ members have moved significantly beyond NIMBYism (not in my backyard) and incorporated the environmental-justice principle of NIABY (not in anybody's backyard) in their daily work.[44]

CCAEJ's organizational staff in 2015 was majority Latina, with Glen Avon local Penny Newman continuing as director. In July 2011, CCAEJ celebrated its role in helping to mobilize rural voters for the successful incorporation of Glen Avon and nearby areas into the city of Jurupa Valley. While it is still too early to say *how* incorporation will influence local struggles against environmental burdens and what role CCAEJ might play in Jurupa Valley politics, cityhood is certainly preferable to the historic marginalization of the region's residents and brings new resources to these overlooked (and today predominantly minority) constituencies.

In what way is the story of Stringfellow a case of environmental justice, and do we run the risk of stretching the concept too far? Certainly, the concept of environmental justice is vulnerable to conceptual fuzziness or "stretching" if it is expanded to include *any* instance of community mobilization against environmental harm as a case of environmental justice. However, for environmental justice to be a useful concept (and if claims are to have traction), it must be bounded—defined not only by what it includes but also what it excludes. In this regard, mobilization on the part of wealthy communities against locally undesirable land uses—while certainly an example of organizing against environmental harm—is more about NIMBYism than about challenging manifestations of social inequality. Indeed, when wealthy, highly educated communities have mobilized against the siting of toxics or demanded cleanup of sites that pose contamination risks, they have generally been successful.[45] At the very least, such communities have had access to resources (including media and political attention) that have enabled them to address their concerns in a meaningful and timely fashion. The same cannot be said for more marginalized communities.[46]

In contrast to a narrow NIMBY politics, Stringfellow may be considered a case of environmental justice on the basis of several axes of marginalization, including gender, class, and geography. Just as in the case of Love Canal, mothers bore the disproportionate burden of caring for ill children and advocating on their behalf. The gendered composition of CNA advocates was also a liability, as male government agency officials consistently dismissed their concerns and referred to them as "hysterical housewives."[47] State employees also obfuscated information on site risks and remediation options by presenting information at community meetings in highly technical jargon, incomprehensible to most non-experts. Similar dynamics pervaded Glen Avon litigants' interactions with the legal community over the period of the lawsuit. In spite of such gender and class inequalities, CNA prevailed in its struggle for environmental justice.

Activists in Glen Avon also addressed the concerns of a broader swathe of affected residents, including homeowners and renters, because they framed their organizing in terms of "neighborhood" rather than on the basis of (racialized) property ownership. Although the demographics of the area in the 1980s were primarily working class and white, Latino residents were part of the litigant pool and received compensation from the final settlement. This more inclusive vision for mobilization based on locality thus enabled multi-racial alliances among working-class residents rather than perpetuating dynamics of environmental racism within a larger context of class inequality. Moreover, this early multi-racial organizing enabled CNA to incarnate as CCAEJ a decade later and have legitimacy in working with Latino communities fighting environmental racism.

Cases like Stringfellow also shed light on the dynamics of geographic marginalization, especially for those living in rural and unincorporated areas. Unlike residents in incorporated cities who have proximate access to systems of political accountability, including mayors and city council members, those living in unincorporated areas often find it difficult to gain access to elected and appointed officials. County offices are often physically far from the unincorporated areas, making it more challenging for government officials to relate to resident concerns and for residents to attend meetings to hold officials accountable. Furthermore, county supervisors and planning directors are usually more beholden than their city counterparts to the commercial groups and industries that generate significant tax revenue that is central to financing county services. (By contrast, most city governments rely primarily on residential property taxes.)

The concerns of Glen Avon residents were thus neither visible to nor prioritized by decision-makers in the county seat of Riverside. CNA activists responded to their geographic marginalization with a strategy of highly visible protests outside the homes of politicians and industrial polluters who lived in the city of Riverside. The group also made links with national groups, including the then-recently formed Citizens Clearinghouse for Hazardous Wastes (founded by Lois Gibbs from Love Canal). The more recent incorporation of the city of Jurupa Valley is the latest in a string of strategies to counter the geographic marginalization of residents in the area.

Conclusion

What might a more expansive concept of environmental justice look like, and what are the potential benefits of self-consciously bringing a larger repertoire of cases and communities into environmental-justice scholarship? In engaging with this question, I want to make clear that my argument here is not to "move beyond race" or advocate a politically regressive call for "color-blindness." Racism today is alive and well and has far more subtle (and insidious) manifestations than any explicit act of intentional discrimination.[48] To expand the environmental-justice concept "beyond environmental racism," therefore, is not a move to forego critical understandings of racism and the need for anti-racist practice. It is, by contrast, to broaden the umbrella of consideration beyond only the most marginal groups and examine the ways multiple axes of difference come into play in struggles for environmental justice. A more expansive framework of environmental justice that incorporates race, class, and gender would thus allow us to examine the ways different dimensions of marginality intersect and produce varying aspects of injustice for different actors and groups.

More centrally, examining cases of low-income whites burdened by environmental injustice, for example, *may* dilute the claims-making potential of environmental justice, conceived primarily in terms of environmental racism. Yet this assumes that communities are somehow racially monolithic and ignores investigating the existence of relationships *between* different groups in affected areas. Some might also worry that broadening environmental justice to incorporate environmental burdens in predominantly working-class white communities would distract from combating pervasive racism in the United States of America, especially given the protests of Black Lives Matter and in the context of rising hate crimes and growing anti-immigrant policies. This is a valid concern in the current US political climate and in a cultural and media context in which stories like Erin Brockovich are glamorized in Hollywood blockbusters while other communities and activists are relegated to the margins. Yet broadening the environmental-justice umbrella might encourage us to see the contingent links between ostensibly disparate issues (siting of prisons, access to food, right to local self-governance, clean air and water) and the ways various places and bodies are differentially impacted by and implicated within white capitalist hetero-patriarchy. This rendering would not let go of a critical understanding of racism, just as it also would not let go of understandings of classism and sexism.

The path toward greater intersectional analysis and more nuanced explanations for environmental injustice is being forged, for example, by scholars in the humanities who explore environmental marginalization within the context of racialized ecologies in the United States.[49] In the social sciences, too, recent studies examine how complex intersections of class, race, place attachment, and historic geography help explain the existence of urban inequality in communities white, black, brown, and transnational.[50] And on the ground, in the United States and abroad, activists in often overlapping movements for climate justice, indigenous rights, and poor people's access to land embody a highly intersectional politics that is at once anti-racist, anti-colonial/imperial, and anti-oppression and framed within the broader context of global inequality and disproportionate impact.[51]

In the United States, a history of white supremacy, land dispossession through violence, and racial capitalism over-determines the conditions under which different groups experience vulnerability to environmental burdens.[52] Robert Bullard's point that "race continues to be an *independent* predictor of where hazardous wastes are located, and it is a stronger predictor than income, education, and other socioeconomic indicators" must not be forgotten.[53] This should not mean, however, that we only focus on the struggles of the most oppressed in ways that silo their connection to other groups and movements or simplify the dynamics of particular struggles. Fights for environmental justice in the United States need to be anti-racist, anti-capitalist, and anti-oppression more generally. They also require a broad coalition of forces, across race, gender, and class lines. An examination of the actual experiences of particular cases of community mobilization against environmental harm shows that the formation of such coalitions is contingent, complicated, and often fraught with tension. Yet such alliances are not altogether impossible and have achieved meaningful, if limited, victories for impacted communities. Broadening the concept of environmental justice to more fully engage with the operations and intersections of various axes of difference thus not only cracks open a particular scholarly narrative or canon but also helps sow hope and alliances for social change. Fortunately, and in light of the challenges ahead, these developments are already under way.

Notes

1. Robert Bullard, *Dumping in Dixie: Race, Class, and Environmental Quality* (Boulder: Westview, 1994); Steve Lerner, *Sacrifice Zones: The Front Lines of Toxic Chemical Exposure in the United States* (Cambridge, MA: MIT Press, 2010); J. Timmons Roberts and Melissa M. Toffolon-Weiss, *Chronicles from the Environmental Justice Frontline* (Cambridge: Cambridge University Press, 2001).

2. Deborah Ferruccio, "Our Road to Walk: Environmental Justice Yesterday and Today," *Our Road to Walk*, n.d., http://environmentaljustice-pollutionprevention.org/.

3. Laura Pulido, "Conversations in Environmental Justice: An Interview with David Pellow," *Capitalism Nature Socialism* 28, no. 2 (April 3, 2017): 45, doi:10.108 0/10455752.2016.1273963.

4. David Pellow, "Environmental Inequality Formation: Towards a Theory of Environmental Injustice," *American Behavioral Scientist* 43 (2000): 581–601.

5. Robert Bullard, Paul Mohai, Robin Saha, and Beverly Wright, *Toxic Wastes and Race at Twenty 1987–2007* (Cleveland, OH: United Church of Christ Justice and Witness Ministries, March 2007), 17, http://d3n8a8pro7vhmx.cloudfront.net/united churchofchrist/legacy_url/27850/toxic20.pdf?1418457960.

6. Ramachandra Guha, *Environmentalism: A Global History* (New York: Longman, 2000); James Gustave Speth, *Red Sky at Morning: America and the Crisis of the Global Environment* (New Haven, CT: Yale University Press, 2005).

7. William Cronon, George Miles, and Jay Gitlin, "Becoming West: Toward a New Meaning for Western History," in *Under an Open Sky: Rethinking America's Western Past*, ed. William Cronon, George Miles, and Jay Gitlin (New York: W. W. Norton, 1992), 3–27; Carolyn Merchant, "Shades of Darkness: Race and Environmental History," *Environmental History* (July 2003): 380–94.

8. Dorceta Taylor, "American Environmentalism: The Role of Race, Class, and Gender in Shaping Activism 1820–1995," *Race, Gender, and Class* 5, no. 1 (1997): 16–62.

9. Eileen McGurty, *Transforming Environmentalism: Warren County, PCBs, and the Origins of Environmental Justice* (New Brunswick, NJ: Rutgers University Press, 2007), 103.

10. Eileen McGurty, "Warren County, NC, and the Emergence of the Environmental Justice Movement: Unlikely Coalitions and Shared Meanings in Local

Collective Action," *Society and Natural Resources* 13 (2000): 373–87; Paul Mohai, David Pellow, and J. Timmons Roberts, "Environmental Justice," *Annual Review of Environment and Resources* 34 (2009): 405–30.

11. Commission for Racial Justice, United Church of Christ, *Toxic Wastes and Race in the United States* (New York: United Church of Christ, 1987), 15.

12. Douglas L. Anderton, Andy B. Anderson, John Michael Oakes, and Michael R. Fraser, "Environmental Equity: The Demographics of Dumping," *Demography* 31 (1994): 229–48; Vicki Been, "Analyzing Evidence of Environmental Justice," *Journal of Land Use and Environmental Law* 11, no. 1 (1994): 1–36; Vicki Been, "Locally Undesirable Land Uses in Minority Neighborhoods: Disproportionate Siting or Market Dynamics?" *Yale Law Journal* 103 (1994): 1383–1422; Vicki Been and Francis Gupta, "Coming to the Nuisance or Going to the Barrios: A Longitudinal Analysis of Environmental Justice Claims," *Ecology Law Quarterly* 24, no. 1 (1997): 1–56; Laura Pulido, "Rethinking Environmental Racism: White Privilege and Urban Development in Southern California," *Annals of the Association of American Geographers* 90, no. 1 (2000): 12–40.

13. Bullard, Mohai, Saha, and Wright, Toxic Wastes and Race at Twenty 1987–2007.

14. McGurty, *Transforming Environmentalism*, 117–18.

15. Julian Agyeman, *Sustainable Communities and the Challenge of Environmental Justice* (New York: New York University Press, 2005); Bullard, *Dumping in Dixie*; Robert Bullard, "Poverty, Pollution, and Environmental Racism: Strategies for Building Healthy and Sustainable Communities," July 2002, http://geotheology.blogspot.com/2007/03/poverty-pollution-and-environmental.html; Luke W. Cole and Sheila Foster R., *From the Ground Up: Environmental Racism and the Rise of the Environmental Justice Movement* (New York: New York University Press, 2001); Lerner, *Sacrifice Zones*; Roberts and Toffolon-Weiss, *Chronicles from the Environmental Justice Frontline*.

16. Charles Lee, ed., *Proceedings: The First National People of Color Environmental Leadership Summit* (New York: United Church of Christ, 1991), 88.

17. Dorceta Taylor, "The Rise of the Environmental Justice Paradigm," *American Behavioral Scientist* 43, no. 4 (2000): 538.

18. "The Principles of Environmental Justice (EJ)," First National People of Color Environmental Leadership Summit, October 24, 1991, http://www.ejnet.org/ej/principles.pdf.

19. Bullard, *Dumping in Dixie*; Stella M. Capek, "The 'Environmental Justice' Frame: A Conceptual Discussion and Framework," *Social Problems* 40, no. 1 (1993): 5–24; Steve Lerner, *Diamond* (Cambridge, MA: MIT Press, 2005); Judith Perrolle, "Comments from the Special Issue Editor: The Emerging Dialogue on Environmental Justice," *Social Problems* 40, no. 1 (1993): 1–4.

20. US Environmental Protection Agency, "Executive Order 12898," 1994, www.epa.gov/region2/ej/exec_order_12898.pdf.

21. J. Timmons Roberts and Melissa M. Toffolon-Weiss, *Chronicles from the Environmental Justice Frontline* (Cambridge: Cambridge University Press, 2001), 101–36.

22. Ryan Holifield, Michael Porter, and Gordon Walker, eds., "Spaces of Environmental Justice: Frameworks for Critical Engagement," special issue of *Antipode* 41, no. 4 (2009): 591–612; Mohai, Pellow, and Roberts, "Environmental Justice"; Andrew Szasz and Michael Meuser, "Environmental Inequalities: Literature Review and Proposals for New Directions in Research and Theory," *Current Sociology* 45 (1997): 99–120; Julie Sze and Jonathan London, "Environmental Justice at the Crossroads," *Sociology Compass* 2, no. 4 (July 2008): 1331–54; Robin L. Turner and Diana P. Wu, *Environmental Justice and Environmental Racism: An Annotated Bibliography with General Overview, Focusing on the US Literature, 1996–2002* (Berkeley: Berkeley Workshop on Environmental Politics, University of California, 2002); Gordon Walker, "Beyond Distribution and Proximity: Exploring the Multiple Spatialities of Environmental Justice," *Antipode* 41, no. 4 (September 2009): 614–36, doi:10.1111/j.1467-8330.2009.00691.x; Robert W. Williams, "Environmental Injustice in America and Its Politics of Scale," *Political Geography* 18 (1999): 49–74.

23. Pulido, "Rethinking Environmental Racism."

24. Kimberle Crenshaw, "Demarginalizing the Intersection of Race and Sex: A Black Feminist Critique of Antidiscrimination Doctrine, Feminist Theory, and Antiracist Politics," *University of Chicago Legal Forum* (1989): 139–67; Kimberle Crenshaw, "Mapping the Margins: Intersectionality, Identity Politics, and Violence against Women of Color," *Stanford Law Review* 43, no. 6 (1991): 1241–79.

25. Mary Hawkesworth, "Congressional Enactments of Race-Gender: Towards a Theory of Race-Gendered Institutions," *American Political Science Review* 97, no. 4 (2003): 529–50; Leslie McCall, "The Complexity of Intersectionality," *Signs* 30, no. 3 (2005): 1771–1800.

26. Doreen Massey, *Space, Place, and Gender* (Minneapolis: University of Minnesota Press, 1994); Pulido, "Rethinking Environmental Racism"; Edward Soja, *Postmodern Geographies* (New York: Verso, 1989).

27. Giovanna Di Chiro, "Nature as Community: The Convergence of Environmental and Social Justice," in *Uncommon Ground: Rethinking the Human Place in Nature*, ed. William Cronon (New York: W. W. Norton, 1996), 298–320; Dolores Greenberg, "Reconstructing Race and Protest: Environmental Justice in New York City," *Environmental History* 5, no. 2 (2000): 223–50; Amy M. Hay, "Recipe for Disaster: Motherhood and Citizenship at Love Canal," *Journal of Women's History* 21, no. 1 (2009): 111–34; Andrew Szasz, *Ecopopulism: Toxic Waste and the Movement for Environmental Justice* (Minneapolis: University of Minnesota Press, 1994); Jennifer Thomson, "Dredging

the Canal: The Buried Local of Environmental Justice," presented at the Annual Meeting of the American Society for Environmental History, Madison, WI, 2012.

28. Alison Alkon, "Reflexivity and Environmental Justice Scholarship: A Role for Feminist Methodologies," *Organization and Environment* 24, no. 2 (2011): 130–49; Celene Krauss, "Women and Toxic Waste Protests: Race, Class, and Gender as Resources of Resistance," *Qualitative Sociology* 16, no. 3 (1993): 247–62; Michelle Murphy, *Sick Building Syndrome and the Problem of Uncertainty* (Durham, NC: Duke University Press, 2006): 111–30.

29. Evelyn Brooks Higginbotham, "African-American Women's History and the Metalanguage of Race," *Signs* 17, no. 2 (1992): 274.

30. Pellow, "Environmental Inequality Formation," 582.

31. Murphy, "Uncertainty, Race, and Activism at the EPA," 113.

32. McGurty, *Transforming Environmentalism*, 94–95.

33. Ibid., 95.

34. Szasz, *Ecopopulism*; Sze and London, "Environmental Justice at the Crossroads"; Turner and Wu, "Environmental Justice and Environmental Racism."

35. Elizabeth Blum, *Love Canal Revisited: Race, Class, and Gender in Environmental Activism* (Lawrence: University of Kansas Press, 2011).

36. Ibid.

37. Lois Marie Gibbs and Murray Levine, *Love Canal: My Story* (Albany: SUNY Press, 1982), 12.

38. Patricia Hill Collins, *Black Feminist Thought: Knowledge, Consciousness, and the Politics of Empowerment* (Boston: Unwin Hyman, 1990), 74–75.

39. Certainly, one might argue that similar dynamics were on display decades later in relation to the federal government's excruciatingly slow response to working-class and black victims in the aftermath of Hurricane Katrina. "There's No Such Thing as a Natural Disaster," June 11, 2006, http://understandingkatrina.ssrc .org/Smith/.

40. Blum, *Love Canal Revisited*, 74–75.

41. The wastes dumped at Stringfellow included numerous organic compounds (including PCBs, DDT, phenols, and trichloroethylene), inorganic compounds, elements and residues (including arsenic, cadmium, and chromium), and acids (including chromic acid, hydrochloric acid, and sulfuric acid). H. K. Hatayama, B. P. Simmons, and R. D. Stephens, "The Stringfellow Industrial Waste Disposal Site: A Technical Assessment of Environmental Impact" (Berkeley, CA: Hazardous Materials Management Section, California Department of Health Services, March 1979), Box 11, folders 9 and 10, Stringfellow Archive, University of California at Riverside.

42. Penny Newman, *"It's the Pits": Remembering Stringfellow* (Glen Avon, CA: Center for Community Action and Environmental Justice, October 2, 2004); Hatayama,

Simmons, and Stephens, "The Stringfellow Industrial Waste Disposal Site"; Donald O. Lyman, "Letter from Department of Health Services (Donald O. Lyman, MD, Deputy Director, Public and Environmental Health Division) to Donald Boling, Director of Environmental Health, Riverside County," May 10, 1979, Box 11, folder 10, Stringfellow Archive, University of California at Riverside.

43. *Penny Newman et al. v. J. B. Stringfellow Jr. et al.*, no. 165994MF, Riverside County Superior Court (1995).

44. Michael Heiman, "From 'Not in My Backyard!' to 'Not in Anybody's Backyard!' Grassroots Challenge to Hazardous Waste Facility Siting," *American Planning Association Journal* 56, no. 3 (1990): 359–62.

45. Susan Cutter, "Race, Class, and Environmental Justice," *Progress in Human Geography* 19 (1995): 111–22; "Why Does Affluent Porter Ranch Get More Urgent Environmental Relief than Working-Class Boyle Heights?" *Los Angeles Times*, January 29, 2016, *Latimes.com*, http://www.latimes.com/opinion/editorials/la-ed-exide -20160131-story.html.

46. Cole and Foster, *From the Ground Up*.

47. Personal communication, Penny Newman, June 2011.

48. Michael Omi and Howard Winant, *Racial Formation in the United States* (New York: Routledge, 1994).

49. Lindsey Dillon and Julie Sze, "Police Powers and Particulate Matters: Environmental Justice and the Spatialities of In/securities in US Cities," *English Language Notes*, 2016, http://www.academia.edu/26904303/Police_Power_and_Particulate _Matters_Environmental_Justice_and_the_Spatialities_of_In_Securities_in_U.S. _Cities; Lindsey Dillon, "Race, Waste, and Space: Brownfield Redevelopment and Environmental Justice at the Hunters Point Shipyard: Waste, Race, and Space," *Antipode* 46, no. 5 (November 2014): 1205–21, doi:10.1111/anti.12009.

50. Diane Sicotte, *From Workshop to Waste Magnet: Environmental Inequality in the Philadelphia Region* (New Brunswick, NJ: Rutgers University Press, 2016); Isabelle Anguelovski, *Neighborhood as Refuge: Community Reconstruction, Place Remaking, and Environmental Justice in the City* (Cambridge, MA: MIT Press, 2014).

51. Joan Martinez Alier, Isabelle Anguelovski, Patrick Bond, Daniela Del Bene, and Federico Demaria, "Between Activism and Science," *Journal of Political Ecology* 21 (2014): 19–60; Jessica Grady-Benson and Brinda Sarathy, "Fossil Fuel Divestment in US Higher Education: Student-Led Organising for Climate Justice," *Local Environment* 21, no. 6 (2016): 661–81; Rob Nixon, *Slow Violence and the Environmentalism of the Poor* (Cambridge, MA: Harvard University Press, 2011); Joni Adamson, Mei Mei Evans, and Rachel Stein, *The Environmental Justice Reader: Politics, Poetics, and Pedagogy* (Tucson: University of Arizona Press, 2002).

52. Cheryl Harris, "Whiteness as Property," *Harvard Law Review* 106, no. 8 (1993): 1710–91; Omi and Winant, *Racial Formation in the United States*; Pulido, "Rethinking Environmental Racism"; Cedric J. Robinson, *Black Marxism: The Making of the Black Radical Tradition* (Chapel Hill, NC: University of North Carolina Press, 1983).

53. Bullard, Mohai, Saha, and Wright. *Toxic Wastes and Race at Twenty 1987–2007*, xiii, emphasis added.

3

Power to the People

*Grassroots Advocacy for Environmental
Protection and Democratic Governance*

CODY FERGUSON AND PAUL HIRT

> Human uses of the environment are matters of governance, not merely of
> individual choice or economic markets.
> *Richard N.L. Andrews[1]*

When residents mostly in rural eastern and central Tennessee learned
that their communities were slated for construction of some of the largest waste dumps in the country in the late 1980s, many were concerned.
Despite promises of new jobs and benefits to their local economies, they
worried about how the massive landfills might affect the health of their
families, property values, and their land and water. When they learned that
the landfills were being built to handle garbage and toxic materials from
cities hundreds of miles away, they were outraged. Some organized. As
one might expect, they advocated for new environmental regulations and
even outright bans on the construction of landfills. Notably, however, they
promoted greater democratic participation in decision-making as their
central strategy.

DOI: 10.5876/9781607328483.c003

This was a familiar tactic for the members of Save Our Cumberland Mountains (SOCM, pronounced "sock 'em"), a grassroots, member-based conservation group that had originally formed in opposition to coal strip mining in the 1970s. When SOCM lobbied the state legislature for a new law governing waste dump siting in Tennessee in the 1990s, instead of emphasizing more stringent environmental protection regulations, the group lobbied to require the state to notify nearby communities of proposed landfills before approving permits. This was designed to provide citizens with the right to appeal state permit decisions and to establish a process by which residents could vote by referendum to allow or deny such a development in their community.[2] In short, the group fought for democratic reforms to protect communities from environmentally destructive practices. SOCM had honed those strategies twenty years earlier when it helped gain passage of landmark strip mining, reclamation, and water-quality laws. Importantly, those environmental protection laws and many others from the 1960s and 1970s contained citizen participation rules that transformed US environmental planning and decision-making. Conservation organizations in the 1990s capitalized on and extended these democratic reforms of governance. SOCM's strategies mirrored those of thousands of environmental activists working through hundreds of groups across the United States in the second half of the twentieth century. While they were concerned about water and air pollution and the health of their families and communities, their understanding of environmental issues was tightly woven into ideals of good government and the notion that citizens ought to have a right to participate in decisions that affect their lives. For the members of many grassroots conservation groups during this period, justice and democratic process were inextricable from environmental protection goals.

The connection between democratic advocacy and environmental advocacy in the United States (and elsewhere in the world) since the 1970s is deeper and more significant than generally acknowledged in traditional historical scholarship. With a few notable exceptions, environmental historians and political historians alike have mostly ignored the important relationship between environmental reform and democratic reform.[3] In fact, the two have been inseparable: environmentalists have often helped lead successful efforts to make government agencies and decision-making processes more transparent, accountable, and responsive to citizen input. As Sarah L. Thomas has argued, Rachel Carson's pesticide reform work in the early 1960s "contributed to a growing emphasis on access to information and public participation, both of which emerged as key tenets of the new environmentalism."[4] Environmentalists championed public participation, right-to-know laws, and judicial standing for citizens to challenge government decisions. They supported laws that required federal and state agencies to assess the environmental and social impacts of proposed actions, disclose them to the public, invite and respond to feedback, publish decision records, and treat formal citizen appeals with due process. Accompanying these reforms of government decision-making, environmentalists organized extensively at the grassroots level to ensure the faithful implementation of laws designed to protect the human and natural environment. Organized citizen oversight and advocacy is the primary means for ensuring that policy intentions established at the legislative level are fulfilled at the local and community level. Environmentalists advocated for a whole new body of citizen rights that made their way into mainstream acceptance: the right to a healthful environment, the right to know the ingredients in our foods, the right *not* to be exposed to harmful chemicals, the right of communities to protect themselves from developments that would harm their local environments and quality of life. Since the 1960s, environmental reforms have democratized governance.

This has been neither accidental nor merely incidental to environmental protection but central to the reform agenda and larger social vision of postwar environmentalists—among both the leadership and the rank and file. Indeed, democratic reforms have often been a *primary* aim for many environmental groups, particularly at the grassroots level. This chapter describes the role of democratic advocacy in the environmental movement since the 1960s, a hopeful story of successful citizen action to advance, incrementally, democratic governance and to promote the faithful implementation of hard-won environmental protection policies.

The Evolution of Environmental Advocacy since the 1950s

At an organizational and strategic level, the environmental movement evolved through three distinct but overlapping phases after the 1950s: an initial phase from the 1960s through the mid-1970s, focused on reforming environmental law and administration; a second phase from 1977 through the Reagan era, focused on professionalizing environmental organizations and defending the gains won in the earlier period; and a third phase extending from the 1980s through the 1990s that focused more on decentralized grassroots campaigns with greater attention to democratic action and environmental justice.[5]

In the first phase during the 1960s and continuing to a crescendo in the mid-1970s, the movement's leaders focused on passing new environmental laws, most notably at the federal level but also with successes at the state and local levels. The US Congress, for example, enacted an unprecedented surge of legislative reforms between 1964 and 1977, resulting in a complete reformation of environmental policy, government accountability, corporate responsibility, and citizen empowerment. As we are now steeped in this political and cultural milieu, it is hard to imagine the world before this statutory revolution. As with many of the democratic reforms of the civil rights era, effective implementation of the new laws often depended on citizens "watchdogging" government and industry.[6] Most reforms involved some redistribution of costs and benefits or restraint of someone's liberty or authority. Consequently, every reform had advocates and opponents. In the recent history of environmental protection around the world, it appears that the difference between a well-intended law that does little and a law that brings meaningful change often depends on citizens' propensity and capacity to engage their government. For example, a study of environmental law and enforcement in China by a visiting scholar at Harvard, Ying Zhao, notes that while significant environmental protection laws exist, "China still lacks the will to achieve compliance with and efficient enforcement of environmental requirements." Zhao points to inadequate procedures for public hearings and public disclosure, along with poorly organized citizen involvement, as key reasons for the inadequate enforcement of environmental laws in China. His prescription for improving enforcement: "Encourage public organizations, such as labor unions, youth leagues, and the women's federation[,] to participate in environmental protection." Organized public awareness and environmental knowledge, he says, would "promote their ability to voluntarily protect the environment, report violations, and superintend the government"[7]—exactly the role environmental groups started playing in the United States in the 1960s and 1970s.

The second phase of the modern environmental movement was characterized by a focus on building organizational memberships, honing environmental advocacy skills, and defending the gains of the 1970s against a backlash in the 1980s. Robert Gottlieb referred to this era as one of "Professionalization and Institutionalization."[8] We can trace its beginnings to the first Earth Day in 1970, the mass popularity of which surprised everyone. Indeed, environmentalism caught on with a fervor that so greatly exceeded expectations that environmental organizations spent the next two decades catching up with its popularity and possibilities. An estimated 20 million people participated in Earth Day events in 1970. In just three years, between 1969 and 1972, membership in the Sierra Club increased from 83,000 to 136,000, while membership in the Audubon Society nearly doubled, from 120,000 to 232,000.[9] This rapid rise in public support for environmental organizations had started in the mid-1960s, and Earth Day accelerated the trend.[10] But progress on environmental reform proved to be short-lived. The ascendance of the Reagan administration in 1981 and its unapologetic hostility toward the previous decade's environmental reforms stalled and even reversed some environmental gains. This, however, had the ironic effect of boosting the membership and financial resources of mainstream environmental organizations.[11] As opportunities to pursue new environmental reforms in Washington, DC, slowed after 1976, environmental leaders focused on institutionalizing their previous gains, educating and motivating their burgeoning memberships, expanding and professionalizing their paid staff, and fighting efforts by the legislative and executive branches of the government to weaken the hard-won environmental reforms of the first era. Those environmental organizations with legal expertise pursued environmental goals in the courts, too. In essence, this second era witnessed a subtle but significant shift from establishing environmental policies to preserving and enforcing those policies.

The third phase of the movement evolved during the long legislative stalemate of the late 1980s and the 1990s. While Reagan's anti-environmental initiatives had been largely blunted by his second term, most new environmental protection initiatives were similarly blocked by a well-organized opposition, including the Wise Use movement, property rights think tanks, and an oppositional Republican resurgence in Congress during the Clinton administration.[12] This political opposition consciously engendered a culture of distrust of the federal government and reified an economic libertarianism that made strong regulatory action an increasingly difficult strategy to pursue. The Reagan era ended strong bipartisan support for environmental initiatives and turned distrust of the federal government into a potent and persistent force in contemporary political culture. By the mid-1980s, the decline of environmental leaders in the Republican Party,[13] increasing popular disdain for federal institutions, and a persistent partisan gridlock in Congress undermined the usefulness of the legislative branch as a key arena for environmental action.

The decline of the legislative strategy paralleled the rise of a bottom-up strategy of mobilizing grassroots environmental watchdogs to ensure the implementation of existing policies. As mentioned, the extraordinary growth of mainstream environmental memberships during the 1980s and a remarkable flourishing of new local and regional groups enabled this grassroots strategy. Most of the new grassroots organizations started out independent of the national groups but often sought advice and resources from experienced environmental leaders. Many of these "alternative" grassroots groups, as Robert Gottlieb calls them, consciously distanced themselves from the mainstream environmental movement and were "predominantly local in nature, more participatory and focused on action." Moreover, their activism crucially relied on promoting "citizen empowerment."[14] The democratic reforms incorporated into environmental laws of the 1960s and 1970s enabled this shift of activism from dues-paying letter writers to citizen participants and enforcers. Environmentalists learned that a robust system of public participation resulted in tangible environmental benefits, and so protecting citizens' ability to participate in natural resource decisions became a vital component of environmental work.

A number of scholars in the 1980s, especially Nicholas Freudenberg, Robert Bullard, and Robert Gottlieb, identified a clear pattern of citizen mobilization within these grassroots environmental organizations. In an essay titled "Not in Our Backyards: The Grassroots Environmental Movement," Freudenberg and his colleague Carol Steinsapir described these groups as composed mostly or entirely of volunteers and amateurs organized at the community level. More racially and occupationally diverse than the typical environmental professionals, with women more frequently in leadership positions, these organizations sprang up in response to local concerns, especially pollution and public health problems. They typically began by documenting a hazard or threat, then lobbied government or industry to fix the problem, which brought them into extensive interactions with politicians, business representatives, scientists, public agencies, and the media. Leaders of these groups learned the intricacies of citizen participation in environmental governance. According to Freudenberg and Steinsapir, "The initial objective is usually to correct a specific problem, not to effect broader policy changes. Failure to achieve goals at this level can lead groups to enter the legal system . . . or to move into the political arena where they lobby for legislation, endorse candidates, or propose ballot initiatives. The cumulative effect of these activities can lead to dramatic changes in political consciousness for activists."[15]

The case study of SOCM, mentioned above and profiled below, reveals the importance of democratic reform in on-the-ground environmental advocacy and shows how efforts to protect environmental and human health are closely tied to notions of community welfare, justice, and participatory democracy.[16] SOCM represents only one example of the kinds of grassroots environmental organizations that proliferated after the 1970s. Like hundreds of other grassroots groups, SOCM was a membership-based organization founded on democratic principles to address immediate threats to its members' land, health, and community. And, like its counterparts around the nation, it pursued primarily democratic solutions to the environmental threats it faced.

Communities and Landfills in Tennessee

By the late 1980s, the United States produced more trash per capita than any other country in the world—more than 260 million tons, or roughly 1 ton per person annually.[17] As cities and surrounding suburbs grew, disposing of waste became a pressing problem. City and state governments as well as waste industry officials looked for solutions, such as shipping the garbage from cities like New York and Chicago to less populated parts of the country. The recipients of such waste, however, could be reluctant to accept it. In one highly publicized incident in 1987, a barge of trash was shipped south from Long Island to be processed into methane in Morehead City, North Carolina. When officials there rejected it, citing new environmental regulations, the barge began a months-long epic journey south as its handlers searched for a place to dispose of the garbage. The Mexican Navy prevented it from entering its country's waters. In Belize it was finally turned around and sent back to New York, where its contents were incinerated.[18] The "Garbarge" fiasco demonstrated just how contentious trash disposal could be. In spite or perhaps because of such highly publicized events, many still saw opportunity in garbage. Waste management corporations and the nation's major cities increasingly looked to the economically depressed rural areas of the American South and West to ship their waste, arguing that massive waste dumps or incinerators would bring jobs, tax revenue, and impact fees to poor rural communities, paying for roads, health clinics, and education. Rural Tennessee, with its history of poverty and environmental degradation associated with sharecropping and boom-and-bust coal mining, was a prime candidate. For local business interests and elected officials representing communities starved for jobs and industry, processing out-of-state waste represented an attractive proposition. But many people who lived in the communities slated for these mega-landfills or waste incinerators saw them as an assault.

The move to locate waste management facilities in impoverished, rural parts of Tennessee during the late 1980s and 1990s followed a pattern identified by environmental-justice activists and scholars: powerful, wealthy, politically well-connected industries shifting the costs of doing business onto the poor and politically disenfranchised. Multinational corporations like Browning-Ferris Industries and Waste Management, Inc., justified their proposals to ship waste from the nation's major cities to its rural areas as facilitating much-needed economic development for often-desperate poor communities. They described their plans as mutually beneficial to all involved, but in fact their plans mostly benefited cities and corporations. The site communities received some jobs, an increased tax base, and impact fees, yet they also received the garbage—millions of tons of it—and the polluted air, soil, and water and traffic associated with it. At best, it could be a nuisance, fowling air with its putrid stench. At its worst, the garbage leached harmful chemical compounds into local streams and groundwater, could cause respiratory and cardiovascular problems, and was potentially linked to cancer and birth defects (such as spina bifida, Down syndrome, and heart and lung defects). Landfills also depressed property values, further entrenching poor communities in a cycle of poverty. Waste management companies looked specifically to rural, impoverished communities because property was cheap and local politicians and business interests were hungry for economic development. They also chose these communities because the residents—poor and often people of color—usually had little political power.[19] A decades-long tradition of rural organizing among the residents of eastern Tennessee, however, stymied some of the waste industry's ambitions and ensured better outcomes for the communities where mega-landfills were eventually sited.

SOCM quickly took up the cause. Forged in the crucible of prolonged battles against coal strip mining in the previous two decades, SOCM was organized according to a radically democratic philosophy that drew on the interests, local knowledge, and skills of its members. SOCM members, organized in local chapters, brought their concerns before the monthly meetings of its board of directors, composed of elected representatives from the chapters. Responding to a number of proposals for new waste facilities across rural Tennessee and citizen exposés of environmental problems associated with existing landfills, SOCM members formed a thirteen-member Toxics Committee in 1990 to investigate landfill and incinerator proposals, document environmental and code violations by existing landfills, and empower citizens to participate in landfill siting decisions.[20]

SOCM's campaign built on an existing body of environmental protection laws and relationships forged with state environmental agencies. It also made effective use of its members' research and communications skills honed over twenty years of activism. The Toxics Committee began delving into the history of code and environmental violations by existing landfills and incinerators. With the help of a paid organizer, the volunteers reviewed what information they could find from the Tennessee Department of Environment and Conservation—the state agency responsible for solid-waste regulation enforcement—and compared their research with what they found in newspaper articles and the on-the-ground experiences of members who monitored landfills. Members also took their concerns to agency officials. The committee concluded that the fundamental problems with waste management in the state resulted from state regulations reliant on self-reporting by landfill and incinerator operators, inadequate oversight by state agencies, failure of those agencies to enforce water- and air-quality laws, and the absence of processes that allowed citizens to review, comment on, and appeal waste management permitting decisions.

Early in its campaign, SOCM realized that passing new laws and regulations at the federal and state levels would be challenging and unlikely to happen quickly enough to stop the massive importation of out-of-state garbage into Tennessee. So the group instead focused its efforts on local solutions. SOCM adopted a county-by-county strategy promoting greater authority for town councils and county commissions to regulate activities within their jurisdictions. It based this local campaign on what became known as the "Jackson Law." In 1989, general assemblymen from counties confronting the construction of massive new landfills pushed through a state law with SOCM's support that required that county governments have final say on the siting of a landfill in their county. The Jackson Law did not automatically apply to counties across the state. Instead, local governments had to vote to "opt in" to the law and claim the local control it provided.[21]

Over the next year, SOCM organized residents across eastern Tennessee to pressure their county commissions and city councils to opt in. Drawing on its experience in mobilizing citizens, SOCM used public service announcements on the radio, letters to the editors of local newspapers, house meetings, and door-to-door organizing to spread its message. It gathered hundreds of signatures on petitions encouraging county commissioners in the group's historical strongholds of Campbell, Anderson, Roane, and Morgan Counties to opt in to the Jackson Law. Each county adopted the law, and by the end of the year the county commissions in each of those counties had used the law to stop construction of contentious landfills.[22]

While SOCM pursued its county-by-county campaign, it simultaneously sought to strengthen state law, with mixed results. For the 1991 session of the Tennessee General Assembly, the group proposed legislation that would add citizen representatives to the Solid Waste Board, require advance public notice of permit applications, guarantee citizen rights to appeal landfill permitting decisions, and, through a referendum process, create a legal mechanism by which citizens could have ultimate say regarding landfill permitting decisions in their counties. In addition, SOCM proposed extending or making permanent the Jackson Law, which was scheduled to expire in July of that year. The group also advocated policies permitting county governments to charge adequate "impact fees" so that landfill companies could not shift the environmental costs of their facilities onto communities and the state. Failing to find success in the legislature in 1991 and 1992, SOCM packaged these provisions into a comprehensive Environmental Justice Bill introduced in 1993, but the group was still unable to muster sufficient political support to pass the bill.[23] The state did pass a limited landfill law in 1993, but only a few of these democratic reforms were included. Landfill supporters argued that increased citizen participation would hamper the ability of Waste Management, Inc., and

Browning-Ferris to locate large landfills in Tennessee, leading to the potential loss of hundreds of jobs and millions of dollars in tax revenues. SOCM did win an extension of the Jackson Law, first until 1995 and then indefinitely, and helped pass a "bad boy" law that prohibited solid-waste companies from opening landfills in Tennessee if they had violated environmental laws in Tennessee or other states. The other legislative proposals, however, met defeat.[24]

Learning from its experience fighting coal strip mining in the previous decades, SOCM realized the potential strength that could be drawn from working in coalition with groups across state borders. Rural communities in other parts of the South and in the West were also confronting proposals for out-of-state waste dumps. From 1991 to 1995, SOCM joined a consortium of grassroots groups organized by the Western Organization of Resource Councils to advocate for a federal "Right to Say NO" bill to enable states to refuse to accept the introduction of solid, hazardous, and biomedical wastes from out of state. Ultimately, opponents' arguments against the bill—that it violated the interstate commerce clause of the US Constitution and created unnecessary and onerous regulatory burdens for the waste management industry—led to a legislative stalemate.[25] This failure in the state and federal legislative arenas was a common experience for most environmental organizations in the 1990s, as the political consensus surrounding environmental issues during the 1970s had all but evaporated. The inability of grassroots environmental groups to successfully influence the passage of new landfill and waste laws contrasted markedly with environmental gains made at the local level during the same period as a result of vigorous public involvement. In county commission and city council meetings, activists leveraged neighborly relations to offset the influence of industry in a way they could not in Nashville or Washington, DC. Accordingly, organizations concerned about pollution from landfills saw democratic participation at the local level as their key tool in the fight to protect their environment and communities.

Over the decades since its formation, SOCM had increasingly learned the importance of participating in the nitty-gritty of agency rule making and environmental law enforcement. When the legislative process failed to deliver solutions against the threat of out-of-state waste, citizen activists were forced to wade further into this murky area of civic participation in which success or failure was rarely clearly defined. Watchdogging government agencies and industry became central to SOCM's work in the 1990s. Its efforts were organized along two lines: (1) participating in the rule-making process for the limited laws passed in 1991 and the "bad boy" law, and (2) completing a comprehensive study of enforcement of waste management laws by the state and of regulatory compliance by landfill and incinerator operators.[26]

The momentum behind SOCM's campaign culminated in 1996 when the organization released its landfill enforcement study. More than three years of research by members, SOCM organizers, and paid consultants revealed systematic failures by the state in enforcing existing waste management and air- and water-quality regulations. The study concluded that most of the necessary laws to prevent degradation of air and water quality by landfills were already in place, but lack of transparency in permitting decisions and the absence of procedures facilitating citizen oversight of agency actions contributed to the ineffectual administration of the laws. In publicizing its findings, SOCM called on the Tennessee Department of Environment and Conservation to meet with the organization to discuss the study and address the problems it identified. The department took SOCM up on the offer. Members were pleasantly surprised when the director of the department and the administrators of the solid-waste program conceded most of SOCM's conclusions in the landfill study. The agency agreed that landfill enforcement was plagued by inconsistent enforcement practices, ineffective communication between department offices, lack of transparency in agency decision-making, limited public access to information, and poor record keeping.[27]

SOCM members and agency officials met over the course of the next year to work out a plan for improving environmental performance and regulatory compliance with vigorous citizen involvement. The department and citizen activists agreed to a list of actions each side would take, set a schedule to meet each objective, and scheduled future meetings to evaluate their progress. For its part, the department would require its inspectors to document the rationale for their enforcement practices and set deadlines for correcting violations. SOCM would share its findings with the department about which field offices it found most and least responsive to citizens. The department also committed to standardize its record keeping and enforcement practices across the agency and field offices and to implement a comprehensive inspection program by July 1996 and make the results accessible on a publicly available computer database.[28] When SOCM members and the department came together in later meetings, however, the citizen activists were often disappointed at the state's slow progress. They realized that increased participation and oversight was only the first step toward ensuring environmental compliance. SOCM members had to commit to long-term engagement with department staff and apply sustained pressure on the department to fulfill its obligations.[29]

This deeper form of democratic participation is at once profound and tedious. Unlike passing a law, there is no clear victory or endpoint in the day-to-day struggle to keep the train moving down the tracks. But this is where democratic governance succeeds or fails; it is the arena where intentions yield results or reveal themselves as mere rhetoric. By rolling up its sleeves and engaging in a collaborative process, a mostly volunteer grassroots community organization partnered with state institutions to enhance public participation in environmental governance and improve the performance of state environmental agencies. This is the kind of citizen participation, enabled by environmental laws providing the means for public involvement and oversight, that scholar Ying Zhao identified as crucial to the successful implementation of environmental policy: citizen groups organized to "protect the environment, report violations, and superintend the government."[30]

Although SOCM and its allies in Tennessee failed to persuade state lawmakers to create new protections for communities from the importation of garbage, sustained activism increased citizens' ability to influence decisions that affected the health and environment at the county level. By the mid-1990s, most of the mega-landfills and waste incinerators proposed for Tennessee to handle garbage from the nation's major cities were scrapped. Out-of-state waste foes found a powerful tool in the "bad boy" law and used it to challenge landfill and incinerator permits by operators who had a history of violations in other states, but much of their success came from their dogged engagement with the Tennessee Department of Environment and Conservation, which resulted in increased enforcement of existing laws. In their campaign to stop out-of-state waste, SOCM members expanded what counted as democratic participation to achieve tangible results that benefited the health and environment of their communities.[31]

A Wider View...

The experience of SOCM provides one example of citizens seeking solutions to environmental problems by promoting democratic participation in decision-making and citizen involvement in environmental compliance. Naturally, such a confined study has limitations; most notably, SOCM was historically composed of predominantly Anglo members. Environmental-justice scholars emphasize that environmental degradation and toxic contamination tend to be disproportionately experienced by people of color and the poor. A community's success in correcting these issues is often contingent on the race and class makeup of its members.[32] At the time it was fighting proposed mega-landfills, however, SOCM also began actively organizing in African American communities in central and western Tennessee on toxics and waste issues and began a "dismantling racism" campaign to encourage its members to understand the relationships among race, class, and environmental injustice in their communities and in their work as activists. Allying with predominantly African American groups and eventually forming chapters in central and western Tennessee broadened SOCM's membership and undoubtedly contributed to its success. This began a shift in the organization that resulted in it describing itself as a "social, economic, and environmental justice" group by the early 2000s and changing its name to Statewide Organizing for Community eMpowerment [*sic*] (to retain the acronym SOCM, the organization capitalizes the "m" in "empowerment").

Class also played a significant role in the group's abilities to affect change. Unlike some citizen activists in other parts of the country who could argue for protection of the environment and public health based on their rights as property owners, SOCM's primarily working-class members rarely enjoy such privilege. Instead, they stress threats to public health and the injustice of dumping other states' waste on Tennessee's rural working poor. Scholars also acknowledge a power differential based on gender within mainstream environmental organizations and the fact that women and men tend to emphasize different arguments, rhetoric, and strategies for righting environmental wrongs. But this case study and others, including Elizabeth D. Blum's examination of the famous Love Canal issue, demonstrate that gender does not seem to handicap activists' success at the grassroots level. On the contrary, in SOCM and at Love Canal, women's ability to appeal to the public and decision-makers on behalf of the health of their children and communities appears vital to organizational success.[33]

During the last decade of the twentieth century and in the early twenty-first century, the environmental-justice movement brought widespread critical attention to the success differential between predominantly Anglo and middle-class environmental organizations and working-class and/or non-white groups. A common emphasis on justice and increasing citizen participation in the decisions that affect community and environmental health and welfare linked grassroots groups like SOCM to this movement in philosophy and strategy, even if in many cases the groups themselves remained predominantly Anglo or middle class and did not explicitly identify as "environmental-justice" organizations. After vigorous lobbying by environmental-justice activists, President Bill Clinton issued Environmental Justice Executive Order (EO 12898) in February 1994, directing federal agencies to address how federal actions affected environmental and human health in minority and low-income communities.[34] Responding to the rise of the environmental-justice movement, traditional environmental groups paid increasing attention to environmental injustices. Sierra Club leaders embraced environmental-justice issues in the 1990s, prodded by environmental-justice leaders who felt the mainstream environmental movement was insufficiently concerned about the needs of urban poor and minority communities. By the year 2000, the Sierra Club had created a formal environmental-justice program with ongoing regional campaigns.[35] All of this was facilitated by the democratic reforms enacted in the 1960s and 1970s and defended and expanded by local, regional, and national groups in the 1980s and 1990s.

Like their local and regional grassroots counterparts, national environmental organizations also pursued democratic strategies and goals to address environmental issues. In a 2010 interview, Rob Smith, Southwest regional director of the Sierra Club at that time, emphasized that the citizen participation rules included in state and federal environmental laws were among environmentalists' most important accomplishments of the last generation. Involved in dozens of campaigns over more than thirty years, Smith credits public participation rules and citizens' rights to appeal government decisions for much of the movement's success. But because these public participation rules have been effective in blocking or stalling many environmentally destructive proposals, they are "always under assault," according to Smith, by those who would like to see development projects fast-tracked. Pro-industry and pro-property rights lobbies and their supporters in the US House and Senate have continually sought to weaken citizen participation provisions of laws such as the National Environmental Policy Act (NEPA), which mandates environmental analysis, transparency, and vigorous avenues for public involvement in federal decision-making. Often, developers and their allies seek to exempt projects from required environmental reviews. "They call it 'streamlining,'" Smith said, but "they're going after the public participation stuff."[36] In essence, while environmental reforms served to expand public participation in decision-making, anti-environmental initiatives often sought to reduce citizen participation. Environmental organizations defended participatory democracy when they defended public participation rules.

The democratic current has been foundational even for organizations that do not accomplish their work directly through grassroots volunteers. For example, the Center for Biological Diversity (CBD), a national environmental group founded in Arizona in 1989, has primarily employed a judicial strategy, suing to force federal and state agencies to implement environmental laws when those laws are ignored or circumvented. Unlike SOCM, which privileged local knowledge and "people power" over that of professional experts, the CBD has employed lawyers and scientists to protect endangered species and millions of acres of important wildlife habitat through administrative and judicial procedures codified through the democratic reforms of the 1960s and 1970s. While its approach focuses on litigation, CBD views its work in much the same vein as grassroots groups: as a strategic defense of democracy, law, citizen rights, and nature. The opponents of environmentalists have repeatedly portrayed the latter's legal strategies as obstructionism. CBD co-founder Kieran Suckling suggests that the public often overlooks the judicial branch of government as a legitimate part of a working democracy, equal in power to the executive and legislative branches. Likewise, we argue that the judicial strategy of the CBD and other groups that specialize in court procedures is crucial to the effective implementation of environmental law and crucial as well to a successful democracy. This point requires some elaboration.

According to Suckling, in the early years of the CBD's existence, its leaders discerned two core values in American environmental law: that decision-making should be based on the best science available and that the public should be deeply and meaningfully involved in decision-making. Documents the CBD obtained through the Freedom of Information Act—the law the CBD claims it uses more than any other—revealed many examples of government science being falsified and experts silenced for political reasons.

Suckling concluded, "You can fake the best science . . . the only protection against that is public oversight."[37]

Like our informants in the Sierra Club and SOCM, Suckling and other CBD leaders argued that transparency in government decisions and citizen participation made real differences in environmental protection. In a chapter written for a book reviewing the successes and failures of the Endangered Species Act (ESA) thirty years after its passage, Suckling together with CBD biologist and Endangered Species director D. Noah Greenwald, and executive coordinator of the National Parks Association of Queensland, Australia, Martin Taylor, put that hypothesis to the test. They found that from 1974 through 2003, the listing of species for protection under the ESA passed through four distinct phases, with the quantity of listings closely related to the level of meaningful public participation.[38]

In the first phase, 1974–81, there were no rules for how species should be listed, so many species that deserved protection under the law did not make it onto the list. Phase two began in 1982 when Congress amended the ESA by establishing two paths for listing—one in which the US Fish and Wildlife Service (USFWS) proposed a species for listing and a second process by which citizens could propose a listing. Congress also required the US Department of the Interior to act on citizen petitions for listings within a reasonable time line. These two reforms were based on the presumption that citizen participation would improve the policy performance of the agency authorized to implement the law. Nevertheless, the 1982 amendments lacked a vigorous enforcement mechanism, so the Department of the Interior simply delayed making decisions on controversial species.

In the third phase, which the authors date to a series of lawsuits in 1991, environmental groups were finally successful in forcing the department, through the courts, to act on a number of stalled proposals. Listings increased dramatically, from about forty species per year to an average of seventy-three per year until 1995, when Secretary of the Interior Bruce Babbitt introduced an administrative rule that once again slowed the listings by requiring quick action only for citizen petitions. In the fourth phase, from 1996 onward, listings declined markedly and remained low into the first decade of the twentieth century through the administration of George W. Bush. The Bush administration, generally hostile to ESA listings, implemented additional administrative rules that further stymied citizens' ability to force the government to implement the ESA. Remarkably, from 1974 to 2003 (the period studied by Suckling, Greenwald, and Taylor), citizens acting through environmental organizations accounted for 71 percent of all the species federally listed as threatened or endangered. Citizen participation was integral to the protection of endangered species and the habitat that sustained them.

While the CBD specializes in monitoring and forcing compliance with the Endangered Species Act, several older organizations—such as the Environmental Defense Fund, the Natural Resources Defense Council, and Earth Justice—also use the courts extensively to defend existing environmental laws, helping ensure that they are preserved and faithfully implemented. These groups have in a very real sense become an institutional enforcement arm of national environmental policy, evolving out of the legal reforms that empowered citizens to play that role. Architects of the citizen participation rules enacted in the 1960s and 1970s purposefully put those rules in place knowing that citizen oversight and pressure would help ensure that environmental protection policies were not ignored or subverted when those policies became inconvenient to powerful special interests.

"Power to the People"

As environmental protection efforts evolved through the three phases we identified from the 1960s through 1996, the ways in which citizens participated in environmental decision-making evolved—from promoting legislation to expanding and strengthening the movement to defending environmental laws and working to ensure their enforcement. Particularly in the 1960s and 1970s, citizens organized according to the hopeful notion that the passage of a well-written law would solve environmental problems. What they learned, however, was that the laws they helped enact were only as good as the ability and commitment of citizens to ensure their enforcement. The best way to do that was to maintain and, when possible, expand the democratic reforms that accompanied environmental protections in the 1960s and 1970s and maintain constant oversight and participation.

While SOCM passed little legislation to regulate solid waste in Tennessee during the 1990s, it ultimately defeated the proposals to import out-of-state garbage by defending and expanding the role of citizens to participate in decision-making. One of the key lessons of SOCM's campaign—and of the

environmental movement in the postwar era in general—is that environmental protection is an ongoing process whose success is intimately tied to
Americans' ability to participate in the decisions that affect them. Herein lies
a message of hope. Citizen involvement profoundly shaped the outcomes
of every reform movement in this nation's history. Since 1970, a substantial,
unbroken majority of Americans have consistently stated that they favor
environmental protection policies. How those values translate into on-the-
ground environmental accomplishments is determined in daily struggles by
committed volunteers and paid professionals engaging in the democratic
process, exercising their rights as American citizens to participate in governance. Our research reveals that the lived-experiences of environmental
activists are defined as much by a commitment to democratic rights as a
commitment to environmental protection. And as these stories reveal, so
long as citizens maintain the ability to influence decision-making, they can
positively influence environmental outcomes.

In a sense, the environmental protection system that evolved in the United
States resembles the ecological systems it aims to conserve. Ecosystems
require a degree of resiliency to sustain themselves—an ability to respond
to change while maintaining the integrity of the system over the long term.
Public participation mandates enshrined in America's system of environmental protection laws provide a similar kind of resiliency. While it may
never result in an environmental utopia like the one Ernest Callenbach
imagined in 1975 in his book *Ecotopia*, the ability of citizens to affect environmental decisions holds the promise of better and more responsive environmental governance in solving problems and protecting public goods. We have
these participatory rights and privileges only because committed activists
demanded them and, once secured, fought tirelessly to preserve them.

Notes

1. Richard N.L. Andrews, *Managing the Environment, Managing Ourselves*, 2nd ed.
(New Haven, CT: Yale University Press, 2006), 1.

2. "1993 Environmental Justice Bill: SOCM Works to Stop Corporate Criminals
and Out-of-State Waste," *SOCM Sentinel*, January 1993, 1–3, private collection, Statewide Organizing for Community Empowerment, Lake City, TN.

3. Among those who have noted the relationship between environmental and
democratic advocacy are Robert Gottlieb, *Forcing the Spring: The Transformation*

of the American Environmental Movement, rev. ed. (Washington, DC: Island, 2005), 134–48; Adam Rome, "'Give Earth a Chance': The Environmental Movement and the Sixties," *Journal of American History* 90 (September 2003): 525–54; Michael Egan, *Barry Commoner and the Science of Survival: The Remaking of American Environmentalism* (Cambridge, MA: MIT Press, 2007). Some contemporary writers who are not historians have noticed and written about this relationship, too. See William A. Shutkin, *The Land That Could Be: Environmentalism and Democracy in the Twenty-First Century* (Cambridge, MA: MIT Press, 2001); Charles Sabel, Archon Fung, and Bradley Karkkainen, "Beyond Backyard Environmentalism," chapter 1 in the book by the same title edited by Joshua Cohen and Joel Rogers (Boston, MA: Beacon, 2000). Of course, there have been numerous books and articles claiming environmentalism to be distinctly anti-democratic, including Alston Chase's polemical *In a Dark Wood* (New York: Houghton Mifflin, 1995); Robert Bullard's *Dumping in Dixie: Race, Class, and Environmental Quality*, 3rd ed. (Boulder: Westview, 2000); and numerous analysts who emphasize the elitist character of the old-line conservation movement. While not denying the existence of some authoritarian impulses, we argue here that democratic commitments are much more the norm among American environmental activists of the last fifty years.

4. Sarah L. Thomas, "A Call to Action: Silent Spring, Public Disclosure, and the Rise of Modern Environmentalism," in *Natural Protest: Essays on the History of American Environmentalism*, ed. Michael Egan and Jeff Crane (New York: Routledge, 2009), 185–203. Quote is on p. 186.

5. The authors of this chapter propose this novel articulation of three "phases" to the post-1950s environmental movement based on a synthesis of secondary sources and our own primary research. Evolutionary models proposed in much of the extant literature are outdated or inadequate or inattentive to grassroots environmental strategies. For example, Samuel Hays breaks the postwar environmental movement into three phases (1957–65, 1965–72, and 1972 onward) that emphasize the predominant environmental issues of each phase. See *Beauty, Health, and Permanence: Environmental Politics in the United States, 1955–1985* (Cambridge: Cambridge University Press, 1987), 54–56. This periodization misses important developments after Reagan and emphasizes the most visible campaigns rather than organizational and strategic developments.

6. Hays, *Beauty, Health, and Permanence*, 63.

7. Ying Zhao, "A Survey of Environmental Law and Enforcement Authorities in China," *Proceedings of the Fourth International Conference on Environmental Compliance and Enforcement*, vol. 2, 1996 https://www.inece.org/4thvol1/4toc.htm. Quotes are from p. 14 of Zhao's paper.

8. Gottlieb, *Forcing the Spring*, chapter 4.

9. Robert Cameron Mitchell, Angela G. Mertig, and Riley E. Dunlap, "Twenty Years of Environmental Mobilization: Trends among National Environmental Organizations," in Riley E. Dunlap and Angela G. Mertig, *American Environmentalism: The US Environmental Movement, 1970–1990* (Washington, DC: Taylor and Francis, 1992), 13.

10. The best study of Earth Day and its aftermath is Adam Rome, *The Genius of Earth Day: How a 1970 Teach-In Unexpectedly Made the First Green Generation* (New York: Hill and Wang, 2013). Regarding membership, see the Annual Membership Growth table in Stephen Fox, *John Muir and His Legacy: The American Conservation Movement* (Boston: Little, Brown, 1981), 315.

11. On the Reagan backlash and the resulting strengthening of environmentalism, see Hays, *Beauty, Health, and Permanence*, chapter 15. As Hays noted, "Reagan's policies actually strengthened public support for environmental organizations. Membership, resources, and organizational capabilities grew" (505). See also Mitchell, Mertig, and Dunlap, "Twenty Years of Environmental Mobilization," 15, for more data on membership growth in these years. See also Andrews, *Managing the Environment, Managing Ourselves*, chapter 13.

12. Two classic scholarly studies of the environmental opposition of the 1970s–90s are R. McGregor Cawley, *Federal Land, Western Anger: The Sagebrush Rebellion and Environmental Politics* (Lawrence: University Press of Kansas, 1993); and Jacqueline Switzer, *Green Backlash: The History and Politics of Environmental Opposition in the U.S.* (Boulder: Lynne Rienner, 1997).

13. Before the 1980s, many Republicans such as Nelson Rockefeller and Russell Train were leaders in the environmental movement. President Richard Nixon signed into law more far-reaching environmental laws than any of his postwar predecessors. Even arch-conservative Barry Goldwater said in *The Conscience of a Majority* (New York: Prentice Hall, 1971), "While I am a great believer in the free enterprise system and all that it entails, I am an even stronger believer in the right of our people to live in a clean, pollution-free environment." Historian Adam Rome reflects on this nearly forgotten legacy of conservatives advocating for the environment in his blog http://discourseinprogress.com/what-happened-to-conservative-conservation/.

14. Gottlieb, *Forcing the Spring*, chapter 5, quotes on p. 227. Of course, Gottlieb was not the first scholar to remark on this proliferation of grassroots environmental groups after 1970. Nicholas Freudenberg and Carol Steinsapir documented the phenomenon in the early 1990s in "Not in Our Backyards: The Grassroots Environmental Movement," in Riley E. Dunlap and Angela G. Mertig, *American Environmentalism: The US Environmental Movement, 1970–1990* (Washington, DC: Taylor and Frances, 1992), 27–37.

15. Freudenberg and Steinsapir, "Not in Our Backyards," 27–31. See also Robert Bullard and Beverly Wright, "The Quest for Environmental Equity: Mobilizing the African-American Community for Social Change," in Riley E. Dunlap and Angela G. Mertig, *American Environmentalism: The US Environmental Movement, 1970–1990* (Washington, DC: Taylor and Frances, 1992), 39–49; Robert Gottlieb and Helen Ingram, "The New Environmentalists," *The Progressive* 52 (1988): 14–15.

16. Research and writing for these case studies occurred first as part of a dissertation and then in conjunction with writing the book manuscript for *This Is Our Land*. See Cody Ferguson, *"This Is Our Land": Grassroots Environmentalism in the Late Twentieth Century* (New Brunswick, NJ: Rutgers University Press, 2015). The case studies are used here to illuminate the especially close alignment of democratic and environmental reform in the minds and actions of activists. *This Is Our Land* expands parts of the arguments presented here while providing a deeper investigation of the origins and growth of grassroots conservation organizations and the transformation of these organizations and their members over the first three decades of the modern environmental era.

17. From "Table 4, Per Capita Hazardous Waste Generation of Selected Countries," n.d., no author, solid-waste research, private collection, Statewide Organizing for Community Empowerment, Lake City, Tennessee, cited as from Harvey Yackowitz, "Harmonization of Specific Descriptors of Special Wastes Subject to National Controls of Eleven OECD Countries," in *Transformation Movements of Hazardous Wastes* (Paris: Organization for Economic Cooperation and Development, 1985), 53. Like the previous case study, this is a condensed version of a case study that appears in Ferguson, *This Is Our Land*; see Ferguson, *This Is Our Land* for a more detailed account of SOCM's solid-waste campaign during the 1990s.

18. H. Lanier Hickman, *American Alchemy: The History of Solid Waste Management in the United States* (Santa Barbara: Forester, 2003), 524.

19. David Naguib Pellow, *Garbage Wars: The Struggle for Environmental Justice in Chicago* (Cambridge, MA: MIT Press, 2002); Robert J. Brulle, *Agency, Democracy, and Nature: The US Environmental Movement from a Critical Theory Perspective* (Cambridge, MA: MIT Press, 2000), 212; Bullard, *Dumping in Dixie*. Pellow traces this phenomenon—how people of color, immigrants, and low-income populations came to bear a disproportionate share of the burden of wastes—in Chicago dating back to 1880; Brulle recounts a report prepared for the California Waste Management Board in 1987 in which the authors recommended siting municipal waste and toxic waste incinerators in communities that did not find the developments offensive, characterized as low-income, low-education, high-minority populations and those desperate for economic development.

20. Ferguson, *This Is Our Land*, 161; Bill Allen, "Save Our Cumberland Mountains: Growth and Change within a Grassroots Organization," in *Fighting Back in Appalachia: Traditions of Resistance and Change*, ed. Stephen L. Fisher (Philadelphia: Temple University Press, 1993), 85; "AN UPDATE ON THE PRIVATE DUMP ISSUE IN HUMPHREYS COUNTY," Citizens against Pollution, Waverly, Tennessee, n.d., private collection, Statewide Organization for Community Empowerment, Lake City, Tennessee; "Group Fights Landfill Expansion," *Commercial Appeal* (Memphis), August 26, 1993; "Toxics Committee Off and Running," *SOCM Sentinel*, January 1990, 4. Allen traces the origins of internal discussion about landfills and whether SOCM should work on toxic issues back to a leadership retreat in 1988. By the following year, it was a high priority for the group.

21. Ferguson, *This Is Our Land*, 157–58, 161; Duncan Mansfield, "East Tennessee Residents Picket over Landfills," *Greenville Sun* (Tennessee), May 10, 1990; Betsy Kauffman, "Protesters Accuse State of Landfill Laxity," *Knoxville News-Sentinel*, May 10, 1990; "State Hears from SOCM about Waste," *SOCM Sentinel*, December 1990, 8–9; "SOCM's Legislative Efforts End after Roller Coaster Ride," *SOCM Sentinel*, June 1991, 5–7; State of Tennessee General Assembly, *Senate Journal of the Ninety-Seventh General Assembly of the State of Tennessee*, Nashville, Tuesday, January 14, 1992, Second Regular and First Extraordinary Sessions (Nashville: Tennessee General Assembly, 1992).

22. Ferguson, *This Is Our Land*, 162–63; "Campbell County Chapter Gains Great New Members and Several New Issues in One Community," *SOCM Sentinel*, July 1990, 2; "Campbell County Chapter Victorious with Jackson Law," *SOCM Sentinel*, September 1990, 11; "Oliver Springs Victory: County Holds Firm," *SOCM Sentinel*, December 1990, 1–2; "Landfill Case Goes to Trial," *SOCM Sentinel*, January 1991, 9–10; "Yeah . . . We Won!" *SOCM Sentinel*, January 1991, 11; "Oliver Springs Celebrates Victory," *SOCM Sentinel*, February 1991, 1, 7.

23. Ferguson, *This Is Our Land*, 163–65; "SOCM's Legislative Efforts End after Roller Coaster Ride," *SOCM Sentinel*, June 1991, 5–7; *Senate Journal of the Ninety-Seventh General Assembly of the State of Tennessee*.

24. Ferguson, *This Is Our Land*, 164–65; "SOCM Drafts Bill to Stop Out-of-State Waste," *SOCM Sentinel*, November–December 1992, 18; Maureen O'Connell, interview by Cody Ferguson, Lake City, Tennessee, June 25, 2010; "1993 Environmental Justice Bill: SOCM Works to Stop Corporate Criminals and Out-of-State Waste," *SOCM Sentinel*, January 1993, 1–2.

25. Ferguson, *This Is Our* Land, 167–68; Sara Kendall, Western Organization of Resource Councils, to People Interested in Right to Say No, memorandum, June 19, 1995, private collection, Statewide Organizing for Community Empowerment, Lake City, Tennessee; "Right to Say No Federal Bill Update," no author, September 9,

1994, private collection, Statewide Organizing for Community Empowerment, Lake City, Tennessee; "Comparison of Right to Say 'No' Bills," Save Our Cumberland Mountains, n.d., private collection, Statewide Organizing for Community Empowerment, Lake City, Tennessee; "Action Alert," Western Organization of Resource Councils, n.d., private collection, Statewide Organizing for Community Empowerment, Lake City, Tennessee.

26. Ferguson, *This Is Our Land*, 168–69.

27. Ferguson, *This Is Our Land*, 170; "*Landfill Enforcement in Tennessee*: A Study of Enforcement of Regulations Governing Class I Solid Waste Disposal Facilities in Tennessee," November 1, 1995, Save Our Cumberland Mountains, Lake City, Tennessee; "Solid Waste Study Released! Toxics Committee Set to Meet with D.E.C Officials," *SOCM Sentinel*, November–December 1995, 5.

28. Ferguson, *This Is Our Land*, 170; "*SOCM Wins Major Improvements in Landfill Enforcement*: Toxics Committee Meets with D.E.C. Deputy Commissioner Wayne Scharber and Other Officials, Wins Concessions," *SOCM Sentinel*, January–February 1996, 1, 4.

29. Ferguson, *This Is Our Land*, 170; "UPDATE: SOCM LANDFILL ENFORCEMENT STUDY AND FOLLOWUP," April 15, 1996, Save Our Cumberland Mountains, private collection, Statewide Organizing for Community Empowerment, Lake City, Tennessee.

30. Ferguson, *This Is Our Land*, 183; Zhao, "Survey of Environmental Law and Enforcement Authorities in China," 14.

31. Ferguson, *This Is Our Land*, 172; O'Connell interview; Franz Raetzer, interview by Cody Ferguson, Harriman, Tennessee, July 1, 2010.

32. Joni Adamson, Mei Mei Evans, and Rachel Stein, eds., *The Environmental Justice Reader: Politics, Poetics, and Pedagogy* (Tucson: University of Arizona Press, 2002), 4. See Bullard, *Dumping in Dixie*; David Naguib Pellow and Robert J. Brulle, *Power, Justice, and the Environment: A Critical Appraisal of the Environmental Justice Movement* (Cambridge, MA: MIT Press, 2005).

33. Vera Norwood, *Made from This Earth: American Women and Nature* (Chapel Hill: University of North Carolina Press, 1993), xiv, 148. Blum observes that in the Love Canal case, of the citizen activists who spoke out publicly on the toxics issue, women tended to emphasize traditionally maternal values in conjunction with arguing for their rights as citizens and taxpayers to justify protecting the health of their children and community, whereas men tended to emphasize economic arguments such as the loss of property value as a result of toxic contamination. She notes, however, that at times women used the economic argument and men the health and welfare argument and that middle-class men and women tended to frame their arguments in environmental terms, whereas working-class and African

American activists tended not to do so. Elizabeth D. Blum, *Love Canal Revisited: Race, Class, and Gender in Environmental Activism* (Lawrence: University of Kansas Press, 2008), 6, 31, 49, 50. In some instances, women of color faced challenges distinct from those of Anglo women in addressing environmental issues in their communities. Andrea Simpson documents how the local media's unwillingness to interview local female African American activists who were not scientific "experts" hindered mobilizing an African American community to address toxic contamination in Memphis, Tennessee, during the early 2000s. See Andrea Simpson, "Who Hears Their Cry? African American Women and the Fight for Environmental Justice in Memphis, Tennessee," in *The Environmental Justice Reader: Politics, Poetics, and Pedagogy*, ed. Joni Adamson, Mei Mei Evans, and Rachel Stein (Tucson: University of Arizona Press, 2002), 82–104.

34. https://www.epa.gov/laws-regulations/summary-executive-order-12898 -federal-actions-address-environmental-justice, accessed March 27, 2016.

35. https://www.sierraclub.org/environmental-justice, accessed March 27, 2016.

36. Rob Smith, interview by authors, Phoenix, Arizona, December 9, 2009.

37. Kieran Suckling, interview by authors, Tucson, Arizona, November 22, 2009.

38. D. Noah Greenwald, Kieran F. Suckling, and Martin Taylor, "The Listing Record, 2006," in *The Endangered Species Act at Thirty: Renewing the Conservation Commitment*, ed. Dale D. Goble, J. Michael Scott, and Frank W. Davis (Washington, DC: Island, 2006), 55–61.

Spatial Dynamics

4

Returning to the Slough

Environmental Justice in Portland, Oregon

ELLEN STROUD

When I first learned about the Columbia Slough some twenty-odd years ago, it was a slow-moving, filthy mess of a marshy stream, winding through a neighborhood of decent but not great housing mixed with light industry. Some people living nearby remembered it as an oasis of nature on the city's edge, but little of that former life remained.[1] Its lamentable claim to fame was as a surprisingly toxic waterway in one of the only non-white neighborhoods in Portland, Oregon.[2]

Now in the second decade of the twenty-first century, it is by most measures a far cleaner, safer waterway, and environmental organizations host kayaking and birding outings there—sometimes in Spanish—to introduce Portlanders to nature at their doorsteps. Blue herons, red-tail hawks, bald eagles, great-horned owls, otters, turtles, and even salmon now call the slough home. But multilingual warning signs are still posted along the route: visitors are told in fourteen languages—including Ukrainian, Vietnamese, and Swahili—that the water is dangerous. As habitat for non-human animals, the slough is much improved. For people, things are better but still not great.[3]

DOI: 10.5876/9781607328483.c004

When the slough is in the news, the health of the waterway for people gets far less emphasis than does its health for birds and fish. For humans, the primary benefit touted is "open space" for recreation. Perhaps this has been useful: the language of bird and salmon habitat may have been more broadly compelling than campaigns for cleaner soil and air. Successfully packaging the slough as a slice of nature in the city may have been precisely what was needed to secure funding for restoration and for recreational programming, which are in turn connected to new regulations and initiatives that have stopped the most egregious polluters.[4]

For much of the twentieth century, millions of gallons of Portland's raw sewage were dumped into this slow-moving waterway each month, and more than 200 industries along its banks contributed to the accumulated contamination. The first businesses along the waterway included slaughter-houses, stockyards, a meat-packing plant, a dairy farm, a shingle company, and a lumber mill; and their sewage flowed directly into the slough. The area's association with industry intensified when the wartime shipbuilding industry came to town.[5] De-icing fluid from Portland International Airport, pesticides from farms and golf courses, and toxins leaching from a municipal landfill all drained to the water as well. Toxic sludge lines the slough's floor.[6]

In the 1990s, the Portland environmental group Northwest Environmental Advocates charged that the city had allowed the slough to become and remain polluted because the communities affected were primarily communities of color. According to Richard Brown, a community activist who worked with Portland's Black United Front, many of the people who fished for years for subsistence along the slough were African Americans and recent immigrants. Although danger signs had been posted to discourage people from eating slough fish, those who lived near the slough were at continued risk of expo-sure to the toxins concentrated there.[7]

Economic vulnerability, housing discrimination, and a lack of political clout have hampered the ability of North Portland residents to resist pollu-tion in their neighborhoods or to choose to live in cleaner areas. However, the history of this discriminatory landscape cannot be entirely explained by explicit racism in politics, housing, and employment. The politics and geog-raphy of industrial location, wartime changes in Portland's population and economy, the limitations of the goals and achievements of Oregon's envi-ronmental movement, and changing perceptions of the North Portland neighborhoods have all contributed to the area's social and environmental landscapes. Throughout the second half of the twentieth century, the land near the Columbia Slough appeared on the cognitive map of many Portlanders as a throwaway place, an area best suited to industry and waste. That perception, which had a multiplicity of origins, was as much a cause as an effect of the environmental disaster at the slough. Portlanders in power thought the North Portland Peninsula was a disaster, and so it was. But since the 1990s, hard work by civil rights and environmental activists alongside ecologists and local residents has begun to shape a new image of the slough and its environs—as wildlife habitat and nature preserve. The slough's legacy as a sacrificed waterway endures, but many more constituencies now see it as a resource to invest in and protect.

Pollution was rampant at the slough before the settlement of a significant minority population nearby, and the concerns of the slough's residential neighbors have a long history of being subordinate to business interests. However, when the area became identified with minority residents during World War II, the assault on the local environment intensified. For industrial developers, city planners, and, later, environmental activists, the association of the North Portland Peninsula with African American residents contributed to a perception of the area as degraded and therefore as an appropriate place for further degradation. Likewise, recent white gentrification has accompanied recent improvements, both as cause and effect.

Until the 1940s, most people who lived on the North Portland Peninsula near the slough were working-class people of European ancestry. The jobs that accompanied the industry-friendly development of the peninsula, which was encouraged by the area's proximity to the confluence of the Willamette and Columbia Rivers, helped maintain the respectable working-class reputation the area had earned. Like other waterfront areas, the North Portland Peninsula attracted industry because of the transportation and sewage disposal options the waters offered.[8]

The outbreak of World War II pushed Portland's already strained housing situation to a crisis. When industrialist Henry J. Kaiser realized that the lack of housing was threatening his ability to recruit the army of workers the wartime production schedule at his Oregon Shipbuilding Corporation factories demanded, he took matters into his own hands. Kaiser went straight to the federal government and secured funding to build his own worker housing complex. Once the project was under way, the Housing Authority of Portland had little choice but to accept administration responsibilities for the project from the Federal Public Housing Authority, which oversaw the construction.[9]

In August 1942, the Federal Public Housing Authority approved Kaiser's plan to build cheap wood apartment buildings on 650 acres of lowlands near the Columbia Slough, just outside Portland city limits. Before the construction of Kaiserville, which was later renamed Vanport City, this area between the slough and the Columbia River had been marsh, pasture, and farmland. It was bounded on all four sides by dikes between fifteen feet and twenty-five feet high, which had kept the waters of both the slough and the river from flooding the farmland. To the south of Vanport, the county drainage district had built a dike in 1920, and a dike to the north held back the waters of the Columbia River. Dikes to the east and west served the double purpose of keeping back water from the surrounding marshes and providing transportation routes across their crests. Denver Avenue, a link in the Seattle–Los Angeles Highway, ran atop the eastern dike, and the tracks of the Spokane, Portland, & Seattle Railroad topped the dike to the west. People who lived in this walled city described the uneasy feeling of living in a place with no horizons.[10]

By January 1943, about 6,000 people were living in two-story, box-like apartment buildings on the former, though still muddy, wetland. By the end of March, 10,000 people called Vanport home. By early November of that year, the population had reached 39,000, making it Oregon's second largest city. The population remained near 40,000 until shipyard production waned at war's end. By July 1946, the population had dropped to about 26,000 and was continuing to fall. After residency requirements were relaxed, allowing people who did not work at the shipyards to settle in Vanport, the postwar population finally stabilized at around 18,500. It remained at that level until the city was wiped out by a flood in 1948. Despite its short life, Vanport had a dramatic effect on the image of the peninsula and thereby the condition of the slough.[11]

Although the Housing Authority of Portland eventually administered sixteen different wartime housing projects, Vanport housed more people than those other projects combined.[12] Indeed, Vanport was not only Oregon's largest wartime housing complex, it was the largest in the nation. However, the Vanport homes were not intended as permanent housing. Rather, they were built as temporary wartime accommodations. The Portland establishment, including the members of the Housing Authority, expected the war industry workers to head home once peace was declared. In fact, throughout the war, members of the Housing Authority of Portland maintained that the site where Vanport was located would be most appropriately used for industry after the war's end, and the fact that public housing had been located on the peninsula seemed to accelerate rather than retard the push for industrial development. Politicians and planners argued that the kinds of people public housing attracted demonstrated that public housing was not in the peninsula's best interest.[13]

During the war, the North Portland Peninsula acquired a reputation as an area of industry, housing projects, and black residents. The first two characterizations were accurate, but the third was not. Nevertheless, the identification of North Portland with African Americans contributed to the perception of the area as blighted, suitable only for industry and for those who could not afford to live elsewhere. Many white city residents, politicians, and businessmen were beginning to see North Portland as a throwaway zone.

Although North Portland was not a predominantly black area in the 1940s, the promise of jobs at the Kaiser shipyards had attracted large numbers of African Americans to the Portland area for the first time, and many of them, along with many white migrants, found housing on the peninsula. In 1940, only 1,800 black people lived in Oregon. By 1944, that number had grown to about 15,000, with over one third living in Vanport.[14] Although many white families moved out of Vanport at the war's end, most black families remained, in part because racist real estate practices and restrictions kept them from moving to many places in Portland.[15]

Having black neighbors was a new experience for most Portlanders, and although African Americans never accounted for more than 28 percent of the population of Vanport or more than 18 percent during the war years, the community quickly acquired a reputation as a "negro project"; the Housing Authority of Portland was very worried about what it termed the "negro problem."[16] As early as 1943, Housing Authority commissioners were regularly spending portions of their meetings anxiously discussing the "negro situation." Among their concerns were Vanport events they described as "mixed dances (negro & white)." The Vanport sheriff reported that the dances, "from a police standpoint, cannot be tolerated." Separate recreational facilities for black and white residents were considered, but the housing commissioners were concerned that federal rules against discrimination in housing projects might interfere with that plan. The authority was unable to decide on a solution to what it had come to believe was a crisis.[17]

As early as February 1945, the Housing Authority of Portland was making plans for the destruction of Vanport, despite the fact that it was still 95 percent occupied at the time.[18] But it wasn't until May 1948 that Vanport was destroyed, with floodwaters washing the city away. On Memorial Day of that year, heavy rains and particularly warm weather had brought the waters of the Columbia River, behind Vanport's northern dike, and Smith Lake, behind the western dike, to fifteen feet above the city floor. The water in the Columbia Slough, to Vanport's south, was quickly rising, too. That morning, the sheriff's office assured Vanport residents that there was nothing to fear. But shortly after 4 p.m., floodwaters crashed through the railroad dike to the west, and a ten-foot wall of water careened through Vanport, sweeping buildings off their flimsy foundations. More than 2,000 people were initially declared missing in the flood; 15 people were confirmed dead and another 18 were missing. The next day, the Denver Avenue dike to the east of Vanport gave way as well, and Vanport apartment buildings began floating through the breach toward the present-day site of the Portland Meadows Race Track.[19]

The Columbia River had reclaimed its floodplain. Vanport was not rebuilt, and its 18,000 residents had to find housing elsewhere. While white residents scattered throughout the city, most black residents moved to Albina, a run-down part of town south of the North Portland Peninsula, just across the Willamette River from Portland's Central Business District. Historically, Albina had been a stopover district for recent immigrants of European descent, and it held the most densely built housing in the city. The neighborhood was one of the few areas in Portland from which black people were not excluded by racist white homeowners and real estate agents, who employed tactics ranging from restrictive housing covenants to outright violence to exclude African Americans from most neighborhoods. By the 1930s, Albina had become the center of Portland's small black community, and when the flood destroyed Vanport, the development's black residents had little choice but to seek housing in that already overcrowded district.[20]

Although black residents had left the North Portland Peninsula and would not move back there in large numbers until the 1960s, the area's reputation as a black neighborhood would continue to encourage the placement of industry there. The disappearance of this major housing project on the peninsula, coupled with the endurance of a reputation of blight, helped clear the way for intensive industrial development nearby at a time when environmentalists were beginning to secure gains elsewhere in the city and the state.[21]

In the early 1950s, conditions of the slough became so bad that mill workers refused to handle logs that had traveled through the water. Meat-packing plant waste, hog ranch waste, and lumber and shingle mill waste would cling to the logs as they floated down the slough to the mills.[22] Related concerns drove many of the industries that relied on navigation of the slough to relocate in the early 1950s, and by 1965, all commercial traffic on the slough had stopped.[23] Industrial developers who chose sites near the slough after this point saw proximity to the waterway as a benefit not for transportation purposes but rather for the disposal of wastes.

Until the 1950s, Portland's sewers dumped the city's waste, untreated, into the Willamette River and the Columbia Slough. In an attempt to clean up the local waterways, the city of Portland finally began building a sewage treatment plant in the late 1940s, which began operating in 1951. Unfortunately, this by no means solved the peninsula's sewage woes. The plant, which provided for the treatment of much of Portland's sewage before discharging it into the Columbia River, contributed significantly to the improvement of the water quality of the slough and the rivers. However, the city placed the plant itself on the banks of the slough. The peninsula was still collecting the city's sludge.[24]

Also, despite the new plant, not all sewage was treated before it reached the waterways. Although many of the industries that had been dumping their sewage into the slough began to send it to the treatment plant, a number of businesses that were not connected to city sewers continued to send their waste directly into the slough. In addition, although the city sewers had been rerouted to the treatment plant, the plant was not always able to handle all the sewage sent there. When storm water mixed with the sewage, it exceeded the treatment plant's capacity. At these times, the sewers would overflow and a mixture of sewage and storm water would spill over weirs, or gates, in the sewer pipes and fall into the Willamette and the slough. Such an occurrence, frequent in rainy Portland, is called a "combined sewer overflow," or CSO. Although this arrangement was far superior to dumping all raw sewage directly into the water, CSOs were still a serious problem facing the slough.[25] Not until a twenty-year sewer infrastructure project was completed in 2011 was the system largely (although not completely) fixed.[26]

In those same decades, the Portland Planning Commission continued to see North Portland as most appropriate for industrial uses. Factors the commission considered when choosing where to site industry in the city were indicated in a handwritten outline for a commission report on expanding the city's industrial sector, listing "housing condition and population characteristics" as key. The population characteristics the outline specifically called attention to were "stability," "income," and "non-white" status. The implication was that low-income minority neighborhoods were the most appropriate for industry. Other neighborhoods would be protected from industrial blight. This practice of placing industry in areas seen as already blighted would continue throughout the 1970s and 1980s.[27]

The impression left by Vanport that the peninsula was a "minority" area encouraged the siting of industry there. Among the businesses that opened along the slough in the postwar years were numerous metal production plants and chemical plants, a wood treatment facility, and a construction materials plant, which contributed to the accumulation of lead, pentachlorophenol (PCP), polychlorinated biphenyls (PCBs), cyanide, chromium, hydrochloric acid, dioxins, and other pollutants in the slough. Ironically, by the time African Americans returned to the North Portland Peninsula in substantial (although not majority) numbers, they were finding affordable housing in neighborhoods that had been devalued and rendered toxic, in part by the idea that black residents called the place home.[28]

At the same time Portland's industry was being concentrated around the slough, Oregon was beginning to acquire what has become an enduring reputation as a place where environmentalists are in charge and people live in balance with the natural world. The Columbia Slough, however, is not simply a forgotten waterway that missed the environmental fervor. Rather, it is a sacrificed waterway. Oregon's shiny green veneer was paid for in part by the filth of waterways like the slough and neighborhoods like those of the North Portland Peninsula.

Tom McCall, Oregon's governor from 1967 to 1974, was largely responsible for Portland being able to bask in its reputation for environmentally friendly development.[29] During his first term as governor, McCall oversaw the creation of the Oregon Department of Environmental Quality and the concerted effort to clean up the Willamette River, which had been so polluted that fish suffocated in its waters. He also pushed through the five "B" bills, which "required removal of billboards, reasserted public ownership of ocean beaches, set minimum deposits on beverage bottles and cans, allocated money for bicycle paths from highway revenues, and tied bonding for pollution abatement to the growth of total assessed values."[30]

Perhaps the most dramatic environmental accomplishment of McCall's administration was that final "B," which came to stand not so much for "bonds" as for "boundaries." His administration established the Land Conservation and Development Commission in 1973, the job of which was to oversee local compliance with newly established statewide land-use planning goals. Among the goals were the preservation of farmland, the energy-efficient use of land, and the definition of urban growth boundaries to set limits on urban sprawl.[31]

The urban growth boundaries in particular changed the face of land-use planning in Oregon. In the 1950s and 1960s, Oregon had been experiencing rapid suburban growth. Single-family homes on large plots were eating away at the state's open space and at the land on which Oregon's farming and resource industries depended. The urban growth boundaries contained that sprawl by encouraging the intensive development of urban areas and by setting limits on development outside the boundaries. Metropolitan growth began to be seen as environmental degradation, and Oregonians wanted to protect against the peril of "Californication."[32]

The main goal of limiting growth beyond urban borders was not to preserve open space or wilderness but to support "the vitality of the agricultural and forest industries."[33] In addition, as historian Carl Abbott has argued, the programs of this land-use plan "protected middle and upperclass neighborhoods and residents and benefited the metropolitan economy. It is certainly true that the same programs neglected the needs of the poor and failed to share out the costs of growth equally."[34]

Although planners paid much attention to the regional economic and environmental aspects of metropolitan planning, they did not give much consideration to the experiences different groups would have with the new rules.[35] At the slough, land-use regulations worked against the working-class and minority people who lived there. At a time when much of the state was being cleaned up, the Columbia Slough stagnated. Industries continued to dump sewage into the slough, and the Port of Portland continued to invite new industries to the area. The residents protested, but their complaints had little effect. This had become an industrial area, one of the few places in the state that was allowed to remain filthy so that industry could thrive while the rest of Oregon was provided with a cleaner, healthier environment.[36]

North Portland residents protested what they saw happening to their neighborhoods. In 1971, an article in the *Oregonian* quoted Oregon State Marine Board director Robert Rittenhouse describing the Columbia Slough as "the rottenest stream in the Northwest." The same article explained that the Port of Portland saw the slough as "playing a key role" in the area's long-range industrial planning and hinted at the reason the waterway was not included in cleanup plans: "The slough is close to thousands of North Portlanders, many retired and with low incomes—people with little political power." The article went on to describe how many of the neighborhood people favored using the slough not as a drainage or sewage canal and not for navigation but for recreation and for food. "Fish caught there in the past have supplemented the diet of some people with skimpy grocery budgets," the article reported."[37]

However, in the early 1970s, the Port of Portland was not focusing on the slough as a neighborhood resource. Rather, it was concentrating on the possibilities for expanding industrial development in the slough area. Port officials argued that the slough was so filthy that more industrial development was really all the area was good for. The port's primary question about the slough was how to best manage it for industry, and that meant a choice between managing for flood control or managing for navigation. The port, which was one of the more powerful of the many government agencies involved in planning for this area and which framed the terms of the debate for many of the other government participants, favored flood control. Cleaning the slough, though still discussed, began to be portrayed as a lofty but impractical goal.[38]

The Oregon State Game Commission, in assessing the ecological impact of the port's plan for the Columbia Slough area, wrote in approval that "concentrating, rather than scattering, industry and residential areas minimizes damage to wildlife by preserving natural habitat and open spaces. The public often comments about the lack of fish and wildlife, yet thinks nothing of the adverse effect on wild animals from scattering houses and factories throughout our best habitat." The North Portland area was being sacrificed so that the "best habitat," in other parts of the city and state, could be preserved.[39]

Residents of the peninsula were not pleased with the proposals, and they resented the process by which decisions had been made. As early as 1971, area residents were upset that the public had had no part in the planning of a large industrial district on the peninsula.[40] By 1973, area agencies were finally beginning to solicit public participation in the decision-making processes. However, the agencies that requested public input often paid little attention to what residents actually said.

In response to public demands for attention to neighborhood concerns, the US Army Corps of Engineers held a public workshop in June 1973 to try to form a citizens' advisory committee, but at the meeting, residents felt intimidated by the presence of so many government agencies. Meeting with representatives of the Army Corps of Engineers were officials from the Port of Portland, the Columbia Region Association of Governments, the Multnomah County Planning Commission, the Oregon State Marine Board, the Oregon State Water Resources Board, the City of Portland Parks Bureau, the US General Accounting Office, Bonneville Power Administration, and the Oregon State Highway Division. In addition, representatives from many area industries, including the Union Pacific Railroad Company, Moar Lumber Company, and Upland Industries Corporation, were there. Fewer than half of the almost seventy people who filled out attendance cards after the meeting identified themselves as area homeowners, residents or members of neighborhood organizations.[41]

Residents did not feel welcome, either. Mary Runyon complained at the meeting, "The residents have been pushed around by various agencies and the fact that there are so many agencies represented here tonight gives us the feeling we are being overpowered." Clifford Nelson agreed with her. "Many of the people who are doing so much talking do not live down here. Why is there so much talk if they do not live down here?" he asked. Joe Heidel of the Army Corps of Engineers told him that living in the area was no prerequisite to being interested in the slough.[42]

The meeting was a confusing affair. The Corps of Engineers wanted to limit the topic of discussion to its area of jurisdiction—flood control—and the related issues of recreation, water-quality improvement, and fish and wildlife habitat. However, area residents wanted a more wide-ranging conversation. Their interests included public health, industrial zoning, proximity of housing to industry, rights of property owners, and more. There was no clear sense of what the meeting was intended to accomplish, and many

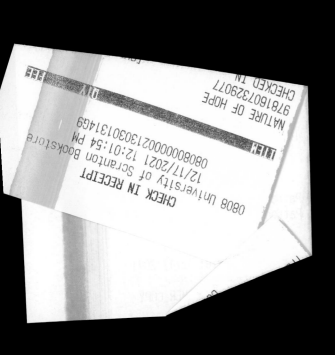

people were left irritated and confused. Bond Easly commented toward the end of the workshop, "I don't know what you have been talking about tonight." Virginia Monroe hoped to understand more when she read the minutes of the meeting later. "When you send out the minutes of the meeting, would you please explain some of these terms you are using such as 'pondage'?" she asked.[43]

In October 1974, the North Portland Citizen's Committee held a conference titled "North Peninsula Environment '74: Lakes, Lands & Livability." Sharon Roso, who compiled the conference report, had participated in the Army Corps of Engineers' workshop the previous year. This conference was designed specifically with the needs of community residents in mind. The purpose of the conference, according to Roso, was "to find out agency plans for and needs of that area, and for local people and agency people to ask specific questions regarding lakes, land and livability, e.g., traffic generation and patterns, air quality outlook, recreational uses, noise generation, water quality, funding possibilities, recycling possibilities and mass transit potential." Among the agencies the committee invited to participate in the conference were the Army Corps of Engineers, the Port of Portland, the Portland Landfill, the Department of Environmental Quality (DEQ), the Multnomah County Planning Bureau, the Portland Planning Bureau, and the Columbia Region Association of Governments. The conference culminated with North Portland residents mapping their priorities for their environment, which they then presented to the various agencies.[44]

Water pollution was one of the citizens' primary concerns. Roso wrote in the conference report, "We believe no industry should be allowed to pollute, in any way, any of the water [in the] Willamette River, Columbia River, Columbia Slough, [or in] Smith or Bybee lakes. We feel the DEQ should make arrangements for cleanup of the Columbia Slough, and enforce a policy of no pollution there." Water quality was something the residents did not want to see compromised in any way.[45]

The citizens were also highly concerned about air quality. "We feel the Port's marketing practices encourage polluting industries," Roso wrote. The citizens' requests made it clear that they felt as though their neighborhood was being used as a dumping ground. "Treat the North Portland Peninsula as a natural resource rather than as an area for dumping industry unwanted in cleaner areas, or a site for maximum development, or maximum profit," they requested of the port. Area residents were also concerned with noise pollution and increased traffic on their streets.[46]

Almost all of the community's requests were ignored. The slough area was zoned for heavy industry, and the St. John's Landfill on the banks of the slough was kept open until 1991, when it could hold no more garbage. The DEQ continued to issue permits to polluting industries, including those that dumped factory waste directly into the slough. And the North Portland Peninsula remained a dumping ground for industry that no one wanted anywhere else. The planning bureaucracy handed down the decision to continue developing North Portland as a haven for heavy industry, with little regard for the people living there.[47]

Also during the 1970s, the peninsula's minority population was on the rise, as greater numbers of African Americans and recent immigrants began to find housing in the neighborhoods near the slough. In 1950, when only 4 percent of Portland residents were classified as non-white in the federal census, the census tracts along the slough reported similar numbers. By 1970, in most of the census tracts along the lower Columbia Slough, the percentage of non-white residents was at least twice as high as the city-wide average.[48] In 1990, the census reported that the minority proportion of the population on the peninsula had continued to increase. That year, 7.6 percent of residents of the Portland metropolitan area were classified as black, and 15 percent were classified as non-white. In contrast, in seven of the nine census tracts along the lower slough, 17 percent of the residents were classified as black and over 23 percent as non-white. One tract was 44 percent black and 51 percent non-white; another was 62 percent black and 67 percent non-white. By this time, fully one quarter of Portland's African American residents lived in the immediate vicinity of the slough, and the proportion living in the old Albina district had significantly declined.[49]

The decline in the number of African American residents in the Albina district resulted in part from urban renewal projects undertaken there during the 1950s and 1960s. Many Albina residents were displaced by the construction of the Portland Coliseum in the 1950s and by the construction of Interstate 5 in the 1960s. Although a US Supreme Court ruling had outlawed restrictive covenants in 1948 and Oregon state law had outlawed all discrimination in housing in 1959, many African Americans continued to face opposition when they sought housing in many Portland neighborhoods. Census statistics show that most African American Portland residents found housing near the Albina district even after large blocks of housing were razed to make way for the sports arena and the highway, and then in the later twentieth century, the center of Portland's African American population shifted to the north, toward the Columbia Slough.[50]

Indeed, housing closer to the slough was better in many ways than that in the old Albina district, and income information from the census suggests that a move from the Albina area to the neighborhoods of the North Portland Peninsula was a move up the socioeconomic scale. The homes there were in better condition, there was more space between houses, and there were more and bigger lawns. The sewage and industrial filth that polluted the neighborhoods were not so visible at first glance. Better housing for many African American in Portland meant worse water and worse air.[51]

The pollution and industrial development that kept property values lower on the peninsula, a decrease in turn encouraged by assumptions about the types of people who did and should live in these neighborhoods, meant that relatively inexpensive housing was available for African Americans, working-class white Portlanders, and recent immigrants. At the end of the twentieth century, half of the census tracts along the slough had a significantly higher population of both recent immigrants and African Americans than the city-wide average as well as more people who spoke no English at all, trends that have continued in recent years.[52] As part of its mid-1990s campaign to educate people against eating fish caught in the Columbia Slough, the Portland Bureau of Environmental Services commissioned a survey that suggested that the majority of people who were eating fish caught in the slow-moving waterway were recent immigrants. Hence the multilingual warning signs posted at the slough.

Fishing for food remains a danger there and is discouraged. Yet both canoeing and kayaking are now enthusiastically promoted, as are hiking, cycling, and birding. Boating the slough in particular is strategically important: paddling events connect a broad constituency to the slough in a visceral way while also confirming that it is a navigable waterway and thereby subject to the provisions of the federal Clean Water Act. In fact, much of the area around the slough is far prettier—and much cleaner and safer—than it was twenty years ago. That said, a slough that is lovely but not healthy is not yet a slough that is clean enough; substantial improvements can and should continue.[53]

A long history of development and zoning decisions coupled with discriminatory housing practices and inequitable environmental policies have created the North Portland landscape of the early twenty-first century, in which the most toxic neighborhoods in the city also have the highest proportion of minority residents. City planners, politicians, developers, real estate agents, homeowners, landlords, and environmentalists have all contributed to the creation of the Portland landscape in which inexpensive housing is most accessible to working-class whites, African Americans, and recent immigrants in the most toxic part of the city.

Yet recent developments offer hope: the slough is far cleaner today than it was twenty years ago, thanks in large part to the virtual elimination of the combined sewer overflows that had been pumping raw sewage into the waterway for decades. Since the completion of the upgraded sewer system in 2011, habitat improvement projects along with recreation and education programs have begun to recast the slough and its environs not as an industrial corridor but as a green oasis in an ever more densely developed city. The slough water continues to be filthy, but part of it is now a pretty place to kayak, and the slough and its banks serve as a rich ecology classroom for area schoolchildren.[54] For much of its length, the slough retains its character as a hard-to-reach industrial waterway, but recent history is encouraging nonetheless. As more people come to value urban waterways like the slough as natural systems worthy of attention, seeing such places as vital ecological components of the complex environments in which we all live, the more hope we will have of securing truly broad access to healthy water, soil, and air.

Notes

An earlier version of this chapter appeared as "Troubled Waters in Ecotopia: Environmental Racism in Portland, Oregon", in Radical History Review Vol. 74: 1999, pp. 65–95. Copyright 1999. MARHO: Radical Historians Collective. All rights reserved. Republished by permission of the present publisher, Duke University Press.

1. A slough (pronounced "sloo") is a swampy waterway or marsh with very little current, if any. An earlier version of this article appeared as "Troubled Waters in Ecotopia: Environmental Racism in Portland, Oregon," *Radical History Review* 74 (1999): 65–95.

2. Northwest Environmental Advocates, "Warning: The Columbia Slough Is Polluted" [pamphlet] (Portland: Northwest Environmental Advocates, n.d.);

"Posting the Sewer Next Door," Portland *Oregonian*, December 10, 1992, D8; "Beware of Tainted Waterways," Portland *Oregonian*, September 9, 1994, B5. For more on the phenomenon of environmental racism and campaigns for environmental justice in the United States, see United Church of Christ, Commission for Racial Justice, *Toxic Wastes and Race in the United States: A National Report on the Racial and Socio-Economic Characteristics of Communities with Hazardous Waste Sites* (New York: Public Data Access, 1987); Paul Mohai and Bunyan Bryant, "Race, Poverty, and the Environment: The Disadvantaged Face Greater Risks," *EPA Journal* 18 (March–April 1992): 6–8; Andrew Hurley, *Environmental Inequalities: Class, Race, and Industrial Pollution in Gary, Indiana, 1945–1980* (Chapel Hill: University of North Carolina Press, 1995); Julie Sze, *Noxious New York: The Racial Politics of Urban Health and Environmental Justice* (Cambridge, MA: MIT Press, 2006); Dorceta E. Taylor, *Toxic Communities: Environmental Racism, Industrial Pollution, and Residential Mobility* (New York: New York University Press, 2014). For a more international perspective on environmental inequities, see, for example, Rob Nixon, *Slow Violence and the Environmentalism of the Poor* (Cambridge, MA: Harvard University Press, 2011).

3. Joe Fitzgibbon, "Columbia Slough Slowly Nurtured Back to Health," Portland *Oregonian*, October 8, 2001, Sunrise edition, Portland Zoner East Mid County, C02; Kara Briggs, "Watchdog of the Waterway," Portland *Oregonian*, December 29, 2004, Sunrise edition, East Zoner Mid County Zoner, B03; Joe Fitzgibbon, "Exploring Columbia Slough," Portland *Oregonian*, June 23, 2005 Sunrise edition, Portland Zoner Mid County East, B03; Melissa Jones, "Slough Enthusiasts Celebrate Its Slow Flow Back to Health," Portland *Oregonian*, September 1, 2005, Sunrise edition, East Zoner, 3; Eric Bartels, "Slough Outruns Poison Past," *Portland Tribune*, July 24, 2006, Features Section; Steve Law, "Natural Area Preserved along Slough," *Portland Tribune*, December 13, 2012, News section; Scott Learn, "Fish Destined for Table Surprisingly Toxic," Portland *Oregonian*, October 19, 2012, Sunrise edition, Local News section. Multilingual warning signs are posted, among other places, along the slough at Kelley Point Park in North Portland.

4. See, for example, Erin Hoover Barnett, "Golf Course Sale Spurs Land Fight," Portland *Oregonian*, September 16, 2008, Sunrise edition, Local News section, D01; Joe Fitzgibbon, "Eco-Activists Using Grant Money to Improve Watersheds," Portland *Oregonian*, February 26, 2009, Sunrise edition, Metro Portland Neighbors: In Portland section. See Matt Klingle, *Emerald City: An Environmental History of Seattle* (New Haven, CT: Yale University Press, 2007) on political uses of nature imagery.

5. *St. John's Review*, November 11, 1904, 1; July 8, 1910, 1; September 16, 1910, 1; August 30, 1918, l; Rowland and Fortiner, *Map of Portland and Vicinity*, 1:31,680 (Portland, OR: The Company, 1908); *Portland Evening Telegram*, August 5, 1916, 20; March 23, 1920; September 1, 1928, 1; Portland *Oregonian*, June 4, 1966; American

Map and Reproducing Company, *Map of Portland and Vicinity*, ca. 1:24,000 ([Portland, OR]: The Company, 1912): Carl Abbott, *Portland: Planning, Politics, and Growth in a Twentieth-Century City* (Lincoln: University of Nebraska Press, 1983), 68; Columbia-Willamette River Watch, *Toxic Waters* [map], 1:62,500 (Portland, OR: Northwest Environmental Advocates, 1992); City of Portland, "The Columbia Slough: Its History and Current Status," 1972, 2, Section 7706–06, Location 10–09–33/1, folder 1/2, City of Portland Stanley Parr Archives and Records Center, Portland, OR [hereafter Parr Archives]; City of Portland Columbia Slough Environmental Improvement Program, "Historical Summary," 1977, Series 0462–02, Location 16–04–01, folder 1/27, Parr Archives; City of Portland, Bureau of Environmental Services, "Columbia Slough Planning Study Background Report," February 1989, 2–1.

6. Columbia-Willamette River Watch, *Toxic Waters*; Joe Fitzgibbon, "Now-Ailing Slough Has Rich History," Portland *Oregonian*, September 16, 1993, 5.

7. Columbia-Willamette River Watch, *Toxic Waters*; Brown quoted in Henry Sessions, "Fishing in Polluted Waters," on *Crossroads* (a National Public Radio program), May 14, 1993; City of Portland, "Technical Memorandum on the Results of the Dry Weather Fish Consumption and Recreational Use Surveys," unfiled report, 1995, Parr Archives.

8. E. Kimbark MacColl, *The Shaping of a City: Business and Politics in Portland, Oregon, 1885–1915* (Portland: Georgian Company Press, 1976), 460; *Sixteenth Census of the United States: Population and Housing Statistics of Census Tracts by Cities; Statistics for Census Tracts, Portland, Oregon* (Washington, DC: Government Printing Office, 1942), 13, 20; Portland City Planning Commission, "St. John's Area: A Plan for the Development of a North Portland Community," April 1959, in Minutes of Portland City Planning Commission, vol. 16, Parr Archives. This report characterized the North Portland Peninsula as having a "predominance of manufacturing workers in its population." It went on to say that this peninsula had "always been a manufacturing community."

9. Abbott, *Portland*, 133.

10. Abbott, *Portland*, 133; Manly Maben, *Vanport* (Portland: Oregon Historical Society Press, 1987), xii, 6–7, 10, 31, 106; Bernard Raymond La Plante, "The Negro at Jefferson High School: A Historical Study of Racial Change," PhD dissertation, University of Oregon, Eugene, 1970, 87; E. Kimbark MacColl, *The Growth of a City: Power and Politics in Portland, Oregon, 1915-1950* (Portland: Georgian Company, 1979), 111, 578.

11. Maben, *Vanport*, 18–21; La Plante, "The Negro at Jefferson High School," 87.

12. "National Housing Agency Federal Public Housing Authority War Housing Projects" (Portland: Housing Authority of Portland, 1944), Series 2012–30, Location 13–07–15/2, folder 2/16, Parr Archives.

13. Housing Authority of Portland Meeting Minutes, May 4, 1944, Series 0605–02, Location 06–06–58, folder 4/17, Parr Archives; Housing Authority of Portland Meeting Minutes, February 15, 1945, Series 0605–02, Location 06–06–58, folder 4/26, Parr Archives; MacColl, *Growth of a City*, 595; "National Housing Agency Federal Public Housing Authority War Housing Projects"; Abbott, *Portland*, 157.

14. Maben, *Vanport*, 87.

15. Maben, *Vanport*, 88; La Plante, "The Negro at Jefferson High School," 74; MacColl, *Growth of a City*, 269.

16. Abbott, *Portland*, 144, 157; Housing Authority of Portland Meeting Minutes, May 18, 1944, Series 0605–02, Location 06–06–58, folder 4/17, Parr Archives; Maben, *Vanport*, 88.

17. Housing Authority of Portland Minutes, July 1943, Series 0605–02, Location 06–06–58, folder 4/7, Parr Archives; Housing Authority of Portland Minutes, April 20, 1944, Series 0605–02, Location 06–06–58, folder 4/16, Parr Archives; Housing Authority of Portland Minutes, September 16, 1943, Series 0605–02, Location 06–06 58, folder 4/9, Parr Archives; Maben, *Vanport*, 89–90.

18. Housing Authority of Portland Minutes, February 15, 1945, Series 0605–02, Location 06–06–58, folder 4/26, Parr Archives.

19. Maben, *Vanport*, 106, 113, 120–22.

20. Abbott, *Portland*, 23–24; Stuart McElderry, "The Problem of the Color Line: Civil Rights and Racial Ideology in Portland, Oregon, 1944–1965," PhD dissertation, University of Oregon, Eugene, 1998, 1, 57, 235, 238, 326.

21. La Plante, "The Negro at Jefferson High School," 93; American Automobile Association, *Street Map of Portland*, ca. 1:40,550 ([San Jose, CA]: H. M. Gousha, a division of Simon and Schuster, 1993).

22. Lawrence Barber, *Columbia Slough* ([Portland: Columbia Slough Development Corp.], 1977), 10; Fitzgibbon, "Now-Ailing Slough Has Rich History," 5; League of Women Voters of Portland, "The Columbia Slough: A League Action Program to Rescue a Waterway," November 1972, Series 7706–06, Location 10–09–33, folder 1 /3, Parr Archives.

23. City of Portland, "The Columbia Slough: Its History and Current Status," 1972, 2.

24. MacColl, *Growth of a City*, 546; Portland *Oregonian*, October 7, 1951, 21; League of Women Voters of Portland, "The Columbia Slough."

25. Fitzgibbon, "Now-Ailing Slough Has Rich History," 5; Columbia-Willamette River Watch, *Toxic Waters*. CSOs still plague the slough. During the rainy season, 70 percent of the lower slough's flow comes from CSOs.

26. Beth Slovic, "Portland's \$1.4 Billion Big Pipe Project Comes to an End after 20 Years," Portland *Oregonian*, November 25, 2011.

27. Portland City Planning Commission, handwritten outline of report [1960s], Series 7706–15, Location 10–10–14, folder 3/2, Parr Archives. The planning commission was following a standard national convention by making investment and development decisions based on the perceived stability of neighborhoods. See Kenneth T. Jackson, *Crabgrass Frontier: The Suburbanization of the United States* (New York: Oxford University Press, 1985), chapter 11, for a discussion of Federal Housing Administration redlining practices.

28. Columbia-Willamette River Watch, *Toxic Waters*; Oregon Department of Environmental Quality, Northwest Region, *Columbia Slough Total Maximum Daily Loads (TMDLs) For: Chlorophyll a, Dissolved Oxygen, pH, Phosphorus, Bacteria, DDE/ DDT, PCBs, Pb, Dieldrin, and 2,3,7,8 TCDD* (Portland: Oregon Department of Environmental Quality, September 1988).

29. Abbott, *Portland*, 248–49.

30. Abbott, *Portland*, 250–51; Brent Walth, *Fire at Eden's Gate: Tom McCall and the Oregon Story* (Portland: Oregon Historical Society Press, 1994), 327.

31. Abbott, *Portland*, 248, 251–52.

32. Abbott, *Portland*, 248, 250.

33. Carl Abbott, Deborah Howe, and Sy Adler, eds., *Planning the Oregon Way: A Twenty Year Evaluation* (Corvallis: Oregon State University Press, 1994), xv.

34. Abbott, *Portland*, 270.

35. Abbott, Howe, and Adler, *Planning the Oregon Way*, xx.

36. League of Women Voters, *Solid Waste* (Portland: League of Women Voters, 1972).

37. Jim Kadera, "Polluted Columbia Slough Faces Clean-Up Problems," Portland *Oregonian*, August 1, 1971, 11.

38. Kadera, "Polluted Columbia Slough Faces Clean-Up Problems," 11; "Port Presses Plan to Close River Slough," Portland *Oregonian*, May 22, 1969, 32.

39. Quoted in "The Columbia Slough: Its History and Current Status," City of Portland Report, June 1972, Series 7706–06, Location 10–09–33/1, folder 1/2, Parr Archives.

40. Letter from Joan Binnenger, Topic Chairman, This Beleaguered Earth study group, Portland Branch of the American Association of University Women, to Columbia Slough Environmental Task Force, August 25, 1972, Series 7706–06, Location 10–09–33/1, folder 1/3, Parr Archives.

41. "Rivergate–North Portland Survey Study Workshop Attendance," 1–9, Columbia School, Portland, OR, June 14, 1973, Series 7706–06, Location 10–09–33/ 1, folder 1/3, Parr Archives.

42. "Rivergate–North Portland Survey Study Workshop Notes," 3, 5, Columbia School, Portland, OR, June 14, 1973, Series 7706–06, Location 10–09–33/ 1, folder 1/3, Parr Archives.

43. "Rivergate–North Portland Survey Study Workshop Notes," 1–10.

44. Sharon Roso, compiler, "North Peninsula Environment '74: Lakes, Lands, and Livability—a North Portland Conference" (Portland: North Portland Citizen's Committee, 1974), 1, Series 5000-1000-01, Location 09-07-22, folder 2/35, Parr Archives.

45. Roso, "North Peninsula Environment '74," 11.

46. Roso, "North Peninsula Environment '74," 2, 3.

47. "Cleanup Cost Estimated at Nearly $1 Million," Portland *Oregonian*, March 2, 1994, B2; "Time Bomb, Time Capsule," Portland *Oregonian*, October 29, 1992, 1; "Lawyer Says Settlement Covered Cost at Landfill," Portland *Oregonian*, July 29, 1992; Portland Development Commission, "Columbia Corridor Economic Analysis," November 1988, 45, Series 044–02, Location 17–03–38, folder 4/28, Parr Archives.

48. *1950 United States Census of the Population, Portland Oregon: Census Tracts*, vol. III, chapter 63 (Washington, DC: Government Printing Office, 1952), 7–9; *1970 United States Census of Population and Housing: Census Tracts no. 165, Portland-Oregon-Washington: Standard Metropolitan Statistical Area* (Washington, DC: Government Printing Office, 1972), P-7 to P-15.

49. *1990 United States Census of Population and Housing, Characteristics for Census Tracts and Block Numbering Areas, Portland Oregon Primary Metropolitan Statistical Area* (Washington, DC: Government Printing Office, 1993), 118–22; Abbott, *Portland*, 128 (map); "Black Community Remains Small," Portland *Oregonian*, November 24, 1991, C1; US Bureau of the Census, *Census of Population and Housing, 1990: Summary Tape File 3 on CD ROM* [machine-readable data files] (Washington, DC: The Bureau [producer and distributor], 1992).

50. Abbott, *Portland*, 26; McElderry, "Problem of the Color Line," 235, 315, 325.

51. *1990 United States Census of Population and Housing*, 415–23.

52. *1990 United States Census of Population and Housing*, 415–23; Portland, Oregon, population data by census tract, Social Explorer, based on data from US Census Bureau American Community Survey 2014 (five-year estimates), https://www.socialexplorer.com/, accessed June 25, 2017; Adolfson Associates, "Technical Memorandum on the Results of the 1995 Fish Consumption and Recreational Use Surveys: Amendment no. 1" (Portland, OR: Adolfson Associates, 1995), 7.

53. Scott Learn, "Fish Destined for Table Surprisingly Toxic," Portland *Oregonian*, October 19, 2012; Steve Law, "Natural Area Preserved along Columbia Slough," *Portland Tribune*, December 13, 2012; Casey Parks, "Department of Environmental Quality Wants Comments on Proposed Slough Clean Up Near St. Johns Landfill,"

Portland *Oregonian*, May 1, 2014; Nina Bell, "Symposium: Environmental Injustice Posed by Oregon's Water Quality Standards," *University of Oregon Journal of Environmental Law and Litigation* (2005): 85–110; Douglas Carstens, Michelle Black, and Staley Prom, "Isn't That Special? The EPA's Special-Case Determination for the Los Angeles River Extends Clean Water Protections Cast in Doubt by the Army Corps and the United States Supreme Court," *Golden Gate University Environmental Law Journal* (Spring 2011): 251–75; Nick Bjork, "Debate Arises over Portland Industrial Land Use," *Daily Journal of Commerce* (Portland, OR), August 30, 2010; Nick Bjork, "Oregon's Gov. Kitzhaber Calls for Quicker Industrial Permitting," *Daily Journal of Commerce* (Portland, OR), February 18, 2011.

54. See the Columbia Slough Watershed Council website for information on recreation and educational programs at the slough, accessed June 25, 2017, https://www.columbiaslough.org/.

5

Streetscape Environmentalism

*Flood Control, Social Justice, and Political Power
in Modern San Antonio, 1921–1974*

CHAR MILLER

You can locate Zarzamora Creek on the map: type in its coordinates on Google Earth—N 29°31, W 98°34—and you will have pinpointed its cartographical location. But that digital representation will tell you little about its environmental significance or its cultural meaning to the city of San Antonio. Often bone-dry, the Zarzamora is an eight-mile dusty channel that falls away from the low hills ringing the downtown core to its northwest. The creek first twists and turns in a southwesterly direction, then breaks south and east before flowing into a retention pond known as Elmendorf Lake, merging there with Apache Creek. Their combined stream flow then presses into the San Pedro a mile or so above its confluence with the San Antonio River. The Zarzamora is thus a small part of the San Antonio's 4,180-square-mile drainage system.

Perhaps the Zarzamora's frequent dryness and small size are why the Spanish, who gave the creek its name, neglected to demarcate its presence on their eighteenth-century maps of this sprawling watershed, which made arable the river valley where they sited five religious missions, built a civilian community and a presidio, and irrigated innumerable farms and ranches. For

DOI: 10.5876/9781607328483.c005

these colonists, like most modern-day San Antonians, Zarzamora Creek left an almost invisible mark on the South Texas landscape.

Yet the Zarzamora has a habit of becoming noticeable when it rains. Then, what appears unimportant and practically indecipherable becomes overwhelming in significance and force. To account for this startling transformation, start with the confluence of meteorology and topography. San Antonio lies just east of the 100th meridian, long identified as the break point between the humid East and the arid West. This meteorological boundary is not as fixed as the meridian appears on a map, and depending on whether the Pacific Ocean is in an El Niño or a La Niña cycle, San Antonio oscillates between deluge and drought. The amount of rain that can fall is startling: the prevailing southeasterly breezes pull supersaturated air up from the Gulf of Mexico that rises as it reaches San Antonio and the Hill Country. Should this uplift collide with a wall of high-pressure air or a cold front pushing down from the north, the resultant storms can produce lightning and earthshaking thunder and can quickly drench and race across parched ground.

In late June and early July 2002, for instance, upward of thirty-five inches fell in seven days, and the two major rivers that cut through the city, the San Antonio and the Medina, registered record heights; tragically, twelve people lost their lives. On October 17–18, 1998, the same scenario had occurred after a cold front slammed into the region's high humidity, which was then supercharged by "a plume of moist mid- and high-level air . . . streaming across the area from Hurricane Madeline off the west coast of Mexico." More than twenty inches of rain fell in twenty-four hours, killing eleven.[1]

The problem was not solely how much precipitation slanted down as where and how it landed. The Hill Country, and the larger Edwards Plateau of which it is a part, serve as an elevated catchment basin; as rainwater hits and cascades down its slopes, it will be funneled into channels that over the millennia have been carved into the limestone terrain. From Austin to San Antonio, a series of rivulets, creeks, and streams carry these turbulent floodwaters to the flatlands, where they power into the Little Colorado or San Marcos, Guadalupe or San Antonio Rivers, which carry the churning flow south and east into the Gulf of Mexico. This complex combination of weather patterns, geological structures, and riparian systems, along with the killer surges they regularly produce, has led the National Weather Service to dub south-central Texas "Flash-Flood Alley."[2]

Zarzamora Creek has contributed its share to that alley's periodic destructiveness. Consider the aftermath of a torrential downburst that erupted over San Antonio on August 8, 1974, as a weak cold front moved across the area and smacked into thick, moist Gulf air. As often happens on such occasions, the creek quickly filled up and burst over its banks, inundating the low-lying neighborhoods that had been platted along its course. The roiling waters flushed more than forty families from their homes, swept away a bridge spanning the creek, and swamped nearby streets. Once the fetid waters finally receded, they left behind a tangled mass of old tires, broken bottles and dented tin cans, sodden mattresses, tree limbs, and grass-choked shopping carts.[3]

Such damage was normal on the west side of San Antonio, a massive Latino barrio whose environmental stressors and public health concerns seemed as integral to its social ecology as the Zarzamora was to its physical geography. Few in this community felt they had the power to alter what appeared natural; few believed they had the ability to make themselves heard in City Hall. Their perceived sense of powerlessness was a logical (and intentional) outcome of a community under the control of a closed, Anglo-dominated power elite. "San Antonio was run by a fairly well-knit oligarchy of well-off, very well-off people," organizer Ernesto (Ernie) Cortés Jr. asserted, adding "all of whom, mostly whites and WASPS, lived in the northeast quadrant of the city and kind of dominated the politics and economics of the city." Because these elites did not spend "a whole lot of time and energy and attention or resources . . . on the older areas of the city," they ignored those citizens' plight whenever thick, dark clouds blew up on the horizon.[4]

The 1974 storm was different, however; the hard-driving rain and its filthy aftermath provoked a public outcry that could not be contained within the narrow boundaries that had long defined San Antonio's restricted civic arena. Making ready use of this storm was a handful of grassroots activists. Over the previous year and under the banner of Communities Organized for Public Services (COPS) and led by Ernie Cortés, who had trained at the Saul Alinsky–founded Industrial Areas Foundation, they had been quietly organizing among community activists, union organizers, and Catholic parishes on the city's west side. Cortés estimated later that he held more than 1,000 face-to-face, one-on-one interviews with potential allies, paying special attention to members of the local machinist union and the American Federation of Government Employees. He interviewed innumerable pastors about the key figures in their parishes, met with women who worked in and out of the home, and discovered along the way what issues were paramount on the west side and who among its mainly Latino residents were willing to go public with their collective grievances.[5] Among the pivotal issues that emerged from these conversations were the twinned issues of drainage and flood control, so when the small flood of 1974 blew through the community, its residents quickly turned its damaging presence to their advantage—building momentum for a well-planned assault on discriminatory public policies that forced the poor and disadvantaged to scramble for high ground every time rampaging waters cut through their communities.

Wielding what we now refer to as the language of environmental justice, these protestors challenged the social inequities they endured, the political discrimination from which they suffered, and the disproportionate burden they bore; they did so through an intense process of self-education that laid bare the political context of the physical world they inhabited. This, in turn, allowed them to identify the means they could employ to protect their lives and livelihoods, make their community less flood-prone and more habitable, and, along the way, wrest power from a local white elite whose privilege had rarely been contested. Theirs was a classic example of what theorist Antonio Gramsci and, more recently, scholars James Scott, Laura Pulido, and others call a "subaltern" struggle. "This new form of environmentalism," Pulido argues about the Chicano movement in the Southwest, is counterhegemonic, existing "in opposition to prevailing powers." The emergence of such "explicitly oppositional" organizations depends in part on the movement's ability to alter "the perceptions and meaning of environmental problems and actions on the part of both observers and actors, as subordinated groups' responses to continued economic and political marginalization, struggles over identity, concerns for quality of life, and the continued degradation of the physical environment." The ultimate goal, she notes in language that dovetails with COPS's aspirations, is "to change the distribution of power and resources to benefit the less powerful."[6]

Strikingly, COPS's subaltern resistance has not been incorporated into scholarly analyses of the origins and significance of the environmental-justice movement. Instead, historians have focused almost exclusively on events that occurred in the late 1970s and early 1980s in Warren County, North Carolina. There, a grassroots organization emerged to rally local citizens—mostly

African American—against the county's and state's decision to locate a toxic waste landfill in their community. After the Tar Heel State announced in 1978 that roughly 40,000 cubic yards of polychlorinated biphenyl (PCB)–contaminated material would be trucked to former farmlands the state had purchased in Warren County, residents fought back in the courts. Four years later, when their legal challenges against the dump's potential to compromise local groundwater and hinder other economic development failed, they tried to disrupt the transfer of the contaminated soil. Making shrewd use of local, state, and national media; gaining the attention of civil rights leaders such as Benjamin Chavis, then the head of the United Church of Christ's Commission for Racial Justice; and demonstrating a willingness to go to jail for the cause (there were more than 500 arrests), activists devised what is often thought to be a new form of environmental protest. By locating the toxic dump in the predominately African American county, they alleged, the state was practicing "environmental racism," a term Chavis is credited with coining. "The community was politically and economically unempowered," one resident declared. "That was the reason for the siting. They took advantage of poor people of color."[7]

This melding of concerns about social inequality and environmental quality has had a profound impact on the political arena. The emerging environmental-justice movement sparked a new generation of civil rights activism and provoked mainstream environmental organizations, such as the Sierra Club and the National Resources Defense Council (NRDC), to widen their hitherto almost exclusive focus on wilderness protection to include emphases on degraded human habitats. It has also compelled local, state, and federal governmental agencies to better account for the risks they often imposed on disenfranchised people and disempowered communities and to open up their decision-making processes. These transformative responses, Eileen McGurty argues, are what make Warren County so central to the defining narrative of the emergence of environmental justice as a movement: "The Warren County events . . . were significant in the crystallization of environmental justice in three ways: opponents of the hazardous waste landfill were arrested for civil disobedience, people of color were involved in a disruptive collective action against environmental regulatory agencies, and national-level civil rights activists supported an environmental issue through disruptive collective action." Comparing these consequences to those that emerged in the aftermath of the bruising early twentieth-century battle over the damming of Hetch Hetchy Valley in Yosemite National Park, McGurty notes how each moment helped "articulate [a] common purpose, create a mechanism for building solidarity among movement participants, and allow for the development of ongoing strategic collective action." Even though this particular uprising failed to stop the construction of the landfill, McGurty argues that the "importance of Warren County for the development of the movement cannot be overemphasized."[8]

Of similar (and earlier) import were COPS's protests in the 1970s over the inequities of flooding in San Antonio. Drawing on the political heritage of Latino activism in the city that had emerged during World War II, the new organization's potent challenge to the city's willful neglect of low-lying, poor neighborhoods gave voice to Latinos and morphed into a full-scale attack on an array of related social, environmental, and public health issues that culminated in the rewriting of the city's governing charter. San Antonio was transformed, and as COPS's organizing tactics spread to other urban centers with large Hispanic populations, its energy helped alter the political dynamics of the Southwest.[9]

To understand this volatile context requires an analysis of another, earlier flood in San Antonio whose punishing power laid bare the intertwined character of the city's topography and politics and the degree to which its economic disparities were built into a segregated landscape. Without knowing what happened in September 1921, when floodwaters spectacularly tore San Antonio apart, it is impossible to comprehend the significance of COPS's actions in the aftermath of the much smaller August 1974 flood.[10]

The summer of 1921 was typical for South Texas: each day was as hot and dry as the next. By September, the unrelenting heat had scorched ranchlands and urban lawns, and on September 9, when light rains swept across the region—the first since June—they offered a wonderful respite. Not only had these "most timely showers" put an end to a "prolonged drought," the *San Antonio Express* reported, they had done so without damaging crops or flooding low-lying neighborhoods. Over the next twenty-four hours, however, violent thunderstorms crashed overhead, dropping more than twenty inches of rain in some areas and triggering a series of frightening flash floods. San Antonio was particularly hard hit: its rainfall measured but seven-and-a-half inches, yet most of that amount fell within a few hours when a storm cell stalled just north of the city, concentrating over the watershed of the San Antonio River. Later that evening its major west-side tributaries—the San Pedro, Apache, Zarzamora, Alazán, and Martínez Creeks—swept over their banks, becoming "swift torrents" of destruction. They ripped through the crowded barrios of the west and south sides of the city, pulling so many houses from their foundations and sweeping them away that no official tally was kept; left behind were fifty-foot piles of debris choked with tree trunks, siding, cars, and parts of chairs. The floodwaters also killed more than fifty people, most of whom were sucked into the raging creeks during the early morning hours. Finding their bodies was no easy task. For the rest of the week, able-bodied civilians and soldiers were stationed on downstream bridges to spot, then attempt to retrieve, corpses entangled in the sodden detritus. "What occurred in the blackness of the night," the New York Times mourned, "when scores of men, women, and children met death in the oil-coated waters of the flood, as houses collapsed, bridges were swept out, trees and electric and telephone poles crashed, is something that will be never known in detail."[11]

A somewhat less ghastly job awaited those who cleaned up from the flooding associated with Olmos Creek, which flowed through the city's north side. Around midnight it had surged into adjacent neighborhoods and urban parks, driving out residents and campers. When its crest smashed into the San Antonio River, it forced a five- to ten-foot wall of water through the central business district—inundating the bottom floors of most office buildings, damaging a considerable portion of the commercial inventory, tearing up miles of street pavement, and washing away or weakening the structural integrity of the Alamo City's many bridges. Located downtown, too, were the sources of San Antonio's basic utilities—water, electricity, and telephone—which were consequently shut down for several days. Ruptured fuel storage tanks only added to the mess, spreading an oil slick several miles long and wide. Although early estimates of the overall damage were set at $3 million, by the time the cleanup was completed several months later, the costs had escalated to more than $4 million. Certainly, San Antonians knew that by any form of measurement—by the height of floodwaters, the number of deaths and injuries, or the financial costs—the 1921 flood was a disaster, the greatest in the city's history.

The flood's impact went well beyond any specific tally of human loss or physical destruction. Indeed, a greater and long-term consequence was the community's response to the critical question of how to control future floods. The initial response was swift and telling. The pressrooms of the city's rival newspapers, the *San Antonio Express* and *San Antonio Light*, had not been pumped dry when each newspaper began to editorialize fervently in support of the construction of a citywide network of canals and the erection of a retention dam spanning the Olmos Valley to prevent another such tragedy. That was the least the citizenry could do, for the "mass of wreckage" left in the flood's wake was mute testimony that "the elements, when loosed from the gates of hell, are no respecters of persons, class or creed." It was high time for San Antonians to recognize this fact of nature, the *Express* trumpeted. "The storm waters must be controlled," for only then could the city be rehabilitated.[12]

The precise storm waters that would be controlled, and thus what portions of the community would undergo rehabilitation, would be decided in the political arena, which proved fairly respectful of the discriminatory powers of race and class. That remained true for the next fifty years. When completed in 1927, for instance, the 1,941-foot-long Olmos Dam helped articulate land-use patterns within San Antonio. Its mere presence intensified the central core's already established economic functions by encouraging once wary financiers to invest heavily in the city's post-flood downtown skyline; the 1920s construction boom produced some of the city's finest and largest buildings, from the Smith-Young Tower to the Scottish Rite Temple and the Medical Arts Building. The dam also made it possible to conceive and then develop the much-acclaimed Riverwalk. Without it there would be few tourists strolling along the river's (now) placid waters, visitors who have become one of the mainstays of San Antonio's modern economy. Because of these ramifications, the Olmos Dam is arguably the single most important public works project in the community's history.[13]

Yet the dam was also a failure, in the sense that the decision to build it depended on a disturbing and remarkably skewed distribution of public benefits in one of America's poorest big cities. That is not what San Antonio's Anglo leadership announced, of course, when it floated a $3 million bond issue to underwrite the dam, ensuring the central business district's prosperous future. Simultaneously, it also voiced a commitment to establish a flood-control plan for the waterlogged barrios. This action, civic leaders conceded, was only just, for the vast majority of those who had died in the 1921 flood had been Hispanics living along the west side's dangerous creeks and whose neighborhoods remained well outside the proposed dam's protective zone. From this concession, *The Survey*, a national Progressive-era reform organ, took hope, believing that the 1921 flood set the stage for San Antonio to do more than just build prosaic storm sewers. By sweeping away the dense tracts of "rude shacks built in a hit or miss manner," the devastating flood-waters gave San Antonio the perfect "opportunity for bettering the lives and sanitary conditions of the Mexican population."[14]

The local power elite chose instead to ignore for half a century the legendary (and interlocking) problems on the west side that flowed from poor drainage, bad housing, and inadequate sanitation; the west siders' plight was theirs alone. Nothing more perfectly captures the elite's willful disregard and the disdain that underlay it than a paired set of announcements that emanated from the city council in August 1924. At the same time it declared the release of millions of dollars to fund construction of the Olmos Dam, the council also indicated that it had voted to spend $6,000 to cut brush along the San Pedro and Alazán Creeks. This remarkable discrepancy in investment and technology meant that those who had died in the 1921 flood had died in vain. The devastating storm, in short, did nothing to disrupt the Anglo domination of San Antonio politics in this era while the Hispanic population remained threatened by periodic flash flooding and consistent under-representation in local government.[15]

The dire and discriminatory consequences of the management of San Antonio's floodwaters, channeled along ethnic divisions and class lines, continually resurfaced. The city's master plans dating from the 1930s focused almost exclusively on the main course of the San Antonio River, reports that highlighted the construction of the Olmos Dam and praised the downstream straightening of critical sections of the San Antonio River that once had bent and curved through the city. This work demonstrated its value later in the 1930s when a series of powerful storms swept across the watershed. As designed, the Olmos Dam retained the upstream waters, and below it, the newly constructed cutoff channel, a 70-foot wide and 750-foot long conduit that sliced through the urban streetscape, quickly sluiced water out of the central core. The interests of the city's political and economic elite were secured, but no such protective infrastructure existed on the west side, so once again murderous floods cascaded through the barrios.[16]

The same thing happened on September 26–27, 1946: a massive storm dropped more than seven inches of rain in thirty-six hours. The Olmos Dam performed as expected, holding back an estimated 5,000 acre-feet of water; below it, newly completed channelization projects captured and diverted an equal amount of water, minimizing damage to the central business district. These measures, however, were of no value to those living in the city's western sectors. According to a report from the US Geological Survey, shortly after the heaviest rainfall began, San Pedro Creek and its tributaries were in full flood. As they poured into adjacent neighborhoods and commercial districts, six people died, "flimsy structures were washed down [the] roaring creeks," and nearby stockyards were inundated. Thousands of citizens and cattle were left homeless.[17]

So consistent was this pattern that after a punishing June 1951 storm churned up Alazán and Martínez Creeks, killing three people, one newspaper casually labeled these streams "those old trouble spots." The fact that these waterways were known to be so troublesome and that fatalities were an expected outcome of such routine flooding produced no discernible political response. This failure is consistent with a larger national pattern historian Ted Steinberg has identified, in which natural disasters serve as "a kind of grand metaphor for rationalizing life under our economic system." When the San Antonio elite ignored the continued rush of water through west-side barrios, they were acting as did their peers elsewhere. "By disavowing moral responsibility for disaster, we are rationalizing the kinds of economic oppression," Steinberg argues, that explain "why some people get adequate protection from floods and others do not, why some live and some die."[18]

City planners, in contrast to the local politicians, were designing systemic responses to disruptive flooding. Some of their efforts were showcased in the 1951 master plan for San Antonio. Although the bulk of that document's section on "Flood Control and Drainage" was concerned with ongoing projects to hasten the movement of water through the central core, it acknowledged that "little or no provision has ever been made in residential areas to provide an adequate system of surface water drainage; and the development of the city streets has been accomplished with little or no thought being given to the effect of surface water on them." One result of this inattention, with which west-side residents were fully familiar, was that "houses have been built in low areas which in time of heavy rain become flooded and the streets in the area impassable." The plan's authors concluded that "money spent in building streets where drainage facilities are not provided is wasted money," a calculation that would not become policy for more than twenty years.[19]

A similar calculus framed the actions of the region's lead flood-control agency, the San Antonio River Authority (SARA). Founded in 1937 as the San Antonio River Canal and Conservancy District, its original purpose had been to plan for a 150-mile barge canal to the Gulf of Mexico. Ten years later, the US Army Corps of Engineers determined that the canal would not carry water—its projected costs were inordinate and its predicted returns minuscule. In conjunction with the devastating aftermath of the 1946 flood, the agency dropped all navigation work on the river in favor of flood-control studies. SARA (it assumed its new name in 1953) followed suit. Yet the research collaboration, for all the expertise it brought to bear, came to a not-so-startling conclusion: as bad as the flooding problems were on the west side, the central concern of the San Antonio River Channel Improvement Project would be the river's main branch that ran from downtown to its confluence with San Pedro Creek. Subsequent work shifted to eastern portions of the larger drainage system. Throughout the 1960s, SARA built dams and channels to control the Salado, Calaveras, and Escondido Creeks. In 1965, after a severe storm alerted SARA to the need to expand its earlier channelization of the San Antonio's main course, it secured more funding from the Bexar County commissioners to resolve the ongoing problems in this troublesome sector. Those taxpayers who lived within the web of west-side creeks waited until the 1970s for much-needed infrastructure on the Apache, Alazán, Martínez, and Zaramora Creeks. In its implementation strategy, SARA, consciously or otherwise, was mimicking the pattern of neglect the city leadership had practiced since the 1921 flood.[20]

That is not how the agency's official history describes its actions, however. Its master narrative, which covers SARA's first fifty years, from 1937 to 1987, is at once devoid of politics and implies that the organization operated outside the political realm; its engineers and experts simply crafted logical plans and adopted neutral policies in its battle against urban flooding. Although the text acknowledges, for instance, that public tax dollars underwrote its projects, it never discusses the democratic tug-and-pull that produced those funds or whether or how specific interests might have shaped the bond packages to determine the priority, siting, need, or timing of its actions. This absence is especially obvious in SARA's recounting of its activities during the explosive 1970s and in the passive voice it employed to describe its actions:

> SARA's flood control work involved the completion of the channelization of the Alazán and Martinez [sic] Creeks. Also, SARA was cooperating with the Urban Renewal Agency and the Model Cities staff of the City of San Antonio to complete local requirements for the Apache Creek flood control improvements. SARA coordinated the project and constructed the 19th Street Bridge-Dam at Elmendorf Lake, the Urban Renewal Agency acquired the necessary land rights, and the City of San Antonio paid all the costs from funds made available through the Model Cities program of the U.S. Department of Housing and Urban Development . . . By 1975 channelization of Alazán Creek was completed, and most of San Pedro and Martinez [sic] Creeks were completed. The channelization of Apache Creek was completed in 1976.[21]

COPS framed its version of these same events differently, employing a more active narrative voice to reflect its oppositional stance. After all, it was in the early 1970s that the new organization began to exert intense public pressure on city officials and, by extension, SARA to fund flood-control and drainage projects throughout the west side. It is no surprise, then, that its chronology begins with a direct clash of wills that erupted on August 13, 1974, at the first public meeting between COPS and Sam Granata, the city manager. Mere days before, Zarzamora Creek had rushed out of its earthen embankment, yet another wet slap in the face of those long threatened with flooding—an event that infused the 500 COPS members who gathered at Kennedy High School with a renewed sense of outrage; it even "bolstered our faith in God," one organizer later laughed.[22]

No one was amused at the time, though, as an unsuspecting Granata discovered when he walked into the school's auditorium. An irate audience "demanded action on drainage improvements in the neighborhoods. They told the city manager they were not interested in long-winded explanations; he could keep his responses to 'simple yes or no answers.'" To bolster their case, they screened photographic images of the long-standing pattern of neighborhood flooding and the havoc it routinely caused. "Scenes like these have been there for years and are still the same," activist Ray Kaiser told Granata. "We have decided to not take it anymore. We have decided to make our problem your problem." When a flustered Granata confessed that he did not have the authority to resolve their concerns—"To give a 'yes' and not be able to deliver would be a fraud. I can't do it"—the rambunctious crowd asked him who had the authority. Told that city council was the appropriate body, COPS immediately asked him to place the issue on the following week's agenda.[23]

What happened at that session has taken on a legendary cast. Hundreds of COPS supporters jammed city council chambers well beyond capacity, and, a reporter recounted, the crowd "broke all the time-honored rules about how citizens are supposed to address the council on a sign in basis, one at a time." With a theatrical sense of its emerging clout, the audience rose as one when its chief spokeswoman, Mrs. Hector Aleman, walked to the podium microphone and crowded up next to her as she hammered the council into stunned submission. Telling the representatives that her west-side neighborhood lay smack within the Zarzamora's floodplain, she related how every time it poured, houses, streets, the local park, even the parish church went under water. Her voice cracked: "How would you feel getting out of bed in the morning and stepping into a river right in your house?" Aleman's supporters roared.[24]

Aleman's personal pitch came with a sharp edge. COPS researchers had burrowed deep into the city's archives to locate the 1945 master plan, which contained provisions to reconstruct the Zarzamora as it swung past Mayberry Street, site of many of the bank-busting floods to which Aleman had alluded and close to her still sodden home. Bond monies had been committed at that time but were never spent. Charles Becker, recently elected mayor, swiveled to ask Granata if Aleman's account was accurate. Told that it was, he queried, "You mean to tell me this project has been on the city's list that long and never received a thin dime?" Yes, Granata said. "Well, that's a damn shame," Becker replied. "How many people does this affect?" When advised that the number was upward of 40,000, the shocked mayor gave city staff four hours to locate the financing for the Mayberry Street project and then commanded council and COPS to return later that evening to learn the results. The staff complied; flood control was suddenly and emphatically on the city's agenda.[25]

It remained that way because COPS proved relentless. In November it cajoled the city council into calling a special bond election that would fund fifteen west-side drainage projects to the tune of $46.8 million; the measure passed easily. Over the next three years, COPS would reorient the way city council and staff crafted the city's budget, demanding and receiving commitments to underwrite $100 million for neighborhood improvements that ranged from flood control and street repair to trash pickup and water and sewer infrastructure. Within a decade its organizing efforts had netted an estimated $500 million for local environmental and public health projects. As those robust figures suggest, COPS had become adept at finding untapped federal dollars and new uses for previously committed local funds. COPS also compelled the city and SARA to tap into monies from the US Department of Housing and Urban Development to build the new channels, dams, and culverts that began to dry out the oft-soggy west side.[26]

For all its success at the street level, COPS understood the broader implication of its demands for a more habitable landscape—a shift in the city's power dynamics. To do so, it also helped start up similar organizations on the largely African American east side and on the ethnically mixed south side. Within a year of the raucous 1974 city council meeting, it had formed as well an alliance with north-side (mostly Anglo) environmentalists to battle against a massive housing development over the recharge zone of the Edwards Aquifer, successfully protecting the city's sole source of drinking water.[27]

These achievements had ramifications for local politics, making San Antonio a more democratic place—a transformative effect that gained even greater force as some COPS members joined with the Mexican American Legal Defense and Education Fund to force the rewriting of the city's charter. For the preceding twenty years, that governing document had mandated that city council elections be run on an at-large basis. This form of governance had enabled the Good Government League, a north-side political machine, to dominate local politics. Its dominance was reflected in its distribution of the public fisc—it freely spent tax dollars to underwrite the expanding suburbs in which its supporters resided and the central business district in which they worked. The US Department of Justice (DOJ) entered the fray after charter-revision forces sued the city in federal court, arguing that the at-large political structure violated provisions of the Voting Rights Act of 1964–65. The DOJ compelled the city to submit a revised charter to voters in January 1977 that created ten city council districts, and the plan was narrowly approved, with 52 percent of the vote.[28]

Get-out-the-vote campaigns on the west side were critical to the new charter's passage; its precincts reported nearly 90 percent voting in support

of a new, more equitable government. Four years later, this newly empowered west-side electorate made one of its sons, Henry Cisneros, mayor of
San Antonio, and he gave voice to their plight and prospects: "Over the last
decade, generations of Mejicanos have worked their fingers and shoulders
raw and driven themselves to premature old age in order that their sons and
daughters could take their rightful places in society," the thirty-three-year-old
mayor thundered. "That legacy of sweat and tears provides a moral impera-
tive that this generation assert itself to fulfill its most sacred dreams . . . We
have a generation of men and women who are hungry for what they can
achieve as only those who have been barred from the table can be hungry."[29]

Their fight for environmental justice had schooled COPS supporters
in the need for political power, new identity formation, and the broader
and democratic benefits that could flow from their subaltern resistance
movement. Some of its activists began carrying this galvanizing message
across the Southwest. Ernie Cortés, COPS's lead organizer in San Antonio,
moved on to East Los Angeles to launch a similar set of initiatives. Others,
all trained at "the University of COPS," fanned out to organize in Latino
neighborhoods in Houston and El Paso, Tucson and Phoenix. Willie
Velásquez, another San Antonio activist, added to this transformative
energy when he founded the Southwest Voter Registration and Education
Project with the goal of bringing Hispanic and underrepresented communities into the political process. Just as Atlanta was an incubus for the black
civil rights movement, so San Antonio was a formative ground in which
Latino activists conceived, trained for, and tested their ability to reconstruct
regional political life. Just as the civil rights movement found its source
in multiple communities' activism, so too with the environmental-justice
movement—its origins can now be traced back to Warren County, North
Carolina, and Bexar County, Texas.[30]

Still, locating when and where a protest movement originated is of little
moment to those swept up in the rush of its development. Much more crucial for them was clarifying the interwoven set of problems they felt impelled
to resolve. At its tenth anniversary celebrations, COPS's first president, Andy
Sarabia, reminded his audience of what they had once confronted: "Ten
years ago, city leaders said, 'Leave them alone. They're Mexicans. They can't
organize.' Today, we have power, we have our culture, we have our faith, we
have our communities, we have our dignity, and we're still Mexicans. They

feared the successful revolution from a government of the few by the few to a government of the people by the people and for the people. The significance is that the powerless do not have to stay powerless."[31]

The way this disenfranchised people secured power is no less significant. COPS's members first had to place themselves on the map, to recognize that the historic and ongoing flooding of the Zarzamora and other west-side creeks was a consequence of nature *and* politics, of the landscape they inhabited and the political geography in which they were located. Only then could they identify the need for a social response to this occasionally deadly environmental force. To achieve that level of identification required, in turn, that they understand their marginal location within local politics, develop a new framework by which to articulate their community's newfound identity, fight to insert themselves into the center of the civic arena, and, once there, use their authority to transform the physical terrain they called home. This process, at once transformative and reciprocal, legitimized their mobilization around a streetscape environmentalism that made it possible for them to imagine a future that was more just and sustainable—and a good deal less wet. Nature, the source of so much damage, death, and disarray on San Antonio's west side, had also become the catalyst of its residents' liberation.[32]

Notes

An earlier version of this chapter appeared in the *Southwestern Historical Quarterly* (CXIV [4], October 2014: 159–77) and is reprinted with its editors' kind permission.

1. *South Texas Floods, October 17–22, 1998* (Washington, DC: US Department of Commerce, 1999), 1.

2. See http://www.floodsafety.com/media/ffa/contents_index.htm, accessed August 13, 2018.

3. Mary Beth Rogers, *Cold Anger: A Story of Faith and Power Politics* (Denton: University of North Texas Press, 1990), 12–13.

4. Green Peyton, *San Antonio: City in the Sun* (New York: McGraw-Hill, 1946); David R. Johnson, John A. Booth, and Richard J. Harris, eds., *The Politics of San Antonio: Community, Progress, and Power* (Lincoln: University of Nebraska Press, 1983), 3–27, 191–212; Rodolfo Rosales, *The Illusion of Inclusion: The Untold Political Story of San Antonio* (Austin: University of Texas Press, 2000); Char Miller, ed., *On the Border: An Environmental History of San Antonio* (San Antonio: Trinity University Press, 2005), 12–13; Ernesto Cortés Jr. to Lynnell J. Burkett, May 27, 1994, interview transcript,

Institute of Texan Cultures Oral History Collection, San Antonio, 4–5, accessed August 13, 2018, http://digital.utsa.edu/cdm/ref/collection/p15125coll4/id/275.

5. Cortés to Burkett, May 27, 1994, 13–20; Ernesto Cortés Jr. to David Todd and David Weisman, April 12, 2002, *Texas Legacy Project*, interview transcript, accessed August 13, 2018, http://www.texaslegacy.org/bb/transcripts/cortesernietxt.html; Joseph Daniel Sekul, "Communities Organized for Public Service: Citizen Power and Public Policy in San Antonio," in *The Politics of San Antonio: Community, Progress, and Power*, ed. David R. Johnson, John A. Booth, and Richard J. Harris (Lincoln: University of Nebraska Press, 1983), 175–90; Carlos Muñoz Jr., "Mexican Americans and the Promise of Democracy: San Antonio Mayoral Elections," in *Big City Politics, Governance, and Fiscal Restraints*, ed. George E. Peterson (Washington, DC: Urban Institute Press, 1994), 105–20; Rosales, *Illusion of Inclusion*, 79–40.

6. Stephen Morton, *Gayatri Spivak: Subalternity and the Critique of Postcolonial Reason* (Malden, MA: Polity, 2007), 96–97; James Scott, *Weapons of the Weak: Everyday Forms of Peasant Resistance* (New Haven, CT: Yale University Press, 1985); Laura Pulido, *Environmentalism and Economic Justice: Two Chicano Struggles in the Southwest* (Tucson: University of Arizona Press, 1994), 4, 24; Laura Pulido, "Rethinking Environmental Racism: White Privilege and Urban Development in Southern California," *Annals of the Association of American Geographers* 90 (March 2000): 14–40. See also Paul Mohai, David Pellow, and J. Timmons Roberts, "Environmental Justice," *Annual Review of Environment and Resource* 34 (November 2009): 405–30.

7. Eileen McGurty, *Transforming Environmentalism: Warren County, PCBs, and the Origins of Environmental Justice* (New Brunswick, NJ: Rutgers University Press, 2007), 4 (quotation); Robert D. Bullard, *Dumping in Dixie: Race, Class, and Environmental Quality*, 3rd ed. (Boulder: Westview, 2000); Martin V. Melosi, "Equity, Eco-Racism, and Environmental History," in *Out of the Woods: Essays in Environmental History*, ed. Char Miller and Hal K. Rothman (Pittsburgh: University of Pittsburgh Press, 1997), 194–211. Robert Gottlieb, *Forcing the Spring: The Transformation of the American Environmental Movement* (Washington, DC: Island, 2005) argues correctly that the antecedents of the environmental-justice movement extend back to the Progressive era, but much of the historical scholarship follows McGurty, continuing to focus on Warren County as the source of its modern impetus.

8. McGurty, *Transforming Environmentalism*, 7. See also Robert D. Bullard and Glenn S. Johnson, "Environmental Justice: Grassroots Activism and Its Impact on Public Policy Decision Making—Statistical Data Included," *Journal of Social Issues* 56 (Fall 2000), doi.org/10.1111/0022-4537.00184, accessed August 13, 2018.

9. Cortés to Burkett, May 27, 1994, 4–5; Cortés to Todd and Weisman, April 12, 2002.

10. The following paragraphs draw in part on Char Miller, *Deep in the Heart of San Antonio: Land and Life in South Texas* (San Antonio: Trinity University Press, 2004), 61–66.

11. *San Antonio Express*, September 10, 1921; "San Antonio, TX Flood," *New York Times*, September 11, 1921 (all quotations); J. H. Jarboe, "The San Antonio Flood of September 10, 1921," *Monthly Weather Review* (September 1921): 494–96. See also Jonathan Burnett, *Flash Floods in Texas* (College Station: Texas A&M University Press, 2008), 28–36.

12. *San Antonio Express*, September 13, 1921 (quotations); September 18, 1921.

13. Miller, *On the Border*, 12–13.

14. J. B. Gwin, "San Antonio—the Flood City," *The Survey* (October 1921): 45–46.

15. Miller, *Deep in the Heart of San Antonio*, 61–66. These discrepancies were manifest as well in the maldistribution of potable water in San Antonio: Heywood Sanders, "Empty Taps, Missing Pipes: Water Policy and Politics," in *On the Border: An Environmental History of San Antonio*, ed. Char Miller (San Antonio: Trinity University Press, 2005), 141–68.

16. *A Preliminary Report on a System of Major Streets for San Antonio, Texas* (St. Louis: Harland Bartholomew and Associates, 1930), 322–28.

17. Seth D. Breeding, *Flood of September 1946 at San Antonio, Tex.*, circular 32 (Washington, DC: US Department of the Interior, 1948), 2–3; *San Antonio Express*, September 28, 1946.

18. Ted Steinberg, *Acts of God: The Unnatural History of Natural Disaster in America* (New York: Oxford University Press, 2000), 201.

19. Walter H. Lilly and M. Winston Martin, *San Antonio Takes Stock and Looks Ahead: A Comprehensive Master Plan for San Antonio, Texas* (San Antonio: [n. pub.], 1951), 192–207.

20. The Flood Control Act of 1954, Section 203, San Antonio Channel, reads: "The project for flood protection on the Guadalupe and San Antonio Rivers, Texas, is hereby authorized substantially in accordance with the recommendations of the Chief of Engineers in House Document Numbered 344, Eighty-Third Congress at an estimated cost of $20,254,000." See *Guadalupe and San Antonio Rivers, Texas—Chief of Engineers Report (February 1954)*, an Army Corps of Engineers report that served as the decision document for the authorized project, H. Exec. Doc. 344, 83rd Cong., 2nd Sess. This report concluded in part "that a serious flood problem exists within the city of San Antonio, an important military center and distribution point for a vast area in southwest Texas, and that a flood-protection project for this city to eliminate the flood menace is economically justified." Further, the report recommended "that a channel improvement project in San Antonio, Texas, be authorized at this time for construction by the Federal Government, substantially

as outlined in this report, at an estimated first cost to the United States of $12,906,900."

21. *San Antonio River Authority, 1937–1987* (San Antonio: San Antonio River Authority, 1988), 11.

22. Rogers, *Cold Anger*, 111; Jan Jarboe, "Building a Movement: Mexican Americans Struggle for Municipal Services," *Civil Rights Digest* (Spring 1977): 39–46; Mark Warren, "A Theory of Organizing: From Alinsky to the Modern IAF," in *The Community Development Reader*, ed. James DeFillipis and Susan Saegert (New York: Routledge, 2008), 194–203; Richard Buitron, *The Quest for Tejano Identity in San Antonio, Texas, 1913–2000* (New York: Routledge, 2004); Patrick J. Hayes, "COPS: Putting the Gospel into Action in San Antonio," in *Living the Catholic Social Tradition: Cases and Commentary*, ed. Kathleen Maas Weigert and Alexia K. Kelly (Lanham, MD: Rowman and Littlefield, 2005), 139–50.

23. Rogers, *Cold Anger*, 105–26.

24. Jarboe, "Building a Movement," 44.

25. Rogers, *Cold Anger*, 113 (quotation); Jarboe, "Building a Movement," 44; Jan Jarboe Russell, "By Exposing Good Government League Becker Made History," *San Antonio Express News*, June 26, 2006.

26. Jarboe, "By Exposing Good Government League Becker Made History"; Heywood Sanders, "Empty Taps, Missing Pipes," in *On the Border: An Environmental History of San Antonio*, ed. Char Miller (San Antonio: Trinity University Press, 2005), 141–68.

27. Cortés to Burkett, May 27, 1994, 3–4; Cortés to Todd and Weisman, April 12, 2002; Laura A. Wimberley, "Establishing 'Sole Source' Protection: The Edwards Aquifer and the Safe Drinking Water Act," in *On the Border: An Environmental History of San Antonio*, ed. Char Miller (San Antonio: Trinity University Press, 2005), 169–81; Robert Brischetto, Charles L. Cotrell, and R. Michael Stevens, "Conflict and Change in the Political Culture of San Antonio in the 1970s," in *The Politics of San Antonio: Community, Progress, and Power*, ed. David R. Johnson, John A. Booth, and Richard J. Harris (Lincoln: University of Nebraska Press, 1983), 75–94.

28. Thomas A. Baylis, "Leadership Change in Contemporary San Antonio," in *The Politics of San Antonio: Community, Progress, and Power*, ed. David R. Johnson, John A. Booth, and Richard J. Harris (Lincoln: University of Nebraska Press, 1983), 95–113; Tucker Gibson, "Mayoralty Politics in San Antonio, 1955–79," in *The Politics of San Antonio: Community, Progress, and Power*, ed. David R. Johnson, John A. Booth, and Richard J. Harris (Lincoln: University of Nebraska Press, 1983), 114–29; Heywood Sanders, "Building a New Urban Infrastructure: The Creation of Postwar San Antonio," in *Urban Texas: Politics and Development*, ed. Char Miller and Heywood

Sanders (College Station: Texas A&M University Press, 1990), 154–73; Rosales, *Illusion of Inclusion*, 83–158.

29. Cited in Richard Garcia, *Rise of the Mexican American Middle Class: San Antonio, 1929–1941* (College Station: Texas A&M University Press, 1991), 260.

30. Rogers, *Cold Anger*, 42–46; Mark A. Warren, "Building Democracy: Faith-Based Community Organizing Today," *Shelterforce*, January–February 2001; Char Miller, "Street Talk," in *A Tale of Two Cities: Atlanta and San Antonio: Proceedings of the 2005 Earl M. Lewis Symposium*, ed. Char Miller (San Antonio: Urban Studies Department, 2005), 4–13; Henry Cisneros, "People Make Change," in *A Tale of Two Cities: Atlanta and San Antonio: Proceedings of the 2005 Earl M. Lewis Symposium*, ed. Char Miller (San Antonio: Urban Studies Department, 2005), 127–43.

31. Rogers, *Cold Anger*, 125–26.

32. Rogers, *Cold Anger*, 125–26; McGurty, *Transforming Environmentalism*, 9–11; Pulido, *Environmentalism and Economic Justice*, 13; Jarboe, "Building a Movement," 38–43; Moises Sandoval, "The Decolonization of a City," *Alicia Patterson Foundation Newsletter*, https://web.archive.org/web/20061002100025/, http://aliciapatterson.org/APF001977/Sandoval/Sandoval04/Sandoval04.html, accessed August 13, 2018.

6

When the Sky Opened

*The Transformation of Tachikawa Air Base
into Showa Kinen Park*

Adam Tompkins and Charles Laurier

American bombs rained on Tachikawa and Sunagawa through the first half of 1945. This part of the Musashino Plain to the west of the then twenty (now twenty-three) wards of central Tokyo experienced profound change with the escalation of Japanese imperialism, transitioning from a predominantly agricultural area to a place with a mixed rural, military, and manufacturing character. The Japanese Imperial Army Air Force established Tachikawa Airfield in 1922 in a location previously covered with sericulture farms.[1] Tachikawa Aircraft Company began building civilian planes in the late 1920s but shifted production in the years following to eventually manufacture approximately one-tenth of Japan's military aircraft.[2] Hitachi Aircraft Corporation also housed its biggest engine factory there.[3] The size of Tachikawa mushroomed as the need for workers increased into the tens of thousands.[4] Neighboring Sunagawa largely managed to keep its agricultural character intact through the war years. As the Empire of Japan weakened in 1945 and the United States bombed cities on the main island of Honshu at will, manufacturers of war materials dispersed operations into adjacent neighborhoods.[5] This action saved neither the planes nor

DOI: 10.5876/9781607328483.c006

the surrounding Sunagawa homes from bombardment.[6] The air base runway, however, remained in remarkably good shape at the end of the war.[7]

Sunagawa farmers expected that land around the base and perhaps even property previously confiscated by the Japanese military would be returned for cultivation with the coming peace.[8] American forces, however, soon cleared bombed debris with bulldozers, rebuilt the base, and assumed control of its operations. Many local residents felt they lacked any right to complain because Japan had lost the war. The US military took advantage of the acquiescent mood and lack of organization, seizing farmland to expand the base perimeter and runway to better accommodate larger American airplanes.[9] A 1955 proposal to again extend the length of the runway northward through Sunagawa threatened to dissolve the bonds of community and jeopardize agricultural lifeways. This time, however, residents and their supporters proved less compliant as they embraced the spirit of democracy fostered by the United States during the postwar occupation and rallied to thwart a plan jointly supported by the United States and Japan.[10] The resulting mass movement, known as the Sunagawa Toso (struggle), successfully stalled the expansion plans and ultimately led to closure of the base.

The Sunagawa Toso embodied the spirit of environmental-justice activism decades prior to the drafting of Principle 15 at the 1991 First National People of Color Environmental Leadership Summit, which established the environmental-justice movement's opposition to "military occupation, repression and exploitation of lands, peoples and cultures, and other life forms."[11] Tachikawa Air Base caused environmental disturbances with the constant noise from its aircraft operations and posed a seemingly inexorable threat to the Sunagawa community with its plan to expropriate land owned by farm families for generations. The long campaign of nonviolent civil disobedience undertaken by residents and their supporters preceded other well-documented efforts of marginalized people in places like Hawaii, Puerto Rico, and Okinawa to retain or often regain control of land claimed for use by the US military in the post–World War II era.[12] The Japanese activists saved the land in Sunagawa from ruin, yet their improbable victory is not well preserved in the public memory, in part because land-use decisions made by the Japanese government after the announced closure of the base marginalized the Sunagawa narrative in an attempt to foster better citizen-government relations.

Saving Sunagawa

The American occupation of Japan ended in 1952, but the security treaty signed the previous year authorized the United States Armed Forces to maintain a presence under the auspices of protecting the non-militarized country from attack and securing peace in the Far East. The bases in Okinawa and Japan, which remained under US control, became centrally important installations for American operations in Asia. Okinawa had the greatest concentration of military installations, but US bases still dotted other areas of Japan and housed approximately 40,000 troops.[13] Tachikawa Air Base experienced an escalation of activity with the onset of the Korean War. It functioned as the largest military supply depot in the northern part of the Asian Pacific, handling nearly 12,000 tons of material and transporting approximately 100,000 personnel every month in the mid-1950s.[14]

The city of Tachikawa experienced dynamic change in the postwar years because the base exited east to the main thoroughfare close to the Chuo rail line that fed directly into central Tokyo. The city's population doubled from 30,000 to 60,000, with an economy driven largely by military services.[15] With a favorable to the United States exchange rate of 360 yen to the dollar, businesses catered to servicemen. Some clubs even restricted access to Americans only.[16] Extensive black markets, an estimated 325 prostitution houses and 1,450 sex workers, and 400 drug dealers operated in town by the end of 1954.[17] The base also attracted Japanese seeking employment opportunities. Many women worked as maids, nannies, or laundresses; men found employment in a variety of positions ranging from translation to carpentry to medical services.[18]

Base commanders tried to develop good relations with Japanese in the surrounding area but failed to satisfactorily address environmental issues. The Tachikawa mayor filed suit against the United States in 1952, charging that the military had contaminated 3,165 wells with gasoline. The status of forces agreement did not hold the United States responsible for environmental damage done in Japan, however, so the city bore the financial and logistical burden of delivering clean water to residents.[19] Spilled gasoline also reportedly caused fires in the vicinity of Tachikawa Station and along the Midori River that ran through town.[20] The Tachikawa City–US Forces Advisory Council, established in 1953, worked to resolve a variety of issues relating to roads, utilities, sewage disposal, and hygiene.[21] The base periodically welcomed visiting community groups, hosted friendship festivals and art exhibitions, and offered English conversation classes. Problems persisted nonetheless and ranged from stray gunfire hitting residential houses to aircraft interfering with television signals.[22]

Sunagawa, which abutted the runway at the base's northern end, attempted to maintain its agricultural character and generally experienced a different relationship with the US Air Force than did Tachikawa. Tachikawa welcomed the base because of the business traffic it brought, whereas Sunagawa farmers who suffered a loss of land viewed it less favorably. Sunagawa resident Kurihara Masao asserts that the farmers "lost their livelihood and all they got in return was wind and dust" from takeoffs and landings.[23] Occasionally, aircraft would fail to gain sufficient speed for takeoff and plow into bordering fields.[24] Crime in neighboring Tachikawa ranged from theft to heroin possession, but Sunagawa residents recall the sex trade being the most visible illicit activity.[25] Kurihara says it was "common knowledge to keep the girls inside," as soldiers would sometimes roam the streets and there were even stories of men "going into people's houses and actually looking for women."[26]

Noise pollution proved to be a more constant source of irritation (figure 6.1). Popular author Garret Keizer characterizes noise as sound that is imposed on individuals against their will and contends that "noise is a weak issue . . . because most of those it affects are perceived, and very often dismissed, as weak [and] the ones who dismiss them, in addition to being powerful, are often the ones making the noise."[27] This proved acutely true in Sunagawa, where locals viewed the base as "a foreign country" on the other side of the fence.[28] Japan, in fact, could not impose restrictions on US military flights even though the bases are located on Japanese soil.[29] Residents consequently suffered through noise from the Globemaster, Hercules, F-80 jets, and other large planes that took off and landed approximately 120 times a day. Each incident "created massive, pervasive vibrations and shaking," to the point that "noise became the central, symbolizing identity of the base."[30] Sunagawa resident Fukushima Kyoko remembers that noise regularly disrupted conversations and forced teachers to pause their lessons.[31] Military personnel and their dependents, by contrast, often remember the sound from aircraft engines as un-troubling, which speaks to Keizer's point of the imposition of sound being a central element of noise.[32] Noise complaints, nonetheless, did not catalyze into mass demonstrations. The Sunagawa Toso

FIGURE 6.1. A farmer opposed to the base expansion watches as a US Air Force plane comes in for a landing. Noise from military flights constantly pervaded the daily lives of community residents. *Courtesy*, Sunagawa Heiwa Hiroba.

began when farmers once again faced the prospect of losing precious agricultural land.

The 5,021-foot-long Tachikawa Air Base runway posed problems for some aircraft, so the United States and Japan reached an agreement to extend it northward in 1954, making it easier for heavily loaded cargo planes like

FIGURE 6.2. Sunagawa residents and their supporters engage in a sit-down to interfere with surveying efforts. *Courtesy,* Sunagawa Heiwa Hiroba.

the Globemaster and modern jets to operate.[33] The construction would cut through the middle of Sunagawa and displace an estimated 130 families. Some residents willingly sold their land, in part because of the noise problem, but others steadfastly resisted. Sunagawa resident Hoshi Kiich remembers that "locals' pure affection [for] and sense of intimacy to their community and property, which had belonged to their families for as long as 300 years," inspired them to action as they "strived to preserve the farming village." Noise constituted a significant burden, but Hoshi maintains that the threat posed to the land generated the most concern.[34]

Similar to Meiji-period farmers who launched protest movements to address crop damage from industrial pollutants, locals organized the Sunagawa Village Struggle Committee in May 1955 to block surveying efforts and defend their land and way of life (figure 6.2). This marked the beginning of the long Sunagawa Toso.[35] Sunagawa and Tachikawa lacked well-developed infrastructures, so the government tried to placate holdouts with promises of paved roads and better schools. Still, nearly forty affected families who owned 50 percent of the land to be condemned refused to sell.[36]

Instead, they engaged in nonviolent civil disobedience to keep their community intact. They sprayed the fields with pesticides and warned outsiders that chemical contact would cause sickness or worse.[37] Then, Nichiren Buddhist priests and farmers staged a sit-down on the targeted properties, the men wrapped straw rice bags around their stomachs to symbolize their livelihoods. Women acted more assertively, coating bamboo with night soil and flinging excrement at surveyors and police who tried to enter the properties.[38]

Supporters from farther afield lent their numbers to the local resistance. Zengakuren, a student group founded by the Supreme Commander for the Allied Powers to promote democratic principles during the occupation period, and the labor union Sohyo swelled the ranks and interwove a broader anti-base and antiwar agenda into the campaign.[39] Demonstrators wore headbands with kanji characters that communicated that they possessed an indomitable spirit and would stay steadfastly committed to the cause.[40] They went so far as to erect bamboo flagpoles on private property adjoining the runway in an attempt to interfere with flights.[41] Still, demonstrators did not profess a hatred of the United States or even its military; rather, they took action to oppose the expansion specifically and, more generally, to challenge the constitutionality of a military presence in Japan under Article 9, the non-military clause of the new constitution.[42]

The Tokyo Metropolitan Police readied 2,000 officers and seventy armored vehicles to disrupt the demonstrations (figure 6.3). Upon learning of the police plan, Robert McClurkin, director of the Office of Northeast Asian Affairs, remarked that "the results of using the police at Tachikawa could be disastrous or brilliant [but] unfortunately there is no way to be sure before the fact."[43] The planned use of force continued with the recognition that it would cause a "pretty nasty situation for at least the first few days."[44] The activist professor of philosophy Shibata Shingo wrote of the clash that followed: "They broke through a strong human barricade of 4,000 persons, firmly locked arm-to-arm. Blood was shed on the muddy road and the Japanese police assault upon the Japanese peaceloving people continued under the heart-breaking, thundering whirr of the U.S. Globe-Master Planes flying from the airbase. Farmland was trampled under foot [sic] of the mobbed police and the serious damage of crop was caused."[45]

The police ruined oppositional farmers' sweet potato, wheat, and rice crops and unleashed a fury of baton attacks on protesters.[46] Demonstrators

FIGURE 6.3. A police officer attempts to immobilize a demonstrator. The excessive use of force by the police increased public sympathy for the Sunagawa struggle. *Courtesy,* Sunagawa Heiwa Hiroba.

accounted for over 80 percent of the 1,260 people injured in the encounter.[47] The impression that authorities used excessive force generated sympathy from a range of prominent public figures.[48] The stiff resistance forced surveyors to take measurements from the base side of the fence under the protection of military guards.[49]

The police failed to break the Sunagawa Toso, with demonstrations continuing through the 1960s. The inability of the military to complete the runway extension and meet the space requirements of jet aircraft resulted in Tachikawa Air Base losing its strategic importance.[50] Aircrafts were routed instead to nearby Yokota Air Base, where measurements conducted in 1967 showed jets producing 110 decibels of noise in the flight path.[51] The propeller aircraft at Tachikawa generated less noise than jets but still would have exceeded the 2009 World Health Organization standard of 55 decibels for serious noise annoyance by roughly 35 decibels and likely entered the range of sound that poses potential health risks.[52] Fukushima Kyoko describes the end of flights over Sunagawa, saying "it got quieter [and] the sky got bigger."

The United States announced in 1969 that it would decommission Tachikawa Air Base and return the land to Japan in 1977. The Sunagawa residents who for years had refused to sell their property retained their land. The future of the property on the other side of the fence, however, had yet to be determined.

The Making and Function of Showa Kinen Park

The decision to decommission Tachikawa Air Base roughly coincided with rising environmental concern in Japan that influenced the government's planning. Four big environmental disease cases—Itai-itai disease, Yokkaichi asthma, Chisso Minamata disease, and Niigata Minamata disease—brought sudden attention to the interconnectedness of environment, pollution, and health.[53] Sociologist Jeffrey Broadbent contends that the mass movements of the 1950s and 1960s gave citizens the confidence to vocalize their complaints about pollution and environmental health issues as they embraced their democratic rights and the idea that people were entitled to a healthy living environment.[54] Political scientist Margaret A. McKean contends that pollution "stimulated a tremendous wave of political protest, almost certainly the largest and most significant social movement in Japan's modern history."[55] In its race to recovery after World War II, Japan focused almost singularly on economic growth. It became increasingly clear, however, that this narrow pursuit adversely affected citizens' quality of life. An environmentally conscious citizenry made the Tokyo Metropolitan Government cognizant of the need to establish civil minimums for adequate living that considered urban issues ranging from housing floor space to public parks.[56]

The metropolitan government recognized the necessity of expanding open areas within the city for healthy and satisfying urban living. In 1972 it declared that Tokyo needed a restoration and expansion of greenery because "like other living creatures, man needs space" and a shortage of it would cause people's "living pattern to lose balance."[57] Two years later it crafted a "Basic Plan for the Protection and Restoration of Nature in Tokyo," embracing an understanding that nature underlay human existence and should be interwoven into the daily lives of city dwellers.[58] Yet the government also recognized that acquiring the necessary land to make a more livable city could prove problematic. Skyrocketing property values, caused in part by rampant speculation, made it difficult for the government to purchase land for parks. The city paid 13,000 yen per square meter of land when enlarging Koganei Park in 1968. Property values in the same area rose to 74,000 yen per square meter within five years, dramatically increasing park expansion costs. Speculation in real estate led to sprawl, which ate into precious green space.[59] Only 28 percent of the city's green space that existed in 1932 remained in 1969, and growth showed no sign of slowing. Consequently, a core component of the city's urban renewal plan involved the reacquisition and repurposing of Tachikawa Air Base.[60]

The Tokyo Metropolitan Government preached the importance of involving citizens in urban renewal planning, holding that past failure to do so had resulted in an increased distrust of government.[61] Public opinion in Sunagawa ultimately carried little weight in the decision-making process, though. When Japan's Self-Defense Forces (SDF) proposed using a portion of the base, 80 percent of surveyed residents expressed opposition, stating that the aircraft noise would once again degrade their quality of life.[62] The SDF staged a coup of sorts, moving an air squadron onto the property while the city slept in March 1972.[63] The future of the remaining acreage remained undetermined, and a variety of agencies and private entities drowned out local voices that wanted to independently determine what uses would best meet community needs.[64] The National Land Agency announced that it would allow the SDF to continue using the area it occupied, allocate space for use by the Japanese and Tachikawa City Governments, and construct the largest public park in Tokyo on the remaining portion.[65] Tokyoites complained about "insufficient 'naturalness' of the [urban] environment" and noise pollution, so the establishment of a large green space addressed the needs of the larger metropolitan populace but did not satisfy the desire of the people most responsible for the reversion of the base to Japan.[66]

The park generated some controversy because planners chose the name Showa Kinen Park to commemorate the fiftieth anniversary of the emperor's ascension to the throne. Some Japanese felt this would whitewash the complicated reign of Emperor Hirohito.[67] Trade unions forced the Tachikawa City Government to agree not to enlist municipal employees in opening ceremony preparations. City leaders also promised not to have local schoolchildren greet the emperor with waves. Government concern about demonstrations or worse ran so high that it mobilized 8,000 police officers for the event in October 1983. Police outnumbered protesters sixteen to one in the end.[68]

Planners cast the opening of Showa Kinen Park as a "return of greenery and uplifting of humanity" and embraced the Japanese concept of *machizukuri* to advance their mission.[69] Geographers André Sorensen and Carolin Funck characterize *machizukuri* as the process by which local citizens play a direct role in fostering urban change that results in healthier community environments.[70] Oral histories conducted with Sunagawa residents, however, suggest that many community members do not have a strong affinity for the park and, to a significant degree, do not participate in park programs.[71] This could be attributed to the government effectively marginalizing them during the land planning process. Fukushima Kyoko estimates that 70 percent of Sunagawa residents opposed the park.[72] She states that to her, "the park is still a land with a fence around it . . . [and] is not for everyone" because the "entrance fee is expensive compared to other national parks."[73] Tachikawa, in contrast, supported the proposal and benefited more directly because of its prime location between the rail station and the park's main entrance. The opening of the 163-hectare park with its 2.5 million annual visitors helped Tachikawa rehabilitate its image from "base town" to "cultural city."[74] *Machizukuri* programs played an important role in maintaining the landscape and supporting programs that brought masses of visitors through the city and to the park.

The Komorebi Hill Volunteer Group, whose purpose is to foster the growth of a "symbiotic relation between mankind and nature," provides an excellent example of how *machizukuri* functions at Showa Kinen Park.[75] The hill, constructed out of air base building debris and topsoil, has a series of short trails that offer visitors a sense of solitude and quiet respite.[76] The volunteer group maintains the landscape. Participants nurture the coppice forest: conserving and composting soil, cultivating trees, pruning and thinning vegetation, propagating wild grasses and flowers, and performing trail maintenance.[77] The activities inculcate participants with a sustainability ethic, embodying the vision of the Tokyo Metropolitan Government in 1974 in which citizen "movements of education . . . [elevated] people's awareness in support of protecting and creating more vegetation . . . [while] deepening cooperative relations between citizens and administrative bodies."[78] The program effectively empowers individual participants with decision-making responsibilities, builds relationships within the groups, and adds value to the park and the community.

Showa Kinen Park also offers green space to "reflect in peace and quiet upon the turmoil and upheavals of the Showa Period, and to seek out a life worth living in a whole new era."[79] Next to Komorebi Hill, whose tree-lined slopes cover the ruins of a military past, sits Komorebi Village, a *mukashi furosato* (old hometown) that recreates an early Showa-Period village on the Musashino Plain.[80] The park, using the *machizukuri* process again, calls on volunteers to engage in caretaking, management, and agricultural production.[81] This provides an idealized connection to the past for volunteers and visitors alike. The function bears some comparison to a plot development in the Ishimure Michiko environmental fiction book *Lake of Heaven*, in which a young Tokyoite visiting his grandfather's traditional home village becomes spiritually rejuvenated. The young man realizes that "sound itself has come close to becoming a lethal weapon" in the city, as "if his eardrums were being pulled from his inner ear and trampled beneath people's shoes."[82] The village he visits is drowned by waters from a downstream dam; still, he finds that he can "call it up from the depths" of an abyss created by modern technology and reconnect to a more traditional and harmonious existence.[83] Komorebi Village functions similarly, providing rescue from the din of the city and encouraging people to maintain a link to older lifeways. Yet this is a largely sanitized version of the complex Showa Period that hides the history of the Sunagawa Toso that ultimately led to the abandonment of Tachikawa Air Base.

Planners interwove an environmental and social agenda into the design and management of Showa Kinen Park. Although the history of the park is much shorter, it bears comparison to historian Ian Jared Miller's research on Tokyo's Ueno Zoo, in which he shows how the state blended a political agenda with concepts of nature to inculcate the public with a set of values and understandings deemed favorable at the time.[84] A similar argument can be made with the operation of Showa Kinen Park. Nunokawa Hiroshi argues that "people's historical memories are reconstructed through the process of machizukuri" and that some elements will be shown favor over others.[85] The relaxing and scenic green space underneath often quiet skies provides a place for peaceful reflection and appreciation of a cleaner, peaceful Japan. In what could be construed as an act of historical erasure, though, the middle decades of the Showa Period—the years of militarization, war, occupation, and mass protests—are ignored in favor of a more simplified bucolic past. The Tokyo Metropolitan Government wanted urban green space to strengthen community and cooperative relationships between citizens and government after turbulent periods of protest in the 1950s and 1960s. *Machizukuri* promised progress toward this goal, whereas valorizing the oppositional movement of Sunagawa farmers would do little to advance good-faith citizen-government partnerships. Nonetheless, the Sunagawa Toso deserves greater remembrance and remains a potentially empowering episode. Fukushima Kyoko maintains that "no matter where we live, our right to live happily should not be taken away" and hopes that the success of the Sunagawa Toso will encourage younger generations to act as a "voice of peace."[86]

Notes

Special thanks to Sue Sayaka, Mizutani Ritsuko, Yanagawa Haruhi, Kobayashi Mai, Ando Mayu, Aonuki Yurika, Niida Michika, Carl Gabrielson, and Hirasawa Nene for the translation assistance. Thank you also to the people who contributed to the oral histories as interviewees and interviewers. Japanese names in the text follow the Japanese form of the given name following the surname.

1. A/1C Robert P. Garnet, ed., *Once around Tachi: Guide to Tachikawa Air Base* (Tachikawa: Office of Information Services, Northern Air Material Area, Pacific, Tachikawa Air Base, Japan, 1957), 9, copy in possession of author, provided by historian Robert Sligh at Yokota Air Base, Fussa, Tokyo, Japan; Donald Eugene Shoop, "Sunagawa Incident," PhD dissertation, University of Denver, Denver, CO, 1983, 1.

2. United States Strategic Bombing Survey, *Tachikawa Aircraft Company (Tachikawa Kikoki K K)*, Corporation Report no. X (Airframes), Aircraft Division (Washington, DC: United States Strategic Bombing Survey, 1947), 1, 12.

3. United States Strategic Bombing Survey, *Hitachi Aircraft Company (Hitachi Kokuki K K)*, Corporation Report no. VII (Airframes and Engines), Aircraft Division (Washington, DC: United States Strategic Bombing Survey, 1947), 48.

4. United States Strategic Bombing Survey, *Tachikawa Aircraft Company*, 4; United States Strategic Bombing Survey, *Hitachi Aircraft Company*, 49.

5. United States Strategic Bombing Survey, *The Japanese Aircraft Industry*, Aircraft Division (Washington, DC: United States Strategic Bombing Survey, 1947), 2.

6. Kurihara Masao (Sunagawa activist) and Fukushima Kyoko (daughter of Sunagawa activist), interview by authors and Carl Gabrielson, March 21, 2015, Sunagawa Heiwa Hiroba Museum, Sunagawa, Tokyo, Japan.

7. *Tachikawa Kichi* (Tachikawa: Tachikawa City Government, 1972), 17.

8. Nagatani Rokuya (union leader/Sunagawa activist) and Hoshi Kiich (Sunagawa resident), interview by Kobayashi Mai, Niida Miichika, and Adam Tompkins, July 13, 2015, Sunagawa Museum, Sunagawa, Tokyo, Japan.

9. Kurihara Masao and Fukushima Kyoko interview; 17; *Tachikawa Kichi*, 17.

10. Fukushima Kyoko (daughter of Sunagawa activist), interview by Sue Sayaka, February 3, 2015, Sunagawa Heiwa Hiroba Museum, Sunagawa, Tokyo, Japan.

11. The First National People of Color Environmental Leadership Summit, "Principles of Environmental Justice," Washington, DC, October 27, 1991.

12. See, for example, Mansel G. Blackford, "Environmental Justice, Native Rights, Tourism, and Opposition to Military Control: The Case of Kaho'olawe," *Journal of American History* 91, no. 2 (2004): 544–71; Carmen I. Aponte, "US Navy versus Vieques, Puerto Rico: Social Justice through Civil Disobedience," *Journal of Poverty* 8, no. 4 (2004): 59–73; Tanji Miyume, "US Court Rules in the 'Okinawa Dugong' Case: Implications for US Military Bases Overseas," *Critical Asian Studies* 40, no. 3 (2008): 475–87.

13. Thomas R.H. Havens, *Fire across the Sea: The Vietnam War and Japan, 1965–1975* (Princeton, NJ: Princeton University Press, 1987), 8–9, 85.

14. Garnet, *Once around Tachi*, 1, 19–20, 24; Shoop, "Sunagawa Incident," 5.

15. Garnet, *Once around Tachi*, 9–10.

16. Nagatani Rokuya and Hoshi Kiich interview; Kurihara Masao and Fukushima Kyoko interview; [Tachikawa Air Base Guide] (Tachikawa: Office of Information Services, Northern Air Material Area, Pacific, Tachikawa Air Base, Japan, 1957), 35, copy in possession of author, provided by historian Robert Sligh at Yokota Air Base, Fussa, Tokyo, Japan.

17. Shoop, "Sunagawa Incident," 6. The number of prostitutes attracted to the area by the base reportedly climbed as high as 5,000. *Tachikawa Kichi*, 18, 39.

18. Mike Murphy (US Air Force), interview by Maeno Yumi, July 21, 2015 (via email); Al Andre (US Air Force), interview by Inagaki Yuna, July 16, 2015 (via email).

19. Shoop, "Sunagawa Incident," 5–6; Sharon K. Weiner, "Environmental Concerns at US Overseas Military Installations," Defense and Arms Control Studies Working Paper, Massachusetts Institute of Technology, Cambridge, MA, 1992, 26.

20. Nagatani Rokuya and Hoshi Kiich interview. The Midori River became the street Midorikawa Dori after it was paved over like many other waterways in Tokyo. For a discussion of this phenomenon, see Rebecca Milner, "Rediscovering Lost Tokyo," *Japan Times* (Tokyo), July 19, 2014.

21. Garnet, *Once around Tachi*, 9.

22. *Tachikawa Kichi*, 32, 35.

23. Kurihara Masao and Fukushima Kyoko interview.

24. Kurihara Masao and Fukushima Kyoko interview; National Transportation Safety Board, *Aircraft Accident Report: Airlift International, Inc. Douglas DC-7C, N2282 Tachikawa Air Base, Tokyo, Japan, September 12, 1966*, (Washington, DC: National Transportation Safety Board, 1966), 1–4.

25. *United States v. Airman Third Class Robert T. Martin*, United States Air Force Board of Review (1954); *United States v. Staff Sergeant Ezell Turks Jr.*, United States Air

Force Board of Review (1953); Nagatani Rokuya and Hoshi Kiich interview; Kurihara Masao and Fukushima Kyoko interview. Japan waived its jurisdictional right to prosecute in 97 percent of the 12,581 charges brought against American servicemen between 1953 and 1956, which sometimes contributed to negative perceptions of military personnel. Yasuyuki Kimura, "The Defense Facilities Administration Agency: A Unique Support Organization for US Forces in Japan," *Asia-Pacific Policy Paper Series* 16 (Washington, DC: Edwin O. Reischauer Center for East Asian Studies), 25.

26. Kurihara Masao and Fukushima Kyoko interview. The Tachikawa City Government also reported that "soldiers have broken into homes in the middle of the night, and have raped women, and citizens have not been able to do anything about it." *Tachikawa Kichi*, 18.

27. Garrett Keizer, *The Unwanted Sound of Everything We Want: A Book about Noise*, Kindle ed. (New York: Public Affairs, 2010), Location 127 (quotation), 2038.

28. *Tachikawa Kichi*, 18.

29. Japan still lacks the ability to restrict US military flights. "Noisy Nighttime Military Flights," *Japan Times* (Tokyo), May 26, 2014; "Reducing Military Jet Noise," *Japan Times* (Tokyo), August 9, 2015.

30. *Tachikawa Kichi*, 18.

31. Fukushima Kyoko interview. This noise can represent a true health threat. Researchers identified a link between low birth-weight babies and noise from military aircraft in Okinawa. Gwyn Kirk, "Environmental Effects of US Military Security: Gendered Experiences from the Philippines, South Korea, and Japan," in *Gender and Globalization in Asia and the Pacific: Method, Practice, Theory*, ed. Kathy E. Ferguson and Monique Mironesco (Honolulu: University of Hawaii Press, 2008), 312.

32. Susan Shorter (US Air Force dependent), interview by Arakawa Maho, July 18, 2015 (via email); Talbot N. Vivian (US Air Force), interview by Kodama Kanta, July 18, 2015 (via email).

33. National Transportation Safety Board, *Aircraft Accident Report*, 10; Shoop, "Sunagawa Incident," 8–9.

34. Nagatani Rokuya and Hoshi Kiich interview.

35. Shoop, "Sunagawa Incident," 8. For a discussion of the Meiji-era protests, see Miyamoto Ken'Ichi, "Japanese Environmental Policy: Lessons from Experience and Remaining Problems," trans. Jeffrey E. Hanes, in *Japan at Nature's Edge: The Environmental Context of a Global Power*, ed. Ian Jared Miller, Julia Adeney Thomas, and Brett L. Walker, Kindle edition (Honolulu: University of Hawaii Press, 2013), Location 5349–5369.

36. Memorandum of Conversation between Mr. Fukushima and R. L. Sneider, "Runaway Extension Program," September 30, 1955, Record Group 59, 58-D-118

and 58-D-637, Records of the Office of Northeast Asian Affairs, Japan Subject Files, 1947–1956, Box 8, National Archives, Washington, DC [microfilm], Reel 38, #0232; Fukushima Kyoko interview; Liaison and Protocol Section, Bureau of General Affairs, ed., *Tokyo for the People: Concepts for Urban Renewal* (Chiyoda-ku: Tokyo Metropolitan Government, 1972), 41.

37. Shoop, "Sunagawa Incident," 11.

38. Nagatani Rokuya and Hoshi Kiich interview.

39. Zackary Kaplan, "Anti-Americanism in Zengakuren 1957–1960," *Studies on Asia* (March 2012): 58; David E. Apter and Nagayo Sawa, *Against the State: Politics and Social Protest in Japan* (Cambridge, MA: Harvard University Press, 1986), 82, 112; Shoop, "Sunagawa Incident," 12.

40. Fukushima Kyoko interview.

41. Shoop, "Sunagawa Incident," 19.

42. Nagatani Rokuya and Hoshi Kiich interview; Kaplan, "Anti-Americanism in Zengakuren 1957–1960," 51, 56–57. Seven activists charged onto the base and used the courts as a vehicle to argue that Article 9 prohibited an American military presence in Japan. A lower court ruled in the activists' favor, but the United States wielded influence over the Japanese Supreme Court, which reversed the decision. See Alfred C. Oppler, "The Sunakawa Case: Its Legal and Political Implications," *Political Science Quarterly* 76, no. 2 (1961): 241–63; "Sunagawa Incident Retrial Request May Throw Wrench into Self-Defense Push," *Japan Times* (Tokyo), May 14, 2014.

43. Robert J.G. McClurkin to J. Graham Parsons, July 25, 1955, M. 2.1/6 Runway Extension, Record Group 59, Lot Files 58-D-118 and 58-D-637, Records of the Office of Northeast Asian Affairs, Japan Subject Files, 1947–1956, Box 8, National Archives, Washington, DC [microfilm], Reel 38, #0232 (quotation); "Extension of Tachikawa Air Base and Resulting Riots at Sunakawa" [Confidential Report], October 16, 1956, Record Group 59, 58-D-118 and 58-D-637, Records of the Office of Northeast Asian Affairs, Japan Subject Files, 1947–1956, Box 8, National Archives, Washington, DC [microfilm], Reel 38, #0232.

44. J. Graham Parsons to Robert J.G. McClurkin, July 18, 1955, Record Group 59, 58-D-118 and 58-D-637, Records of the Office of Northeast Asian Affairs, Japan Subject Files, 1947–1956, Box 8, National Archives, Washington, DC [microfilm], Reel 38, #0232.

45. Shibata Shingo to Friends (Quakers), October 14, 1956, in Alice Hertz and Shibata Shingo, *Phoenix: Letters and Documents of Alice Herz: The Thought and Practice of a Modern-Day Martyr* (Amsterdam: Grüner, 1976), 101.

46. Fukushima Kyoko interview.

47. Shoop, "Sunagawa Incident," 23–24.

48. "Extension of Tachikawa Air Base and Resulting Riots at Sunakawa"; Nagatani Rokuya and Hoshi Kiich interview. Some of the supporting politicians included Katayama Tetsu, Kazami Akira, and Arita Hachiro. Academic supporters included Shibata Shingo, Kaya Seiji, Suekawa Hiroshi, and Ouchi Hyoe. Shibata Shingo to Friends (Quakers), 101. Some American military personnel guarding the fence perimeter also felt empathy for the peaceful demonstrators. Dennis Banks, *Ojibwa Warrior: Dennis Banks, and the Rise of the American Indian Movement* (Norman: University of Oklahoma Press, 2004), 52–54.

49. Shoop, "Sunagawa Incident," 26–27.

50. American Embassy in Tokyo to Secretary of State, "Phasedown of Tachikawa Air Base," September 4, 1969, DEF 15—Japan-US, Record Group 59, Records of the Department of State, Central Foreign Policy Files, Subject-Numeric Files, 1967–1969, for Japan, National Archives, College Park, MD [microfilm], Reel 4, #0097.

51. Measurements taken 5 kilometers from the end of the runway tested as high as 90 decibels. Liaison and Protocol Section, Bureau of General Affairs, ed., *Tokyo Fights Pollution: An Urgent Appeal for Reform* (Chiyoda-ku: Tokyo Metropolitan Government, 1971), 152–53.

52. Liaison and Protocol Section, Bureau of General Affairs, *Tokyo Fights Pollution*, 146; Birgitta Berglund, Thomas Lindvall, and Dietrich H. Schwela, eds., *Guidelines for Community Noise* (Geneva: World Health Organization, 1999), 17.

53. Miyamoto Ken'Ichi, "Japanese Environmental Policy," Location 5391–431.

54. Jeffrey Broadbent, *Environmental Politics: Networks of Power and Protest* (Cambridge: Cambridge University Press, 1998), 104–16.

55. Margaret A. McKean, *Environmental Protests and Citizen Politics in Japan* (Berkeley: University of California Press, 1981), 1.

56. Liaison and Protocol Section, Bureau of General Affairs, ed., *Tokyo for the People: Concepts for Urban Renewal* (Chiyoda-ku: Tokyo Metropolitan Government, 1972), i–ii; Thomas R.H. Havens, *Parkscapes: Green Spaces in Modern Japan* (Honolulu: University of Hawaii Press, 2011), 14.

57. Liaison and Protocol Section, Bureau of General Affairs, *Tokyo for the People*, 130.

58. *Protecting Tokyo's Environment*, trans. Simul International, Inc. (Tokyo: Tokyo Metropolitan Government, 1985), 85.

59. Liaison and Protocol Section, Bureau of General Affairs, ed. *Land in the Tokyo Metropolis in 1974: Aspect and Program* (Chiyoda-ku: Tokyo Metropolitan Government, 1976), 8–9, 34.

60. Liaison and Protocol Section, Bureau of General Affairs, *Tokyo for the People*, 108, 130.

61. Liaison and Protocol Section, Bureau of General Affairs, *Tokyo for the People*, 72–74.

62. "Most Tachikawa People Oppose SDF Use of Base," *Japan Times* (Tokyo), November 11, 1971.

63. The US Air Force reached agreement with the SDF regarding use, even though Tachikawa Air Base would not be fully reverted back to Japan until 1977. "GSDF Unit 'Sneaks' into Tachikawa Base under Cover of Night," *Japan Times* (Tokyo), March 9, 1972.

64. "Control of Tachikawa Air Base Reverts to Japan after 32 Years," *Japan Times* (Tokyo), December 1, 1977; "Plan Bared for Use of Tachikawa Base," *Japan Times* (Tokyo), June 23, 1971; "Relocating the Capital," *Japan Times* (Tokyo), January 12, 1976; "Tokyo U. Eyes Site at Tachikawa AFB," *Japan Times* (Tokyo), February 14, 1977; *Tachikawa Kichi*, 33.

65. "Land Agency Plans Park at Tachikawa Base Site," *Japan Times* (Tokyo), December 24, 1977; "Proposals Aired for Use of Tachikawa Base Site," *Japan Times* (Tokyo), October 24, 1978.

66. *Protecting Tokyo's Environment*, 15. Other former military spaces in Yoyogi, Ōizumi, Musashino, Fuchū, and Higashi Yamato were also converted to parks. Havens, *Parkscapes*, 117.

67. "Police Mobilize against Park Protesters," *Japan Times* (Tokyo), October 25, 1983.

68. "Showa Nat'l Park Partially Opened," *Japan Times* (Tokyo), October 27, 1983; "Police Mobilize against Park Protesters."

69. The wording of the first quotation varies slightly in three different sources, although the idea is consistent. "Japanese Stamp News," *Japan Times* (Tokyo), October 1, 1983; "Basic Ideology behind the Showa Kinen Park," Showa Kinen Park Official Website, accessed August 6, 2015, http://www.showakinen-koen.jp/about. See also, "Council Reveals Plan for Park," *Japan Times* (Tokyo), August 1, 1979.

70. Sorensen and Funk suggest that the Japanese environmental movement initiated "a new tradition of local mobilization" and ignore mass movements like the Sunagawa Toso and the more widespread peace campaigns in Japan that predate the environmental movement by several years. André Sorensen and Carolin Funck, "Introduction," in *Living Cities in Japan: Citizens' Movements, Machizukuri, and Local Environments*, ed. André Sorensen and Carolin Funck (New York: Routledge, 2007), 1–2, 16.

71. Fukushima Kyoko interview; Kurihara Masao and Fukushima Kyoko interview; Nagatani Rokuya and Hoshi Kiich interview.

72. Kurihara Masao and Fukushima Kyoko interview.

73. Fukushima Kyoko interview.

74. *10th Anniversary of Showa Kinen Koen*, ed. Inoue Tadayoshi (Tokyo: Construction Ministry, Kanto Regional Office, 1993), 3; Mitsui Yuichiro, Kuramoto Noboru,

Itagaki Kumiko, Nishikawa Yoshiteru, and Mochiduki Kazuhiko, "Development of Park with Citizen Participation," *Japanese Institute of Landscape Architecture* 3 (2005): 66–67.

75. Handa Mariko, "Good Practices toward New Capabilities of Parks and Recreation," presentation to the International Federation of Parks and Recreation Administration, Hong Kong, November 15–18, 2010, 2, accessed May 30, 2015, http://www.lcsd.gov.hk/specials/ifpra2010/download/paper/mariko.pdf.

76. *10th Anniversary of Showa Kinen Koen*, 6, 18.

77. Handa, "Good Practices toward New Capabilities of Parks and Recreation," 2.

78. *Protecting Tokyo's Environment*, 90.

79. "Basic Ideology behind the Showa Kinen Park."

80. *10th Anniversary of Showa Kinen Koen*, 18.

81. Terashima Etsuko and Hiramatsu Reiji, "The Function of Citizen Participation Activities in Showa Kinen Park," *Japanese Institute of Landscape Architecture* 3 (2005): 62.

82. Ishimure Michiko, *Lake of Heaven*, trans. Bruce Allen, Kindle ed. (Lanham, MD: Lexington Books, 2008), Location 490, 2276.

83. Ishimure, *Lake of Heaven*, Location 3484.

84. Ian Jared Miller, *The Nature of the Beasts: Empire and Exhibition at the Tokyo Imperial Zoo* (Berkeley: University of California Press, 2013), 13. See also, André Sorensen, "Changing Governance of Shared Spaces: Machizukuri as Institutional Innovation," in *Living Cities in Japan: Citizens' Movements, Machizukuri, and Local Environments*, ed. André Sorensen and Carolin Funck (New York: Routledge, 2007), 62, 71.

85. Hiroshi Nunokawa, "Machizukuri and Historical Awareness in the Old Town of Kobe," in *Living Cities in Japan: Citizens' Movements, Machizukuri, and Local Environments*, ed. André Sorensen and Carolin Funck (New York: Routledge, 2007), 172.

86. Fukushima Kyoko to teachers and students at Lakeland College Japan, June 12, 2015. Copy in possession of authors.

7

Friendship Park

Environmental Placemaking at the US-Mexico Border

Jill M. Holslin

It all started to change in November 2009 when a border patrol agent decided to help plant white sage and California goldenrod at the US-Mexico border. Not your regular border patrol agent. No green uniform with the yellow and black US Border Patrol arm patch. No FLIR Recon BN-10 tactical night-sight thermal binoculars. No ultra-bright CREE T6 LED aerospace-grade aluminum body flashlight. No wap, wap, wap of the white and green helicopters circling relentlessly overhead.

No, this day was a sunny, clear-sky Saturday at Friendship Park, and this border patrol agent looked like all the other volunteers that day, dressed in jeans and work boots and a navy blue Adidas T-shirt, holding his young son by one hand, garden trowel in the other. Our group of volunteer gardeners had gathered at Friendship Park to replant the Binational Friendship Garden of Native Plants that had nearly been destroyed by the recent construction of the border wall.

Located at the southwestern corner of the continental United States, in San Diego County, Friendship Park is situated directly on top of the international

DOI: 10.5876/9781607328483.c007

boundary, near the delta and lagoon where the Tijuana River drains into the sparkling Pacific Ocean. The site is not unlike the famous Four Corners Monument in the Navajo Nation of the Southwest, where a granite and brass plaque and a visitor center mark the abstract boundary where four US states come together in the middle of the desert. Here, a white marble boundary monument marks the site where the United States and Mexico agreed to establish the international boundary in 1848.[1]

Standing directly on the boundary line in the Binational Friendship Garden amid the bright yellow blossoms of native coast sunflower, you can reach out your arms and be in both countries at once. On any given day, from Tijuana you might catch the ethereal wail of a mariachi trumpet as it rises up and is gone, the ocean breeze carrying laughter and the rich aroma of grilled shrimp and fish tacos. In San Diego, you might see flocks of California Least Tern and Snowy Plover dart back and forth on the beach, pecking wildly for bugs under the wet sand.

Enjoyed for decades by local families who came from nearby Tijuana and San Diego to gather at the border for weekend picnics, the park and beach were open for surfers and beachgoers to wander from San Diego over to the Playas de Tijuana side for tacos or fruit drinks and come back. The park became the site of local immigrant rights organizing in the late 1990s. In response to cruel federal workplace raids that tore families apart, local human rights advocate Roberto Martinez chose Friendship Park as the site for an annual Christmas celebration, La Posada Sin Fronteras, a traditional Mexican ceremony that reenacts Mary and Joseph's search for shelter in an unwelcoming Bethlehem. Inspired by these original posada events, today a binational border church offers Sunday communion services, and the park welcomes groups for yoga classes, beach cleanups, and music concerts. This park on the border has empowered people from Mexico and the United States to overcome fear and create a sense of belonging through place.

And so for decades this site on the US-Mexico border has been a critical locus of binational friendship and cooperation. Yet it is also the location of the first US border walls, making it the initial test site of late twentieth-century border militarization.

Under a logic of militarization, the US-Mexico border has been secured since 9/11, and crossing the border in San Diego has been recoded as a deviant, potentially threatening mobility. For lots of us here, the rhythm of everyday life is created by cross-border visits to family and the daily commute to work, and intrusive surveillance and biometric tracking systems make life on the border an annoying and sometimes scary experience.[2] This logic is evident at Friendship Park: the constant surveillance of the San Diego Sector Border Patrol along with a prison-like atmosphere of high steel bars, lights, cameras, and ground sensors now shape the experience of visitors. In response to the post–9/11 national hysteria linking unauthorized migration with terrorism, the US Department of Homeland Security (DHS) appropriated fifty-three acres of land along the border here in San Diego—including Friendship Park—to build border security infrastructure.[3] By 2009, the new wall divided the park in two. The park is now federal property, and a massive eighteen-foot-high wall of rusty steel bars divides the native plant garden, the beach, and even the ocean waters into US and Mexican sides. Our goal as advocates for the park crystallized in this moment: take back our park and garden. The border patrol allows public access to the park, but the space is just as much "an enforcement zone" as a park.[4] In a meeting in May 2015, the border patrol agent in charge of the park stressed this dual function: he noted that "the park has national security value as well as sentimental and historical value. And so, we've got to meet in the middle."[5]

Its location near the rich Tijuana River delta on the international border makes Friendship Park a unique but absurdly frustrating space for us as advocates. After a long, bitter year arguing with the border patrol in 2009, we got our park back. But this was only the first step of many. We would face endless negotiating in coming years to protect the place we were creating. Our struggles in Friendship Park are a great example of the way grassroots environmental organizing can be a mechanism for democratizing the political arena. Here we were together on this sunny November day in 2009, on the very boundary line of the United States and Mexico, stubbornly replanting a garden in a park that refused to go away. The San Diego Sector Border Patrol has acknowledged that it is "confident that we, too, can come to an agreement that similarly addresses the Border Patrol's mission, the spirit of binational friendship and cooperation, and the safety of everyone involved."[6] Armed with hand trowels, rakes, and garden hoses, it felt as if by digging our hands deep into the rich coastal wetland soil, we could find a source of growth and fertility to lead us all beyond the acrimonious national debate about immigration and the border. This was only the beginning.

An Estuary or a Theater of War?

This was not the first time militarization had disrupted the natural cycles of human migration and settlement in the Tijuana River Valley. The history of the valley is one of conflicting priorities. Friendship Park is located at the delta of the Tijuana River Watershed where it reaches the Pacific Ocean, a 1,750-square-mile region divided by the international boundary. The first inhabitants of this region, ancestors of the Kumeyaay Native people, found sustenance in the marine life, shellfish, and waterfowl in this rich lagoon.[7] Spanish conquest in the eighteenth century displaced the coastal communities of Chiap and Melijo. Real estate developers struggled to settle the estuary, competing with the natural cycles of river flooding in the salt marsh.[8] By the 1940s, the political imperatives of two world wars had turned the fertile lagoon into a degraded staging area for military aircraft landing strips and a machine gun and bombing training center.

Beginning in the 1960s, San Diego conservatives campaigned to fence off the border with Mexico, real estate developers eyed the beach-front estuary for a marina,[9] and environmental activists worked to save this precious coastal wetland.[10] In 1971, "Border Park" and Friendship Park were established when the land was granted to California by President Richard Nixon.[11] Over the next thirty years, environmental leaders transformed the barren area into a fertile, healthy wetland with over half a billion dollars in local, state, and federal investment in the restoration of the Tijuana estuary. But in the panic over national security, political leaders too often overlook environmental concerns.[12] In 1986, President Ronald Reagan began militarizing the border to fight the drug trade.[13] By 1996, the Illegal Immigration Reform and Immigrant Responsibility Act (IIRIRA) authorized the construction of fences and roads along the border and called for a 14-mile triple barrier fence in San Diego. As a result, the borderlands were once again turned into a theater of war. In 1990, construction on a new 14-mile fence was begun in San Diego, its heavy panels made from Vietnam War aircraft carrier landing mats. The war had come home.[14]

The terrorist attacks of September 11, 2001, accelerated border militarization. New border bills were proposed in the US Congress and one, the Real ID Act of 2005, includes a provision, Section 102(c), which authorizes the secretary of Homeland Security to waive any federal, state, or local law the secretary deems an impediment to the construction of border security infrastructure, thus granting one appointed official unlimited authority to reconstruct US borders.[15] The act includes language by San Diego congressman Duncan Hunter mandating the closure of a 3-mile gap in San Diego's ongoing 14-mile border fence project.[16]

Driven by the mandate of the Secure Fence Act of 2006 to build 700 miles of barriers across the US-Mexico border, the Bush administration and Secretary of Homeland Security Michael Chertoff pushed the rapid construction of border walls all along the US-Mexico border beginning in 2006.[17]

In an argument all too familiar to us now that President Trump has put the border wall at the center of his national agenda, local activists argued back in 2006 that Congressman Duncan Hunter's push for a border wall was "an opportunistic tactic to play on the fears of the American people."[18] Attitudes were one thing, but the new border legislation was the real game changer. The new Real ID Act authorizing DHS to waive environmental laws to speed up construction of the border wall made traditional environmental litigation extremely difficult.[19] But it fostered new kinds of action. Our commitment to Friendship Park and the Binational Garden pushed us into citizen activism, local grassroots organizing, and coalition building. And eventually we found ourselves negotiating directly with the border patrol.

Hard Bargain: Working with and against the Border Patrol

In May 2008, I first learned about the new border wall project standing high up on the cliffs on the Mexican side of the border looking into the United States above Smuggler's Gulch. A local activist, Dan Watman, had been clandestinely documenting the US Army Corps of Engineers's construction of preliminary border walls since 2006 and posting the videos on YouTube. Dan heard that they were going to fill in Smuggler's Gulch with 2.2 million cubic yards of earth to build a border patrol road over the top of it, and so here we were. Smuggler's Gulch was a 200-foot drop straight below, a quarter of a mile wide and over a mile long. From here we could see the ocean miles away in the distance. To fill in a canyon seemed an act of unimaginable hubris. The federal government was secretive, and local reporters had their hands tied by editors who were tired of the border story. And so following Dan Watman's lead, I decided to document the construction on my blog, learning what I could from the few documents available, from rumors and off-the-record conversations with public employees who were afraid to speak out.

From a colleague in my university faculty organization, I learned of a national group, No Border Wall,[20] that had organized to oppose the construction of border walls in Texas. I dedicated myself to reading everything I could find and joined weekly national conference calls. Here, members of the Sierra Club and Defenders of Wildlife joined with the national immigrant rights groups to strategize how to save our borderlands and communities from the coming seige. Suddenly, I saw the big picture. On my blog, I began to put San Diego's struggles in a border-wide context. In the summer of 2008, I joined members of the local immigrant rights community and a host of others opposing the border wall, and Friendship Park and the Binational Friendship Garden became a center for our organizing. San Diego Methodist minister John Fanestil held communion services at Friendship Park every Sunday, and Dan Watman worked patiently planting and tending native plants in impossibly hostile, dry soil. I would often arrive early or stay afterward to hike along the border and document more of the construction. Out of these gatherings our coalition emerged, and we dedicated our efforts to stopping the wall and saving Friendship Park.[21]

With the election of President Barack Obama in November 2008, members of our group, Friends of Friendship Park, had renewed hope that help might come from Washington. We lobbied our local political leaders and sent letters to Obama's transition team, asking them to halt construction on the border wall and take more time for environmental review. In April 2009, I traveled with members of our coalition to Washington, DC. While lobbying, I shared my photographs of the border construction, and staffers were shocked to see the damage. But what became clear in this moment was that the political climate had not changed since 2005–6. In Washington, comprehensive immigration reform was linked to the border wall project, and no one in the US Congress was willing to oppose the wall. Regardless of the environmental damage, the political costs of pushing back against border security were too high.

In January 2009, the San Diego Sector Border Patrol closed public access to Friendship Park, and construction began. In July, we appealed to DHS secretary Janet Napolitano to stop the construction, and we learned that public access to Friendship Park would be decided by local border patrol using standard risk assessment criteria.[22] At this point, we changed our strategy. Rather than fight to stop the wall, we decided to intervene in its construction. We invited architect James Brown of PUBLIC Architecture and Planning to join our group. Brown had just returned from a year at Harvard, where he developed a design for a binational city centered at Friendship Park and Boundary Monument 258.

We started having regular quarterly meetings with the San Diego Sector Border Patrol, and at first they politely tolerated our ideas. Over time, we noticed divisions among various agents. While a few were genuinely interested in ways to make the park space more comfortable for everyone, with sun shades, seating, and other enhancements, other border patrol leaders grew increasingly condescending and dismissive, showing little interest in an architectural design for a space they viewed as a theater of operations. Meetings more often than not were a source of frustration and misunderstanding. Yet regular talks gave us access to key information and a deeper understanding of the complex and enigmatic corporate culture of the border patrol as a federal agency.[23] Slowly, in our meetings with border patrol, we developed a proposal for a park design that would offer "dignified and controlled access" to park visitors at three locations: the monument, the binational garden, and the beach. An issue paper drafted by US Customs and Border Protection in June 2009 indicated that indeed, our pressure to keep the park open was paying off. The long-term outcome of the plan recognized public access as a legitimate use of the park: "Achieve a lasting balance between the demands of the mission to maintain operational control of the area; and the demands of the public for access to an area of cultural and historical significance."[24] Indeed, it was clear that our ability to apply political pressure and our consistent engagement in personal meetings with border patrol leaders were beginning to shape policy around the park.

In November 2009, to restore public access to the park, the border patrol put up an additional ad hoc fence inside the enforcement zone to prevent visitors from reaching out and touching their loved ones through the bars. The "cage," as we called it, kept park visitors five feet away from each other as though they were inside a prison visiting area; it was demeaning and horrific. Families were being torn apart by a new wave of deportations and family separation under the Obama administration.[25] For families separated by the border, physical touch was essential, we argued, and we stressed that a design should be adopted that would allow these families to hug and touch each other at Friendship Park. At first, the border patrol leadership was stubbornly and absolutely opposed. Soon, our quarterly meetings evolved into interminable discussions about congressional appropriations bills, contractors, and obscure bidding processes for federal construction projects; these discussions dragged on throughout 2010 and 2011.

By early 2011, the long-awaited federal appropriations had been approved and local San Diego Sector Border Patrol leadership was suddenly willing to accommodate our requests. In addition, the deputy chief told us that many of the design details were discretionary decisions he could make at the local level without consulting Washington, DC. We wanted regular access to the garden to plant, water, and allow it to grow. No problem. We wanted the public to have access to the garden with a pathway marked by movable bollards. Yes, we can do that, the border patrol assured us. We wanted a rolling gate that would open up to sixty feet and create a wide open space for big annual events. Yes, we can do that, too, they said. And we wanted to make sure people could come up to the fence and touch their loved ones on the other side. To our astonishment, not even that request was a problem anymore, they told us. They proposed a compromise. Either choose a "cage-like" structure to keep visitors at least five feet away from the primary fence, making it impossible for them to have intimate conversations or touch their loved ones. Or open up the area but put a triple layer of iron mesh on the bollards, allowing visitors to approach the fence without being able to pass contraband through the bars. Our architect agreed to draw up a model, and after considering what it might look like, we agreed to the mesh. A devil's bargain, it turned out. Today, a thick mesh covers the bars, and visitors can get up close but can put only their fingertips through to touch loved ones.[26]

Placemaking and the Building of Community on the Border

"What garden?" asked the deputy chief border patrol at one meeting when we put discussion of the binational garden on the agenda. To most of the agents, the native plants that had survived multiple rounds of construction and regular trampling by border patrol agents looked like a big patch of weeds. Thinking that our aim was primarily aesthetic, the deputy chief asked why we couldn't just plant some nicer-looking plants over in the state park away from the border wall and the enforcement area, clearly resisting our attempts to reframe the meaning of their enforcement zone. What we wanted was official permission for our binational garden to remain on the boundary line of the US-Mexico border.

But in the meantime, the garden continued to grow. Located about fifty feet directly east of the boundary monument inside Friendship Park, the garden situates the border wall as the central axis of three themed circles of plants, while a pathway called the "White Sage River" crosses through each circle and moves back and forth across the borderline, symbolizing the course of the Tijuana River. A cactus garden features cholla and coast prickly pear, while California buckwheat and Nevin's wooly sunflower and Coyote brush bring bright color to the garden. Through the tireless efforts of Dan Watman, who was often forced to carry water in buckets to keep the plants alive, the garden began to draw a social network around it. The Surfrider Foundation, Wildcoast, and I Love a Clean San Diego joined as part of the Tijuana River Action Network on the US side, while on the Mexican side a coalition of twelve Tijuana environmental organizations led by Margarita Díaz and Ricardo Arana Camarena of Proyecto Fronterizo de Educación Ambiental (Border Project of Environmental Education) and individual volunteers on both sides of the border. Remarkably, for one year, a teen group called the Border Explorers, sponsored by US Customs and Border Protection, joined with volunteers to cultivate, plant, and tend the garden weekly. Friendship Park and the binational garden have attracted families, students, ecologists, and environmental advocates from both sides of the border to join in a true binational cooperative effort. The space brings together people from Mexico and the United States to educate visitors and volunteers about native plants in the microhabitat of the Tijuana River Watershed and estuary.

On the Mexican side, this new community has literally used the space as a means of confronting the effects of violence and corruption. Mexico City artist Pedro Reyes linked his efforts to the binational garden in Tijuana–San Diego in 2010 with the campaign Palas por Pistolas (Shovels for Guns). Reyes, a conceptual artist, developed a binational campaign that literally turned weapons into shovels. After collecting guns throughout Mexico, the group melted them down and turned them into functional shovels that were distributed to community gardening groups and used to plant trees.[27] Projects like these give people a lot of hope, according to Ricardo Arana Camarena, co-director of Tijuana's Proyecto Fronterizo de Educación Ambiental and leader of the movement Cultiva Ya! (Plant Now!), a group and movement that teaches communities how to build and maintain organic urban gardens. "In the context of so much corruption," Arana notes, "people become very cynical and they stop trying to do anything at all. Seeing that these kinds of projects are possible creates a huge change and motivates people to work together on other things."[28] These interactions that bring local environmentalists and community members together from both sides of the border are a model of what we believe the border environment can be: a place of gathering, of encounter, a place where committed people can work together to solve problems.

Containment intensified in 2015 when the San Diego Sector Border Patrol began to impose new, seemingly arbitrary restrictions. The border patrol frequently closes the garden, they have mowed down entire areas of native plants, and they have now removed the "wishing stones" containing messages written by children who have visited their families at the park. Media access has been restricted, and the border patrol prohibits all but the most staged form of interviews. We learned in August 2015 that our local border patrol leaders in San Diego were using Friendship Park as a model of success in national meetings with border patrol leaders in Tucson and Washington, DC.[29] The meetings are part of the border patrol's Border Community Liaison Program, which mandates public outreach to the community.[30] On the one hand, this policy may indicate that our work has garnered results, opening up new avenues for grassroots activism to play a role in shaping national policy. On the other, the increased restrictions on media access, photography, and filming at the park suggest that the border patrol is now anxious to control the narrative and appropriate the success of Friendship Park as their own. In a meeting in May 2015, local San Diego Sector Border Patrol leaders explained why they had removed messages park visitors had painted on the wishing stones in the garden. They explained that the park is "their house," stressing that no one would be allowed to come in and disrespect "their house" with critical or negative messages.

Less than two years later, on the fifth day of his presidency, Donald Trump issued an Executive Order titled "Border Security and Immigration Enforcement Improvements" that frames the US-Mexico border once again as a site of danger, a place where "transnational criminal organizations operate sophisticated drug- and human-trafficking networks and smuggling operations," thus justifying expanded militarization with more border walls.[31] An expansion that signals the struggle over this space will continue and is a reminder that space and place—especially on the border—are always contested terrains. The environmental placemaking we are engaged in here at Friendship Park on the US-Mexico border puts the earth at the center of our common coexistence. The antagonistic logic behind sealing our borders and keeping out others will not guarantee our security if we forget that our sustenance springs from the earth: clean water, fresh air, and fertile soil fulfill human needs, not just American needs. The ebb and flow of the Tijuana River, the ocean tides, and the cycles of the seasons remind us that we are all visitors, we are all migrants living in a shared ecosystem. Our garden, its abundance of shoots and branches and blossoms pushing up from beneath the rusted steel bars of the border wall, is the very image of hope in the face of violence and despair. For this reason, the garden draws people close, it fascinates, and most of all it inspires us to believe that together, what we create will matter.

Notes

1. The boundary monument overlooking the Pacific Ocean just south of San Diego became a popular tourist attraction after it was dedicated in 1851, drawing more than 100,000 visitors a year by the end of the nineteenth century. See Barbara Zaragoza, *San Ysidro and the Tijuana River Valley* (Charleston, SC: Arcadia, 2014), 19–21.

2. The San Ysidro and Otay Mesa Ports of Entry between San Diego, California, and Tijuana, Baja California, are the busiest land ports in the Western Hemisphere. Here, an average of 60,000 personal vehicles cross daily into San Diego from Tijuana, and 32,000 pedestrians cross the border daily on foot. US Department of Transportation, Bureau of Transportation Statistics, Border Crossing Entry Data, accessed August 17, 2018, https://data.transportation.gov/Research-and-Statistics/Border-Crossing-Entry-Data/keg4-3bc2/data.

3. On April 28, 2008, a condemnation order was filed in US District Court by the federal government for the taking of fifty-three acres of land from Border Field State Park. *The United States of America v. the State of California*, 2005, US District Court, Southern District of California. (April 28, 2008). A general federal EIS covering the entire US-Mexico border was completed but did not take into account

the specific qualities or features of the area and thus prompted the first of two major public-interest lawsuits on behalf of a host of local and state organizations spearheaded by the San Diego law firm of Cory Briggs. In successive arguments in 2004 and 2007, Briggs challenged the adequacy of "generic" environmental impact statements and later the constitutionality of federal waivers of environmental laws. See my earlier article, Jill M. Holslin, "Saving Friendship Park: A History of the San Diego Coalition Friends of Friendship Park," in *Wounded Border/Frontera Herida: Readings on the Tijuana/San Diego Region and Beyond*, ed. Justin Akers Chacón and Enrique Dávalos (San Diego: City Works Press, 2011), 124–42.

4. In our meetings with them, San Diego Sector Border Patrol officials have routinely referred to an area inside the secondary wall located 150 feet to the north of the monument and park center as "the enforcement zone." The area north of the secondary border wall is a California State Park property called Border Field State Park.

5. Meeting Minutes, Friends of Friendship Park Meeting with Border Patrol, May 20, 2015. Minutes archived in author's personal files.

6. Internal email communication between San Diego Sector Border Patrol and Friends of Friendship Park, November 9, 2009. Email communications archived in author's personal files.

7. The park is the location of archaeological sites varying in age from 7,300 years ago to yesterday, a full and rich record of the occupation of this estuary of primarily Pleistocene geologic age. Prehistoric archaeological sites CA-SDI-222 and CA-SDI-4281 in particular are of note (Therese Muranaka and Cynthia Hernandez, "Time Has No Boundaries: Archaeological Sites along the US-Mexico Border," paper presented at the Fifth World Archaeological Congress, Washington, DC, June 21–26, 2003; published by California Department of Parks and Recreation, accessed August 17, 2018, http://www.parks.ca.gov/?page_id=23632). The communities of Chiap and Melijo fought back in 1837 and again in 1851, when Mexican military officer and commander of the presidio Santiago Argüello was given a land grant of 10,000 acres, including all of what was then Rancho Tia Juana, and his son, Emigdio Argüello, was granted an additional 10,000 acres of Rancho Melijo. The family holdings extended from the Pacific Ocean through the entire Tijuana River Valley. Zaragoza, *San Ysidro*, 10–16.

8. The first border barrier was built in 1911 on the San Diego–Baja California border as a simple barbed-wire fence to impede the crossing of cattle. Throughout the twentieth century, chain-link border fences were constructed in San Diego County on the international border with Tijuana, Baja California, Mexico.

9. "Imperial Beach Awaiting Marina," *San Diego Union*, June 21, 1969, p. 18. For more on the environmental battle to save the Tijuana estuary from real estate

development, see Serge Dedina, *Wild Sea: Eco-Wars and Surf Stories from the Coast of the Californias* (Tucson: University of Arizona Press, 2011).

10. For several decades in the mid-twentieth century, San Diegans clamored for a border fence, but the federal government could not agree on which agency should pay for it. The US Department of Agriculture was tasked with the responsibility but did not want to take on the cost of expansion. In 1949 the US Senate approved a project for a 545-mile fence across the US-Mexico border at an expected cost of $2.5 million, ostensibly to manage cattle crossings; but the project was also supported by the US Department of State, which noted that the fence would prevent both illegal entry of non-citizens and smuggling of contraband. The project was proposed over and over but was never approved by the House of Representatives. But fencing continued in San Diego. In 1955, according to Bay Cities Press, 22,000 feet of chain-link fence was built in the Tijuana River Valley, and the reason cited was to prevent illegal immigration. Then in 1979, under President Jimmy Carter, more of this chain-link fence was built, creating a huge controversy. The fence, called "the tortilla curtain," was derided as a racist act. In the early 1990s the Vietnam War–era landing mat material was used to build first the 7-mile wall, which was expanded to a 14-mile wall, primarily justified to control drug trafficking. The project was continued under the Clinton administration through Operation Gatekeeper in 1994.

11. "Border Park" in San Diego was one of 39 parcels totaling 4,200 acres of federal land valued at $10.5 million that President Richard Nixon was deeding to states under the Legacy of Parks program to promote public park use in his first term in office. "Mrs. Nixon to Act at Park Ceremony," *San Diego Union*, August 17, 1971, p. 17.

12. Stephen P. Mumme, "The Real ID Act and San Diego–Tijuana Border Fencing: The New Politics of Security and Border Environmental Protection," paper presented at the Annual Association for Borderlands Studies, Phoenix, AZ, April 19–22, 2006.

13. Immigration Reform and Control Act of 1986 (IRCA), Pub. Law 99–603. Among other provisions, IRCA described "an increase in the border patrol and other inspection and enforcement activities . . . to prevent and deter the illegal entry of aliens into the United States" as an "essential element" of immigration control, and it authorized a 50 percent increase in border patrol staffing. See Marc Rosenblum, "Border Security: Immigration Enforcement between Ports of Entry," Congressional Research Service, Library of Congress, Washington, DC, January 6, 2012. See also Paul Gootenberg, "Cocaine's Blowback North: A Pre-History of Mexican Drug Violence," *LASA Forum* 42, no. 2 (Spring 2011): 7–10.

14. Using authority granted to the attorney general by the Immigration and Nationality Act, 8 USC §1103(a)(5), to control the US border, in 1990 the US Border

Patrol and Army Corps of Engineers (Department of Defense) began the con-
struction of a 14-mile-long border barrier made of 10-foot-high welded steel panels.
See Blas Nuñez-Neto, "Border Security: Fences along the US International Border,"
Congressional Research Service, Library of Congress, Washington, DC, May 9,
2005. See also Lee Romney, "US Erects Last Strip of Border Fence Barrier: Holdout
Landowner Settles Suit, Allowing the Government to Close a Half-Mile Stretch
along Otay Mesa Boundary," *Los Angeles Times*, August 5, 1992; Joseph Nevins,
*Operation Gatekeeper: The Rise of the "Illegal Alien" and the Making of the US-Mexico
Boundary* (New York: Routledge, 2002).

15. Determination Pursuant to Section 102 of IIRIRA as Amended by Section
102 of the REAL ID Act of 2005, 70 Fed. Reg. 55622 (September 22, 2005). For a legal
analysis of the waiver authority, see Jenny Neeley, "Over the Line: Homeland Security's Unconstitutional Authority to Waive All Legal Requirements for the Purpose
of Building Border Infrastructure," *Arizona Journal of Environmental Law and Policy*
(Spring 2011), accessed November 12, 2015, https://www.ajelp.com/articles/over
-the-line-homeland-securitys-unconstitutional-authority-to-waive-all-legal-require
ments-for-the-purpose-of-building-border-infrastructure/.

16. For the debate on the Real ID Act, see the Congressional Record—House,
vol. 151, part 2, 1399–1400, February 9, 2005.

17. Secure Fence Act of 2006, Pub. Law 109–367, §2(b).

18. Gig Conaughton, "Congressmen Lobby to Complete Border Fence," *San
Diego Union Tribune*, March 30, 2005.

19. For a full discussion of San Diego lawsuits against the Department of Homeland Security, see Holslin, "Saving Friendship Park." Also available on Academia
.edu.

20. No Border Wall was started in May 2007 by Scott Nicol, Stefanie Herweck,
Betty Perez, and Phyllis Evans in La Joya, Texas, in response to plans by the
Department of Homeland Security to construct new border walls in the Lower Rio
Grande Valley. Texas landowners rose up en masse and filed over 200 individual lawsuits against the government, slowing down construction and giving people time
to organize. In one celebreated case, settled in March 2008, the University of Texas,
Brownsville, successfully stopped the government from building a wall through the
middle of the university campus. Nicol went on to found the Sierra Club Borderlands Campaign but continues to maintain the No Border Wall website.

21. The following twenty-six organizations signed a coalition statement in June
2008 condemning the border wall as an "offence to the peoples of San Diego and
Tijuana": Activist San Diego, American Civil Liberties Union (San Diego and Imperial Counties), American Friends Service Committee's US-Mexico Border Program,
San Diego Audubon Society, Border Angels, Border Meetup Group, California

Native Plant Society, Center for Social Advocacy, Citizens Oversight Projects, San Diego Coastkeeper, Endangered Habitats League, Environmental Health Coalition, Foundation for Change, San Diego Friends Meeting, Fundación La Puerta, Green Party of San Diego County, Immigrants Rights Consortium, Interfaith Coalition for Immigrant Rights, Lipan Apache (El Calaboz) Women Defense, Peace Resource Center, Proyecto Fronterizo de Educación Ambiental, Save Our Heritage Organization, Sí Se Puede Immigrants Rights Organization, Sierra Club (San Diego), Surfrider Foundation, and WildCoast/CostaSalvaje.

22. Napolitano's recommendation anticipated by several years the strategy of risk assessement the border patrol would adopt in the *2012–2016 Border Patrol Strategic Plan* for border security. The strategic plan, only the third such plan in the agency's history, stressed that border security operations would be "risk-based, intelligence-driven." The agency contrasted the new "risk-based" strategy with the "resource-based" strategy of its 2004 strategic plan. US Customs and Border Protection, *2012–2016 Border Patrol Strategic Plan: The Mission Protect America* (Washington, DC: Department of Homeland Security, 2012), accessed August 17, 2018, https://www.hsdl.org/?abstract&did=707938.

23. I have not named any of the specific border patrol agents or sector leaders in this section to preserve their anonymity.

24. US Customs and Border Protection, "Issue Paper: Public Access to Friendship Park," June 22, 2009. This document was drafted and circulated locally among stakeholders in the San Diego area. As indicated on the bottom of each page, the document is a "working draft, not for public distribution." This document is archived in the author's personal files.

25. According to the Pew Research Center, deportations reached a record high in fiscal year 2013, when the Obama administration deported a record 438,421 unauthorized immigrants. See Ana Gonzalez-Barrerra and Jens Manuel Krogstad, "US Deportations of Immigrants Reach a Record High in 2013," Pew Research Center, October 2, 2014, accessed November 13, 2015, http://www.pewresearch.org/fact-tank/2014/10/02/u-s-deportations-of-immigrants-reach-record-high-in-2013/. All told, there were 5,281,115 deportations during the eight years of the Obama administration. Migration Policy Institute, accessed August 17, 2018, https://www.migrationpolicy.org/article/obama-record-deportations-deporter-chief-or-not.

26. In conjunction with the new border wall replacement project in San Diego started in 2018, San Diego Sector Border Patrol reported that they plan to move the current wall back to its original position, placing Boundary Monument 258 directly in the center rather than on the south side of the wall, open to the public on both the north and south sides of the wall. They plan to remove the mesh and place a barrier fence to keep the public 5 feet away from the wall. Meeting Minutes of

Friends of Friendship Park, June 13, 2018. Minutes and email correspondence are archived in the author's personal files.

27. For more on Pedro Reyes and his ongoing projects, see his essay at http://creativetimereports.org/2013/05/20/disarm-transforming-guns-into-art-from-mexico-to-the-united-states/, accessed August 17, 2018.

28. Ricardo Arana Camarena, interview by author, December 21, 2015. Tijuana, Baja California.

29. "Communities of Interest," meeting with US Border Patrol, Tucson, Arizona, July 27–30, 2015.

30. Department of Homeland Security, *2012–2016 Border Patrol Strategic Plan: The Mission: Protect America*; US Customs and Border Protection, *2012–2016 Border Patrol Strategic Plan*.

31. Executive Order: Border Security and Border Enforcement Improvements, January 25, 2017, accessed June 24, 2017, https://www.whitehouse.gov/the-press-office/2017/01/25/executive-order-border-security-and-immigration-enforcement-improvements.

Healthy Politics

8

From Bomb to Bone

Children and the Politics of the Nuclear Test Ban Treaty

Jeffrey C. Sanders

In 1962, the *Berkeley Daily Gazette* featured a full front-page photograph of a Berkeley-area mother named Sandra Napell flanked by her three-year-old son Bruce and her nineteen-month-old son Anthony. The caption explained that they were placing a "note in their milk bottle discontinuing milk delivery for eight days after every atmospheric nuclear test." The missive was an adapted version of one an organization called Women Strike for Peace (WSP) had begun circulating in its national publication *Memo* in the first years of the 1960s. "To My Milk Company," one of the flyers read. "As you may know, the nation's milk supply will become increasingly contaminated by radioactivity this year. This can affect the health of our children. As your customer, I ask you to represent my interests in this matter. Please write or wire President Kennedy, urging him not to resume atmospheric testing."[1] As the test ban debate heated up in 1962, mothers like Napell were part of a nationwide, decentralized movement that began to send out an "urgent call to action," suggesting ways local groups of women could adapt the message about radiation in the food supply to their local conditions. Local groups began

DOI: 10.5876/9781607328483.c008

designing and distributing flyers that emphasized the connection of radiation and the milk their children drank. One such flyer, revised and adapted by the Bay area group, depicted a milk jug emblazoned with the message "Our children are paying the price of atomic testing—in birth deformities, leukemia, cancer."[2]

In the early 1960s, the bones, blood, and thyroids of children living in the United States moved to the center of the political debate over nuclear testing and inspired a movement. But what conditions made such a public discussion of pollution and imperiled children even possible, all but eclipsing the strict foreign policy considerations that had mostly dominated discussions of the bomb for the previous decade?

In the decades immediately after World War II, most government scientists and many politicians were reluctant to make the connection between atomic tests and cancer in kids. Each year, as a parade of successive pink fallout clouds moved east in widening arcs over the United States, downwinders across the continent had been mostly left to their own devices, reckoning with the fallout. Alone, they interpreted the apparent risks of radioactive materials that potentially sickened their neighbors and intermittently leaked from the reports and mouths of government officials.[3] But as the atomic winds continued to blow, by the late 1950s and early 1960s three important factors bore children's health aloft as the impetus for a nascent politics of postwar environmentalism.

The specific context of domestic containment provided fertile soil in which a new approach to environmental risk could take root. As historian Elaine Tyler May argues, the domestic space was tenuous in the Cold War era: "While the home seemed to offer the best hope for freedom, it also appeared to be a fragile institution, subject to forces beyond its control."[4] Children occupied the center of this fragile institution. They embodied hope as well as profound vulnerability in the age of childhood consumer dangers and new understandings of potential psychological damage.[5] As the baby boom exploded, middle-class white mothers in particular found themselves in an onerous but powerful position: they were expected to be experts in modern childrearing. That expectation produced action. An emerging citizen-driven, decentralized science revolution began to fill the vacuum of information left by a tight-lipped national security state in the 1950s, a revolution that invited women—particularly mothers—to participate as both scientists and activists.

Concerns about consumption and children's well-being provided an acceptable opening for new forms of political activism on the local level, like the work of Sandra Napell and her sons. Ultimately, Cold War ideology and the baby boom set the very conditions and contradictions that activists, fearing for their children, would confront.

We often take children for granted, assuming that childhood is a constant throughout history. But children's environmental health and well-being, for instance, has not always been an obvious focus of public concern. The proper feeding and care of children has varied drastically over the last several hundred years. Even as few as thirty years before the atomic decade, children—depending on factors including race, class, gender, and location—were often treated more like little adults, routinely put at risk in various potentially harmful environments including mines, factories, slaughterhouses, and farms. They were a critical part of the workforce for many extended families. The twentieth century, however, and the decade of the 1950s in particular, presented a watershed moment in the constant reinvention of childhood when the conditions of modern mass childhood emerged in tandem with postwar prosperity, a national consumer culture, and the surging population of the baby boom.[6] Faced with a proliferation of new products, advice, and threats after the war, Americans struggled with how to integrate new meanings of childhood health into the imperatives of an unprecedented mass consumer society. In this context, women were tasked with ever greater responsibility as consumers and caretakers to make informed decisions about how to raise healthy children. Many took this job seriously.

"Nuclear war, whether you are for or against it," as Rebecca Solnit observed, "is supposed to be a terrible thing that might happen someday, not something that has been going on all along." Solnit referred to the deserts of the Southwest where the United States simulated the conditions of nuclear war year in and year out at the Nevada Test Site (NTS) beginning in 1951. Before the first moratorium on testing in 1958, the Atomic Energy Commission (AEC) detonated at least ninety bombs of various sizes and compositions aboveground at the Yucca Flats proving ground. Each of the series of bombs had odd names like "Buster-Jangle" (1951), "Upshot Knot-hole" (1953), "Teapot" (1955), and "Plumbbob" (1957). The NTS employed hundreds of scientists, engineers, and tradespeople from the region to perform a multiplicity of interesting experiments with the new technology. "Each Nevada test has successfully added to scientific knowledge," the AEC explained in its public relations propaganda. "Most tests have been used additionally for basic research, such as biological studies." For locals who read these pamphlets, the AEC added, "You people who live near the Nevada Test Site are in a very real sense active participants in the Nation's atomic test program."[7]

Many of the early tests released a mélange of radioactive chemicals and debris into the atmosphere, rock and dirt sent skyward from the desert floor. Some of the explosions launched from atop metal towers in the desert produced mobile clouds of metal fragments and radioactive chemicals. Journalists noted during the "spring series" in 1953 that the tests were "showering radioactive particles on communities 100 miles away." Such fallout, close to ground zero, created "dangerous radiation fields extending several hundred miles downwind from the crater." The larger particles could burn bodies on contact. They came down out of the sky faster and usually close to the point of detonation. Scientists hoped the finer particles would dissipate in the stratosphere, but particles easily moved into the stratosphere and traveled long distances. They came down in rain over Missouri and New York State, for instance.[8]

Three of the chemicals released in these tests were potentially most dangerous when they made their way into children's bodies: Iodine-131, Strontium-90, and Cesium-137. Most children who died of leukemia in the small southern Utah towns closest to the test site in the period of three to six years after each major test series likely died from high exposure rates to Strontium-90. This radioactive element is similar chemically to calcium and concentrates in milk, especially in the skeletons of developing bodies. In high doses it can cause leukemia, a malignant cancer of the bone marrow that affects the production of blood cells. Young people were especially vulnerable.

But leukemia was not the only threat to young people. Iodine-131 would become of special interest to public health officials in the years during the tests because it was traceable through the food supply. When released in US and Soviet tests, Iodine-131 was directly absorbed into air, water, soil, and plants. Grazing animals in particular breathed these particles and ate them as part of their forage over the vast open range and newly irrigated fields of the Southwest and in other places far downwind in the United States. This radiation accumulated in the thyroids of animals, and in the case of children, whose bodies were still developing, it absorbed easily and was very destructive, residing in the thyroid where it emitted gamma rays that destroyed tissue. Finally, Cesium-137 concentrates in the muscles of humans and other animals and can lead to genetic damage because it affects reproductive organs. Although they are only three of the many forms of radiation produced in each explosion, these three had the greatest impact on children in the 1950s and 1960s.[9]

During the 1956 presidential contest, vigilant mothers paid close attention to the new ways children's health and disease began to enter public debate, as the news aroused concern about their children consuming contaminated food. Adlai Stevenson, Dwight D. Eisenhower's liberal Democratic challenger for office that year, was the first high-profile politician to force a public discussion of the potential dangers of radioactive fallout. "Nuclear weapons and fallout have become major issues in the presidential campaign," noted the *New York Times* in a special article meant to explain the technical issues of fallout for Americans. The piece noted the short-term effects of burns and ingestion of radiation such as those experienced by people downwind from the NTS and in the Marshall Islands but added another ominous ripple: "Over a very long period radiation is hazardous because it is capable of altering the agents of heredity in animals and plants by damaging genes and reproductive cells. Such effects might not be readily apparent, 'as in the birth of freaks' but might form shortened lifespans or susceptibility to common disease and then only in grandchildren or great-grandchildren of victims."[10] The emerging stories about radiation struck at the heart of a Cold War society obsessed with reproduction and family.

In that year's presidential campaign, Stevenson went further, pointing to the perils of radiation already loose in the atmosphere. He was blunt about potential contamination, accusing President Eisenhower's administration of concealing information about contaminated milk in the American food supply. Echoing the *Times* coverage, Stevenson placed children squarely at the center of this emerging debate as well: "Growing children are the principal potential sufferers from the radiostrontium content of milk," he asserted and admonished Eisenhower's administration for "keeping facts from the American people that directly concern their health and the future of their children."[11] Radiation in the atmosphere conjured science fiction scenarios of potential genetic mutations and threats to reproduction, not to mention government duplicity.

Following the election, a series of widely read articles about radiation's effects on children captured the attention of the magazine-reading public. One of the more persuasive voices linking the threat of radiation fallout to children's health was former US Navy nuclear physicist Ralph Lapp. Lapp published informative and readable articles throughout the 1950s in the *Bulletin of Atomic Scientists*, and he testified numerous times before congressional committees about the links between radiation and children's cancer. Around the time of the 1957 hearings before the US Congress, Lapp reached beyond the more limited science and policy audience, moving into the realm of popular publications at a moment in American history when the availability of mass media contributed to a growing and shared national culture.[12] Lapp and his coauthor, Jack Schubert, published an essay in the *New Republic* titled "Our Irradiated Children." That same year the authors also published a mass audience book titled *Radiation: What It Is and How It Affects You*. Lapp had a talent for making radiation worrisome in an everyday way. He warned of excess use of the ubiquitous fluoroscopes in shoe stores, for instance. Marshaling recent evidence about post-Hiroshima cancers in children, Lapp also cautioned parents to limit excessive unnecessary X-rays at the dentist's or doctor's office to avoid increased risk of thyroid cancer. Lapp and Schubert described a host of everyday radiation hazards in American society, some of which could affect the "unborn child," and argued for a better system for measuring radioactivity and especially for "assaying the uptake of radiostrontium substances in plants, animals, and humans." The world, they suggested in reference to testing, had "suddenly become a small sphere—too restricted in surface area for the 'safe' testing of super bombs."[13]

Few popular press articles about children and radiation hit home as hard as Paul Jacobs's widely read and broadly circulated—especially among politicians and activists—1957 article in *The Reporter* magazine. Jacobs related the story of families living downwind from the Nevada Test Site and linked their experiences to a more universal threat to public health. The Laird family at the center of this influential piece lived so close to the test site that their door had been blown in at least once by the powerful blasts. The Lairds' son, the "towheaded kid everybody called 'Butch,'" Jacobs wrote, "died last year of leukemia."[14] Jacobs's article highlighted the silence and tight control that characterized AEC policy during the 1950s near the site, making it difficult to determine the effect of fallout and the perils that faced the people living nearest to the NTS, much less far afield. When the story of children's cancer and fallout was told in the press at all during the 1950s, it was most often presented as hypothetical or described in abstract terms. But Jacobs changed that perception by grounding the story in place and in the specifics of one representative child and family in the Atomic West for an American audience overwhelmed by competing opinions and inadequate information.[15]

Faced with competing bits of information and the AEC's general dismissal of legitimate public concern, a new breed of public and citizen-driven science entered the debate, informing and mobilizing a new constituency. One of its leaders was a not-yet-famous Barry Commoner, who published an article in *Science* in 1958. He explained: "There is[,] I believe, no scientific way to balance the possibility that a thousand people will die from leukemia against the political advantages of developing more efficient retaliatory weapons." Such an equation "requires a moral judgment," he argued.

In their desire for secrecy and the control of information during the Cold War, the AEC and other federal agencies tightly limited the flow of scientific information related to fallout. The spirit of free scientific inquiry had been significantly quashed in this intense national security atmosphere. Many scientists avoided the difficulties of doing radiation-related research altogether outside a government structure, although there were exceptions. As a result, according to Commoner, "the fallout question has not yet become an integral part of the freely flowing stream of information which is the vehicle of scientific progress." Science required openness and debate, he believed. In the end, American scientists suffered from a profound deficit of actual baseline science on which to found authority. In fact, it was the "nonproduction of knowledge" that characterized the early postwar period during which government scientists mostly controlled the study of radiation and regularly made unfounded statements about risk.[16] AEC scientists, for instance, argued that Strontium-90, a hazardous by-product of tests in Nevada and the Pacific, would remain in the stratosphere for many years, therefore posing little threat to the general population. Few federal dollars were spent to study potential hazards of Strontium-90 as a result. But in the early 1950s other groups of scientists throughout the country began to notice much higher levels of background radiation and pegged surges in their measurements to fallout after detonations and the debris that came down in heavy rains in places like upstate New York.[17] Scientists knew a great deal more about how to make a bomb and detonate it, Commoner explained, than they understood about the biological effects of the by-products fission created. Faced with such new technologies, it was critical that the public better understand this uncertainty and potential risk.[18]

Commoner's article acted as a miniature manifesto for what historian Michael Egan terms the "politico-scientists" of this period, including Commoner, Linus Pauling, and Rachel Carson, among others, who in the years before the Partial Test Ban Treaty of 1963 collectively reshaped public understanding of fallout and other risks, heightening the public's expectations for better information. On a foundation of transparency, they cultivated a new constituency and shaped a more democratic atmosphere of postwar science and risk assessment, directly challenging the national security state's authority.[19] The lives and physical bodies of baby boomer children were crucial to forming the crucial link among the moral, political, and scientific landscape of the nuclear age.

Along with his colleagues Louise and Eric Reisse, both in the dental school at Washington University in St. Louis, Commoner created the Greater St. Louis Citizen Committee for Nuclear Information (CNI) and launched its nationally influential newsletter *Nuclear Information* (NI).[20] During the 1950s, according to the Public Health Service, St. Louis had experienced some of the highest levels of fallout measured in the United States, reaching 23 percent of the maximum permissible dose. Downwinder children in Utah and Nevada were the most at risk, but through the provocative and informative NI, Commoner and his colleagues helped Americans see the ecological connection between tests in the desert and the ecological systems in other parts of the country. The committee circulated NI widely, especially among public libraries, Parent Teacher Associations, and the League of Women Voters. NI explained the strange new language of atomic science for concerned Missouri residents and a broad public, women's groups in particular. With headlines such as "Carbon 14 May Be Greatest Fallout Danger" and "Yearly Number of Explosions," NI demystified the language of radioactive fallout, detailing the rate of nuclear explosions at the Nevada Test Site from year to year and familiarizing readers with the terms and vocabulary related to radioactive elements loosed into the atmosphere.[21] The newsletter cultivated the informed doubt: "It must be said that we do not yet know with any certainty the consequences of the intake of Strontium 90 in to the human body." The reason, NI explained, was that "the present human generation is the first to receive any Strontium 90."[22]

While it asked questions and sowed doubt about continued nuclear testing, the committee's crucial contribution to public debate was far more innovative.

The committee gave citizens something to do. The CNI directly engaged non-experts, women in particular, in the empowering act of collecting the baseline data necessary for assessing the presence of radiation in the nearby ecology, including their children's bodies. The plan was to collect the deciduous teeth of St. Louis's children. Dr. Louise Reisse led the subcommittee that initiated the baby teeth study, which included Barry Commoner and others. With a sense of urgency, the December issue of NI announced the plan to "collect 50,000 baby teeth a year to provide an important record of the absorption of radioactive strontium 90 by children in the St. Louis area." This collection of baby teeth "must begin at once," the committee argued, because "teeth now being shed by children represent an irreplaceable source of scientific information about the absorption of strontium 90 in the human body."[23]

Throughout the late 1950s, families participating in the greater St. Louis–area study began to make the baby teeth study part of their children's tooth fairy rituals. After slipping a dime under their sleeping children's pillows or in a glass of water on the night table, thousands of worried young mothers placed their children's precious teeth in little envelopes and sent them away to Washington University to be tested by the committee's scientists. The people-driven St. Louis study stood in stark contrast to the distant, secret "big science" performed at the Nevada Test Site and labs throughout the West. The study brought the potential perils of radiation down to a more intimate, personal, and understandable scale. By placing the teeth of these baby boom children at the center of its citizen-driven science, the CNI brought the issue of radiation and environmental problems directly into the private realm of postwar life.

Yet the outcome of the study, which confirmed a 300 percent increase in cancer-causing Strontium-90 in midwestern children's teeth between 1951 and 1955, may have been just as important in the final consideration as the empowering experience of women who participated in the study.[24] By asking families to sacrifice a piece of their children to science while educating them about their children's vulnerability, the CNI cultivated increased public attention toward radiation risks. The profound and simple act of collecting data for the study forced families to acknowledge their households' connection to a larger global ecosystem. Particularly for mothers, who were tasked with protecting their children amid the fraught, family-focused ideological climate of the early 1960s, participating in the study might have felt both empowering and daunting. If radiation released at the arid Nevada Test Site and distant Soviet tests could make its way to the verdant fields of the Midwest, to the middle-class homes of St. Louis, and into the teeth of children, then what about people closer to the site itself?

This outpouring of interest and participation in the baby teeth study nurtured curiosity. The study also beckoned middle-class homemakers and professional women in particular who, armed with scientific data they had helped create, could now picture themselves as crucial political actors in a new campaign on behalf of children and soon much more. This campaign took the concerns of the supposedly private realm of home and family and transposed them into the public sphere.

A grassroots group calling itself Women Strike for Peace (WSP) paid close attention to the baby tooth study and the trickle of news about radiation in the food supply. Not long after results from the first CNI study began to circulate among women's groups across the country, the WSP began to incorporate concerns about children's health, consumption, and radiation into its existing peace activism. As American women grappled with their roles in a postwar consumer economy that had become increasingly difficult to navigate, they also used their decisive role as consumer activists to effect change in this context. As historian Lizbeth Cohen points out, Americans of the period had more discretionary income and "aimed to improve through their consumption of mass-produced goods the quality of their own lives and the vitality of America's economy and democracy."[25] She adds that the "growing complexity of the flourishing marketplace also made new kinds of demands on consumers that they sought help in managing: advanced technologies, new synthetic materials." Confronting the limits of their knowledge about a plethora of postwar goods only "fueled consumer agitation."[26] In this context, groups like the WSP turned societal expectations and their authority as private consumers to their advantage in a public forum.

Many of the activists in the WSP were former members of the activist group Committee for a SANE Nuclear Policy (SANE) who had grown disillusioned with that organization's emphasis on foreign policy considerations and its male leadership in the antinuclear debate. In 1961, Women Strike for Peace burst onto the public stage with its mix of the personal and the political with a call for a walkout, or what it called a "housewives' strike," that brought over 50,000 women out of their middle-class homes and into the streets to challenge continued atomic testing.[27] The WSP produced important local and national leaders who would go on to shape the peace and women's movements during the 1960s. A popular children's book illustrator from Washington, DC, Dagmar Wilson, who founded the first chapter in her Georgetown garden, became the WSP's charismatic national face. But the organization remained distinctly decentralized. As Wilson noted in an interview with the *New York Times*, "We're all individuals. Not really an organization."[28] In the years just before the publication of *Silent Spring* and *The Feminine Mystique*, Wilson—who described herself as a housewife—exemplified the organization's strategic and conservative brand of activism. Yet she and the organization helped channel the pent-up power of white middle-class women throughout the country.[29] With Wilson's leadership and her tireless lectures around the country, the message and organizing power of Women Strike for Peace spread quickly from coast to coast.

Although Wilson and activists in New York and Washington, DC, were the most recognizable faces of the movement, the organization's decentralized nature made it flexible and distinct. This flexibility also allowed for a variety of approaches to the test ban issue, a set of shared sentiments knitted together by nationally distributed newsletters, including *Memo: The National Bulletin of the Women Strike for Peace* and *Women Peace Bulletin*. The West Coast movement was active and notable for its direct action efforts. Many of the members' proximity to the actual Atomic West also made a difference. The Los Angeles chapter soon published its own newsletter, *La Wisp*, which became the organization's important West Coast voice. The Seattle group called itself Women Act for Peace, and the Bay area chapter also published its own local newsletter, *Women for Peace*. The number of local newsletters suggests the decentralized ways these local versions of the national WSP could blend the national story of radiation risk with their specifically western concerns for children's health in the early 1960s.[30]

The Bay area group, for instance, began meeting in Methodist church basements and nursery school classrooms in 1961. Its founding "Statement of Purpose" explained that the group members had "committed themselves to work tirelessly and for the sake of our children" to achieve disarmament and, in the short term, an immediate end to "nuclear testing by any nation." Like their SANE comrades, the members implored public officials to end the arms race. But unlike SANE, the Bay area WSP worked to more directly confront the specific issues that faced children, including contaminated milk, civil defense in schools, and especially the continued testing at the Nevada Test Site. In each instance of protest or demonstration, the Bay area group—like its nationwide counterparts—used children as the central feature of the protest actions.

Between 1961 and 1963, women in the Bay area repeatedly took their protest into the streets. During the spring and summer of 1962, the group held ongoing vigils outside the Federal Building in San Francisco to protest continued nuclear testing. In one of its largest demonstrations, the Bay area group led a nine-mile-perimeter march around the city on August 5, 1962, to commemorate the anniversary of the Hiroshima bombing.[31] Unlike their East Coast counterparts, the West Coast activists saw a more obvious geographic link to the legacy of bombing Japan. They also understood how close the Nevada Test Site was to major cities like Los Angeles and San Francisco, making the fear of bombs and radiation more visceral and immediate. A pamphlet from the Hiroshima anniversary events underlined the connection between Japanese children who survived the attack and the work of the WSP: "There is an ancient legend in Japan that a crane lives one thousand years. Following the bombing of Hiroshima in 1945 the children who had been hospitalized from radiation effects developed a story of their own drawn from that legend—that if a child could make one thousand paper cranes, he would be granted his wish to live." The WSP asked each protester to send a paper crane to his or her senator as a gesture of protest.[32] The solemn procession ended at "ground zero," the San Francisco Civic Center, where Ava Helen Miller (who was married to Linus Pauling) gave a speech to the marchers.[33]

During each such protest—in the middle of the day at the Federal Building, at the state capitol in Sacramento, or in larger mass protests—the Women for Peace activists brought their kids along, partly out of necessity but also as a powerful symbol of the concern and moral authority. It was often easier to bring the kids than to organize childcare (which the group regularly did for its strategy meetings). Press coverage of events consistently mentioned the children and invariably featured photographs of children marching next to their mothers, being carried by protesting women, or playing on the ground nearby. In one march on city hall, the *San Francisco Chronicle* featured a photograph of children playing on the floor in the corridor outside the mayor's office while their mothers carried placards. "Mothers and children crowded Mayor Christopher's office" the newspaper explained, as the mothers "waited to deliver a plan for disarmament."[34] Women for Peace members incorporated their children self-consciously, helping to underline the stakes in the nuclear arms race and especially ongoing testing. Children's presence also helped sanction the activists' interventions in the public debate.[35]

As radiation from aboveground testing in Nevada, the Soviet Union, and the Pacific continued into the 1960s, levels of radiation detected in milk throughout the United States had begun to rise by the end of decade. Since the mid-1950s, milk had been of particular interest as a measure of radiation in the food supply because, according to the Public Health Service (PHS), it represented "the logical course by which strontium-90[,] the highly poisonous radioactive material[,]" can "enter the human body." Strontium-90 bonded with calcium in milk and human bone. In announcing the first program to monitor milk in 1956, the *New York Times* noted that the PHS had "become 'concerned' with the problem of radioactive contamination of milk because of the obvious importance of milk in the human diet."[36]

Milk obviously had great symbolic power in postwar America, at a time when fewer Americans questioned their food supply. The association of milk and radiation therefore touched a nerve with postwar parents and had profound political consequences. Milk consumed in large amounts by children and young people epitomized health and purity, and it could be associated with reproductive fertility, a replacement for mother's milk. During the 1940s and 1950s, dozens of dairy operations on the outskirts of American cities and towns afforded the morning ritual of people finding fresh milk, cream, and butter in their doorstep milk boxes. The growing concern over the milk supply, then, struck at the heart of domestic life and the health of children that mothers/consumers were meant to protect.[37] If milk indeed had high levels of Strontium-90 or Iodine-131, then it was children who would concentrate that poison in their growing bones at higher rates than adults. In the chain of causation, the closer children were to cows that were eating grasses contaminated by higher than normal levels of fallout, the higher the incidence of radiation in milk and the higher potential for cancers. Milk and the politics of consumption changed the equation. If "the family seemed to be the one place where people could control their destinies and perhaps even control their future," as Elaine Tyler May argues, then mothers found both a threat to that institution and a calling to challenge government policy. Instead of a bulwark against communism, the family and especially the health of children became a platform of political resistance to government policy.[38]

As early as 1961, the national WSP saw the efficacy and urgency of linking its ongoing disarmament work to the emerging science of radiation's effect on children's bodies. The organization's files from the 1960s are packed with news articles and CNI publications about radiation and children's health. Between 1961 and 1963, legitimate public fears about milk and radiation built to a crescendo with influential studies published in *Consumer Reports*, stories in women's magazines, and the widely publicized NI studies that circulated to women's groups like the WSP.[39]

The national organization worked to publicize radioactive milk, with a particularly powerful impact. Women Strike for Peace member Jean Bagby, who would later speak at the Senate subcommittee hearings on radiation risks in August 1963, led the WSP's "radiation committee to address contaminated milk" and mobilized milk radiation committees across the country. Adopting the slogan "pure milk not poison," the WSP sent representatives to speak at PTA meetings and other women's groups throughout the United States. According to Amy Swerdlow, a member and the group's historian, while other "traditional peace groups tended to concentrate on foreign-policy and disarmament issues[,] WSP emphasized contaminated milk as a key strategy in shaping the test ban debate."[40] During its 1962 boycott of milk, the group adopted an information strategy similar to CNI's. Women Strike for Peace, therefore, was able to capitalize on this concern for children and consumption while deftly employing its membership's identities as women and homemakers.

The West Coast activists, sensitive to the proximity of the tests and the potential threat to their homes, also linked the milk issue directly to the ongoing work at the Nevada Test Site as they walked and held vigils. "Dear Friend," one frequently circulated pamphlet read, "Did you know that LEAKAGE FROM NEVADA UNDERGROUND TESTS IS SUSPECTED BY SCIENTISTS AS A SOURCE OF IODINE-131?" The group emphasized that "our knowledge of this poison, and its possible effects on children, is one of the reasons why we are protesting atomic testing." As they marched among lunch-time crowds in downtown San Francisco, group members underlined that Iodine-131 increases the "Number Of Thyroid Cases, Particularly Among Infants." In leaflets used in the milk campaign, the WSP cited Commoner's CNI and emerging evidence of Iodine-131 in Utah's milk and the building evidence that Iodine-131 was a hazard that presented "maximum risk" involving "the infant thyroid."[41]

Women Strike for Peace also made the link between Iodine-131 and another recent high-profile risk to children's health: Thalidomide. Thalidomide, a sedative and anti-nausea drug popular in Europe during the 1950s, had been found to cause shocking deformities and deaths in children. By 1961, the European story had made it into the American press and provoked US Senate hearings regarding American drug safety policy. Unlike Thalidomide, which "caused deformity in thousands of babies," however, "poisoned air cannot be removed from the market," the WSP argued. Yet the consumer marketplace, as the group had shown in its role as informed consumers, clearly played the central feature of the activism and authority the WSP claimed in the public realm.[42] The Thalidomide scare, along with Rachel Carson's serial publication of *Silent Spring* in the *New Yorker* beginning in June 1962, only heightened awareness among consumers and would-be activists in what one historian termed a "single chaotic year."[43]

The West Coast groups augmented consumer politics and vigils to create a more confrontational politics as well, linking their own consumption to products of the Nevada Test Site. Five women from Berkeley, for instance, traveled to Geneva, Switzerland, as citizen diplomats during the test ban talks and regularly appeared at protests in Washington, DC. Activists on the West Coast, however, took their protest right to the epicenter of the radiation that was potentially poisoning their children. The group's September 20, 1962, newsletter related the story of its "Nevada Trip." That summer, forty-four WSP members from San Francisco and Los Angles descended on the streets of Las Vegas, Nevada. The "busload" of activists garnered plenty of press attention in Las Vegas newspapers and CBS television, which inter-viewed six of the women and announced that "nuclear energy and female energy expanded in Las Vegas today."[44]

The activists chose "two of the flossiest, busiest blocks" in the tourist city (where gamblers could regularly view the test site explosions from the strip), raised their signs aloft, and began picketing and handing out leaflets. According to one of the participants, several women "pushed empty baby-carriages" as they paraded near the strip, explaining to surprised high rollers that their carriages were "empty because of stillbirth. Empty because of Leukemia. Empty because of cancer."[45] Later the next day, the bulletin reported, a group of women traveled to Mercury Base, outside the gates of the Nevada Test Site, "to case the joint." One of the participants described that they were "welcomed by the sheriff (who took careful note of their names)." The NTS protest would be one of the first of many, as WSP on the West Coast continued to protest at the site well after the aboveground Test Ban Treaty had been signed.[46]

Women Strike for Peace's use of its members' authority as women and mothers to claim a place in the public debate was not new in the history of feminist politics and women's political activism. But this latest iteration of women asserting themselves in the public sphere by way of their authority as mothers coincided with an era in which the ideology of home—which placed the care of the baby boom's children at its center—gave their movement yet greater power and legitimacy. The WSP capitalized on this context, using among its members' many roles those of consumers, women, and mothers to effect political change. Children, a critical segment of these consumers, justified and, as this chapter argues, even helped to make sense of the emerging radiation science and activism. Toxins in the food chain, in the atmosphere, and specifically in children's bodies provided a political opening for a new politics.

Women Strike for Peace may have organized in a decentralized fashion, acting locally as consumers and mothers, but members ultimately took their sense of authority directly to the seat of power. Between 1961 and 1963, according to Swerdlow, "WSP organized an uninterrupted stream of visits to congressional representatives." Even West Coast WSP members made the trip. By spring of 1963, WSP's numbers and supporters throughout the country had grown exponentially. On May 7, a demonstration in Washington, DC, was the most impressive display yet. Members crowded into Barry Goldwater's office lobby to make their demands for a test ban heard. Most lawmakers did their best to avoid them.[47] "Women Besiege Capitol, Demanding Test Ban," *New York Times* reporter Marjorie Hunter announced: thousands of women "took over the Capitol Hill" waving "paper sunflowers." They called the protest that day "a 'Mother's Day gift'—the precious gift of life, health, and security for our children."[48]

As the hearings approached, the WSP stepped up its direct action campaigns against the backdrop of the unfolding science and consumer distress about the radiation in milk. That May, the "Mothers' Test Ban Lobby" gathered on the steps of the US Capitol with a large turnout and the familiar signs emblazoned with children's faces. Later in the day, the activists crowded into a meeting room in the Old Senate Office Building, which they used as a base of operations as groups of women moved methodically through the halls to lobby. Reporting on the protest and massive lobbying effort, the *New York Times* noted that "hour after hour, footsore but determined, they tramped the corridors of the Senate and House office buildings, searching out members of Congress." The meeting room became "an exhilarating forum of women reporting back from interviews" with senators and their aids. In the WSP report on the May 7 events at the Capitol, the group recounted its visits. One of the most encouraging was a visit to the office of Frank Church, the Idaho Democratic senator who had a longtime commitment to the Test Ban Treaty and who, they happily remarked, "welcomes [the] support of women." In contrast, one "group sat in the office of Senator Barry Goldwater, Republican of Arizona, for 30 minutes. They never saw him." But the press took note.[49]

During the hearings in August, Georgia Republican senator Richard B. Russell brought some levity to the otherwise serious hearings. He addressed Glenn Seaborg, the renowned scientist and powerful head of the AEC.[50] "Dr. Seaborg," he began, "I read in the paper, I believe the day before yesterday, that there is twice as much radiation in milk today as there was 3 years ago. Is that approximately right?" Seaborg noted that such a measurement would vary by place but confirmed that there might be parts of the country where there was indeed "twice as much strontium 90 in the milk now." Russell continued: "Has that yet reached a point where it is sufficient to endanger the human family?" Seaborg assured him, "No sir." Russell: "It is a long way from it?" Seaborg: "It is a considerable distance from it, yes sir." Then Russell noted: "I must express my surprise that you did not refer to any advantages to be gained from lessened fallout. Some of our practicing politicians have been predicating their vote on this treaty on what they call very cynically and irreverently 'the mother vote,' because the treaty would lessen the dangers of increasing the fallout." Seaborg, a supporter of the test ban, did not mean to minimize the problem of fallout: "Certainly the less fallout we have the better for everybody," the director noted. "I feel better about it myself and I am not a mother or even a father," Russell answered. His remarks set off a ripple of laughter in the chamber.[51] That laughter was revealing.

Despite the men's chuckles at women's expense, the "mother vote" and the supposedly gendered concerns it represented had developed into a serious force to reckon with by the time of the hearings. In fact, by 1963, white middle-class women—and the children they championed—had profoundly transformed the test ban debate. When lawmakers sat down to discuss whether to ratify the agreement, the "mother vote" had become a nationwide grassroots political movement in opposition to nuclear testing. Children offered the moral ammunition of this new Cold War brinkswomanship. Contaminated milk, deformed babies, leukemia, and thyroid cancer—once thought to be the hysterical fears of housewives and "eggheads"—had moved toward the center of the hearings. Activists working coast to coast made it clear that the fallout produced in the Pacific, the Southwest, and the Soviet Union had become a burden that all American children might potentially bear. The moment of laughter therefore betrayed uneasiness about the subject matter and also about the constituency that had pressed it forward. As the WSP members stalked the hallways of the US Capitol and testified before Congress, a fair portion of the testimony over the eleven days was devoted to the questions and concerns they had helped raise. By the time of the hearing, politico-scientists active in the deserts of Utah and Nevada, for instance, had also generated new data that only confirmed the findings of the burgeoning public and citizen science community, tracing the route of radioactive products through the American food chain from the Nevada Test Site to children's teeth and bones.

The mainly white middle-class activists who challenged the federal government's nuclear testing program drew from their racial and class privilege to effect change as well. Indeed, they had the time and the access to power not afforded to most working-class people and people of color in the 1950s and early 1960s. The emphasis on middle-class consumption—how radiation might enter children's bones through their ingestion of milk, for instance—created tradeoffs. On the one hand, these activists used their class position as concerned consumers to underline a broadly shared threat to all children and brought attention to an experience of toxic pollution that spanned the globe. They heightened public awareness of shared ecological systems and threats. Like radiation, they crossed borders. Their politics emphasized the intersection of the human body and ecology. In addition, they brought consumer power to bear on environmental problems in a way that would become increasingly familiar. In this way, they offered a preview of late twentieth-century environmental activism and thought. This approach to activism, however, tended to privilege consumption rather than production, and at a cost.[52]

If concern for children's bodies could connect people and places, consumer-based environmentalism could also obfuscate the places and people that were often the most at risk. Had their activism focused on the horrors faced by Marshall Islanders or Navajo uranium miners and their children—people who often lived in the places that produced, processed, and tested these materials—the story and potential allies would look different and perhaps form an even more persuasive coalition. In the 1950s and 1960s, the people most affected by toxics did not have such allies in government or their access to power. Indeed, the federal government knew this and took advantage of marginalized people and places in the name of national security. On the other hand, these efforts to connect far-flung causes and effects ultimately lay the groundwork for future claims of environmental justice.[53]

Yet it was this specificity and the place-based experience of children in the deserts of the Southwest that may have helped turn the tide of public concern. During the hearings in 1963, when it was Hubert Humphrey's turn to question Willard Libby, a scientist at the University of California, the future vice president emphasized "great concern over radioactive fallout." Reading aloud from a recent report's findings, Humphrey underscored the disturbing risks of radiation specific to the Atomic West and embodied in its children. "Several thousand children in Nevada and Utah have probably received hazardous doses of fallout radiation from nuclear testing in Nevada over the last 12 years," he explained to his colleagues in the chamber.[54] By that time children, like the ones who died of leukemia in the Atomic West, had finally been made a more concrete part of the public discourse.

The US Senate voted to approve the Test Ban Treaty in September 1963. In his speeches that summer, John F. Kennedy embedded the significance of radiation's threats to children, speaking directly to the concerns and constituency the WSP strategy had cultivated over time:

This treaty can be a step towards freeing the world from the fears and dangers of radioactive fallout . . . The number of children and grandchildren with cancer in their bones, with leukemia in their blood, or with poison in their lungs might seem statistically small to some, in comparison with natural health hazards. But this is not a natural health hazard—and it is not a statistical issue. The loss of even one human life, or the malformation of even one baby—who may be born long after we are gone—should be of concern to us all. Our children and grandchildren are not merely statistics toward which we can be indifferent.[55]

If the culture of Cold War containment encouraged Americans to think of the walls of their homes as protective shields guarding a fragile nuclear family in an uncertain age, then the threat of radiation in air, food, and ultimately in children struck at the heart of this sense of safety and control. Groups like the WSP responded to this conundrum by encouraging white middle-class women to use their power and their societally sanctioned domestic concerns for children and extend them outward, mixing the politics of consumption, foreign policy, and feminism with a dawning public awareness of ecology to become a powerful public force.

During the postwar era, children in the arms of their concerned mothers became the salient measure of environmental risk and the important indicator species for an emerging postwar environmental movement. As the baby boom exploded in the 1950s and 1960s, children were the critical figures at the center of a web of historically contingent relationships. Citizen scientists and groups like the WSP drew on this empowering combination of knowledge and activism. In the process, they helped both to democratize scientific knowledge and to make it visceral and personal. But their political work also showed how ecological connections could tie the domestic and private realm of the postwar family to a national and even international environmental scale of concern. Historical context was crucial in this process. Women who worked to make the science of radioactive risks legible—participating in studies and even crafting their own local studies of milk and teeth—did so within a specific historical moment in which baby boom children played an outsized role in American culture. These activists showed how children made environmental concerns manifest in their bones and teeth, demonstrating the high stakes of continued nuclear testing. At a time when children and reproduction were central obsessions in American culture, WSP members importantly leveraged their position as legitimate consumer activists and mothers to do political work, with lasting consequences.

More than fifty years later, we may still recognize the potent connections Women Strike for Peace first forged among consumerism, nascent environmentalism, and democratized science. The power in this earlier grassroots movement came in part from its flexibility and its openness to opportunities available in the historical moment. In the case of the WSP, this meant leveraging its position in society to protect the most vulnerable, but it also meant helping itself at the same time to advance gender equality and antiwar politics. In the years since the early 1960s, environmentalists have just as often tended to ignore potential affinities with political allies and other movements. The Women Strike for Peace's movement embodied the holism that ecology suggested in the mix of the personal and the political to achieve its goals.

Notes

1. Florence Doutrit, "Women's Ban on Fresh Milk Gains Support," *Berkeley Daily Gazette*, April 30, 1962, Box 3, folder 24, San Francisco Women for Peace Records, BANC MSS 89/132c, Bancroft Library, University of California, Berkeley (hereafter San Francisco Women for Peace Records); "Dear Neighbor," 1962, Box 3, folder 24, San Francisco Women for Peace Records. For the history of Women Strike for Peace and this moment in feminist politics, see Amy Swerdlow, *Women Strike for Peace: Traditional Motherhood and Radical Politics in the 1960s* (Chicago: University of Chicago Press, 1993), 3; for more on the WSP and its role in the women's, peace, and environmental movements, see also Ruth Rosen, *The World Split Open: How the Modern Women's Movement Changed America* (New York: Viking, 2000), 58–59; Estelle B. Freedman, *No Turning Back: The History of Feminism and the Future of Women* (New York: Ballantine Books, 2002), 329.

2. "Nuclear Tests Cost Lives," Women for Peace, 1962, Box 3, folder 24, San Francisco Women for Peace Records.

3. Downwinders' and fallout history is large, and much of it focuses on the specific history of communities that were contaminated by fallout, their struggles, the health effects of fallout, litigation, and efforts at redress. For examples of these strong histories that help situate events and that were written late in the Cold War, see Howard Ball, *Justice Downwind: America's Atomic Testing Program in the 1950's* (New York: Oxford University Press, 1986); A. Costandina Titus, *Bombs in the Backyard: Atomic Testing and American Politics* (Reno: University of Nevada Press,

1986); Philip L. Fradkin, *Fallout: An American Nuclear Tragedy* (Tucson: University of Arizona Press, 1989). An excellent recent treatment of events in the Southwest downwind area is Sarah Alisabeth Fox, *Downwind: A People's History of the Nuclear West* (Lincoln: University of Nebraska Press, 2014). For a more general approach to the history of the Atomic Age and to fallout, see Paul Boyer's seminal work, *By the Bomb's Early Light: American Thought and Culture at the Dawn of the Atomic Age* (Chapel Hill: University of North Carolina Press, 1994); Paul Boyer, *Fallout: A Historian Reflects on America's Half-Century Encounter with Nuclear Weapons* (Columbus: Ohio State University Press, 1998).

4. Elaine Tyler May, *Homeward Bound: American Families in the Cold War Era* (New York: Basic Books, 1988), 25.

5. For a discussion of domestic containment culture, see Alan Nadel, *Containment Culture: American Narratives, Postmodernism, and the Atomic Age* (Durham, NC: Duke University Press, 1995),1–9; see also, Benjamin Spock, *The Common Sense Book of Baby and Child Care* (New York: Duell, Sloan, and Pearce, 1946).

6. For examples of the literature on the history of childhood, see Paula S. Fass and Mary Ann Mason, *Childhood in America* (New York: New York University Press, 2000); Paula S. Fass and Michael Grossberg, eds., *Reinventing Childhood after World War II* (Philadelphia: University of Pennsylvania Press, 2012); Marilyn Irvin Holt, *Cold War Kids: Politics and Childhood in Postwar America, 1945–1960* (Lawrence: University Press of Kansas, 2014). For an overview of the environmental history of childhood, see Bernard Mergen, "Children and Nature in History," *Environmental History* 8, no. 4 (2003): 643–69.

7. Rebecca Solnit, *Savage Dreams* (San Francisco, CA: Sierra Club Books, 1994), 5. United States Atomic Energy Commission, *Atomic Tests in Nevada*, March 1957, pp. 1–2, in Box 490, folder 3, MSS 20, Wallace F. Bennett Papers, 20th Century Western and Mormon Manuscripts, L. Tom Perry Special Collections, Harold B. Lee Library, Brigham Young University, Provo, UT; Gregg Mitman, *The State of Nature: Ecology, Community, and American Social Thought, 1900–1950* (Chicago: University of Chicago Press, 1992), 137.

8. Charles Mays to Robert Pendelton, "Fallout, Radioactive," July 11, 1962, Box 1, Robert C. Pendelton, Department of Radiological Health, University of Utah Archives, Salt Lake City (hereafter DRHUUA).

9. Mays to Pendelton, "Fallout," DRHUUA.

10. "The Bomb Debate: Answers to Questions Raised in the Campaign," *New York Times*, October 21, 1956.

11. "Stevenson Sees Cover Up on Bomb," *New York Times*, November 3, 1956.

12. For a discussion of this developing national culture, see David R. Farber, *The Age of Great Dreams: America in the 1960s* (New York: Hill and Wang, 1994), 49–66.

13. Jack Schubert and Ralph Lapp, *Radiation: What It Is and How It Affects You* (New York: Viking, 1957), 237; Jack Schubert and Ralph Lapp, "Our Irradiated Children," *New Republic*, June 17, 1957, 9–12.

14. Paul Jacobs, "Clouds from Nevada," *The Reporter*, May 2, 1957, 10.

15. For more on this episode, see Fradkin, *Fallout*; Fox, *Downwind*.

16. Scott Frickel, "On Missing New Orleans: Lost Knowledge and Knowledge Gaps in an Urban Hazardscape," *Environmental History* 13 (October 2008): 643; Barry Commoner, "The Fallout Problem," *Science*, May 2, 1958, 1025.

17. Michael Egan, *Barry Commoner and the Science of Survival: The Remaking of Modern Environmentalism* (Cambridge, MA: MIT Press, 2007), 51.

18. Barry Commoner, "The Fallout Problem," *Science* 127, no. 3305 (1958): 1025; Egan, *Barry Commoner*, 47–50.

19. Egan, *Barry Commoner*, 57–59.

20. Egan, *Barry Commoner*, 66–71.

21. Greater St. Louis Citizen Committee for Nuclear Information, *Nuclear Information* (NI), October 24, 1958, Utah University Library, Salt Lake City.

22. NI, November 24, 1958, 1.

23. NI, December 24, 1958, 1

24. Egan, *Barry Commoner*, 72.

25. Lizabeth Cohen, *A Consumers' Republic: The Politics of Mass Consumption in Postwar America* (New York: Knopf, 2003), 348.

26. Cohen, *Consumer's Republic*, 348–49.

27. Bella Abzug, for instance, was an early member of the WSP. "A Nationwide Peace Strike," *San Francisco Chronicle*, November 2, 1961, 9; Swerdlow, *Women Strike for Peace*, 203.

28. Marjorie Hunter, "Women's Peace Campaign Gaining Support," *New York Times*, November 22, 1961.

29. Swerdlow, *Women Strike for Peace*, 70–73.

30. For an example of the variety of local adaptations to the national message, see "Policy Paper #8," National Information Clearing House, May 27, 1963, Box 3, folder 5, San Francisco Women for Peace Records.

31. "Chronology of Women Strike for Peace Activism," 1962, Box 1, folder 3, San Francisco Women for Peace Records.

32. "Paper Cranes Fly for a Test Ban," 1962, Box 3, folder 24, San Francisco Women for Peace Records.

33. "Hiroshima Walk Planned by Women," July 1962, Box 3, folder 24, San Francisco Women for Peace Records.

34. Jane Eshleman, "200 S.F. Women Appeal to Mayor," *San Francisco Chronicle*, November 1, 1961, Box 1, folder 17, San Francisco Women for Peace Records.

35. "Chronology of Women Strike for Peace Activism," San Francisco Women for Peace Records.

36. "The Bomb Debate: Answers to Questions Raised in the Campaign," *New York Times*, October 21, 1956.

37. Sarah Alisabeth Fox argues that "milk was such an integral part of daily life in the 1950s that fifty years later baby boomers in the downwind region could still recall where their family's milk came from." Fox, *Downwind*, 111.

38. May, *Homemward Bound*, 24.

39. See "The Milk All of Us Drink—and Fallout," *Consumer Reports* 24 (March 1959): 102–11.

40. Quoted in Swerdlow, *Women Strike for Peace*, 81, 83.

41. "Dear Friend," San Francisco Women for Peace Records.

42. "Dear Friend," San Francisco Women for Peace Records.

43. Nancy Langston, *Toxic Bodies Hormone Disruptors and the Legacy of DES* (New Haven, CT: Yale University Press, 2010), 83, 85–98.

44. *Women Peace Bulletin*, September 20, 1962, p. 3, Box 3, folder 20, San Francisco Women for Peace Records.

45. *Women Peace Bulletin*, p. 3.

46. For more on this history and the ongoing protests at the site that by no means ended in 1963, see Rebecca Solnit, *Savage Dreams: A Journey into the Hidden Wars of the American West* (San Francisco: Sierra Club Books, 1994).

47. Women Strike for Peace, "Report—May 7 et seq: Test Ban Lobby," 1963, Box 19, folder 2, Frank Church Papers, 1941–1984, MS 56, Special Collections, Boise State University Library, Boise, ID.

48. Marjorie Hunter, "Women Besiege Capitol, Demanding a Test Ban," *New York Times*, May 8, 1963; Swerdlow, *Women Strike for Peace*, 97–124.

49. Hunter, "Women Besiege Capitol"; "Report," Frank Church Papers.

50. The hearings were a who's who of postwar Senate luminaries. Hubert Humphrey, Scoop Jackson, Barry Goldwater, and J. W. Fulbright were there. The much-anticipated Test Ban Treaty hearings during the summer of 1963 captured the attention of the Senate Foreign Relations Committee, the Armed Forces Committee, and the Joint Committee on Atomic Energy. The men and one woman met for eleven days of testimony before deciding whether to ratify an agreement with the Soviets that would ban nuclear weapons testing "in the atmosphere, in outer space, and under water." United States Congress, Senate Committee on Foreign Relations, *Nuclear Test Ban Treaty: Hearings before the United States Senate Committee on Foreign Relations, and Senate Committee on Armed Services, and Joint Committee on Atomic Energy, Eighty-Eighth Congress, First Session, on Aug. 12–15, 19–23, 26, 27, 1963* (Washington, DC: Government Printing Office, 1963).

51. United States, *Nuclear Test Ban Treaty*, 214.

52. Finis Dunaway, *Seeing Nature: The Use and Abuse of American Environmental Images* (Chicago: University of Chicago Press, 2015), 208–22.

53. United States, *Nuclear Test Ban Treaty*, 658–59.

54. United States, *Nuclear Test Ban Treaty*, 657.

55. John F. Kennedy, "Address to the Nation on the Nuclear Test Ban Treaty," July 26, 1963, accessed September 27, 2015, https://www.jfklibrary.org.

9

Fear, Knowledge, and Activism

Toxic Anxieties in the 1980s

Michael Egan

Historians of environmental activism have long acknowledged fear's implicit influence in their scholarship. Chemical pollution—the manner in which it can infiltrate the body and generate disease or disrupt normal hormonal processes—is a frightening subject, and many grassroots organizations were galvanized into responding to exposures and the future hazards they and their members' families faced. But inasmuch as many environmental and human health struggles since World War II have orbited around some form of latent fear, historians have been reluctant to look that fear in the face. Part of that reluctance might stem from the fact that fear is an unquantifiable abstraction. Another rationale might involve the notion that fear seems a passive center of focus, relegating contaminated communities to victim status. To assume this would be to miss the point. By the final quarter of the twentieth century, fear was the principal (and a universal) response to toxic pollutants in the environment among Americans. Put another way, after World War II, chemical contamination and fear walked in lockstep through American history; nowhere did that tandem leave a

DOI: 10.5876/9781607328483.c009

bigger imprint on the environmental, political, and cultural landscape than in the 1980s.

In the 1980s, toxic fear became an explicit environmental issue in its own right. Although the "Age of Ecology" had begun decades earlier with concerns about radioactive nuclear fallout and widespread interest in the lessons about synthetic chemical use in Rachel Carson's *Silent Spring*, it appeared as though an unparalleled—and often paralyzing—fear of chemicals and chemical wastes reached a crescendo in the 1980s. Newspaper searches for fear in relation to environmental and toxic issues during the 1980s return more hits than the two previous decades combined. Not only were stories of hazardous wastes published more frequently, a growing understanding of the risks associated with polychlorinated biphenyl (PCBs), dioxins, and other chemicals became prevalent in coordination with the discovery of these chemicals having leaked, leached, and escaped from where they were stored. Chemical exposure has been described as "contact between misplaced matter and flesh."[1] The frequency with which misplaced matter was found in drinking water and residential wells; seeping into parks, schools, and gardens; and in the ambient air put paid to the purported benefits of what David Harvey and James C. Scott have called high modernism.[2]

If the chemical threats to health were not enough, many journalists investigated pollution's psychological effects. Numerous references to what they called "toxic time bombs" reflected the malaise many Americans were experiencing on a daily basis. In a 1982 *New York Times* piece, the science writer Maya Pines observed that environmental toxins constituted the potential for a series of "psychological time bombs." In the face of environmental dangers, her byline read, "fears multiply." The article deliberated on the profound psychological impact of environmental catastrophe. In the face of toxic hazard, Pines wrote, "people face the danger of severe illness in themselves or their offspring, now or in the future. But they also face the dangers of stress and anxiety, which can generate physical and emotional illnesses that are often impossible to distinguish from purely physiological diseases."[3]

All manner of indications showed that Americans were afraid. Across the country, Americans phoned in to state health agencies and the Centers for Disease Control at an unprecedented rate to report possible cancer clusters. The insurance industry acknowledged a marked increase in customers seeking coverage from technological disasters. Tort rulings began allowing a fear of future harm from chemical contamination as grounds for claiming damages from polluters. After the near disaster at Three Mile Island, the US Court of Appeals for the District of Columbia ruled that the Nuclear Regulatory Committee would need to conduct a new kind of environmental assessment on subsequent construction projects. The new assessment was designed to review the "psychological stress" felt by residents who neighbored nuclear sites. "We cannot believe that the psychological aftermath of the March 1979 accident falls outside the broad scope of the National Environmental Protection Act," the majority opinion argued.[4] Sociologists got in on the act as well. By the 1990s, Kai Erikson had sufficient evidence to claim that people in general find toxic substances a good deal more threatening than any other natural or technological hazards that do not involve toxicity, even when that fear is drastically exaggerated.[5] Indeed, the 1980s witnessed a chronic contagion of chemical fear and public anxiety. Amid the nuclear scare at Three Mile Island, the neighborhood contamination at Love Canal, the evacuation of Times Beach, Missouri, and countless other incidents of toxic chemical pollution raising alarm bells in communities across the country, Americans became primed to fear strange smells in their ambient air and unclear water in their taps. In many instances every cough, every new ache was interpreted as the first sign of latent disease to which they had been exposed through environmental exposure. Americans even came to distrust the scientific authorities who reassured them that the risks they feared did not exist.

Examining fear in history is difficult and potentially pessimistic. Environmental fears increased in inverse proportion to access to information. But also the reverse: in many instances, fears increased as a result of information overload. If environmental activism during the 1960s sought to highlight the need for greater clarity pertaining to environmental risks, the 1970s were typified by efforts to bolster new environmental legislation. The 1980s, in comparison, witnessed a lot of white noise. This was especially evident in the 1980s in the wake of the Reagan administration's deregulation of federal agencies. As Americans worried about potential sources of chemical harm, the US Environmental Protection Agency (EPA) lacked the resources and the directives to test and evaluate risk effectively. That situation promulgated fear, especially when scarce personnel and resources coincided with emerging environmental hazards in neighborhoods all across the country as well as mounting scientific uncertainty over the veracity of those threats. At the same time, media outlets capitalized on public unrest. Stories in print and on television kept toxic waste and environmental pollution squarely in the mainstream's popular consciousness.

In some cases, however, citizens organized to raise public awareness of their concerns and to gather the requisite scientific information necessary to understand the risks they faced. These grassroots efforts constitute one of the brighter lights in an otherwise bleak period in American environmental history. In gathering information, grassroots activists were forcing a more participatory kind of democracy onto these environmental proceedings. This chapter compares two case studies in which citizens participated in the collection and curation of environmental data to determine the nature of the risks they faced, with an example of how mismanaged information created a maelstrom of exaggerated fears and equally exaggerated anti-environmental rebukes. In each instance, public efforts to produce grassroots information were designed primarily to galvanize policy for their protection by doing the work they felt government agencies were not. The struggle for reliable environmental information as a means of evaluating social risks is an important strategy in confronting toxic fear and constitutes the lifeblood of American environmentalism today. As much as grassroots ecological activism is a social exercise in the "politics of hope," it is also often a communal expression of the fears modern industrial practices have instigated.[6]

Grassroots knowledge production—the independent gathering of environmental data by local community members—was not new to the 1980s. The biologist Barry Commoner devoted a career to promoting public participation in environmental issues through the production of accessible scientific knowledge. After World War II, Commoner reasoned that because people lacked the technical information to understand the dimensions of problems such as nuclear fallout or DDT or dioxin, they were unable to act or express concern to policy-makers. As a means of challenging Cold War conformity and to deflect challenges that he was subverting American values, Commoner invented what he called the science information movement, which consisted of providing a vernacular body of scientific information on the environmental crisis to the public so it could participate in political debate with access to technical data. Much of his research also involved non-scientists participating in the gathering of information and empowering them to use the findings.[7]

This production of knowledge matured during the 1980s and spread through a number of different kinds of citizen groups. Local public health questions became environmental health issues, which is to say that citizens acknowledged the relationship between human health and environmental well-being in their efforts. Moreover, the widespread and independent development of popular epidemiology became a feature of grassroots knowledge production. According to the sociologist Phil Brown, who coined the term, popular epidemiology "is the process by which lay persons gather scientific data and other information, and also direct and marshal the knowledge and resources of experts in order to understand the epidemiology of disease."[8]

Brown introduced the idea in reference to his work on the response to the leukemia cluster at Woburn, Massachusetts.[9] A cancer cluster is a statistically improbable grouping of similar cancer cases, which suggests that some environmental factor might be the primary trigger. Paula DiPerna describes clusters as the "mysterious medical phenomenon loosely defined as an apparent outbreak of disease clumped in time, place, or both."[10] Too many variables creep in to trying to link a particular exposure to an illness that occurs sometimes decades later, so epidemiologists refer to "associations" rather than explicit links. They discuss the statistical likelihood, or probability, of these associations.[11] For example, the average incidence of leukemia without a known cause is 3.74 cases per 100,000 children. In Woburn, a town of 36,000, 26 cases were diagnosed between 1979 and 1985—and most of these cases were among residents of East Woburn in neighborhoods that drew water from two wells. The statistical likelihood of this being a freak occurrence is more than 100 to 1. A single case of childhood leukemia is heartbreaking. A second case might be an unfortunate coincidence. But when local residents start to perceive a pattern, there is the prospect that external—environmental—causes are at work, that the disease might be preventable; and this is the ignition point for local environmental fears. When communities find themselves at risk to a hazard over which they have no control and little understanding, the social response is typically fear.

Between 1969 and 1979, Woburn residents counted nineteen cases of leukemia.[12] The rate of incidence defied statistical probability: this was four times the number that might have been deemed "normal" in a community of this size. Another nine children contracted leukemia between 1983 and 1990. Anne Anderson's son, Jimmy, was diagnosed with acute lymphocytic leukemia in 1972. In her interactions with neighbors and other parents at the hospital where Jimmy was being treated, Anderson became convinced that something in the water was responsible for her son's disease. She requested that state officials test the water but was told that tests "could not be done at an individual's initiative."[13]

Behind the scenes, though, other signs of trouble were afoot. In 1975, Woburn's Board of Water Commissioners identified high concentrations of salts and minerals in two of the town's wells and requested that the chlorination methods be changed. The state Department of Health approved the change but recommended against relying on the water from these wells. Four years later, on May 22, 1979, officials from the Massachusetts Department of Environmental Quality and Engineering ordered the immediate closing of the two affected wells. On September 10, 1979, Charles Ryan reported in the *Woburn Daily Times and Chronicle* that an illicit toxic waste dump had been discovered the previous June.[14] The find—300 acres of lagoons infested with chromium, arsenic, lead, and other wastes—was not reported to the public at the time.[15] Toxic chemicals had broken free of corroded drums and seeped into the wells. Subsequent studies found that the wells that fed Woburn were bowl-shaped and became a sink for the escaped arsenic, chromium, and trichloroethylene.[16]

Woburn residents were no nearer to any resolution on whether the toxic chemicals in their water were responsible for the heightened incidence of leukemia among their children. In the absence of state or federal intervention, they proceeded with their own epidemiological study. Starting in January 1980, volunteer residents canvassed Woburn's neighborhoods under the newly formed For a Cleaner Environment (FACE). By early 1982, the EPA had completed a hydrogeological study that identified two distinct contaminant sources in the water but did not point to the culprits. In May 1982, armed with their data, thirty-three Woburn residents (representing the families of eight leukemia victims) launched a class-action lawsuit against W. R. Grace's Cryovac Division and Beatrice Foods' Riley Tannery, which they held responsible for the contamination of the wells and, by extension, their community's cancer cluster.[17] Technical support from Harvard University's School of Public Health enriched the data, which were completed after the trial had begun. The survey covered more than 4,000 pregnancies between 1960 and 1982 and found little evidence that the water from Wells G and H had contributed to marked birth defects or spontaneous abortions prior to 1970. After 1970, the study revealed some associations with perinatal deaths and childhood health disorders involving kidneys and urinal tract and respiratory problems.[18]

On July 26, 1986, a jury found that W. R. Grace had been negligent in illegally dumping toxic chemicals on its property. Beatrice Foods was acquitted. The next stage of the trial would have involved the plaintiffs needing to prove that W. R. Grace's actions had cause leukemia, but the judge ordered a retrial because he felt the hydrogeological data had been poorly understood by the jury. Before the new trial could begin, Grace settled with the residents, paying damages totaling $8 million.

Cases of illegal and irresponsible dumping—especially when it has a direct impact on local health—almost always require the attribution of white and black hats. Similarly, in pantomime fashion, readers want victims to be rewarded and wrongdoers to be appropriately punished. Cases of environmental contamination, however, are rarely so cut and dry. Nor are allegiances quite so obvious. One might expect that Woburn's residents lined up on one side of the issue and defensive industries on the other. Nothing is ever so tidy, however. Woburn's mayor, among others, worried that the fears might have been exaggerated and that they threatened to hurt the town. New industry might stay away. Property values could decline. "What do I care about property values?" Anne Anderson retorted to a *Newsweek* journalist two years after Jimmy died. "I have an empty room."[19]

It might seem crass to the historical actors at Woburn—especially those who lost loved ones—to measure Woburn's historical significance in terms other than right and wrong, aggrieved and culpable, assaulted and negligent. But situating Woburn's contributions to the process of grassroots activism is worthwhile, both in terms of its place in the larger story of the American toxic crisis and as an object lesson in how communities come together to confront a faceless corporate industrial power. Another important facet of Woburn's story stems from the popular epidemiology practiced by local residents in response to local contamination. Popular epidemiology happened outside the laboratory setting. As a result of the state's refusal to test water and an absence of official confirmation that Woburn constituted a cancer cluster, residents took it upon themselves to shed light on the uncertainty that plagued their case. They sought to build a body of information, seeking answers for themselves and ammunition that could be used in a court of law. At Woburn, the final data were never actually used in the legal proceedings because W. R. Grace settled before the trial proceeded to the point of connecting its contamination of the wells to the cluster of cancer cases in the town. But there is some speculation that the judge ordered a retrial because he was aware that an out-of-court settlement was imminent.[20] In many respects, the popular epidemiological work had put Woburn residents in a position of power.

Although confronting state and federal agencies—and meeting resistance at every turn—was inevitably and unquestionably frustrating, the lack of support resulted in the Woburn activists becoming more independent, conducting investigations and mastering the knowledge and information crucial to accusing, if not proving, the culpability of W. R. Grace and Beatrice Foods in the sickness and deaths in the community. This is one of the slippery slopes of the 1980s neo-liberal turn.[21] On the one hand, participatory democracy invites and even requires public activism and interaction as a part of the political discourse. On the other hand, its nature changed during the shift to the political right that occurred in democracies around the world during the 1980s. Social problems became individual problems; their solutions required individual fixes. The onus of responsibility moved from government and government agencies to a public that had in the previous decade turned environmental oversight and the necessary scientific literacy over to experts who were now finding themselves underfunded or ousted from government offices.[22] If uncertainty and lack of information excited toxic fears, then they were aided by deregulation and the curtailing and hamstringing of government agencies tasked with monitoring environmental health and remediating polluted sites. But inasmuch as the 1980s constituted a dark period for American environmental policy, the result of this expanding individual responsibility for environmental health bred public empowerment. Grassroots ecological activism became increasingly prevalent, taking on different characters in different places and in response to different environmental threats. In such a historical context, it should come as no surprise that the emergence of environmental-justice movements coincided with this shift. Minority groups—frequently poor and disenfranchised—found new voice and charged that environmental racism was behind the siting of dirty manufacturing and toxic waste dumps in their communities.[23]

In working-class Woburn, residents clearly understood they were on their own against the polluting industries. The Reverend Bruce Young, an early ally in Anderson's search for environmental answers to her son's illness, noted the obstacles to their struggle: "For seven years we were told that the burden of proof was upon us as independent citizens to gather the statistics . . . All our work was independent of the Commonwealth of Massachusetts. They offered no support, and were in fact one of our adversaries in this battle to prove that we had a problem."[24] Given the obstacles, the fact that Woburn became a national story and that its popular epidemiological work served as a model for subsequent communities across the United States reveals the importance of activist power in contending with toxic fear and challenging polluters. This seemingly positive development had a negative flip side, however. The rise of popular epidemiology, as evidenced in Woburn, represents the breakdown in the political contract that a government bears the responsibility to keep its citizens safe from toxic threats as well as enemies, foreign and domestic. FACE engaged in epidemiological data collection not to assist an under-resourced state or federal agency but rather to conduct work it thought officials—experts—should have been doing in the first place.

As such, Woburn is also a significant chapter in the development of the American public's distrust of government. Within the context of toxic fear, distrust of government institutions tasked with preserving the safety and well-being of the people provides an unsettling backdrop to the environmental politics of the 1980s and helps us understand the national panic surrounding apples at the end of the decade. During the second half of the 1980s, a slick media campaign followed by extensive news reporting galvanized toxic fear. The popular story goes like this: in 1989, the Natural Resources Defense Council (NRDC) published a damning report titled *Intolerable Risk*, raising alarm bells about the use of daminozide on apples. Daminozide, known commercially as Alar and sold by the Uniroyal Chemical Company, was a chemical growth regulator that helped keep apples from falling before they were ripe. "For the apple industry," wrote Sheila Jasanoff, "daminozide was close to a miracle product. It delayed ripening, reduced preharvest drop, increased shelf life of harvested fruit, and yielded fruits that were redder and firmer than untreated crops."[25]

Earlier in the 1980s, the discovery of daminozide found in apple juice and applesauce raised concerns about its health impact on humans. In the 1989 report, the NRDC urged the EPA to ban daminozide and provided scientific evidence—using the EPA's own data—suggesting that the chemical was 240 times more carcinogenic than EPA standards allowed. The NRDC hired a publicity firm to help coordinate its efforts. The report was released at the end of February in conjunction with a mainstream media campaign highlighted by a primetime segment on CBS's *60 Minutes*, which aired nationally on February 26. "The most potent cancer-causing chemical in our food supply is a substance sprayed on apples to keep them on the trees longer and make them look better," reported host Ed Bradley to open the segment, provocatively titled "'A' is for Apple."[26] A skull and crossbones covering a red apple served as the backdrop.[27] Actress Meryl Streep appeared in support of the ban on the *Today Show* and the *Phil Donahue Show*. She also testified before a US Senate Labor and Human Resources subcommittee, urging legislators to end experimentation on children.[28]

The campaign was remarkably successful inasmuch as it captured national attention and prompted a widespread popular reaction. Part of the success stemmed from the tide of similar chemical intrusions that had entered the mainstream consciousness throughout the preceding decade. Another part was a result of the professional campaign itself. The NRDC and the media dominated subsequent discourse. With growing awareness of the issue and Streep as the public face of the activism, the industry was framed as negligent and mendacious. The EPA was at best overly cautious, at worst incompetent. Alarm ensued.[29] The EPA was deluged with calls from frightened mothers.[30] Why the sudden warning? Why the about-face? Where Love Canal or Woburn had been local incidents, daminozide became a nationwide cause for concern, but one in which government agencies appeared inept at safeguarding the public or in communicating risk. According to one account, state troopers chased a school bus after a desperate call from a mother hoping to intercept and confiscate the apple in her child's lunch. School administrators in many districts removed and destroyed apples and apple products from children's lunch boxes. As one retrospective put it, "Apple markets rotted overnight."[31]

By June, the EPA felt compelled to act on the basis that "long-term exposure" posed "unacceptable risks to public health." Uniroyal announced that it would cease marketing Alar in the United States. In response, apple growers in Washington State filed a libel suit against the NRDC and CBS, claiming that the public outrage against daminozide was spurred by media propaganda creating hysteria through creation or manipulation of toxic fears. The $100 million lawsuit criticized what the state characterized as faulty science that sealed Alar's fate. University of California–Berkeley biochemist Bruce Ames castigated the NRDC's estimates, which he argued well before the media frenzy consisted of "worst case piled on worst case, and none of it is true."[32] In hindsight, Alar seemed far less pernicious than the CBS story and the NRDC had implied. The real victim appeared to be the apple industry, which suffered unprecedented losses as a result of the ban.

In popular accounts, passionate rhetoric rather than dispassionate science sealed daminozide's fate. Americans were scared, and the EPA was forced into action more quickly than it would have liked. Fear had driven policy. In its aftermath, the daminozide case became rich fodder for anti-environmental critics to castigate environmentalists as anti-scientific fearmongers and environmental issues as a socialist plot against American business and industrial issues. The same critics berated environmental organizations for preying on the scientific illiteracy of public audiences by hurling dubious science and polysyllabic chemical names to galvanize anxiety and a public response. On the one hand, the American public was well primed and frankly justified in responding negatively to any polysyllabic chemical name based on the litany of historical events in which chemicals from Strontium-90 in nuclear fallout to DDT and dioxin had poisoned people and landscapes. On the other hand, growing fears over the latency of carcinogens and the emerging understanding of hormone-disrupting chemicals exacerbated hyperbole on both sides of the daminozide debate and others like it across the United States.

While the NRDC report and the subsequent publicity campaign provoke some questions about their scientific reliability and parts of the CBS story are theatrically shrill, pandering to the grotesque, it is inaccurate to argue that daminozide created no risk and was wrongly attacked by the NRDC and the EPA. Moreover, viewing the chemical through the narrow lens of the 1989 tempest distorts the historical record. Somewhere between the toxic fear hysteria on one side and the simplistic narrative of beneficial chemicals and accusations of environmental extremism on the other lies a more complex story that is crucial to understand for not only historical purposes but to illuminate current debates about chemicals, genetically modified organisms (GMOs), and vaccinations. In 1973, studies conducted by Bela Toth found that daminozide and its breakdown component, unsymmetrical dimethylhydrazine (UDMH), caused cancer in lab mice.[33] Subsequent studies showed no signs of tumors in hamsters, but the potential for carcinogeneity nevertheless existed. Toth's study prompted the EPA to put daminozide under special review in 1977. The agency did not proceed with its review until 1984, but it did call on Uniroyal to provide further data on the conversion of daminozide to UDMH.

Technical science was not the lone metric in determining Alar's safety. Rather, a more complex cost-benefit algorithm put scientific knowledge in conversation with industrial interests, economic priorities, public health, and political expediency. In 1985, the EPA's Office of Planning, Policy, and Evaluation balanced the costs to the apple industry against the costs to human health. It was estimated that by suspending their use of daminozide, apple growers stood to lose $32.9 million a year. The potential risks, however, seemed to outweigh the benefits. Based on knowledge at the time, daminozide was deemed at least as dangerous as EDB, a grain fumigant just suspended by the EPA. This assessment coincided with scientific experts—industrial and independent—calling the original studies on daminozide and UDMH into question.[34] As the EPA stalled, the public response gathered steam. In 1986, Massachusetts and Maine "took steps to reduce and eventually eliminate daminozide residues in foods sold in those states."[35] At the same time, the NRDC and Public Citizen, Ralph Nader's consumer advocacy organization, became involved, pressuring large supermarket chains to sell only non-Alar-treated apples. Even if the science was not definitive, the fact that some studies had returned the prospect that daminozide was a carcinogen, they reasoned, ought to be grounds for a ban. Otherwise, Alar threatened to cause further cancers before its use could be restricted. On July 1, 1986, the NRDC filed a petition in New York and Maine to establish zero tolerances for daminozide.

In early 1989, Uniroyal reported on further bioassays, muddying the waters even more. While the company's tests showed no indication of risks among rats, they did find an increase of benign and malignant blood vessel tumors in mice. UDMH studies also found increased carcinogenic signs at high doses. Based on the EPA's risk analysis, these results augured heightened risks for human cancer, especially among children.[36] On February 1, 1989, John A. Moore, the acting administrator, saw fit to accelerate the canceling of

daminozide and wrote to the International Apple Institute asking the industry to take voluntary action before the EPA proceeded. Later that month, the
NRDC report and the *60 Minutes* story served as gasoline, turning a slow-
burning fire into a full-blown conflagration.

In some sense, the Alar story is a curious partner for the leukemia cluster
in Woburn. But it, too, offers a case—albeit markedly different—of citizen
knowledge production and activism. The NRDC report parallels the popular
epidemiology from the Woburn case in several ways. *Intolerable Risk* was a
piece of citizen-based scientific work, drawing on existing literature to raise
awareness of the hazards posed by daminozide's use on apples across the
country. While the report was castigated as poor and faulty science by its critics, the NRDC did not conduct any independent tests. Rather, *Intolerable Risk*
was produced using studies conducted and collected by the EPA. And while
the NRDC's offices and teams of lawyers might suggest few points of comparison with the stricken Woburn parents collecting data from their neighbors, it is possible to draw a straight genealogy between them. Founded in
1970, the NRDC acts as legal watchdog to safeguard Americans against polluters of the environment and denuders of its resources. During the 1980s, the
NRDC became increasingly involved in questions pertaining to toxic waste
and environmental health. Even at the time of the Alar case, the NRDC's
recruitment letters drew on the citizen activism base that inspired so many
smaller grassroots groups. "You have heard a lot of talk these days about the
powerlessness of citizens," one letter stated. "The 'experts' say people can't be
heard . . . [But our record is] a compelling story of how concerned and organized citizens made a world of difference."[37] A similar distrust of government
and industry science pervades the rationale of both groups. At the end of the
1980s, the popular response against Alar suggested that fear, uncertainty, and
the sense that government had failed to keep its people safe persisted.

Possession of knowledge and expertise constitutes a valuable and powerful commodity in environmental struggles. Access to information is
empowering and helps reduce the fears of uncertainty; it also represents an
important source of political power. And this power is rarely available to
the citizenry. Steve Shapin and Simon Schaffer concluded *Leviathan and the
Air-Pump: Hobbes, Boyle, and the Experimental Life*, their brilliant study of early
modern science, with a critique of expertise and science. "Now we live in a
less certain age," they wrote:

Our present-day problems of defining our knowledge, our society, and the relationships between them centre on . . . dichotomies between the public and the private, [and] between authority and expertise . . . We regard our scientific knowledge as open and accessible in principle, but the public does not understand it. Scientific journals are in our public libraries, but they are written in a language alien to the citizenry. We say that our laboratories constitute some of our most open professional spaces, yet the public does not enter them. Our society is said to be democratic, but the public cannot call to account what they cannot comprehend. A form of knowledge that is the most open in principle has become the most closed in practice.[38]

Although much of this chapter considers popular efforts to again wrest some of that expertise from the invisible and inaccessible forces of political and industrial power, we need to be careful about how we treat science and expertise in such grassroots accounts and avoid accepting simple narratives that pit citizens against experts or the politics of local knowledges confronting modern expertise or industry obstruction. There is no obvious progression from the darkness of uncertainty to the clarity of knowledge or that better information necessarily produced better remedial policy. Different knowledges in these two incidents were highly contested, and debates over scientific expertise, results, and the risks they entailed mired environmental struggles in a new politics of information.[39] Further, as Sylvia Noble Tesh observes, many community groups recruited "experts" or relied on their data in their local struggles.[40] At Woburn, public health experts at Harvard and elsewhere assisted local residents in preparing and analyzing the data they collected. And in the Alar case, the NRDC retained its own experts to draw results from studies conducted by the EPA.

In essence, then, rather than drawing narrative binaries between citizens and experts, scholars need to parse ideas about public expertise and the kinds of independent experts who collaborate with grassroots groups to tell more complicated stories that engage how and when expert knowledge finds itself on opposing sides of environmental disputes. Tesh also refers to a 1984 study conducted by Nicholas Freudenberg on grassroots environmental groups. In surveying 242 respondents involved with grassroots organizations, Freudenberg found that activists sought, processed, and used scientific evidence in their activism. "Contact with scientific experts,"

Freudenberg reported, was "rated to be the most valuable source of information" among the community groups he surveyed.[41] So while grassroots organizations invariably felt as though they were confronting some industrial or government Goliath, many girded themselves with the kinds of expert knowledge—even if they were central to its collection—their adversary had frequently used against them.

But: close on fear as an instigating factor in grassroots environmental action. The daminozide scare drove home to Americans the idea that nobody was really safe. Whereas the leukemia cluster in Woburn was restricted to the consumption of water from specific wells in the eastern part of this specific town, apples sprayed with Alar were grown and trafficked around the entire country. Asked why they never considered leaving Woburn, Jenny Andersson and others responded that Woburn was every town and that they lacked confidence that anyplace was still safe from the advances of chemical pollution.[42] That story persists. Invisible poisons continue to provoke fear in communities all over the United States. Similarly, a legacy of citizen action against "misplaced matter" has matured since the 1980s. Local struggles for safer communities and more accessible information about the environmental risks we face on a daily basis are still constructed in the factories of collaborative, informed debate and confrontation. Collaboration, information, and activism are also among the most effective methods of raising the shroud of fear from environmental disasters and converting them into real and lasting change.

Notes

1. Gregg Mitman, Michelle Murphy, and Christopher Sellers, "Introduction: A Cloud over History," in Gregg Mitman, Michelle Murphy, and Christopher Sellers, eds., *Landscapes of Exposure: Knowledge and Illness in Modern Environments* (Chicago: University of Chicago Press, 2004), 13.

2. "High modernism" is an ideological concept introduced by David Harvey and developed by James C. Scott to explain Western societies' unconditional faith in scientific and technical progress since industrialization. Above and beyond the creation of contaminated environments, I contend that toxic fear constitutes a significant social crack in the veneer of its unbridled optimism. For more, see James C. Scott, *Seeing Like a State: How Certain Schemes to Improve the Human Condition Have Failed* (New Haven, CT: Yale University Press, 1998); David Harvey, *The Condition of Post-Modernity: An Enquiry into the Origins of Social Change* (Oxford: Blackwell, 1989).

3. Maya Pines, "Psychological Time Bombs," *New York Times*, June 13, 1982, 10E.

4. "Court Rules, 'Psychological Stress' Must be Weighed at Three Mile Island," *New York Times*, May 15, 1982, 1.

5. Kai Erikson, *A New Species of Trouble: Explorations in Disaster, Trauma, and Community* (New York: W. W. Norton, 1994), 139–57.

6. The warrant for this investigation stems from the need to complicate our historical understanding of American environmentalism writ large and of grassroots environmental action more specifically. The historiography of American environmentalism treats the 1980s as a period of backlash. In response to the Reagan administration's massive funding cuts at the US Environmental Protection Agency, the US Department of the Interior, and other agencies tasked with protecting the environment, more and more Americans became members of local and national environmental organizations. For better and for worse, many of these environmental groups became more litigious, hiring and retaining teams of lawyers to fight government and industrial polluters in the courtroom and in the corridors of political power. A concurrent narrative—and one that frequently supersedes the traditional mainstream account of American environmental activism—engages with questions of environmental justice as a backlash against the mainstream movement. As older and more established environmental groups migrated into political compromise through the three Ls—lobbying, litigating, and lamenting—some critics perceived their efforts as losing touch with the growing sense of urgency felt in many communities. Especially in communities of color, which felt they were not represented by the preordained priorities of the mainstream groups, a push for a new kind of ecological action—local, confrontational, and urgent—manifested itself. Fighting to protect not the sanctity of some abstract "Nature" but rather the places in which they and their families "live, work, and play," environmental-justice activists struggled against threats to human health in their communities. Further, they stressed that hazards posed by toxic waste unequally affected poorer and more marginalized populations of color. Over the past couple of decades, environmental historians have struggled to reconcile these disparate threads. The more successful efforts consist of treating the body as an ecological landscape and reinforcing recent connections between human and environmental health. I submit that toxic fear is another universal trait that synthesizes disparate threads in the historical literature.

7. See Michael Egan, *Barry Commoner and the Science of Survival: The Remaking of American Environmentalism* (Cambridge, MA: MIT Press, 2007), especially chapter 2. For a brief summary of the science information movement, see Michael Egan, "Why Barry Commoner Matters," *Organization and Environment* 22 (March 2009): 1–13.

8. Phil Brown, "The Popular Epidemiology Approach to Toxic Waste Contamination," in *Communities at Risk: Collective Responses to Technological Hazards*, ed. Stephen Robert Couch and J. Stephen Kroll-Smith (New York: Peter Lang, 1991), 135.

9. The seminal academic study on the Woburn cancer cluster is Phil Brown and Edwin J. Mikkelsen, *No Safe Place: Toxic Waste, Leukemia, and Community Action* (Berkeley: University of California Press, 1990). For an excellent narrative account, see Paula DiPerna, *Cluster Mystery: Epidemic and the Children of Woburn, Mass.* (St. Louis: Mosby, 1985). The Woburn story and litigation were popularized as the basis for *A Civil Action*, a popular law thriller written by Jonathan Harr, which was subsequently turned into a 1994 Hollywood movie under the same name starring John Travolta and Robert Duvall.

10. DiPerna, *Cluster Mystery*, 17. "Clusters tug at the national sleeve, pointing out the huge hollow between scientific knowledge and the national need to protect public health and control environmental contamination," writes Paula DiPerna in *Cluster Mystery* (14–15). A cluster—real or imagined—indicates that public safety has been compromised. In many respects, then, the appearance of cancer clusters constituted one of the driving forces of toxic fear as a cultural and environmental phenomenon during the 1980s.

11. Leukemia offers special insight into cancer clusters. Given cancer's latency—it can take up to twenty years for it to manifest itself as diagnosable malignant tumors—it is extremely difficult to trace potential clusters. People move in and out of areas. They are exposed to any number of different carcinogens. Childhood leukemia works on a much faster time line, which allows epidemiologists a slightly clearer view of the disease's trajectory and parameters.

12. The Department of Public Health's count was only twelve, but local activists who collected their own data argued that the official counts failed to acknowledge cases of children who left the area or of nonresidents who spent considerable time in the community. These discrepancies make up part of the story.

13. Brown and Mikkelsen, *No Safe Place*, 11.

14. Charles C. Ryan, "Lagoon of Arsenic Discovered in N. Woburn," *Woburn Daily Times and Chronicle*, September 10, 1979, 1. After mobilizing the US Army Corps of Engineers to investigate the site, the EPA had refrained from communicating its findings to the community or to town officials until after the story broke in September.

15. DiPerna, *Cluster Mystery*.

16. Brown and Mikkelsen, *No Safe Place*, 8–15.

17. In April 1985, the plaintiffs added Unifirst to the suit. Unifirst countersued the families for libel two months later but ultimately settled before trial in early October.

18. Steven Lagakos, Barbara J. Wessen, and Marvin Zelen, "An Analysis of Contaminated Well Water and Health Effects in Woburn, Massachusetts," *Journal of the American Statistical Association* 81, no. 30 (1986): 583–96. For a summary, see Brown and Mikkelsen, *No Safe Place*, 23–26.

19. Melinda Beck, "The Toxic-Waste Crisis," *Newsweek*, March 7, 1983, 24.

20. Brown and Mikkelsen, *No Safe Place*, 30.

21. Neo-liberalism is attracting increasing interest as a method of explaining or organizing the shift in the Western economic landscape in the years after World War II. David Harvey defines it as "a theory of political economic practices that proposes that human well-being can best be advanced by liberating individual entrepreneurial freedoms and skills within an institutional framework characterized by strong private property rights, free markets, and free trade." Harvey, *A Brief History of Neoliberalism* (New York: Oxford University Press, 2005), 2. But neoliberalism is more than just an entrenchment of capitalist free markets; it should also be understood as a political and ideological program designed to undermine social democracy and the welfare state. In addition to Harvey, see by way of primer, Philip Mirowski, *Never Let a Serious Crisis Go to Waste: How Neoliberalism Survived the Financial Meltdown* (London: Verso, 2013); Philip Mirowski and Dieter Plehwe, eds., *The Road from Mont Pèlerin: The Making of the Neoliberal Thought Collective* (Cambridge, MA: Harvard University Press, 2009).

22. Daniel T. Rodgers describes the final quarter of the twentieth century as an "age of fracture" in the United States, a period defined by the breakdown or fragmenting of American cultural norms. The social, moral, and economic boundaries that defined previous American generations lost concrete definition, resulting in new uncertainties. See Rodgers, *The Age of Fracture* (Cambridge, MA: Harvard University Press, 2011).

23. By and large, this chapter bypasses the question and history of environmental justice, but I would submit that toxic fear and the politics of uncertainty during this period are critical catalysts in that movement's history. The literature on environmental justice is growing rapidly. Seminal works include Robert D. Bullard, *Dumping in Dixie: Race, Class, and Environmental Quality*, 3rd ed. (Boulder: Westview, 2000); Marcy Darnovsky, "Stories Less Told: Histories of US Environmentalism," *Socialist Review* 22, no. 4 (1992): 11–54; Giovanna Di Chiro, "Defining Environmental Justice: Women's Voices and Grassroots Politics," *Socialist Review* 22, no. 4 (1992): 93–130; Dorceta E. Taylor, *The Environment and the People in American Cities, 1600s–1900s* (Chapel Hill: University of North Carolina Press, 2009).

24. Quoted in DiPerna, *Cluster Mystery*, 155–61; cited in Brown and Mikkelsen, *No Safe Place*, 14.

25. Sheila Jasanoff, *The Fifth Branch: Science Advisers as Policymakers* (Cambridge, MA: Harvard University Press, 1990), 141.

26. Natural Resources Defense Council, *Intolerable Risk: Pesticides in our Children's Food*, February 27, 1989, accessed August 13, 2018, https://www.nrdc.org/sites/default/files/hea_11052401a.pdf.

27. Aaron Wildavsky, But Is It True? A Citizen's Guide to Environmental Health and Safety Issues (Cambridge, MA: Harvard University Press, 1995), 201–2.

28. Margaret Carlson, "Do You Dare to Eat a Peach?" *The Nation* 133 (1989): 27.

29. Finis Dunaway's excellent analysis of the Alar case highlights the manner in which consumerist fears emerged as a tactic in environmental activism. Dunaway, Seeing Green: The Use and Abuse of American Environmental Images (Chicago: University of Chicago Press, 2015), 208–22.

30. Eleanor Randolph, "Venture in Managing News Backfires," *Washington Post*, March 3, 1989, A17.

31. "An Unhappy Anniversary: The Alar 'Scare' Ten Years Later," American Council on Science and Health, February 1, 1999, 1–4, accessed March 14, 2015, http://acsh.org/1999/02/an-unhappy-anniversary-the-alar-scare-ten-years-later/.

32. Philip Shabecoff, "100 Chemicals for Apples Add Up to Enigma on Safety," New York Times, February 5, 1989, 22.

33. Bela Toth, "1,1-Dimethylhydrazine (Unsymmetrical) Carcinogens in Mice: Light Microscopic and Ultrastructural Studies on Neoplastic Blood Vessels," *Journal of the National Cancer Institute* 50 (1973): 181–87.

34. The best account of the early scientific debate over Alar is Jasanoff, Fifth Branch, 141–49. Wildavsky also provides a comprehensive account of the Alar story. Wildavsky, *But Is It True*, 201–22.

35. Jasanoff, Fifth Branch, 147.

36. The EPA calculated a cancer risk (over the course of a lifetime) of 5 in 1 million for adults and 9 in 1 million for children.

37. Sylvia Noble Tesh, *Uncertain Hazards: Environmental Activists and Scientific Proof* (Ithaca, NY: Cornell University Press, 2000), 89.

38. Steven Shapin and Simon Schaffer, Leviathan and the Air-Pump: Hobbes, Boyle, and the Experimental Life (Princeton, NJ: Princeton University Press, 1985), 343.

39. This facet of environmental knowledge skirts what Robert N. Proctor and Londa Schiebinger have termed "agnotology," the study of ignorance. Just as scientific knowledge can be kept from public participants in environmental debates, ignorance can be used as a strategic ploy to muddy the difference between the signal and the noise. See Proctor and Schiebinger, eds., *Agnotology: The Making and Unmaking of Ignorance* (Stanford, CA: Stanford University Press, 2008). I do not treat

agnotology in this chapter, but it lurks in the background of many environmental struggles.

40. Tesh, *Uncertain Hazards*; see especially chapter 5.

41. Nicholas Freudenberg, "Citizen Action for Environmental Health: Report on a Survey of Community Organizations," *American Journal of Public Health* 74 (May 1984): 445; cited in Tesh, *Uncertain Hazards*, 95–96.

42. Phil Brown and Edwin Mikkelsen observe that "residents rarely leave toxic waste sites except when they are relocated by the government, as in Times Beach, Missouri, and Love Canal, New York." Brown and Mikkelsen, *No Safe Place*, 4.

10

Raising Change

Community Farming as Long-Term Ecological Protest

JEFF CRANE

College students wander around an interior courtyard at a southeastern San Antonio Head Start helping three- and four-year-old African American and Latino children pick out ladybugs to place on pepper, broccoli, and squash plants. University of the Incarnate Word (UIW) professors and students on this day are learning how to produce food in a food desert, providing delicious organic produce for families that can rarely afford or access it. Although seeing college students working with young children is inspiring, the ladybug release also uses beneficial insects to remove aphids that would consume crops while teaching these children basic ecological principles (it turns out that most of the student-teachers do not fully understand these principles either). The children's delight and interest speaks to the power of nature to create awe and catalyze their learning. And while some may hesitate to consider this activity a form of environmental protest, in the United States community farms[1] have become the sites of some of the most significant challenges to the current political economy and the structures of economic and racial injustice in America and the points of resistance to the industrial agricultural economy.

DOI: 10.5876/9781607328483.co10

In this chapter I examine the ways community farming can challenge the dominant industrial agriculture, undermine neo-liberal capitalism, address fundamental inequity in the United States, and help prepare for climate change. In so doing, I also evaluate some of the pitfalls inherent in this movement and crucial next steps. While the discussion is broad, I examine community farming in Detroit, Michigan; Milwaukee, Wisconsin; and San Antonio, Texas. The first two cities are studied as the movement arises from the community in response to serious economic stress and because they provide strong and innovative models for community farming as a site and source of social, economic, and ecological change. The discussion of San Antonio community farming reflects my positionality in the movement and demonstrates a model of activism that has potential for success but can also limit community engagement.

The image most readily called to mind when one imagines environmental protest is often associated with more active forms of direct opposition. For many middle-aged and middle-class Americans, the words *environmental protest* likely evoke Earth Day or the Sierra Club and successful Greenpeace-like direct actions. For many of my students, environmental protest sparks images of the more radical Earth Liberation Front or Earth First! Social media is filled with images of Sioux Indians and allies fighting to protect sacred land from the fossil-fuel industry, Pacific Northwest kayaktivists attempting to block an oil rig destined for the North Slope, Americans everywhere opposing the Keystone XL Pipeline.

Environmental protest as we know it began with late nineteenth-century women cleaning the cities to reduce disease, followed by the classic conservation work of Gifford Pinchot and Theodore Roosevelt. There was also the slower emergence of a preservationist philosophy and strategy exemplified in the failed fight against damming the Hetch Hetchy Valley in the first decades of the twentieth century, the successful efforts to protect Dinosaur National Monument from dam and reservoir construction in the 1940s and 1950s, the publication and powerful public response to Rachel Carson's *Silent Spring* in 1962, and the passage of the Wilderness Act in 1964. The successes of this complex environmental movement peaked in the early 1970s with the creation of an environmental regulatory state that included new congressional legislation such as the Clean Air Act, the Clean Water Act, and the Endangered Species Act, along with the creation of the US Environmental

Protection Agency. The temporary consensus around the need for a healthy environment collapsed after 1973 as Republicans framed environmental efforts as anti-job, anti-prosperity, and increasingly anti-American.[2]

While meaningful environmental legislation has been hard to secure in the ensuing decades, particularly in regard to climate change, this does not mean that environmental reforms and activism have stopped or even slowed in significant ways. Continuing creation and expansion of wilderness areas, restoration of habitat, and dam removals to restore fisheries indicate a thriving environmental movement operating largely at the local or state level. In addition, the growing environmental-justice movement, which primarily targets the dumping of wastes and pollutants in poor communities populated predominantly by people of color, has expanded the definition of environmentalism to include systemic injustice and structural violence rooted in inequitable distribution of wealth and deep-seated racism. The food-justice movement, which has gained wider appeal in recent years, has continued to widen and complicate the concept of environmentalism and environmental protest, creating new strategies and targets for those concerned with natural and human health as well as social justice. Community farming represents a new and potentially powerful form of environmental protest addressing several issues, or as Wendell Berry might say, "solving for pattern."[3]

Social critic Rebecca Solnit would agree, arguing that the community-farming movement is a "second green revolution," an attempt "to undo the destructive aspects of the first one, to make an organic and intimate agriculture that feeds minds and hearts as well as bodies, that measures intangible qualities as well as quantity. By volume, it produces only a small portion of this country's food, but of course its logic isn't merely volume. The first green revolution may have increased yield in many cases, but it also increased alienation and toxicity, and it was efficient only if you ignored its fossil fuel dependency, carbon output, and other environmental impacts."[4] A community farming revolution that is transformative and restorative and that brings production and consumption home to the community holds great promise and constitutes protest against a deeply damaging industrial agricultural system, destructive neo-liberal policies, and ongoing climate-change pollution and inaction. But those active in this movement need to be aware of destructive social and economic policies emanating from neo-liberalism and ensure that community farming does not simply function as a form of mitigation of harmful policies.

Children's bodies are the most vulnerable to the deleterious impact of industrial agriculture and neo-liberalism. Approximately one-quarter of children in the United States experience regular hunger; in over 300 US counties, one-third of children live in food-insecure households. In fact, 49 percent of infants born in this country are born to families collecting food supplements from the Special Supplemental Nutrition Program for Women, Infants, and Children.[5] The issue of access to healthy food for children constitutes a safe middle ground in the discourse of community farming; as farmers and activists engage with the structural issues that cause hunger and embrace food-justice precepts, the agenda and discourse of community farming inevitably pulls hard left. Embedded in it are fundamental critiques of industrial agriculture, the structural inequity of the American economy, trade agreements such as the North American Free Trade Agreement (NAFTA), labor conditions, and the continuing whittling away of the safety net and social services. Community farmers also explicate the role urban agriculture can play in exposing children to nature, offering educational opportunities, building community cohesion, and bringing social discourse back to a more neutral space.[6]

Community farms are a direct response to economic inequality and can help end food deserts. Food deserts are urban and rural areas where access to healthy food is limited by a lack of grocery stores, healthy restaurants, and land and tools for food production. Fast food, convenience-store fare, and traditional cultural foodways that emphasize meat, fried foods, and heavy use of salts and sugars comprise the majority of the diet in food deserts. The high portion of sugar, fat, meat, and starches in food desert diets, combined with low nutrient–value food, results in persistent health problems: high rates of childhood obesity, type 2 diabetes, stroke, and heart disease predominate. Food justice, then, is partially about achieving equal access to healthy food for all people while acknowledging and confronting the structural barriers to healthy food for the poor.[7]

Food-justice advocates also target the means of production in the nation's industrial agricultural economy and its trading partners around the world. Agricultural workers in the United States experience harsh working conditions for low or irregular pay, whether picking apples in eastern Washington or cantaloupe in the Rio Grande Valley:

A survey conducted by Pineros y Campesinos Unidos del Noroeste [Northwest Tree-Planters and Farmworkers United] (PCUN, Oregon's farm-workers' union) of approximately 200 Marion County, Oregon, farmworkers paid by "piece-rate" in the 2009 berry harvests revealed widespread violations of the state's minimum wage law. Ninety percent of workers reported that their "piece-rate" earnings consistently amounted to less than minimum wage, with an average hourly yield of about $5.30—37 percent below the hourly minimum wage at the time—and an average daily underpayment of about $25.00 per worker. In New Mexico, a survey of farmworkers revealed abusive conditions in the fields, including extremely low wages and high levels of wage theft. Sixty-seven percent of field workers were victims of wage theft in the year prior to the survey; 43 percent of respondents stated that they never received the minimum wage, and 95 percent were never paid for the time they waited each day in the field to begin working."[8]

These are but a few examples of common problems across the country.[9] Food-justice activists and community farmers seek to end the reliance on abused labor that makes food artificially cheap and end the abuse implicit in this economy.

In addition to suffering from wage theft and underpayment, agricultural laborers are also frequently subjected to working with herbicides and pesti-cides that are known carcinogens and can contribute to other health issues such as Parkinson's disease, sterility, miscarriage, and birth defects. Because of low pay, the lack of benefits, and no permanent housing in many cases, as well as constant hunger and malnutrition, this class of workers struggles to escape the lowest tier of the American economy.[10] Making between ten dollars and fifteen dollars an hour at most on an irregular schedule of incon-sistent hours, they crowd into expensive apartments or live in shacks and old chicken coops. Ironically, these workers often cannot access healthy produce. Eighty-nine percent of the Salinas Valley farmworker population is obese compared with 69 percent nationally because they simply cannot afford to buy the fresh produce, like leafy greens and broccoli, that they pick all day and live next to. Not only does impoverishment trap many in a permanent agricultural underclass, but this poor nutrition limits the cognitive and phys-ical development of children, further reducing the possibility that they will eventually escape the cycle of poverty.[11]

While advocates of neo-liberalism argue for expanding prosperity and increasing investment opportunities for consolidated capital in the United States and other countries, they fail to take into account many negative impacts arising from trade deals. As a result of NAFTA and trade with Mexico and Latin American countries, American consumers are implicated in an agricultural economy that is even more abusive of agricultural workers in those countries with limited and lightly enforced regulations protecting workers' bodies and the environment. Agricultural chemicals that are illegal in the United States are manufactured domestically and shipped to other countries that produce vast quantities of nuts, fruits, and vegetables for American consumption. High rates of cancer, miscarriage, severe birth defects, and other ailments are common in the agricultural labor population throughout Latin America; these damaged bodies help keep commodity prices artificially low in the United States.[12] Problems such as these are hard to address through protest or policy change, given the influence of industrial agriculture and the chemical industry in Washington, DC, the continuing expansion of a global neo-liberal economy, and Americans' stunning lack of awareness of the effect of their food consumption on other economies and workers.

A central food-justice mandate is that economically and culturally marginalized communities find ways to gain economic and cultural autonomy through local food production and entrepreneurship; community farming is a means to those ends. As an example of how this might happen, consider the local response to the collapse of the Detroit industrial economy and the city's life on the economic edge. With an estimated 45 percent unemployment rate in the city and a population that dropped from around 2 million to approximately 700,000 from its peak in the 1950s to 2015, Detroit has been in crisis for a long time. The city's declaration of bankruptcy—the largest municipal bankruptcy case in US history—captured the country's attention, as did stories of fires unanswered by fire departments, the rise of crime, packs of feral dogs roaming the city, and the destruction of an iconic industrial city.

The lack of access to healthy food, while difficult in other food deserts, is nearly catastrophic in the Motor City. Eighty percent of the population currently relies on convenience stores, pharmacies, gas stations, and party stores for food purchases. Residents responded to this situation by creating an urban agricultural economy throughout the city. As a result, they commenced fashioning a new type of urban economy that may presage the future of cities in the Anthropocene while also engaging in a significant and potentially power-ful form of environmental protest. With more than 30,000 distressed proper-ties and 20,000 acres of available land, many residents took advantage of the space and began squatting on lots and growing their own food. The Detroit Black Community Food Security Network (DBCFSN) led the way in creating a food sovereignty movement, with strong emphases on local food produc-tion and consumption, community entrepreneurship, and building commu-nity strength. Community activists initiated innovative programs such as the Land Bank, a city-managed program that sells side lots for $100.[13]

Even as community-farming activists in Detroit go about turning lots into farms, they are also educating the community about food production, incor-porating youth into these programs, and developing stronger neighborhood cohesion. Several thousand people own backyard or front-yard gardens or work on farms. Keep Growing Detroit[14] is an organization that encapsulates and promotes key tenets of food sovereignty and food justice while confront-ing structural injustice through advocating for and building stronger commu-nity. Consistent with food sovereignty concepts, the goal of the organization is to have most of the fruits and vegetables consumed by Detroit residents grown within city limits. It provides seeds and transplants to thousands of people and offers numerous classes on farming throughout the city as well as technical assistance to gardeners and farmers. This work also emphasizes community solidarity through potluck meals, shared workdays, and open planning meetings.

Integral to building a movement and creating long-term change is Keep Growing Detroit's emphasis on developing community leadership. The organization trains youth and adults to teach classes and take on leadership roles in association with food production and farm management. To nurture economic resilience, the organization supports and promotes approximately seventy farmers who sell their produce in farmers' markets and other outlets across the city, generating economic activity through increased consumption and the sale of Detroit-grown foods.[15]

Michigan Community Farming Initiative's creation of an "agri-hood" in the Northend neighborhood of Detroit represents another innovative form of community farming. It has a 200–fruit tree orchard, a two-acre garden, and an energy-efficient community resource center that includes two com-mercial kitchens. The farm produces approximately 20,000 pounds of food a year, providing nourishment to approximately 2,000 citizens in the area and supporting churches, volunteer organizations, and other community programs. By centering the farm in the community, it provides a place where neighbors can interact and serve each other. But cities will require many more examples like this for community farming to make a deep impact and create long-term and meaningful structural change.[16]

Detroit community farming activists, many of whom trace their direct protest roots back to the Black Liberation struggles of the 1970s, view food-justice activism as direct action against an unjust society. Food sovereignty and reducing or removing dependence on corporate capitalism are central to community health, strength, and activism in the future. Although it is difficult at this early stage to determine the impact of community farming and activism on local democracy, the DBCFSN headed a task force to develop a food policy that has gained support. The Detroit City Council voted to create a Detroit Food Policy Council and to support proposals by the task force leading to food sovereignty, which indicates initial democratization of city politics as the result of community farming.[17]

Milwaukee is another city that struggles with widespread poverty, and, as in Detroit, community farming has gained widespread support. Much of Milwaukee's success in this regard is identified with local entrepreneur and civic leader Will Allen and his nonprofit company Growing Power. Allen comes by his agricultural interests naturally, as his parents were sharecroppers in South Carolina and purchased a small farm in Maryland on which he grew up. Following a collegiate basketball career (he was the first African American to play for the University of Miami) and a stint playing professionally in Europe, Allen began a career in corporate America, working in executive positions for Kentucky Fried Chicken and Proctor and Gamble. He continued small-scale agricultural work on the side during his career, and in 1993 he purchased two lots on a busy street in North Milwaukee. With his children in college, he left his career to farm full-time. Selling produce directly from his garden, he also built a greenhouse to start transplants and provide opportunities for young people to learn and gain employment by working the farm; this strategy remains the bedrock of Growing Power's mission today.[18]

As of 2017, the company managed 300 acres of farmland in and around Milwaukee, producing 200 varieties of crops. While raising fish through hydroponic farming and raising goats, Growing Power also composts more than 40 million pounds of waste each year, capturing important nutrients for farms while reducing landfill use. The multiple farms are important education sites; they offer classes, workshops, and training for the community and are increasingly the subject of university internships and academic research.[19]

The company has sought to energize community farming in other locales, expanding its efforts to Chicago and providing training in Alabama, Ohio, Georgia, Indiana, and New York, to name a few states. Established in Chicago in 2002, Growing Power manages several farms there: Altged Gardens Community Farm is a three-acre site containing eight hoop-houses that allow production during the winter months. Approximately 100 teenagers are employed in the summer working on the farm, and a dozen work there the rest of the year. As at all Growing Power sites, students learn a variety of farming skills, including pest management, composting, and the logistics and operations associated with the transport and sale of farm products. The organization also offers Fresh Moves Mobile, an old transit bus that carries fresh produce into the south- and west-side communities of Chicago, which are stark food deserts. The price of the food ranges from standard rates for those who can afford them to sharply discounted prices for those receiving Supplemental Nutrition Assistance Program (SNAP) benefits.[20]

Under the leadership of Erika Allen, Will Allen's daughter, Growing Power has explicitly addressed food-justice issues, most clearly with the organization's role in the Growing Food and Justice Initiative (GFJI). Built to address the persistence of structural racial inequality and racism, GFJI seeks to undermine racism by building community strength and identity through community food systems.[21]

The community farming revolution occurs in fits and starts in different parts of the nation, and San Antonio, Texas, provides an example of community farming developing in a manner different from the processes in Detroit and Milwaukee. Although San Antonio has not experienced the kind of economic collapse Detroit and Milwaukee went through in the late twentieth and early twenty-first centuries, it suffers from deeply entrenched poverty on its east, south, and west sides. There are also thousands of vacant lots and vast food deserts in these neighborhoods. Because of its more stable economy, however, community farming in the Alamo City has developed more slowly than in its urban counterparts in the Midwest. Green Spaces Alliance, a land trust and community gardening organization, has supplied much of the local leadership; since 2013, it has helped grow the concept of community farming in collaboration with local universities, the San Antonio Housing Authority (SAHA), and an array of local nonprofits.

Ella Austin Children's Garden, located on the city's east side, is a successful community garden that has the potential to transform into a community farm. In collaboration with the Ella Austin Community Center and drawing off the energy and ideas of Stephen Lucke, one of my former students, I helped link the fledgling garden with the UIW. Lucke had developed an on-campus community in 2012; one year later we initiated a series of garden projects on the east and south sides of San Antonio. The focus of our efforts has been to introduce agriculture into local food deserts. The lack of access to healthy food and produce in many of San Antonio's communities has resulted in higher rates of overall and childhood obesity, type 2 diabetes in adults and children, and high rates of heart disease and stroke, among other, related health issues.

The first garden was started at Ella Austin with support from the United Way and was quickly followed by a garden at the Carroll Early Childhood Education Center, a Head Start program that serves approximately 320 children on the southeast side of the city. UIW was a key player in the expansion of these sites, in good measure because such work is consistent with the institution's mission. The Sisters of Charity of the Incarnate Word founded the forerunner of the university in 1881, and the order—and the institution—emphasize social justice and care for the needy. The Catholic Social Teachings, including the preferential option for the poor, the right of participation, and care for creation, reinforce this focus. These theological commitments, with support from the UIW Ettling Center for Civic Engagement and the community organizing work of Ettling Center director Monica Cruz and community coordinator Denise Krohn, found expression in the service-learning projects and workdays UIW faculty and students have devoted to the garden sites. Moreover, student fees provided crucial funding at Ella Austin and Carroll and in the expansion of an existing community garden at the Guadalupe Center, managed by Catholic Charities and located in western San Antonio. Student leaders such as Michelle Wilk, student government president in 2014, provided funding and labor for the gardens and, in the case of Wilk, continued to manage the gardens in later years.

The Ella Austin Children's Garden has grown substantially since 2013 and now contains fourteen vegetable plots that are eight feet by four feet in size, several linear plots totaling approximately 300 square feet of blackberries and grapes growing along fences, and approximately a dozen fruit and olive trees. The garden produces upward of 1,000 pounds of food a year. When finished, with a full orchard and grape and blackberry vines surrounding the site, the garden is anticipated to have approximately twenty-five fruit, nut, and olive trees, including orange, peach, apple, pear, pomegranate, and plum. The intent was to create a mix of annuals and perennials to maximize crop production. Even in years when care is inconsistent, perennials will provide food. Permaculture crops such as berrying plants and fruit trees also build resilience in anticipation of climate change. The five-year goal was for this one garden to generate yields of 3,000 pounds annually, production that is expected to enhance the diets of the children and their families on the east side and thereby increase the neighborhood's access to healthy food. While the garden is still in its early stages and blackberries, grapes, and fruit trees will not produce in large numbers for two to five more years, large harvests of produce such as potatoes, kale, broccoli, tomatoes, peppers, carrots, beets, lettuce, and other crops occur regularly throughout the year. Most of the year we are able to provide weekly distribution of fresh organic produce to families with children in the center's after-school program.

Since autonomy and community strength are central to food-justice philosophy, those managing the garden strived to involve students in grades 2 through 6 from the beginning. All phases of garden construction and expansion have included faculty, college students, and elementary school children in work that includes building plots, hauling soil, fertilizing, planting, and harvesting. The emphasis in these efforts is to educate students on how to build, maintain, and nurture a garden. College and elementary school students are included in ongoing work such as weeding, thinning, fertilizing, and transplanting, with the hope that they will develop a love of and interest in gardening and eventually take over work at these gardens or start their own. This long-term strategy is consistent with the Detroit and Milwaukee models that seek to grow food and nourish community resilience. It also integrates a science, agriculture, and health curriculum in the after-school program that utilizes the garden to teach scientific ideas and concepts as well as food preparation, deepening the children's association of the garden as a site of community action, improvement, and education. While the lessons in the garden for these children do not emphasize direct action and democracy, the lessons of community action, critical thinking, garden management, scientific thinking, and cooperation constitute the crucial foundation for creating activist citizens.

Rapid changes in opportunities for and attitudes about community farming in San Antonio have suggested a potential transformation of local food production. In 2016 the Food Security Council convinced the city government to remove barriers to raising produce for sale within city limits, and SAHA committed to providing $250,000 and a seven-acre piece of land on the east side for a micro-farm operation. The SAHA project holds the potential to be a cutting-edge site, but it also potentially reinforces existing economic inequalities. In the original conception of the micro-farm, with little to no community input, SAHA planned for it to be a Community Supported Agriculture (CSA) operation, selling food to those who could afford locally produced, organic produce, eggs, chickens, and goats. The SAHA sustainability officer proposed a fence around the seven-acre site located in a poor community and food desert populated almost entirely by Latinos and African Americans. SAHA identified its potential customers as those living on the city's more prosperous north side and indicated that neighborhood access would be available only to those who paid a premium "membership" price or those whom more affluent community members "adopted." My students and I generated a different model that integrated the community into the micro-farm, primarily through an asset-based development model; as of this writing, the originally proposed model was being modified to incorporate more active community participation.[22]

Like many community gardeners and food-justice advocates, we expended considerable time and energy writing grant applications to subsidize the creation of jobs in the gardens, offer market options, develop food hubs, launch farmers' markets, and stimulate other programs to produce economic benefits for the community. While well-meaning, these ideas literally and discursively reinforce the very neo-liberal policies that have wrought havoc on these communities. The focus on generating income and economic activity, as well as providing jobs through community farming and farmers' markets, abides by the rules determined by the mandates of ruthless capitalism rather than sustainability, compassion, and care.[23] While for many community-farming advocates a rhetoric of self-reliance through labor may emanate from their readings of Ralph Waldo Emerson and Wendell Berry, the language of labor and individual responsibility potentially reinforces the neo-liberal organization of the world between those who "work" and those who "don't." Alison Hope Alkon and Teresa Marie Mares summarize this ideological minefield effectively in their article "Food Sovereignty in US Food Systems: Radical Visions and Neoliberal Constraints,"[24] arguing:

> Neighborhood residents are not envisioned as citizen-activists capable of forc-
> ing concessions from the state, nor are they and their families a unified group
> of the working class who could potentially unite and transform an economic
> system that has so thoroughly marginalized their community. Instead, they
> are generally constructed as potential entrepreneurs, who, through involve-
> ment in local food systems, can devise new ways to improve their economic
> livelihoods and provide services for their communities, or as consumers of
> their services. Alternately, some residents, particularly youth, *are* conceptual-
> ized as activists, though their activism is limited to changing their own eating
> habits in favor of local organic food, gardening, and educating their communi-
> ties to do the same.[25]

The ideology of self-reliance postulates that individuals bear primary responsibility for flawed policies and structural economic injustice, while it also asserts that those same individuals and communities most harmed by socially destructive policies that shred the safety net, suppress wages, and limit economic mobility can, through their labor on urban farms, improve society as well as their own standing within it. One powerful critique of community farming asserts that by facilitating individual adjustment to neo-liberal policies under the mantra of community organizing and social change, community farming precludes more radical agendas, achieving structural economic and political change; it also puts the burden of dealing with flawed government and economic policy on the already overburdened shoulders of those targeted by these policies. These activists can become culpable for facilitating neo-liberal policies while setting distressed communities up for failure. Community farming activists must understand the broader and complex socio-political landscape in which they and their ideas operate so their efforts to produce food do not reinforce structural violence and inequality.

While attempting to reform society and serve community needs, those working in this area also need to make a living. Community farmers struggle to survive economically, much less to prosper. The movement attracts many idealistic young people, but the difficulties inherent in maintaining these operations often lead to raised plots overgrown with weeds, un-harvested food rotting in plots, and limited distribution of food and marketing as a result of strained circumstances. City Slicker Farms in Oakland, California, provides a good example of this tension. Well-known as a model for community farming and highly successful in its efforts to produce food and educate the community on health and food-justice issues, in 2011 the organization produced 9,000 pounds of food in its public gardens and estimated that the backyard gardening it teaches and manages generated approximately 23,000 pounds that same year. Its money problems have persisted, however. Rebecca Solnit notes, the "food is great, the community relations seem to be thriving, and yet the project faces the same problem so many people in the neighborhood do: money. They have to raise it, there is never enough, and there is no self-sufficiency in sight for the staff of seven and the public farms, whose food is sold at farm-stands on a sliding scale from free to full price. Since they're farming community and skills and hope as much as lettuce, there's no way to put a price on what they produce."[26] When high-profile farms such as City Slicker struggle, it becomes difficult to imagine the success of a community farm from conception to thriving, full-fledged community partner. Because urban farms are so often idealistic in nature and are designed to correct social problems, they offer free food, sliding-scale prices, and other measures that, while popular, undercut their capacity to generate profits and succeed economically.

In an effort to survive or prosper, many community farmers and food-justice advocates turn to foundations, government agencies, and other non-profits for funding support. There are a number of philanthropists willing to invest their capital in these projects. Organizations such as the Nathan Cummings Foundation, the Kresge Foundation, and the Susan and Michael Dell Foundation, for example, offer grants for community farming, food education, childhood health, climate-change preparation, and related issues. These grants can provide large infusions of capital, but they also require a high level of accountability, metrics collection, and analysis of both participation and impact. Grants are also highly competitive; they require expertise to apply for, to manage when they are secured, and to regularly prepare for and respond to required audits. Applicants must also be aware that these foundations and their donors are reflective of the financial rewards awaiting those who have succeeded in the current economy. They are deeply embedded in the US political economy or, if critics of it, they may seek adjustments at its margins but not radical, structural change at its core. Those calling for greater social transformation in their grant applications might find themselves shortchanged. If successful, whatever funding flows to the applicant-organization may generate a level of dependence on the funding sources. That dependence may cause a moderating of rhetoric and even goals as community farmers strive to negotiate the biases and assumptions of wealthy donors and philanthropies. This reinforces the earlier argument that community farming may merely mitigate the extremes of neo-liberal economic practices. Worn out by paperwork, math, and learning the language of foundations and businesses, community farmers can lose sight of their more radical goals in launching these projects and become captured by a hegemonic discourse of capitalism, jobs creation, entrepreneurship, and self-reliance. This limits the ability of community farms to serve as sites of radical change.

While generating enough income to be self-sufficient and serve the community is a persistent problem for urban farms, they also suffer from the popular perception that they cannot generate enough food to offset industrial agricultural production. This brings up a crucial issue—it is essential for community farming to function as a form of environmental protest through the production of significant amounts of locally grown food. The linchpin of yield connects the ideas of change wrapped up in community farming to the actual changes that may occur and that may radically restructure Americans' relationship with nature, land-use policies in rural areas, urban health, and community strength.

One clear example of the ability of communities to produce food is the fact that 40 percent of domestically consumed food during World War II was grown in American Victory Gardens. Another example is what happened during the blockade of Sarajevo in 1992: urban food production there increased from 10 percent to an estimated 40 percent of vegetables and small livestock. Shanghai and Beijing currently grow upward of 80 percent of the produce consumed there, and Dar es Salaam, Tanzania, garners 60 percent of its milk from city dairy production and 90 percent of its leafy vegetables from local production.[27] More recent studies suggest that the agricultural productive capacity in US metropolitan areas is fairly strong. In a study of Cleveland, Ohio's, ability to become self-sustaining, the authors concluded that if the city used all available vacant lots, based on a low-yield projection it could produce 22 percent of its vegetables, fruit, eggs, honey, and poultry.

If rooftops and hydroponic operations were brought into the mix, then Cleveland could produce 100 percent of its vegetable, fruit, and honey needs and approach that percentage in poultry.[28] A study of Oakland, California's, ability to achieve food independence is less sanguine but still suggests that community farming can be a reliable method to improve community health and autonomy and offset industrial agricultural production.[29] Evaluating the productive capacity of vacant lots and underutilized public land in the city against the recommended intake of vegetables, fruits, and other products rather than against the average existing consumption level, as other studies commonly do, the authors concluded that maximum production would reach approximately 13 percent of the recommended intake based on high-yield production on available land. Using current consumption as the baseline, the high-yield projection suggests that 40 percent of these foods could be produced on available public land in Oakland.

The study of food production in Oakland, California, did not incorporate a full-use model, as did the analysis of potential food production in Cleveland. The Oakland analysis may be a more realistic assessment of what is possible in terms of yield and acquiring space for farming, at least in the short term. That said, even using the lower-yield conclusions from the Oakland study, it is clear that cities have the capacity to produce significant amounts of food. That being true, then successful urban farms would have a spin-off effect, encouraging the incorporation of additional sites like rooftops, lawns, and private lands into production.

Community farming provides the means for a potentially radical reorientation of the relationship between city and country. Meaningful food production in urban areas and small towns would also enable rural acreage to be returned to habitat use and to be used for mitigation of and adaptation to climate change. Biologist Edward O. Wilson's recent proposal that half of the earth be set aside for the natural world, while seemingly outlandish, could be achieved with a growing community-farming movement.[30] A good example of such a process of returning land to nature is the Buffalo Commons project, in which the focus is to return Great Plains lands currently producing commodities such as wheat, hay, and cattle to short-grass prairie on which the keystone species—bison—could roam. A nation of cities able to produce half or more of its food would undercut arguments that the landscape is required for industrial production of foodstuffs.

Just as community farming builds economic and cultural resilience, it also strengthens ecological resilience by creating microhabitats. These small operations of a few plots and trees support pollinators such as butterflies, moths, and bees as well as other bugs. Songbirds, dragonflies, and frogs in these ecosystems help prevent a Silent Spring brought about by climate change. The increasingly common larger farms, like the several-acre City Slicker operation, support species listed above, raptors, small mammals, and any number of reptiles and amphibians. As new farms are started and existing ones grow, an urban greenscape will provide deeper and more complex ecosystem resilience. It will benefit migratory bird species as well.

Community farming might also help combat a key area of ecological decline—the eutrophication of the oceans. Eutrophication results from the deposition of the runoff of high amounts of phosphates and nitrates, largely from industrial, commercial agriculture operations such as corn farming and livestock feedlots, as well as from heavily fertilized lawns and golf courses. Coastal waters at the points where rivers enter the oceans around the world are now regular hypoxic zones, essentially dead of life. One of the best-known examples is the "dead zone" at the mouth of the Mississippi River, which carries heavy volumes of nutrients from agriculture, livestock operations, and lawns to the Gulf of Mexico. This zone averages over 5,000 square miles when it grows every summer, and in 2015 it exploded to more than 6,500 square miles.[31] With less than two-parts-per-million dissolved oxygen, nothing can live in this vast marine-scape. While this is the most dramatic dead zone on the coasts of the United States, these hypoxic zones are common, and collectively they reduce the viability and health of ocean ecosystems. These problems are also found in inland freshwater lakes, ponds, and streams. Community farming, following best practices of composting and fertilizing with organic material, will reduce the pollution that causes hypoxic zones. As this form of farming helps restore the capacity of oceans to sustain aquatic life, it may also help offset deterioration from climate change. Acidification of the oceans as a result of the warming of waters and increased carbon load is an unfolding process that is going to get much worse. A crucial mitigation and adaptation strategy, in the face of national and even global unwillingness to limit greenhouse gas emissions, is to repair ecosystems where possible. Removing pollutants from freshwater and the oceans to reduce eutrophication and improve ecosystem health represents a key resilience practice.

Hunger and lack of access to healthy food are issues that haunted our society prior to the Anthropocene, and community farming is a community-based tool that can be employed to address those injustices. Climate-change resilience for vulnerable communities necessitates local food production. Therefore, community farming constitutes an important resilience strategy. But feeding those in need and unjustly punished by a neo-liberal society is only one piece of the food-justice puzzle. It is also possible to enact long-term structural change for workers in the industrial agricultural complex and those removed from their land as a result of neo-liberal policies such as dam construction, land enclosure, and imported, subsidized crops. Farmers forced from their land would be able to put their skills to use in urban areas and villages close to home or even in countries to which they emigrate.

A robust, growing community-farming movement can reduce the impact of neo-liberal policies on international communities. As people grow food and consume it locally, the likelihood of their purchasing produce from distant economies diminishes. Community farming that includes active education about climate change and food-justice issues can convince a larger segment of the population to shop and consume locally. The drying up of the revenue stream into international agricultural conglomerates that benefit from neo-liberal policies and poor treatment of workers has the potential to engender the type of significant long-term structural change that has not been accomplished by activism and protest to this point. The power of producing food locally has great potential for change, but education and activism beyond simple locavorism are crucial.

As noted earlier, much of the change envisioned here, and the goal of much food-justice activism, is predicated on a growing movement and substantial yields. Similarly, the long-lasting impact of community farming is also contingent on radical changes in patterns of consumption. As community farmers and food-justice advocates need to focus on ordinances and legislation that support the movement and target food-justice issues, so, too, is it necessary to use these spaces to educate Americans on changing consumption patterns in a manner that undermines industrial agriculture and neo-liberalism while supporting local economies and food production. Teaching the food-justice and climate-change impacts of buying Chilean blueberries in January (or ever) while offering classes on how to preserve locally grown blackberries, strawberries, blueberries, or whatever is relevant to that region provides clear actions that have ramifications across the world, ecosystems, and the atmosphere. Sustained education and an analysis of food economies that show local solutions represent a clear path forward. Demonstrating how consuming community-grown foods rather than corn or potatoes from an industrial agricultural business in a rural area helps mitigate climate change by reducing fossil-fuel–based greenhouse gas emissions and contributes to climate-change adaptation and resilience by opening up former agricultural lands in rural American to habitat restoration and carbon sequestration can help drive behavioral change as well. But it remains crucial for community farm advocates to clearly explain the linkages between local food production and consumption that incorporate broad structural change.

Philosopher Richard Rorty offers crucial insights into how community farming can function as protest and create a revitalization of American democracy.[32] He argues that small-scale local protest is crucial in energizing democracy. Real change that makes society more democratic is found in citizens getting their hands dirty by cultivating urban farms, challenging the sources of local air and water pollution, pushing ordinances to ban plastic bags, and fighting to restore or preserve local habitat. Rorty also notes the active political role played by the academic left in the first half of the twentieth century and asserts that academics need to take up that mantle again, providing leadership and guidance and doing the hard work of organizing, lobbying, and crafting legislation.

If community farmers are going to transform their neighborhoods and their health while improving the world, they need to move beyond Voltaire's advice to tend our own gardens and frame food production as protest.[33] For these farms to function as sites of dialogue and resistance and not as retreats or signs of resignation, the community farming community must push for supportive local, state, and federal ordinances, policies, laws, and land planning programs to create a vast community-farming system. Farmers and activists need to convince the state to protect urban farms from development and unreasonable taxation, prevent and limit gentrification in community farming neighborhoods, and provide subsidies for urban farm products to make prices low enough for the very poor as well as arrange mechanisms for distribution.

Even as we discuss the means to correct problems arising from ideology, flawed policies, and inequity, climate change is bringing a chaos and an unpredictability for which we are unprepared. Climate change, properly understood, induces despair; it is accurately described as a wicked problem. The consequences of non-action are devastating, and the impacts that are unstoppable will be catastrophic. Despair and fear create pessimistic inaction, an inability to see how to act or to believe that local action can accomplish anything meaningful. Regulatory mechanisms are needed, increased taxation and investing in alternative energy production and storage are needed, government-mandated and enforced limits on pollution are needed. Activism on the local level alone is not enough, but it can accomplish much more than many people assume.

Imagine, then, college students working with younger children to place ladybugs on tomato plant leaves. Or watch the large hands of the basketball team's power forward guide the tiny hands of a young girl as they dig a hole in the bed, insert a tomato plant, and then fill in the soil around its roots. At moments like these, professors, administrators, students ages three to twenty-five, schoolteachers, and parents join in something fundamental and hopeful, the breaking of the soil for plants, the nurturing of gardens to promote health and life. Maybe hope is also a ladybug or a bright red jalapeno pepper waiting for eager hands to touch and hold it. Through this communion of labor and sweat equity, each person helps construct a new kind of community, human and natural. In so doing, they forge relationships across boundaries that have limited social cohesion. What makes these spaces radical, with meaning created by labor and dialogue, is the very real possibility of subverting the hegemonic discourse about race, environment, class, and climate change. Discussions of food justice, environmental justice, economic equity, and climate-change resilience may lead to the creation of ideas and solutions not mediated by "common-sense" voices, grant-funding agencies, and government entities. In that space, "radical" ideas about turning cities into centers of food production challenge the dominance of the industrial agriculture economy. With the potential to affect so many aspects of our economy, society, and environment, community farming might turn out to be the most important, most durable form of environmental protest.

Notes

1. I choose here to use the term *community farming* for a few reasons. Use of the term *gardening* suggests something less than serious intent and labor, hence my

preferred use of *farming*. The term *urban farming* neglects efforts such as the Diné Food Sovereignty Alliance and local food production efforts in rural areas that also struggle with food deserts and food-justice issues. *Community farming* as a term captures rural and urban communities while denoting that these are serious efforts to produce healthy food and even food autonomy.

2. Adam Rome indicates the turning point as the opposition to a national land-use law co-sponsored by Republican president Richard Nixon and Washington State Democratic senator Henry Jackson. See Rome, *The Bulldozer in the Countryside: Suburban Sprawl and the Rise of American Environmentalism* (New York: Cambridge University Press, 2001).

3. Wendell Berry, *The Gift of Good Land: Further Essays Cultural and Agricultural* (Berkeley: North Point, 1981), chapter 9.

4. Rebecca Solnit, "Revolutionary Plots," *Orion Magazine*, July–August 2012, accessed August 17, 2018, https://orionmagazine.org/article/revolutionary-plots/.

5. "Shocking Need: American Kids Go Hungry," ABC News, August 24, 2011, accessed December 20, 2016, https://abcnews.go.com/US/hunger_at_home/hunger-home-american-children-malnourished/story?id=14367230.

6. Nathan McClintock, "Radical, Reformist, and Garden-Variety Neoliberal: Coming to Terms with Urban Agriculture's Contradictions," *Local Environment* 14, no. 2 (2014): 147–71; Green Cities, Good Health Website, University of Washington, accessed August 17, 2018, http://depts.washington.edu/hhwb/; Leo Horrigan, Robert S. Lawrence, and Polly Walker, "How Sustainable Agriculture Can Address the Environmental and Human Health Harms of Industrial Agriculture," *Environmental Health Perspectives* 110, no. 5 (May 2002): 445–56.

7. Anne C. Bellows, Katherine Brown, and Jac Smit, "Health Benefits of Urban Agriculture," Community Wealth.Org, 2004, accessed August 18, 2018, https://community-wealth.org/content/health-benefits-urban-agriculture; Katherine Alaimo, Elizabeth Packnett, Richard A. Miles, and Daniel J. Kruger, "Fruit and Vegetable Intake among Urban Community Gardeners," *Journal of Nutrition Education and Behavior* 40, no. 2 (March–April 2005): 94–101; Kate H. Brown and Andrew L. Jameton, "Public Health Implications of Urban Agriculture," *Journal of Public Health Policy* 21, no. 1 (March 2000): 20–39.

8. Farmworker Justice, "US Department of Labor Enforcement in Agriculture: More Must Be Done to Protect Farmworkers Despite Recent Improvements," 2015, accessed December 14, 2016, farmworkerjustice.org/sites/default/files/Farmwork erJusticeDOLenforcementReport2015%20%281%29.pdf.

9. "Fields of Peril: Child Labor in US Agriculture," Human Rights Watch, 2009, accessed February 7, 2017, https://www.hrw.org/report/2010/05/05/fields-peril

/child-labor-us-agriculture; Philip Martin and Douglas B. Jackson-Smith, "Immigration and Farm Labor in the US," National Agricultural and Rural Development Policy Center, Brief 4, May 2013; "Inventory of Farmworker Issues and Protections in the United States," Bon Appetít Management Company and United Farm Workers (April 13, 2011), accessed February 7, 2017, https://www.oxfamamerica.org/explore/research-publications/inventory-of-farmworker-issues-and-protections-in-the-united-states/.

10. Thomas Fuller, "In a California Valley Healthy Food Everywhere But on the Table," *New York Times*, November 23, 2016, accessed August 19, 2018, https://www.nytimes.com/2016/11/23/us/in-a-california-valley-healthy-food-everywhere-but-on-the-table.html.

11. Fuller, "In a California Valley Healthy Food Everywhere But on the Table."

12. Amalia Laborde, Fernando Tomasino, Fabrizio Bianchi, Marie-Noel Bruné, Irena Buka, Pietro Comba, Lillian Corra, Lilliana Corri, Christin Maria Duffert, Raul Harrari et al., "Children's Health in Latin America: The Influence of Environmental Exposures," *Environmental Health Perspectives* 123, no. 3 (March 2015): 201–9; Fabrizio González-Andrade, Ramiro López-Pulles, and Edmundo Estévez, "Acute Pesticide Poisoning in Ecuador: A Short Epidemiological Report," *Journal of Public Health* 18, no. 5 (October 2010): 437–42; Amalai Cecchi, Maria Gabriella Rovedatti, G. Sabino, and Gladis Magnarelli, "Environmental Exposure to Organophosphate Pesticides: Assessment of Endocrine Disruption and Hepatoxicity in Pregnant Women," *Ecotoxicology and Environmental Safety* 80 (June 2012): 280–87.

13. Amy Padnani, "Anatomy of Detroit's Decline," *New York Times*, August 17, 2013, accessed August 17, 2018, https://www.nytimes.com/interactive/2013/08/17/us/detroit-decline.html?_r=0; Scott Martelle, "The Collapse of Detroit: Deindustrialization, Racism, Stagnation—Is the Motor City Our Future?" *Los Angeles Times*, March 27, 2011; Monica M. White, "D-Town Farm: African American Resistance to Food Insecurity and the Transformation of Detroit," *Environmental Practice* 13, no. 4 (December 2011): 406–17; Amanda Lewan, "The Business of Community Farming Takes Root," *Entrepreneur*, December 2, 2014, accessed December 5, 2016, https://entrepreneur.com/article/239844.

14. Keep Growing Detroit Website, accessed December 9, 2016, detroitagriculture.net.

15. Grown in Detroit Website, accessed December 5, 2016, http://detroitagriculture.net/farms-and-markets/grown-in-detroit/.

16. Taylor Killough, "Detroit Grows First Urban 'Agrihood,'" *Earth Eats*, Indiana Public Media, December 21, 2016, accessed August 17, 2018, https://indianapublic media.org/eartheats/Detroit-grows-urban-agrihood.

17. White, "D-Town Farm," 411.

18. Roger Bybee, "Growing Power in an Urban Food Forest," *Yes! Magazine*, February 13, 2009, accessed February 22, 2016, www.yesmagazine.org/issues/food -for-everyone/growing-power-in-an-urban-food-desert; Karen Herzog and Lee Bergquist, "A Will and a Way for Allen: MacArthur Grant Aids Urban Farmer's Quest to Bring Fresh Food to Inner City," *Milwaukee-Wisconsin Journal Sentinel*, October 6, 2008, accessed February 2, 2016, https://www.jsonline.com/news/mil waukee/32467114.html.

19. Growing Power Website, accessed November 10, 2016, http://www.growing power.org/.

20. Growing Power Website; WGNTV, accessed November 11, 2016, wgntv.com /2016/11/30/mobile-food-trucks-bring-fresh-produce-to-underserved-neighbor hoods.

21. Alfonso Morales, "Growing Food *and* Justice: Dismantling Racism through Sustainable Food Systems," in *Cultivating Food Justice: Race, Class, Sustainability*, ed. Alison Hope Alkon and Julian Ageyman (Cambridge, MA: MIT Press, 2011), 156–57.

22. Sue Calberg, "Sprawling Urban Garden Coming to San Antonio's East Side," KENS5 News, February 9, 2017, accessed June 5, 2017, https://www.kens5.com /news/community/sprawling-urban-garden-coming-to-san-antonios-east-side /406663819.

23. McClintock, "Radical, Reformist, and Garden-Variety Neoliberal"; Alison Hope Alkon and Teresa Marie Mares, "Food Sovereignty in US Food Systems: Radical Visions and Neoliberal Constraints," *Agriculture and Human Values* 29, no. 3 (September 2012): 347–59.

24. Alkon and Mares, "Food Sovereignty in US Food Systems."

25. Alkon and Mares, "Food Sovereignty in US Food Systems," 355, original emphasis.

26. Solnit, "Revolutionary Plots," 7.

27. Sharanbir S. Grewal and Parwinder S. Grewal, "Can Cities Become Self-Reliant in Food?" *Cities* 29, no. 1 (February 2012): 1–11.

28. Grewal and Grewal, "Can Cities Become Self-Reliant?"

29. Horrigan, Lawrence, and Walker, "How Sustainable Agriculture Can Address the Environmental and Human Health Harms of Industrial Agriculture."

30. Edward O. Wilson, *Half-Earth: Our Planet's Fight for Life* (New York: Liveright, 2016).

31. "2015 Gulf of Mexico Dead Zone 'Above Average,' Heavy June Rains, High July Nutrient Runoff Levels Likely Cause for Increased Size," August 4, 2014, accessed December 27, 2016, http://www.noaanews.noaa.gov/stories2015/080415-gulf-of-mexico-dead-zone-above-average.html.

32. Richard Rorty, *Achieving Our Country: Leftist Thought in Twentieth-Century America* (Cambridge, MA: Harvard University Press, 1999).

33. Voltaire, Candide (New York: The Modern Library, 1930), 148.

11

Building Sustainable Communities in Los Angeles

Intersections of Worker Power and Environmental Justice

ANNA J. KIM AND SOPHIA CHENG

The worker is a clear player in new definitions of environmental justice. The worker is an instrumental part of the production process (the conversion of natural resources for human consumption), and in the example of the food chain described by Robert Gottlieb, the worker is present at all stages: production, processing, retail, and service. Definitions of "sustainability" must include workers' rights and protections that allow for a healthy life—one in which workers are sustained mentally, physically, and emotionally without feeling pressed or stretched thin. Ultimately, a sustainable life is one in which workers can, as one worker-activist stated so succinctly, not just survive but truly live and thrive.

Solutions in environmental-justice literature have been characterized by movement on two levels—through redistribution, just moving stuff around (in this case, stuff being polluting environmental factors)—and through some form of procedural change (either legislative or policies) that would work to mitigate current conditions or be preventative. Environmentalism, as a broad category that also includes the civil rights struggle for environmental

DOI: 10.5876/9781607328483.c011

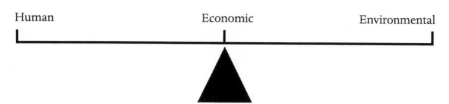

Human   Economic   Environmental

FIGURE 11.1. Three scales of justice

justice, initially focused on distributive inequalities and redistribution as solutions for injustice. For example, Bunyon Bryant writes: "Whereas the term environmental racism focuses on the disproportionate impact of environmental hazards on communities of color, environmental justice is focused on ameliorating potentially life-threatening conditions or on improving the overall quality of life for the poor and/or people of color. Environmental racism is based on problem identification; environmental justice is based on problem solving."[1]

Thus, environmental justice seeks both "justice as fairness" and justice as "mutual respect . . . owed to human beings as moral persons."[2] Drawing from restaurant workers' experiences, this chapter argues for a third level that not only engages policy but moves toward economic restructuring—some dismantling of market-based capitalism and its environmentally harmful products (figure 11.1).

As Laura Pulido reminds us, with the example of Exide Technologies pollution and the company's persistent and deliberate lack of compliance, the costs of doing business are not uniformly passed on to the environment; they are passed on to the environment of the Latino working class because class inequality is a racialized process. It is thus the case that "multiple forms of hierarchy and difference articulate in southern California to create a community that is subject to deliberate and extreme forms of environmental racism."[3]

This connection enters into debates about the right to the city and daily life, as scholars and community leaders in the environmental-justice movement attribute location and spatial processes as their own producer of injustices by race, class, and gender. The increased interest in location is also a causal factor that reemphasizes the notion of scale—or the idea that justice (and injustice) operates at multiple scales in both the city and the region, locally and globally. There has always been tension between moving people and moving place, and herein we argue that the threats to both must be considered simultaneously—especially under a new type of eco-capitalism that may seek to improve the place while also indirectly resulting in the displacement of people into even poorer environmental conditions.

In line with a tradition of expanding notions of environmental inequality and environmental justice, as demonstrated by historic campaigns and victories in Los Angeles, we believe the question of sustainability should be considered at these three different scales of analysis. One scale is the environment itself (what happens at "the place" of interaction, both at home and at work). A second scale is conceived at the individual/human level and involves developing an understanding of the impacts of harmful conditions or toxic chemical exposure on the worker's body. Finally, the third scale gives equal weight to how economic sustainability, or lack thereof, compounds environmental inequality. Sustainability for workers includes, at a minimum, protection from environmental harms in the workplace, as well as fair pay, benefits, and vigorous enforcement of workplace rights so workers can increase their access to health insurance and medical care, green spaces and healthy food, and healthy homes and neighborhoods.

Definition of a Sustainable Community

Environmental and workers' rights movements, organized around a broad definition of "sustainability," combine the power of two distinct yet intertwined movements. In Los Angeles, a number of grassroots organizing and wage theft policy campaigns have raised questions such as: What are our human resources? How do we understand resource scarcity and threats to workers' health? What does a livable community for low-wage immigrant workers and people of color look like in an increasingly unequal urban environment? Wage theft is the non-payment of wages and money owed to workers for labor they have performed, exacerbating economic insecurity and the urgency of these questions.

A sustainable community means, at its heart, understanding the interconnectedness of the urban and the rural, the human and the environmental, the social and the natural. And it is important to not just identify the links between paradigms but also to begin to understand problems of inequality within them as symptoms of problems of the ecosystem; "like much else in the contemporary world, the environment is socially differentiated and unevenly available."[4]

Literature on environmental racism has examined the question of "who moves" and how people of color in particular are disproportionately located next to waste facilities, highways, factories, and other polluting entities. As poor people and people of color are increasingly affected by urban gentrification and often forced to the edges of counties and suburbs with even higher rates of poverty and poorer air quality[5] (San Bernardino County, Center for Community Action and Environmental Justice), how do we ensure access to health services, a living wage, and educational opportunities that lead to access to healthier occupations? How to we ensure a right to healthy places?

Overall, cities are changing, in many ways for the better—streamlining waste processing, educating the public about the benefits of public transportation, creating smaller housing footprints, and developing policy movements for living wages in San Francisco and Los Angeles. And yet cities are becoming even more difficult to access for poor residents, resulting in peoples' articulations of the right to stay, the right to grow, the right to change along with cities, and the right to redefine neighborhood and environmental sustainability.

This chapter proposes that environmental justice should articulate the relationship among labor, capital, and space to include workers' rights and human quality of life in the definition of "sustainability." As a case study, we examine the Los Angeles policy campaign against wage theft to understand the disproportionate environmental burdens, proximity to sites of work (labor), proximity to leisure and consumption (green space and fresh food), the right to physical movement (transportation), and, more recently, the "right to the city" as a part of what environmental justice means for the poor and disenfranchised: "We believe that all communities should have access to fresh whole foods, clean and safe open spaces, and a quality environment. Our organization is committed to addressing health disparities through community development that is not only culturally relevant, but also builds the capacity of individuals to make healthy decisions in their personal lives."[6]

The Pivotal Moment: Distributional Inequality, the Right to the City, and the Bus Riders Union

The struggle for environmental justice (EJ) became more and more inherently spatial because it questioned the reasons and ways certain spaces were unequally created, maintained, and experienced. EJ critiques have evolved today into an understanding that the causal factors of difference do not necessarily lead to a solution to environmental (or other) inequalities as they occur in their spatially diffuse forms.[7] The "Right to the City" is one such movement that involves not just the siting of polluting entities and burdens of environmental inequality but also people's rights to inhabit all spaces equally, overcome spatial segregation, and have equal access to good spaces as well as bad (process and product in one).[8]

Environmental racism helped people understand racism and the spatiality of racism, which means that racism is not a single act but instead is part of sociospatial relationships both constitutive of the city and produced by it: "In any attempt to understand racism, scale is an important analytical tool in that it is both defined by racism and transcends it. Consider the various scales at which racism exists: the individual, the group, the institution, society, the global."[9] Robert Brulle and David Pellow state, many processes and practices need to work together to create a more just and sustainable society—among them, popular epidemiology, the precautionary principle, and policy changes—for to "understand and develop meaningful measures to mitigate ecological degradation, this analysis begins with the development of a theoretical perspective on the social processes by which these problems originate."[10]

Theories of locational discrimination can be traced to the concept of urban space as a site for social justice, as has been debated by many scholars across disciplines. David Harvey dedicates time to a genealogy and geography of "uneven development" across different places. The question of uneven development and locational inequality, as discussed by Harvey, is also a question of scale, wherein the choice to use local or global scales of comparison resulted in drastically different pictures of the degree of inequality: "The geographical landscape which results is not evenly developed but strongly differentiated. 'Difference' and 'otherness' are produced in space through the simple logic of uneven capital investment . . . and the rise of spatially ordered, often segregated social distinctions."[11]

The First National People of Color Summit for Environmental Justice was a groundbreaking event that enabled many organizations to successfully win campaigns. More important, the work of those diverse but coalesced groups reflected the link between locational inequalities and social inequalities and vice versa. A more spatial and place-based perspective has continued to take shape, including the Los Angeles–based campaign that developed out of the Bus Riders Union in the late 1990s. The Second National People of Color Summit for Environmental Justice in 2002 very closely referenced the work of the Labor/Community Strategy Center (LCSC) and the mobilization of transit riders in the city. The second summit centered on transportation justice and reflected the emergence of a more spatial focus than the environmental-justice movement had previously shown.

The Bus Riders Union is an example of a campaign that occurred at a multi-scalar level, not only taking on local issues of urban (spatial) injustice but linking broader access to "public goods" with environmental issues and global economic and environmental forces. Moreover, the fact that the center is self-described as a "civil rights group *on wheels*" points to its spatial mobility—like its constituents, the Bus Riders Union (BRU), as an organization, moves from place to place (and neighborhood to neighborhood) along with the bus passengers.

"It's a progressive civil rights group on wheels," said Eric Mann, veteran organizer and founder and executive director of the project. "We deal with what we call 'the totality of people's lives.' Our main issue might be public transportation and the environment, but we're also involved in global warming and international conditions."[12]

While the BRU did have a localized focus on environmental inequality and the burdens of limited access for residents, the organization focused on mobility and movement throughout Los Angeles in addition to air quality in Wilmington, California, thereby demonstrating how environmental inequality followed residents *through* space and limited people's ability to attend school, find a job, and travel to work. In this conceptualization of environmental justice, place is as dynamic and changeable as people are. And so an important solution to environmental racism emerged, one that focused not just on distributional inequality or locational inequality but on the impact of both.

Right to the City as an organized movement that emerged in the 2000s out of a loosely based coalition of environmental-justice groups is influencing debates at academic and community levels. Currently, the groups in the coalition include the Miami Workers Center, CAAAV—Organizing Asian Communities (formerly known as the Committee against Anti-Asian Violence), Strategic Actions for a Just Economy (SAJE) in Los Angeles, and the Labor/Community Strategy Center and Bus Riders Union. These groups represent labor-, housing-, environmental-, economic-, and transportation-based justice struggles that have historically worked primarily on the local scale but that see the impact of unequal access, environmental degradation, suburban poverty, and their relationship to displacement happening in cities across the world.[13]

Environmental-justice scholars have traced a theory that looks across and between spaces of production and consumption, a production and consumption process that invariably has also reproduced inequality across multiple scales of the environment. In particular, the work of these spatially oriented scholars has studied the economic/environmental nexus, or how industrial chains of production create and produce pollution that unduly impacts working-class groups and communities of color. Andrew Hurley theorizes a race-conscious "working-class environmentalism" in which "one's place in the social and economic hierarchy prove[s] a reliable predictor of one's ability to advance and secure a set of environmental objectives."[14] Drawing from a case study in Gary, Indiana, during the 1960s and 1970s, Hurley argues that a coalition of environmentalists, labor unions, and civil rights groups was successful in mitigating white residents' exposure to pollution, but ultimately, the environmental burden was shifted to black workers and families who were blocked by discriminatory hiring and housing practices from moving into healthier jobs and homes.

Pellow highlights the impact of waste production on waste workers, an important part of the "post-production" process that is often left out of examinations of the impact of waste sites on communities.[15] Pellow points out the irony that recycling facilities, ostensibly dedicated to cleaning and greening the environment, create their own hazards for the workers who recycle the garbage and the residents who live next to these facilities. Labor and laborers are an integral part of each step in the production process and are notable even in the post-industrial, non-manufacturing economy of the West.[16] While the phrase *tech worker* may conjure visions of a programmer working from the comfort of an office, Pellow and Lisa Sun-Hee Park foreground the other tech workers—immigrant laborers subject to chemical exposure while making semiconductor chips.

Beyond Space: Eco-Capitalism and Wage Theft

The spatial turn in environmental-justice movements was very important to demonstrate distributional inequality, but we also understand now that there is more to environmental inequality than causality, siting, and spatial patterns. The metrics for what scholars and activists understand as environmental injustice include housing, income, transportation, food, production, processing, and more: "Environmental inequalities are constituted by more than spatial patterns of proximity and exposure . . . it is necessary to distinguish between inequality and injustice and to reason carefully about why an inequality matters and to whom."[17] Social inequality and environmental inequality are linked processes, and the outcomes of each are tied to race and ethnicity, segregation, wealth, and household income. There is particularly strong evidence showing these "social factors" as significantly connected to poor air and water quality.[18]

Environmental-justice scholars have adapted multiple social indexes, such as the dissimilarity index (which quantifies segregation between racial groups), to measure the disproportionate exposure to ambient air pollution,[19] heat-risk–related land cover,[20] and exposure to air toxics.[21] There are other key factors to consider when linking the social with the economic with the environmental: the top ten corporate air polluters (companies with the highest Risk-Screening Environmental Indicator toxic scores) were responsible for "11% of the total human health risks from industrial air toxics in the United States in 2005."[22]

Consider to whom it matters whether production processes (and products sold) are seen as "green," healthy, and sustainable. Who has the power to make choices about which part of the production process is important and what elements define that process as sustainable? Jenny Price writes about the transition to an era in which "environmental justice" is increasingly related to consumption and consumer spending.[23] Eco-branding (or "eco-frenzy") has led to a type of market-based environmentalism that often excludes the costs to the worker. Food security in low-income neighborhoods, although rapidly becoming a normative part of discussion among policy scholars and "progressive nutrition scientists," can sometimes also underemphasize cultural relationships with food and presuppose capitalist commodification of foods. While it can be easy to take commodified food for granted, food sovereignty scholars and activists direct attention 'outside the box' to consider food systems built on conceptions of rights rather than on capitalist relations."[24]

As Brulle and Pellow argue, "The two key social dynamics that systematically create environmental inequality are (a) the functioning of the market economy and (b) institutionalized racism."[25] Critics of the eco-frenzy and environmental-justice activists have also translated how a focus on production and consumption must connect the work environment to the restaurant table, where more conscious decisions about how to purchase and consume sustainably produced food are made every day. In their book's critical introduction to how labor and food justice align, Robert Gottlieb and Anupama Joshi state: "From seed to table . . . a food justice framework ensures that the benefits and risks of how food is grown and processed, transported, distributed, and consumed are shared equitably."[26]

Building Sustainability through the Food-Justice Movement

Concerns about how food is prepared should and must extend to the health of the persons preparing and serving it: the Food Chain Workers Alliance found that "due to a lack of sick days provided by employers, more than half (53%) of workers surveyed reporting picking, processing, selling, cooking, and serving food while sick."[27] As a whole, consumers have increased their awareness of what healthy means and what organic food should look like, where food should be grown, and how far it should be transported. The Restaurant Opportunities Center–Los Angeles (ROC-LA) builds on the definition of food justice to ensure that the workers who bring food to our tables every day receive living wages, enforcement of basic workplace laws, and opportunities to participate in healthier communities.

ROC-LA is part of Los Angeles's vibrant movement of low-wage worker organizing and part of a community of nonprofit and labor organizations serving and amplifying the concerns of low-wage workers. These groups are organized along as well as across ethnicity, gender, and industry lines—for example, they include retail, grocery, domestic, restaurant, carwash, day laborer, garment workers, and more. Collectively, they are part of an on-the-ground grassroots movement for healthier workplaces, enforceable wages and work standards, and neighborhood sustainability. The activists in the Los Angeles Coalition against Wage Theft, described in this chapter's case studies, connect workplace abuses and low wages with housing instability and food insecurity because "for many activists, an ethic of justice was linked to a language of 'rights' and liberation, contending that ecosystems, animals, and people should be free from oppression and harm."[28]

Meanwhile, Los Angeles is also the center of strong environmental movements concerned with wide-ranging issues, including natural preservation, greening the city, conservation, and sustainable consumption, among others. There is also a creative and promising integration of low-wage worker and environmental sustainability movements. For example, in 2012 the Los Angeles Food Policy Council organized the Los Angeles Unified School District to adopt the Good Food Purchasing Policy for its school meals. The policy defines "good food" in terms not only of nutrition but also of its production using ethical labor standards and environmentally sustainable means.[29]

Given the relative power of the labor and environmental movements, more could—and should—be done to integrate low-wage worker and environmental organizing. One way to begin the conversation is to expand the concept of "sustainability" to apply to low-wage workers on a variety of scales—human, economic, and environmental. In the following section, case studies from Los Angeles workers' rights campaigns articulate workers' own connections of the urban with the environmental, their experiences at work, their lives at home, and how their community fights for justice.[30] Workers explain the relationship among decreased incomes (or stolen income in the case of wage theft), reduced time and increased poverty, and unhealthy work environments.

Human, Economic, and Environmental Sustainability: Stories from Los Angeles

Below, we outline some experiences and stories that emerged from recent campaigns to pass Los Angeles city wage enforcement and minimum wage ordinances that highlight the link among the three scales of sustainability—human, economic, and environmental (as linked through the labor of many Los Angeles residents)—and spearheaded by the Los Angeles Coalition against Wage Theft and the Los Angeles Raise the Wage

Coalition. Quotes from public hearings are from the authors' participation in the campaign.

Example 1: Healthy Environments and Healthy Bodies

"I'M NOT A ROBOT."

Our definition of sustainability and the "environment" includes workplace environments. The environmental-justice movement identifies chemical exposure in the home and workplace as a major source of environmental inequity.[31]

The broad definition of "sustainability" that we propose incorporates a concern for an overall healthy life, with protection from premature aches, pains, and workplace injury. While chemical exposure can result in short- and long-term health problems, unhealthiness among low-wage workers results from more than one discrete source, chemical exposure that can be spot-treated (figure 11.2).

The restaurant industry in Los Angeles is the largest in the nation, with almost 300,000 food services and drinking establishment workers.[32] The restaurant industry is the second largest sector of employment among all private non-farm industries, at 9 percent of total private-sector employment in Los Angeles. Few of these workers receive a living wage; the average annual income reported by workers is less than $18,000—compared to a private-sector median of about $50,000.[33] In summary, the industry is growing and generates billions of dollars in sales for the local and state economy, but wages have remained largely unchanged despite continued growth in the sector. In addition, the difference between a "good job" and a "bad job" for restaurant workers is fairly large: most workers reported no health insurance, no paid sick days, and no vacation time.

Restaurant worker members of ROC-LA prepare and cook food for Los Angeles restaurants, yet they often lack access to the type of fresh food that is served on restaurant tables. Environmentally conscious restaurant employers may have access to organic, sustainable ingredients and provide quality meals to consumers, but they do not always facilitate access to these products for their employees. While the food-justice movement has gained popularity in affluent areas of Los Angeles, where there is a high demand for organic, locally sourced, and seasonal produce and food, one of the goals of ROC-LA is to develop consciousness in low-income neighborhoods where

FIGURE 11.2. Healthy food event with Restaurant Opportunities Center, 2012. Photo: Anna Kim.

residents have little to no access to healthy and sustainable food and where the demand for quality food is growing.

And yet, many restaurant workers normalize their unhealthiness because of the industry's widespread lack of medical benefits, as well as limited enforcement of health and safety standards. Many restaurant workers do not expect to have health insurance; many expect their workplaces to be high-stress, hazardous environments because that is the norm. For example, in Los Angeles, nearly 90 percent of restaurant workers lack basic health protections such as health insurance and paid sick days.[34] Unsafe working and living conditions include unsafe worksites, such as overheated kitchens, and inadequate access to medical care. The normalization of unhealthiness through weak workplace protections is even embedded in policy. For example, the California Occupational Safety and Health Administration (Cal/OSHA)/, California's state agency in charge of ensuring workplace health and safety, regulates heat illnesses in the construction and agricultural industries but not the restaurant industry.[35] The only guideline regarding heat for restaurant workers is prevention of burns.[36]

During conversations with restaurant workers regarding the anti–wage theft campaign, workers often shared stories about what was happening at work. Although the focus was on the minimum wage and wage theft, conversations were wide-ranging. Cooks and dishwashers complained about extreme kitchen temperatures upward of 80 degrees, coupled with a lack of air conditioning and proper ventilation.

Some workers joined the campaign after they were injured at work. One restaurant employee had worked for a decade at a well-known brunch spot in a trendy Los Angeles neighborhood. He worked as a cook for sixteen to seventeen hours a day, seventy–eighty hours a week, and suffered wage theft—for a decade, he did not receive breaks or overtime pay. He stressed that the impact was not only economic; it was also physical and mental. "My stomach hurts from years of working without eating or resting," he said. "I can't sleep well because my stomach and joints hurt." He was ultimately forced to file a workers' compensation claim for the chronic pain built up over years of working in extreme temperatures without safety equipment. The journey to resolve his claim led him to reflect on the wage theft that originally drove him to work long hours to offset the low and, at times, unpaid wages.

For many restaurant workers, the need to reform wages and wage enforcement went hand in hand with the need for safer workplaces. Multiple workers expressed, "I'm not a robot," emphasizing the human need to rest and rejuvenate.

Example 2: Linking Workplace Justice to Human Sustainability

"AFTER WORKING TEN HOURS, NO BREAK, YOU GO HOME AND
TRY TO WIND DOWN, BUT YOU CAN'T."

Human sustainability for low-wage workers takes into account workers' physical, mental, and emotional well-being. That is, it takes into account what is literally needed to sustain a person from day to day and year to year. When day laborer worker centers first established the Los Angeles Coalition against Wage Theft (LA-WTC) in 2009, "wage theft" was a foreign concept in the mainstream media.[37] A key goal of the campaign, especially in the years 2014 and 2015, was to define and popularize the concept of "wage theft" building off the success of San Francisco's passage of its city's landmark Wage Theft Prevention Ordinance in 2011.[38]

The LA-WTC identified early on that leveraging "earned media" through creative direct action and protest was critical to build momentum for an anti–wage theft ordinance. Funding limitations (e.g., there was no staff person assigned specifically to the coalition or campaign; instead, the campaign cobbled together the contributions of coalition member organizations) made "earned media" the only option, as paid radio and newspaper ads and billboards were out of the question. Throughout 2014 and 2015 in particular, the LA-WTC received ample mainstream and ethnic media coverage in English, Korean, Spanish, Tagalog, and Chinese through print, radio, television, and online mediums by staging press conferences, rallies, marches, and direct actions against "bad actors" who violated wage and hour laws and refused to pay their workers.[39]

Wage theft is a crime—when you steal from a store, you go to jail; but if you steal from workers, there is no consequence. Los Angeles is the wage theft capital of the United States, with over $26 million stolen from workers' pockets each week.[40] Common forms of wage theft include lack of overtime pay, lack of meal and rest breaks, stealing tips, illegal deductions (e.g., forcing workers to pay for uniforms and tools), shift pay (i.e., flat payment for a shift of work, regardless of hours worked, resulting in an hourly wage below the minimum wage), off-the-clock work (i.e., pressuring workers to work before clocking in and after clocking out), misclassification as an independent contractor or exempt employee, and finally, complete non-payment (figure 11.3).[41]

Although wage theft in Los Angeles is illegal under both federal and state law, there were no meaningful consequences for employers for committing this theft. Day laborers in Los Angeles founded the LA-WTC in 2009 to address the problem of being unpaid or underpaid for a day's work. Over time, the coalition expanded to include fifteen organizations on the steering committee, representing a broad range of industrial, geographic, and ethnic communities.[42]

A specific crisis Angelenos faced in wage theft was lack of collections even after workers had won wage claims through the State Labor Commissioner's office in California. Filing a wage claim is an administrative process by which a worker can claim unpaid wages and penalties for the previous three years of work. After a settlement conference and a hearing,

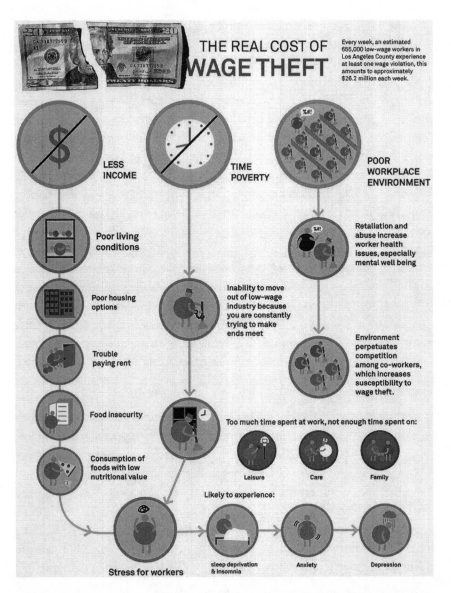

FIGURE 11.3. The real cost of wage theft, human impact partners, and the Los Angeles Coalition against Wage Theft. Artist: Rosten Woo. Permission to reproduce figure obtained.

the State Labor Commissioner's office issues a decision about whether a worker is owed money and, if so, how much. Then the employer is supposed to pay.

In reality, between 2008 and 2011, only 17 percent of workers who won wage claims in California were able to collect even a dime of the money owed.[43] To evade payment, employers closed up shop, changed their business's name, transferred the business to a friend, or in many cases simply ignored the labor commissioner's judgment to pay. There were simply no consequences—no jail time, no increased fines, no impact on future business. The LA-WTC decided to tackle the lack of collections head-on and developed a policy framework of "Collect, Protect, Enforce" that would create more tools for collections, provide stronger protections against retaliation, and establish a city-wide enforcement agency to ensure that policy became reality.

The impact of wage theft is not only economic. Time and again, through group and one-on-one conversations, public testimony, and research focus groups, many of the workers who were leaders and spokespeople in the campaign described the profound mental and emotional impact of wage theft. The LA-WTC incorporated in its campaign talking points about the impact of wage theft on workers' and their families' physical, mental, and emotional well-being.

In 2014, the LA-WTC partnered with Human Impact Partners, a public health research organization, to conduct focus groups and release a research report on the health impact of wage theft.[44] The report includes quotes from focus group participants who suffered wage theft, including:

- When I would get home from work, I would just cry, and I couldn't stop. I would feel so sad.
- After working ten hours, no break, you go home and try to wind down, but you can't. You feel anxious and you can't sleep.
- In reference to health, I can't sleep, I only sleep two–three hours and I'm always tired, I can't stop thinking. I'm constantly thinking day after day [about] the terrible conditions we live under. I think this is affecting me, for sure. I never used to get headaches, but now I do and it affects my work productivity. My headaches are terrible. During the day I'm very sleepy and tired.

The Health Impact Assessment reflected and resonated with one restaurant worker, Sara, in particular.[45] One evening, while preparing for a press conference, Sara began to reflect on what motivated her to join the campaign and what she wanted to share with reporters about wage theft.

Sara began to retrace her work history. Sara began working early, as a teenager, to contribute to the household income. She was only in her twenties during the campaign. Although all of the various food service jobs she had held were low wage, at or hovering above minimum wage, only one was egregious in its wage and hour violations, including non-payment of minimum wage, non-payment for overtime, illegal deductions from paychecks when the cash register was short, meal and rest break violations, and misclassification as an independent contractor so the employer could avoid paying taxes. She filed a complaint with the State Labor Commissioner and ultimately prevailed, falling into the 17 percent minority of workers who are able to collect money after winning a wage claim.

Sara commented that one of the hardest aspects of suffering wage theft was the knowledge that every day she went to work, a crime was being committed against her. This was emotionally taxing, and she lost trust in her employer.

When speaking about sustainability and health, workers often bring up the mental and emotional stressors that are not easily captured in strictly economic statistics on income or wages. To include "human sustainability" as one aspect of a holistic definition of sustainability requires an examination of the physical, mental, and emotional foundation needed to literally survive from year to year on low wages; systemic wage theft; and fear of criminalization, including deportation. Research by the Restaurant Opportunities Center and the Food Chain Workers illustrates that the consumer focus on the "local farm" or the "local distance" of a distribution center to the restaurant table might have less environmental impact than focusing on poor workplace conditions, as well as on the stress-aggravated and environment-aggravated illnesses of the millions of workers who compose the restaurant service industry (8 million nationwide).[46]

Example 3: The Relationship among Time, Space, and Poverty

"I WANT TO LIVE. RIGHT NOW I'M JUST SURVIVING."

Time poverty hurts sustainable living and refers to the strain on workers' personal time as a result of wage theft and low wages. Many low-wage workers hold two or more jobs in order to pay bills and rent. In addition, unpredictable scheduling is the nature of many low-wage jobs. For example, many restaurant workers receive their schedules week by week, waiting and hoping that all will work out with their second jobs, childcare needs, and school schedules. The lack of a secure, stable, and consistent work schedule leaves workers in a permanently precarious situation and has become its own focus of organizing for "predictable scheduling" policies.[47]

Wage theft exacerbates time poverty because it essentially means that workers are compensated for only a fraction of the hours they work, forcing victims of wage theft to seek multiple jobs. During the campaign to raise the minimum wage and pass an anti–wage theft ordinance, the LA City Council's Economic Development Committee organized a series of public hearings throughout the city to gather feedback from the public. Hundreds of community members—including low-wage workers, youth, students, business owners, employers, staff of nonprofit agencies and community-based organizations, and legal experts—attended these hearings to provide public testimony.

Time poverty emerged vividly in these testimonies. Workers expressed frustration with the lack of personal time, the constant grind to rush from one job to another, and the compulsion to seek and schedule more work to make ends meet.

For workers who had successfully filed and won wage theft claims with the State Labor Commission and were unable to collect, time took on a different meaning—the frustration of waiting for justice to be realized. The process to win a claim can take two years, and 83 percent of California workers who win their claims fail to collect a penny.

Speakers expressed hope that a higher minimum wage would translate into the ability to work fewer hours, freeing up time to spend with family and friends and to focus on their own health. They also expressed hope that stronger protections against wage theft would mean a faster, more efficient process to reclaim unpaid wages.

The final regional hearing took place on April 2, 2015, at the Museum of Tolerance in West Los Angeles, one of the most affluent areas of the city. The visual contrast could not have been starker: a line of mostly white male employers queued up to oppose the wage hike, while minimum wage employees—overwhelmingly people of color and many women, transgender, and gender non-conforming individuals—shared their daily struggle to make ends meet on low (and often underpaid) wages.

Employers threatened widespread layoffs and reduced work hours if wages increased. One restaurant worker, a young server, directly addressed the workers' point. She said drily, "I work three jobs—I'm a nanny, a valet, and a waitress. I would actually love to lose one of my jobs because that would mean I'm making closer to a decent wage and surviving on two instead of three jobs." One of the final public testimonies of the evening came from a working mom who also worked three jobs, all on minimum wage pay. She said, "I want to live. Right now I'm just surviving."[48]

Environmental-justice activists have successfully sought change in poor neighborhoods, rightfully identifying injustice in the form of, for example, toxic sites and lack of environmental amenities like parks and green space. Incorporating a broader definition of "sustainability," one that includes workers' rights, ensures that workers have the leisure time to enjoy those new parks and cleaned-up spaces. When an individual is working two to three jobs, this is not possible. One restaurant worker, a single father and busboy with over twenty years' experience in the industry, testified at one of the public hearings: "I wish I had [had] more time with my daughter when she was growing up. I always worked at least two jobs. I regret I was never able to take my daughter to the park even once. Now she's in her twenties."[49]

Notes

Special thanks to the Los Angeles Coalition against Wage Theft and the community activists who contributed stories from their work experiences to this chapter, Human Impact Partners for the "Real Cost of Work" image, and Professor Anna Kim's students: Scripps College student Ally Nkwocha for her map of health code violations in Los Angeles and Georgia Tech doctoral student Andreas Bloom for his assistance with the review of relevant literature.

1. Bunyan Bryant, *Environmental Justice: Issues, Policies, and Solutions* (Washington, DC: Island, 1995), 6.

2. John Rawls, *A Theory of Justice* (Cambridge, MA: Harvard University Press, 2009), 511.

3. Laura Pulido, "Geographies of Race and Ethnicity 1: White Supremacy vs. White Privilege in Environmental Racism Research," *Progress in Human Geography*, 2015, accessed October 1, 2015, doi:10.1177/0309132514563008.

4. Gordon Walker, *Environmental Justice: Concepts, Evidence, and Politics* (London: Routledge, 2012), 214.

5. Omnitrans and BNSF Railyard campaign, Center for Community Action and Environmental Justice (CCAEJ), accessed November 5, 2015, http://www.ccaej.org/#!san-bernardino-campaigns/c1wi.

6. Social Justice Learning Institute, Mission Statement for Health Equity, accessed October 10, 2015, http://www.sjli.org/program/health-equity.

7. E. Soja, "The City and Spatial Justice," *Justice Spatiale, Spatial Justice* 1 (2009): 31–39.

8. US Social Forum 2007, Gentrification in Global Cities: Working Class Communities' Right to the City. Official launch of the Right to the City Alliance.

9. Laura Pulido, "Rethinking Environmental Racism: White Privilege and Urban Development in Southern California," *Annals of the Association of American Geographers* 90, no. 1 (2000): 15.

10. Robert J. Brulle, and David Pellow, "Environmental Justice: Human Health and Environmental Inequalities," *Annual Review of Public Health* 27 (2006): 108.

11. David Harvey, *Justice, Nature, and the Geography of Difference* (Malden, MA: Blackwell, 1996), 295.

12. Eric Mann, 2012 Case Study, Labor Community Strategy Center, 2, published by the Marguerite Casey Foundation, accessed October 1, 2014, http://www.racialequitytools.org/resourcefiles/ferntiger2.pdf.

13. US Social Forum 2007, Gentrification in Global Cities.

14. Andrew Hurley, *Environmental Inequalities: Class, Race, and Industrial Pollution in Gary, Indiana, 1945–1980* (Chapel Hill: University of North Carolina Press, 1995).

15. David Pellow, *Garbage Wars: The Struggle for Environmental Justice in Chicago* (Cambridge, MA: MIT Press, 2002).

16. David Pellow and Lisa Sun-Hee Park, *The Silicon Valley of Dreams: Environmental Injustice, Immigrant Workers, and the High-Tech Global Economy* (New York: New York University Press, 2002).

17. Walker, *Environmental Justice*, 217.

18. Lara Cushing, Rachel Morello-Frosch, Madeline Wander, and Manuel Pastor, "The Haves, the Have-Nots, and the Health of Everyone: The Relationship between Social Inequality and Environmental Quality," *Public Health* 36, no. 1 (2015): 193.

19. Rachel Morello-Frosch and Russ Lopez, "The Riskscape and the Color Line: Examining the Role of Segregation in Environmental Health Disparities," *Environmental Research* 102, no. 2 (2006): 181–96.

20. Bill M. Jesdale, Rachel Morello-Frosch, and Lara Cushing, "The Racial/Ethnic Distribution of Heat Risk–Related Land Cover in Relation to Residential Segregation," *Environmental Health Perspectives* 121, no. 7 (2013): 811.

21. Russ Lopez, "Segregation and Black/White Differences in Exposure to Air Toxics in 1990," *Environmental Health Perspectives* (2002): 289–95.

22. Michael Ash, James K. Boyce, Grace Chang, Manuel Pastor, Justin Scoggins, and Jennifer Tran, *Justice in the Air: Tracking Toxic Pollution from America's Industries and Companies to Our States, Cities, and Neighborhoods* (Los Angeles: Political Economy Research Institute, 2009), accessed November 5, 2015, https://works.bepress.com/cgi/viewcontent.cgi?article=1042&context=james_boyce.

23. Jenny Price, "Remaking American Environmentalism: On the Banks of the LA River," *Environmental History* 13, no. 3 (2008): 536–55.

24. Nik Heynen, Hilda E. Kurtz, and Amy Trauger, "Food Justice, Hunger, and the City," *Geography Compass* 6, no. 5 (2012): 306.

25. Brulle and Pellow, "Environmental Justice," 108.

26. Robert Gottlieb and Anupama Joshi, *Food Justice* (Cambridge, MA: MIT Press, 2007).

27. "Hands That Feed Us," report by the Food Chain Workers Alliance, 2012, p. 63, https://foodchainworkers.org/wp-content/uploads/2012/06/Hands-That-Feed-Us-Report.pdf.

28. David Pellow and H. N. Brehm, "From the New Ecological Paradigm to Total Liberation: The Emergence of a Social Movement Frame," *Sociological Quarterly* 56, no. 1 (2015): 194.

29. Los Angeles Food Policy Council, "Good Food Purchasing Policy," policy implemented October 24, 2012, accessed November 5, 2015, http://goodfoodla.org/policymaking/good-food-procurement/.

30. The anti–wage theft ordinance and minimum wage ordinance were spearheaded by the Los Angeles Coalition against Wage Theft and the Los Angeles Raise the Wage Coalition, respectively. Stories and quotes are from the authors' campaign work with restaurant workers.

31. For example, environmental, feminist, and reproductive justice organizations have united to organize the salon industry against workplace exposure to toxic beauty products, like the Toxic Trio in nail polish and formaldehyde in Brazilian blowout treatments. The National Healthy Nail and Beauty Salon Alliance was founded in 2007 and co-convened by the California Healthy Nail Salon Collaborative and Women's Voices for the Earth. To learn more about the policy agenda against toxic salon workplaces, see California Healthy Nail Salon Collaborative, "Framing a Proactive Research Agenda to Advance Worker Health and Safety in the Nail Salon and Cosmetology Communities: Convening Report," 2010, accessed November 5, 2015, https://www.cahealthynailsalons.org/resourcestim-hi%E1%BB%83u-them/publications-and-media-2/.

32. North American Industry Classification System, 2009 dataset.

33. North American Industry Classification System, 2009 dataset.

34. Restaurant Opportunities Center of Los Angeles, Restaurant Opportunities Center United, and the Los Angeles Restaurant Industry Coalition, "Behind the Kitchen Door: Inequality and Opportunity I Los Angeles, the Nation's Largest Restaurant Industry," February 14, 2011, accessed November 5, 2015, http://rocunited.org/roc-la-behind-the-kitchen-door/.

35. Cal/OSHA, California Department of Industrial Relations, "Heat Illness Prevention Enforcement Q&A," May 14, 2015, accessed November 5, 2015, https://www.dir.ca.gov/dosh/heatIllnessQA.html.

36. Research and Education Unit, Cal/OSHA Consultation Service, Division of Occupational Safety and Health, California Department of Industrial Relations, "Cal/OSHA Guide to Restaurant Safety," State of California, July 2012.

37. http://endwagetheftla.org/, accessed November 5, 2015

38. Rebecca Bowe, "Shelter from the Storm: San Francisco Strengthens Protections for Low-Wage Workers as the Economy Worsens," *San Francisco Bay Guardian*, August 9, 2011.

39. Representative media coverage of the campaign includes, for example, Emily Alpert Reyes, "L.A. Councilmen Make Renewed Push against Wage Theft: Two L.A. City Councilmembers Seek City Ordinance to Criminalize Wage Theft," *Los Angeles Times*, June 24, 2014; Jose Huang, "Little Tokyo Workers Join Growing Numbers Claiming 'Wage Theft,'" *89.3 KPCC Multi-American*, September 3, 2014.

40. Ruth Milkman, Ana Luz González, and Victor Narro, "Wage Theft and Workplace Violations in Los Angeles: The Failure of Employment and Labor Law for Low-Wage Workers" (Los Angeles: Institute for Research and Employment, University of California, 2010).

41. Milkman, Luz González, and Narro, "Wage Theft and Workplace Violations in Los Angeles."

42. The steering committee of the Los Angeles Coalition against Wage Theft is composed of 9to5 Working Women, Los Angeles Black Worker Center, Central American Resource Center, Coalition for Humane Immigrant Rights of Los Angeles, CLEAN Carwash Campaign, Garment Worker Center, IDEPSCA (Instituto de Educacion Popular del Sur de California), Koreatown Immigrant Workers Alliance, National Day Laborer Organizing Network, Pilipino Worker Center, Restaurant Opportunities Center of Los Angeles, UCLA Labor Center, United Food and Commercial Workers Local 770, Strategic Concepts in Organizing and Policy Education, and SEIU United Service Workers West.

43. Eunice Hyunhye Cho, Tia Koonse, and Anthony Mischel, "Hollow Victories: The Crisis in Collecting Unpaid Wages for California's Workers" (Los Angeles: Institute for Research and Employment, University of California, 2013). Report.

44. Human Impact Partners, "Health Impact Assessment of the Proposed Los Angeles Wage Theft Ordinance" (Oakland, CA: Human Impact Partners, June 2014).

45. Alias.

46. Hands That Feed Us report.

47. Steven Greenhouse, "A Push to Give Steadier Shifts to Part-Timers," *New York Times*, July 15, 2014.

48. Sophia Cheng, interview with restaurant worker. April 2, 2015

49. Sophia Cheng, interview with restaurant worker. January 12, 2016.

Challenging Resources

12

Confronting Kennecott in the Cascades

ADAM M. SOWARDS

For Kennecott Copper Corporation, it could have been anywhere. Miners Ridge, in the northern Cascade Range of Washington State, meant nothing to geologists searching for ore or executives searching for profit.[1] Since the nineteenth century, law had acknowledged mining as the highest use on public lands. When the US Forest Service (USFS) designated wild lands, mining's priority did not change. Glacier Peak Wilderness Area may have encompassed Miners Ridge, but Kennecott only saw untapped and available copper. The location mattered hardly at all.

To Northwest conservationists, Miners Ridge, Glacier Peak, and the North Cascades mattered a great deal. This was a protected landscape and a personal one. Take Brock Evans. In the summer of 1965 Evans, a Seattle lawyer and conservationist, and his wife, Rachel, hiked sixty miles over eight days through the Glacier Peak wilderness. An easy drive from the city, it was a world apart. At the end of the road, they found a trail that led through "a primeval forest of huge trees." As they climbed thousands of feet, they emerged "in a sea of flowers on a level ridge." Their view swept "over an ocean of

DOI: 10.5876/9781607328483.c012

jagged peaks" and rested "on the immense white-rising bulk of Glacier Peak."
Then as now, rivers tumble off the mountain and "wheel and arc around the
great mountain to glacial headwaters on the other side." They could see it
all, "a great circle and cycle of cloud, summit, meadow, river, flower, and forest . . . and the trail leads on, to a jewel lake, and from there to other places,
just as beautiful, just as little known." The trip—a "profound experience"—
awakened Evans to all that might be lost, for he and Rachel saw miners
working, which filled them with "alarm and dread." When they returned
the following summer for what they expected to be "the very last time," they
carried with them "very heavy and aching hearts," a burden made worse
as helicopters effortlessly carried in miners and mining equipment several
times a day, creating a noisy interlude "accenting the feeling of dread" that
overcame Evans as he picked his way through "the claims markers and road
survey stakes."[2] Brock and Rachel Evans and a growing troop of activists
organized to keep Kennecott away and protect Glacier Peak. Like most wilderness advocates, those engaged here came mostly from the professional
ranks of the white middle class, including doctors, lawyers, professors, engineers, and ministers, as well as college students and an occasional teenager,
with a mix of men and women.[3]

Their task might have been Sisyphean, for the law was clear. Kennecott
enjoyed every right to dig its pit. It acquired the patented claims in the 1950s,
explored them in the early 1960s, and announced its plan to operate an open-
pit mine in 1966. Although the corporation possessed rights, that did not make
its plans right. Conservationists then did what Americans have always done
when confronted with such situations. They organized. They wrote. They
used moral suasion. They worked to change the offending law. In short, they
protested. To pass this test, they would need to apply old lessons of protest and
write some of their own, even as Kennecott maneuvered for its own interests.

The North Cascades, with their grand peaks and deep valleys, arrest view-
ers who regularly compare them with the Alps.[4] Evans once invited readers
into this world by portraying the mountains in superlative terms: "The trav-
eler who crosses or ventures deeper into these mountains sees an even more
dramatic world. The closer his approach, the more rugged and ever more
wild and beautiful the impact; murmurs and hints of still greater scenic mag-
nificence are tantalizingly revealed in bits and glimpses up long deep valleys."
The qualities in these mountains were outstanding: "Deep rugged precipices

rising sharply above dense rain forests; innumerable creeks and waterfalls fed by glaciers high up on the slopes; deep rushing canyons, and occasional long vistas of finger-valleys, creeping eastward toward the even mightier peaks near the crest of the range." Just to the west of the Cascade crest, Glacier Peak rises over the range with stately presence to create perhaps the most iconic scene in the entire North Cascades: Image Lake, surrounded by alpine meadows and wildflowers, reflecting the glacier-capped volcano.[5]

The scene's natural timelessness masked its human history. Over the next rise, just two miles away from this climactic scene, was Miners Ridge. Beneath the ridge, at the base of Plummer Mountain, low-grade copper ore attracted attention. Prospectors claimed the ore early in the twentieth century, but the ore's low concentration and its isolation made mining it unprofitable and unlikely. Besides, the entire Glacier Peak landscape was protected. National forest land since before the twentieth century, it was designated a recreation area in 1931. A US National Park Service (NPS) study in 1937 endorsed it as a national park. In 1940 it became a "limited area" after Bob Marshall, the US Forest Service's greatest wilderness champion, recommended protection. Twenty years later, the Forest Service created the Glacier Peak Wilderness Area. The North Cascades, Glacier Peak, Image Lake, Miners Ridge—these places, rich in wild beauty, were likewise rich in human stories and aspirations.[6] Conservationists celebrated when the Wilderness Act finally passed in 1964 after eight years plodding through the US Congress. The law created the most restrictive land designation to date for the country's public lands. Howard Zahniser, the longtime executive secretary of the Wilderness Society, largely wrote the act, which defined wilderness as "an area where the earth and its community of life are untrammeled by man, where man himself is a visitor who does not remain . . . [and a place that retains] its primeval character and influence, without permanent improvements or human habitation, which is protected and managed so as to preserve its natural conditions." It kept out roads, commercial enterprises, motors, and "mechanical transport," such as bicycles.[7]

To pass such monumental legislation, lawmakers compromised. Mining was the greatest compromise and Wayne Aspinall the most compromised. Aspinall chaired the powerful US House Interior and Insular Affairs Committee through which any wilderness bill must pass. A proponent of resource development, the conservative Democrat from western Colorado secured a number of changes to the bill the US Senate passed in 1961 to allow Congress to enjoy more power to implement wilderness areas. Aspinall ensured that so-called non-conforming uses, such as grazing and airfields, permitted by the Senate version would be continued. But Aspinall went further, allowing mineral prospecting in designated wilderness areas until 1984. Working mines could continue indefinitely. This loophole was the price conservationists paid to gain statutory protection for wild spaces.[8]

When President Lyndon Johnson signed the bill, the first 9.1 million acres created the National Wilderness Preservation System. That system included the Glacier Peak Wilderness Area of 458,105 acres and the mining loophole.

Like alpine breezes, rumors swirled early and often. Polly Dyer, a long-time northwestern activist who played key roles through many wilderness campaigns, kept alert to emerging threats and learned in 1956 on "extremely good authority" that Kennecott Copper Corporation was "definitely going to mine on Miners Ridge" and construct a town below on the Suiattle River.[9] This rumor died down for a while.

What launched the conservationists' sustained campaign was a 1965 anonymous letter postmarked from Washington, DC, and sent to the North Cascades Conservation Council (N3C). The tip informed N3C that Kennecott would "definitely" begin open-pit operations by 1970, a prospect conservationists found hard to fathom.[10] Contemplating a road to the mine, one activist said, "Oh, how it hurts to say that."[11] Brock Evans confessed, "I have been sick to my stomach since I heard this news, because I know and love the area."[12] Their writing exposed their sense of being violated by Kennecott, an attack from an impersonal corporation that felt anything but.

Despite no official announcements from Kennecott's New York City corporate offices, conservationists harvested information from the mountains and sowed seeds of concern wherever they could. Backpackers reported a variety of activity, including between two dozen and three dozen geologists exploring the site and building nine new shacks. Although the workers made a friendly impression and invited hikers to have coffee, they answered few questions. Daily helicopters and scattered survey stakes pierced the wilderness atmosphere. Such bad news prompted N3C president Patrick D. Goldsworthy to write the *New York Times* in October 1966 to inform the nation's newspaper of record that Kennecott subsidiaries were poised to "start dismembering the heart" of Glacier Peak.[13]

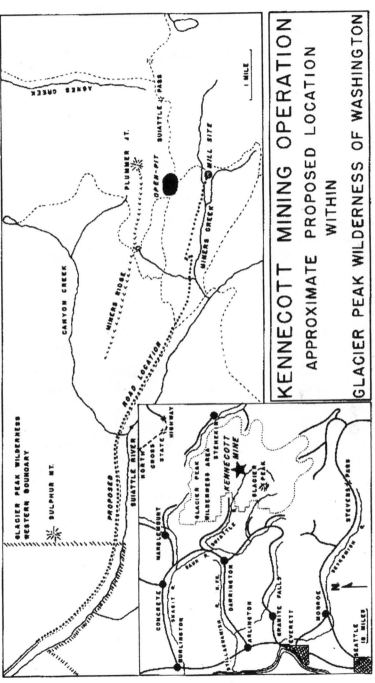

FIGURE 12.1. Map (Caption and Citation). This map shows the location of Kennecott's proposed mine, along with the access road and mill site. It originally appeared in The Wild Cascades (December 1966–January 1967), 7. Used by permission of the North Cascades Conservation Council.

After the rumor festered for more than a year within the Northwest conservation community, Kennecott Copper Corporation finally presented its plans for Miners Ridge a few days before Christmas 1966. Kennecott was no small, struggling concern. The *Mining Year Book, 1966* summarized its business. The corporation and its subsidiaries worked existing or developing mines in Utah, Nevada, Arizona, New Mexico, Missouri, Alaska, and Puerto Rico and abroad in Canada, Nigeria, and Chile. Not only was this geographic reach impressive, but the company's production was rising. The net tonnage increased from 536,005 in 1963 to 619,868 two years later, more than a 15 percent increase. The firm reported a consolidated net income at the end of 1965 of more than $102 million. It thrived.[14]

Yet corporations run on continued profit, and Miners Ridge emerged as a likely source to bolster bottom lines. Although conservationists knew that Miners Ridge contained minerals—it was not called Vista Ridge, after all—they believed its low-grade ore, protected status, and isolation would make exploitation "uneconomical" for any firm interested in dismantling the mountain. However, the Vietnam War boosted copper prices and provided a more attractive market, and some at Kennecott saw it as fulfilling their "patriotic duty" to develop metal mines. In its announcement, the company deflected attention by explaining how the federal government encouraged all copper companies to find new sources to compensate for the world's short supply.[15]

Kennecott referred to an incentive program announced in spring 1966 by the US General Services Administration (GSA). With the war ramping up in Southeast Asia, the GSA sought with its Copper Production Expansion Program to increase domestic copper production. Kennecott also saw its opportunity to develop its Glacier Peak patents and expressed interest. It never formally applied to the program—in fact, when considering a preliminary inquiry, government officials thought the plan too fraught to support—yet the incentive program's very existence spoke of the improved market conditions and a federally sanctioned need. With a needy government and a powerful firm, odds as steep as North Cascades slopes confronted conservationists.[16]

Party lines formed around the plan that, besides the mine, included power lines, a road or railroad, a mill, and a tailings dump. The initial press coverage focused on Kennecott's mine division manager, M. J. O'Shaughnessy, who

THIS IS AN OPEN PIT

THIS IS NOT AN OPEN PIT — NOT YET
December 1966–January 1967

FIGURE 12.2. The cover of The Wild Cascades, the newsletter of the North Cascades Conservation Council, juxtaposes Kennecott Copper Corporation's open-pit mine at Bingham, Utah, with Plummer Mountain in Glacier Peak Wilderness Area where the company proposed a new mine. The North Cascades Conservation Council led conservationists in this campaign and used this contrast often in their campaign to stop the mining company. The Wild Cascades (December 1966-January 1967), cover. Used by permission of the North Cascades Conservation Council.

explained the critical importance of copper and believed the company could "live within a reasonable design to protect the wilderness." Such a comment, although certainly meant to show the firm's accommodating spirit, instead showed just how poorly mining corporations understood wilderness advocates whose worldview could not accommodate mining and wilderness in the same space, on Miners Ridge or anywhere. Paired against O'Shaughnessy, the press pitched Patrick D. Goldsworthy, a University of Washington Medical School biochemist. Goldsworthy, an earnest-looking man who wore a crewcut and dark-rimmed glasses, directed N3C and emphasized not accommodation but the ecological damage such an operation would entail. While informing the public that the Sierra Club would join N3C in a national campaign, Goldsworthy also hinted that efforts were afoot to purchase the property from Kennecott—a vague dream the Sierra Club's David Brower once said was the "only hope" and had roots going back into the 1950s almost as soon as Kennecott picked up the options. More would be needed than hope alone.[17]

The parties tried a summit of sorts, a San Francisco meeting between Kennecott and conservationists barely a month after the corporation's public announcement. Although the company saw this move as de facto evidence of its "willingness to exchange views," the three-hour meeting did nothing to allay wilderness advocates' fears. Instead, activists came away more alarmed than ever about "corporate ruthlessness," since Kennecott plainly planned to push forward with a complex that included a mill to concentrate the copper using a flotation system requiring 5,000 tons of water a day to process 5,000 tons of ore. Somewhere between 5,000 and 7,000 horsepower of electricity would provide energy for the operation the company expected would last for two, maybe three decades and employ 200 men—all to produce less than 1 percent of the nation's annual copper consumption. Altogether, the mine-mill system would cover 200 acres (later estimates placed it at more than twice that), although discarded tailings and new roads—not to mention the blasting noise—would extend its impacts beyond that distance. When closed, the company would plant Australian vetch on the tailings and dump piles—an exotic introduction violating the Wilderness Act—and wait for avalanches to destroy the road. Backpackers, the company claimed, would find waste rocks "indistinguishable from natural talus piles." Despite publicly stating that the company had not yet decided, these plans were obviously well-developed.[18]

Increasing copper production fit within a clear but multifaceted corporate calculus. The nation called for and required copper for its security needs and to lessen its dependence on foreign copper; all copper companies were ramping up production to compensate for losing productivity in existing mines, and corporate profits demanded it. Underlying the situation was the test of precedent. As C. D. Michaelson, the vice president of the metal mining division, put it: "If we are stopped here and half a dozen other places that we plan to develop then we would have to go out of business. We can't afford not to go ahead."[19] This test—of the Wilderness Act's rules, the conservationists' resistance, and the corporation's resolve—mattered.

As important as Michaelson and Goldsworthy were as symbolic agents who would savage or safeguard the North Cascades, they were not alone. Absent from the San Francisco meeting was the US Forest Service (USFS), which administered the North Cascades, including Miners Ridge. Long an agency that favored resource extraction, the USFS also presided over the most protected wilderness, including Glacier Peak. The agency initially opposed the wilderness bill, then reluctantly supported it, and by the early 1960s supported it fully in theory, although many objected to the USFS's practice of wilderness management.[20] The Forest Service in the course of this story bounced between the poles of ambiguity and impotency and grandstanding.

USFS managers at several levels stumbled forward in their attempts to control the story of Miners Ridge. Mt. Baker National Forest supervisor Harold C. Chriswell thought the Wilderness Act's rules were chock full of ambiguity, but he claimed the Forest Service "will exercise all control possible within the law to protect wilderness values." He seemed to have meant it. Although he acknowledged that courts may ultimately decide rules, Chriswell assured the public of the agency's power to "control things. We have told Kennecott it would have to bring in all possible alternatives if, as and when it makes a formal application."[21] However, the agency's associate chief, Arthur W. Greeley, told Goldsworthy: "It is important that our position be clearly stated. The law provides for mining. We cannot nullify the law by writing general regulations that would make mining not possible. We have just as much obligation and desire as ever to maintain wilderness values. But we also have the obligation to administer the mining provisions of the Wilderness Act in a manner consistent with Congress' intent—which is that mining be permitted."[22]

J. Herbert Stone, the regional forester for Region Six (which includes Oregon and Washington), stirred up controversy—and confusion—when he was quoted in the press as saying that an open-pit mine "isn't compatible" with the wilderness character of the North Cascades. Conservationists seized on the statement. Are mine permits required or incompatible in wilderness areas, Representative Lloyd Meeds asked Associate Chief Greeley after hearing of Stone's remarks? Greeley assured Meeds that the press had taken Stone's comments out of context. Stone clarified that despite the incompatibility, the Wilderness Act still allowed mining. Congress, through Aspinall, spoke unequivocally about allowing mining, and Greeley chided conservationists for trying to reinterpret the act to regulate mining out of the wild.[23]

Then into this fracas came Orville Freeman, the secretary of agriculture and thus the Forest Service's ultimate boss. Secretary Freeman was the banquet speaker at one of the Sierra Club's biennial wilderness conferences, this one focused on "Wilderness and the Quality of Life." That April 1967 evening, when he rose to speak in San Francisco's Hilton Hotel, the secretary faced a difficult task of balancing his agency's competing interests in resource development and wilderness protection to an audience often critical of the strength of the former and the weakness of the latter.[24]

Freeman chose the North Cascades to make his case and waxed poetic: "The Cascades are an ocean of mountains, frozen in space and time, wave after cresting wave of stone, dotted with the deep blue-green of alpine lakes, laced with the glacial remnants of another age." The Minnesotan spared no rhetorical flourish, sounding more like a David Brower or John Muir than an agriculture administrator, when he explained to his audience that to understand the North Cascades, one needed to use one's senses: "To hear the wind above timberline, a voice like all the rivers in the world flowing over a thousand miles of granite and green; smell the pine; feel a pebble polished by eons of time." A timeless wilderness, a place where naturalness reigned, protected from humans' games.[25]

At the banquet and an associated news conference, Secretary Freeman dismantled Kennecott's values, much as the company would dismantle the mountain. To be sure, the company possessed the rights to mine there; it could, if it wanted, ignore scenic values and "gouge out its road" and excavate Plummer Mountain. He found this anathema to the public interest and implored the Sierra Club to take the case to the public, who could pressure the management of the copper corporation. American standards of living would not materially lessen and the military's efforts in Vietnam would not falter absent Miners Ridge's paltry copper deposits. Although Kennecott liked to pitch its plans as necessary to American life and security, Freeman dismissed this routine Kennecott ploy and argued instead that other values needed to be considered: "It is not a case, in short, of 'either-or.' It is rather a case of economics, of choosing alternatives; of balancing a priceless, yet intangible, national treasure against ledger sheets and profits." Of course, Freeman had not morphed his identity from agriculture secretary to wilderness director. In fact, he used this controversy to promote the Forest Service's multiple-use strategy. By developing multiple-use plans and getting high production out of other lands, the nation could afford to leave places like Miners Ridge alone.[26]

That April evening, Secretary Freeman channeled generations of Americans who found in nature something divine, something beyond Mammon. Freeman noted suggestively that perhaps "a wise Creator" had put the copper in the mountain "to test whether man could forego material riches for the fullness of the spirit." In saying so, he tapped into his audience, an audience who had long recognized that decision-making required a long-term perspective and non-materialistic criteria. "We are a nation bedazzled by technology and addicted to crash solutions," he said by way of conclusion. "But there are no instant ecologies; no instant wilderness." Our great nation, he feared, stood poised to exercise power without wisdom, and Freeman recognized that this issue in the North Cascades stood as synecdoche of larger struggles: "We now have the power, literally, to move mountains. The next few years will determine if we have the wisdom to refrain from doing so." Time would tell if public interest prevailed.[27]

Although conservationists expressed pleasure, industry responded in an acerbic editorial in its leading professional mouthpiece.[28] The *Engineering and Mining Journal* portrayed a jousting match between Kennecott and "Sir Orville of Agriculture." Complete with mixed metaphors—"Sir Orville of Agriculture galloped off to war in the Wild West last month aboard a mighty stallion. He was looking for a few dragons to slay"—this piece informed readers of the secretary's galling desire for Kennecott to forgo its Miners Ridge investment. Fairly mocking Freeman for speaking at a wilderness conference in San Francisco—"Pearl-by-the-Bay"—the industry organ turned serious by its conclusion, for the writer recognized that Freeman's rhetoric could not be dismissed as "laughable" because of its serious implications. "Sir Orville" meant to close the Wilderness Act's window for prospecting—if not legislatively, at least effectively. Here again was the test. The mining industry saw this as a perversion of public interest to satiate "a pitifully small vocal minority." The editorial, written in parable complete with an errant knight, surely surprised no readers in its content. Its open, mocking hostility indicated at once the industry's fear and confidence.[29]

The industry had no corner on audacity. For the political optics of the developing campaign, public outrage needed a face, preferably a local one. Onto the stage stepped Fred T. Darvill, a doctor from Mount Vernon, Washington, a small city through which the Skagit River (whose tributaries include the Suiattle River and other streams from the Glacier Peak watershed) flows. He began his activism routinely enough, writing letters to the editor and his local US representative Lloyd Meeds. He spoke of Kennecott's actions as "desecrations" and vaunted grassroots efforts that stymied plans for dams in the Grand Canyon, the most recent national victory for conservationists.[30]

Then, Darvill bought three shares of stock in Kennecott for the sole purpose of being able to speak at the annual stockholders' meeting. Expressing his concern as a stockholder in a letter to Kennecott, the Northwest doctor worried that an open-pit mine in the Cascades might result in a "significant deterioration of the corporate image in the eyes of the average American." He insisted on both a discussion and a plebiscite—that is, a formal vote by stockholders—at the next meeting. Kennecott's president, Frank R. Milliken, responded and let Darvill know that regulations prevented the vote but that the company would gladly allow him to make a statement. Milliken cautioned Darvill that the company was "fully aware" of Darvill's and others' aims but that deciding Miners Ridge's fate rested with management, not the stockholders.[31]

At the appointed moment—May 2, 1967, at 10:00 a.m., in the Bowman Room of New York's famed Biltmore Hotel—Darvill spoke eloquently about Glacier Peak wilderness. With an oil painting and a photograph—symbolically bringing the wild mountains to wild Manhattan—the doctor opened with what surely was an uncharacteristic comment for Kennecott Copper Corporation stockholder meetings: "I have come here today to talk about wilderness and beauty." Describing a hike to Glacier Peak through the landscape of flowers and firs, Darvill made Miners Ridge and nearby Image Lake the "acme or heart of the area." After being there amid "unexcelled scenery," a hiker would recall for a lifetime the "grand and memorable experience." The company's production plan—with its open pit, concentrator, and fourteen miles of roads—endangered this beautiful place and his lifetime of memories. All this for an unessential mine, a perspective confirmed by the secretary of agriculture the previous month. Washington's governor, Dan Evans; the district's representative, Lloyd Meeds; the Snohomish County Board of Adjustment; Seattle newspapers; state legislators—all hated the idea. As Darvill told it, "Both high officials in the government and the man on the street corner" concurred. Warning the company of its potential image as a "desecrator of the wilderness," Darvill ended in doggerel, quoted in many newspapers: "Let it not be said, and said to your shame, that all was beauty here, until Kennecott Copper came."[32] The rest of the meeting apparently covered routine business about more mundane company matters, but Darvill had had his say. "I am left with the impression that this corporation strongly wants to go ahead with the mine," Darvill told the *Seattle Times* immediately afterward, "but maybe what was done today will shake it up a bit."[33]

It did shake up the *Washington Post*, which published an editorial the next day under the headline "Crisis at Miners Ridge." Someday, the nation may face a dire copper shortage that justified "leaving a ghastly scar in the place of natural beauty," but the editors thought that day was not at hand. The *Post* moved from the specific landscape of Glacier Peak to general principles and was shocked to realize that corporate calculations, not public agencies, determined whether to mine on public lands—something Secretary Freeman's recent speech, as well as Darvill's gambit, had publicized. For the paper, the decision of whether a crisis merited destroying wilderness "should be made by a responsible national agency rather than a private company interested primarily in profits." The Wilderness Act, the *Post* argued, needed amending to allow private inholdings like Kennecott's to be condemned. Its editorial favored what it described as "one of the most alluring samples of the unspoiled manless world."[34]

Darvill's actions had alerted the national media, but conservationists drew on a much more recognizable ally in their next campaign to stymie the mine. A group, organized as the Statewide Committee to Stop Kennecott Copper and led by David Birkner, drew Supreme Court Justice William O. Douglas to his home state in what was widely called a "camp-in" and in another place a "camp-out, hike-in, love-in, be-in," all playing off the sit-in and teach-in movements that were part of the era's zeitgeist. So in August 1967, Justice Douglas led a protesting group from a Forest Service campground into the woods.[35]

By 1967, Douglas enjoyed veteran status as a wilderness protestor, and he knew Glacier Peak and much of the Northwest intimately. Some years before, he had published *My Wilderness: The Pacific West* and included this wilderness plea: "If the valleys and ridges of this Glacier Peak area are sealed from commercial projects, we will have forever in America high country of enchantment. Those who search them out will learn that an emptiness in life comes with the destruction of wilderness; that a fullness of life follows when one comes on intimate terms with woods and peaks and meadows." A wilderness preserved at Miners Ridge represented humanity's hope. When activists approached Douglas to serve in the cause against Kennecott Copper, he complied.[36]

On August 5, 1967, "a band of 150 adults, kids, dogs, and an assortment of people wearing beards and beads," as the press dubbed the opponents of the open-pit mine, converged on Sulfur Creek Campground, about thirty miles east of Darrington, Washington. The group of all ages milled about, signed petitions, and ate lunch amid the Douglas fir forests where Sulfur Creek spilled into the Suiattle River. After a while, the protestors headed up the trail a short distance to listen to the justice speak. Relying on standard tropes, he celebrated the frontier and beauty: "You've seen the wilderness and its glories and its wonders and its beauty and you may be the last generation to see it . . . the frontier is just about gone." In the next breath, he railed against the materialism symbolized by a corporate mine: "Let's not turn everything into dollars. Let's save something for the spiritual side of man." Photographs captured in newspapers show an impassioned Douglas, eyes and open hands raised to the sky, beseeching his audience huddled around him holding signs of protest. For the conservationists' cause, Douglas brought attention and made clear to Kennecott that resolve remained strong.[37]

Douglas and supporters faced opponents and even rumors of violence, elements that raised the dramatic tension for journalists writing about the protest. Residents from Darrington, a timber town that like other resource-dependent communities was always vulnerable to economic downturns, posted a sign: "Welcome Kennecott." Local citizens saw the protestors as "outsiders [who] want . . . a private playground," while working communities faced certain decline without infusions of new industry. Local millworkers and loggers welcomed the idea of more workers and money in their town and castigated conservationists as just a "bunch of birdwatchers . . . trying to take something away from those who have to work for a living." This critical refrain followed wilderness enthusiasts in the Northwest for a half century, marking a fault line between those who knew nature through work and those who knew it through play. A Democratic state representative from nearby Arlington, Henry Backstrom, also crashed the party, arguing that Kennecott's mine would "be a shot in the arm for the working people." The company would leave the area with a road and a "man made lake after they're through," cheered Backstrom. The counter-protestors, however, were few and impotent, even if the Seattle papers wished to emphasize the confrontation—something Brock Evans characterized as "grossly overplayed." The jobs and development Backstrom and timber workers anticipated would be short-lived and few, and the "man made lake"—a filled-in pit—could hardly compete with a majestic Glacier Peak reflected in Image Lake during a summer sunrise.[38]

Trailside, reporters captured some of Justice Douglas's words, but no one recorded his full remarks. This oversight caused problems, for the Sierra Club was planning a film about Kennecott Copper's threat to Miners Ridge. The following summer Douglas recorded recollected comments as though he were standing on the banks of the Suiattle.[39]

Douglas's comments reflected his long-standing interests in American justice and conservation retooled specifically for this campaign. As a symbol of ultimate legal authority, Justice Douglas addressed the legality of Kennecott's proposed action. Yet he did not challenge that; the Wilderness Act plainly allowed prospecting and mining, but as he told his audience, "just because something's legal doesn't necessarily mean it's right."[40] Instead of urging a lawsuit or seeking legal loopholes—actions increasingly common among activists as Congress passed environmental legislation in the 1960s and 1970s—Douglas pushed protestors: "Try to appeal to the collective conscience of the corporate community represented by Kenn[e]cott Copper, [hoping] to change the minds of stockholders, directors and others who are interested in the corporation, so that the corporation will not become identified in the public eye with the vandalism of the kind that will result if this open-pit operation goes into effect."

Similar to Dr. Darvill's appeal to Kennecott stockholders, Douglas aimed at moral suasion to stoke the corporate conscience to act. However, he expressed marked pessimism; too often in today's society, he lamented, owners directed "their eye only on the dollar sign in disregard of all the spiritual values of the outdoors," a practice that meant America was "destined to become a very, [sic] barren, ugly bit of wasteland." The places here under threat—Glacier Peak, Image Lake, Miners Ridge—constituted "a part of our great wilderness heritage." The area and the threat were representative to Douglas, and he feared, "If we lose this battle with . . . Kenn[e]cott we stand to lose many other battles." The choice was clear to him and his audience, and success depended on two things. First, the nation's constitutional system enshrined majority rule but also protected minority interests, something the justice labored for three decades to secure. In this case, the nation must protect the "rights of minorities . . . who like to backpack, ride horseback, to climb, to escape the noise and din of civilization and find the solitude and peace that is available only in the remote wilderness areas." Second, an aroused public might "appeal to the community's sense of justice, the whole corporate community, the whole body politic" and declare its preference for beauty over "a few paltry dollars." Hope lay in politics—the constitutional system and citizen action—as well as in a moral sense of right. That powerful combination, in Douglas's view, proved cause for resounding optimism.[41]

One of those who recorded Douglas was an Oberlin College sociology student named Benjamin A. Shaine. Unlike most who involved themselves in this fight, when he started Shaine was not a northwesterner, did not work for a conservation organization, and had never tramped or climbed in the Cascades. He personified the 1960s student-activist who combined reasoned intellectual analysis and impassioned personal commitment. As a college junior, he produced a report that urged Kennecott to scrap its plans. Shaine recognized the key dilemma, pointing out that industry, mass recreation, and wilderness cannot coexist in the same place at the same time—a point made repeatedly by all sides in wilderness contests. He ended with a passionate plea that called on the American public to use its influence to stop Kennecott and persuade Congress to revise the Wilderness Act to prohibit "mining and all other inappropriate development in wilderness lands." Only a few years from the movement's great success, the compromises required to pass the wilderness bill no longer seemed tenable. In this way, Shaine, like others, found in Miners Ridge a specific cause that inspired the need for a general reform.[42]

Between his junior and senior years, Shaine worked with Brock Evans, who had left his law practice to work as the Sierra Club's Northwest representative. Shaine returned to Oberlin geared up to make his honors thesis more than an academic requirement and vowed to be "one more voice speaking out" in favor of the North Cascades wilderness.[43] He produced an impressive thesis, but more impressive was his knack for cultivating connections and action. He met with his member of Congress and had a friend on the editorial staff at the *Washington Post* and a professor willing to write something for *Science* related to a petition Shaine compiled opposing Kennecott's actions.[44]

This petition and Shaine's persistence paid off. In April 1969, Shaine secured a meeting with Kennecott president Frank Milliken, delivering a petition signed by 428 scientists urging the company not to develop the open-pit mine. Among the prominent scientists who signed on were Lawrence Slobodkin, a path-breaking ecologist, and Paul Ehrlich, an outspoken scientist and popularizer of global overpopulation who at the time was one of the most visible scientists in the public eye.[45] In a "plush executive suite high above Manhattan traffic," Shaine met Milliken with respect, empathy, and a sense of urgency. The petitioners, he explained to Milliken, represented a growing group who believed that "in our complex, crowded society corporations must accept a responsibility for maintaining the quality of the environment and insist that corporations act in the long-term public interest, even at some financial sacrifice." The student acknowledged the dilemma facing Kennecott with the potential loss of profit and any investment so far made. Despite that sympathy, Shaine steadfastly maintained that mining in Glacier Peak would be a losing proposition for everyone: "Kennecott and the mining industry will encounter a storm of protest which may engender restrictions on all mining. All of the people will lose the tranquil beauty of Miners Ridge." Shaine hoped he provided a perspective and emphasis to persuade Kennecott.[46]

Predictably, Milliken remained equally steadfast, yet his response, evidenced by Shaine's notes, revealed some complications. In the firm's first meeting with conservationists in January 1967, Milliken prioritized profit as the sole factor driving decision-making. By 1969, questions of cost were far from straightforward and constantly changing. Although the company began seriously exploring the possibilities in 1965–66, the cost ratios were unfavorable then; by 1967, costs seemed favorable and the mine inevitable. Nevertheless, the meeting with Shaine occurred two years later; Kennecott had yet to apply to the Forest Service for any permits, and mining had not yet begun—facts that indicated several things. The price of copper was obviously volatile, with the margin between profitable and unprofitable fairly small. In this context, the way conservationists raised attention about the issue—especially calling into question the slight economic benefit compared with the incalculable wilderness loss—created an effect, despite Milliken's claims to the contrary. Milliken referred to the "harassment-legal-publicity" issue, claiming to Shaine that it was just "small peanuts" and "NOT a major factor." Despite Kennecott's many assurances that the various protests did not faze the company, Shaine pointed out that "these busy men rehearsed and attended a meeting with lowly me . . . [which] indicates public opinion really does matter." Milliken enjoyed a reputation as a "scrapper," but despite all this corporate posturing, Shaine recognized openings for continued direct action and grassroots organizing.[47]

Not all elements in the protest against Kennecott could be as dramatic as a criticizing cabinet secretary at a wilderness conference, a protesting doctor at a stockholders' meeting, a marching justice on the trail, or a crusading student in a corporate boardroom. Prosaic politics and macroeconomic forces may have tipped the scales.

Today, a North Cascades map will show a national park, national recreation areas, national forests, and some wilderness areas. There is a gap of many square miles between the North Cascades National Park's southern boundary and Miners Ridge, nestled in Glacier Peak Wilderness Area. However, those borders were not in place in the mid-1960s, and opportunities to map conservation anew in this landscape smashed together the stories of the park and the mine like ore in rock.

For decades, Northwest conservationists worked to determine the best ways to protect the Cascades north of Stevens Pass to the Canadian border. By the 1950s, they saw the regional Forest Service as a functional arm of the timber industry, so they conspired to wrest away the agency's power and shift its management priorities. Creating the wilderness area for Glacier Peak in 1960 whetted but did not sate conservationists' appetite. By the mid-1960s, a full-fledged national campaign developed to carve a national park out of national forests. Such bureaucratic transfers of power brought controversy, which meant slow action.[48] However, Senator Henry "Scoop" Jackson, a Democrat from Everett, practically in Glacier Peak's shadow, championed a North Cascades National Park and pushed the agenda along with S. 1321 passing the US Senate in 1967.

The park bill did not include Glacier Peak Wilderness Area, but that did not mean Miners Ridge did not matter to park advocates. In fact, the wilderness threat by Kennecott Copper Corporation did much to activate public interest. So powerful a motivator was the open-pit mine that Brock Evans once conspiratorially wondered if "we have friends in Kennecott who thought up this proposal to get national attention to this area."[49] The Forest Service's inability to stop Kennecott, even with Secretary Freeman's opposition, also reinforced in the public mind that the NPS, with its ability to ban mining in its units, offered a better bet. To build a public constituency for a park, activists "could beat the Forest Service over the head every day with their helplessness in the face of the mining law. This was of immense help in beating down the Forest Service argument that they could do a good job of protecting the North Cascades." In this telling, Kennecott played a critical role in creating the park.[50]

Soon, hearings opened political space to learn what the public wanted in the North Cascades. Many who wrote to Senator Jackson requesting a place at the hearings referenced Kennecott. The president of the University of Washington's Conservation Education and Action Council, Robert Michael Pyle (since those days a prolific and celebrated writer), was representative, urging Jackson to do all he could because "the snows are melting and disaster is impending."[51] The following spring, 1968, the US House Interior Committee met in Seattle. Evans recalled these hearings as "the real crystallization of the environmental movement in the state of Washington."[52] Whatever they were, they pushed Representative Wayne Aspinall into what the *Seattle Post-Intelligencer* could only call a snit. The controversy had been "blown all out of proportion," according to the inveterate legislator who promoted western resource extraction at every turn. He blamed Jackson and the press for whipping up the public into its agitated state. The Seattle hearings drew 800 people from a variety of socioeconomic positions and political experiences to the Benjamin Franklin Hotel—suggesting the aptness of Evans's characterization—and created a spectacle the legislator found threatening to his own agenda. "I don't know who these people are," Aspinall complained. "Are they hippies or part of a Seattle drive to get out into the country?" Since the hearings had been scheduled for a room with a 130-person capacity, northwesterners obviously overwhelmed and unsettled Aspinall.[53]

Despite Aspinall's snit, the park bill eventually passed, and President Lyndon Johnson signed the legislation in autumn 1968. It was quite an achievement. Conservationists mobilized a powerful constituency in a timber-heavy state against the Forest Service juggernaut doing the industry's bidding. Conservationists wanted a bigger park that would have protected Miners Ridge.[54] So immediately after getting the park, conservationists and allies turned back to Miners Ridge. *Seattle Times* columnist Walt Woodward represented the trend in a note to Jackson's press aide, signing off, "My very best to Scoop and hooray for a good guy who really accomplished something. Now . . . let's figger out a way to keep Kennecott from gouging up the landscape, huh?"[55]

While press attention and conservation action barely dissipated after the park's creation, economic factors also nudged Kennecott off the trail. When Kennecott initially explored opening a pit mine on Miners Ridge, a perceived copper shortage and rising wartime demand attracted the corporation interested in profit. Tracing the many interconnected economic lines resembled the tangled Glacier Peak watershed with myriad tributaries all finally flowing into the Suiattle and then the Skagit River.

Primarily, copper prices and mining costs mattered. Yet these costs bounced up and down like a kite in a Chinook wind. Determining prices in a volatile market for a long-term investment challenged companies' prognosticators and fundamentally revealed just how close to the margin of profitability Miners Ridge copper would be. Kennecott had expended more than $150 million over five years in the early 1960s to expand its domestic operations and needed copper-yielding property. When it found it, extracting the copper was difficult since the high-grade ore had long since been mined. Most available copper ore like that at Miners Ridge was less than 1 percent copper. That meant the company recovered just over a dozen pounds of copper per ton of ore, and first, "over two tons of overburden has to be removed." In the end, Kennecott's president explained, "for each 14 pounds of copper we produce, we must move over three tons of ore." He deployed these data to explain why Miners Ridge attracted the firm. Milliken probably did not see it this way, but his letter paints the picture of a fairly desperate industry.[56]

Organized labor also fit within the economic matrix. Amid the various protests in the Northwest, on July 15, 1967, 37,000 workers struck in the copper industry, closing down 90 percent of the industry into the following year. Only stockpiling just before the union contracts expired, along with high production in Africa and South America and dropping global prices, saved corporations.[57] In this context, organized labor stepped into the wilderness debate. Steel Labor, the steelworkers' paper, featured an article, "Kennecott vs. the North Cascades," in January 1968, a piece Northwest conservationists cooperated in publishing.[58] Recalling Kennecott's pitch of a year earlier, full of patriotic fervor, the United Steelworkers of America now joined with conservationists to oppose Kennecott because the union knew "perhaps better than any other organization . . . the mockery of Kennecott's expressed concern with the national interest." Although unions tended to want jobs for organized labor, the anticipated jobs at Miners Ridge "would be destructive, and this fact must govern our union's position in the matter." In a letter, Evans welcomed the union's support, asking for several hundred article-copies to give to "our union-minded members" to further generate mutual support for wilderness and the strike, adding that Kennecott's treatment of workers—not to mention the land—revealed that the company men "aren't aware that the nineteenth century is over." This was the rare occasion in this campaign when an organized group other than white middle-class professionals (or students) stood up to Kennecott. In this case, the unions' and conservationists' positions matched, each recognizing a valuable ally in the larger fight against corporate interests, albeit from different foundations.[59]

Contemporary sources mixed their messages. Kennecott long claimed domestic need and imbalance in the international market as reasons to pursue Miners Ridge's hidden copper. However, other facts undermined that position. In summer 1967, a 100,000-ton world surplus was reported just a year after the federal program, citing shortages, called for incentives that pushed Kennecott toward Miners Ridge. By 1969, a domestic shortfall seemed to be rooted in exporting too much copper to take advantage of higher global prices. Meanwhile, wearied by frequent shortages and price fluctuations, copper users adapted other materials when possible, finding substitute metals a better long-term strategy to increase independence from copper's unpredictability.[60] When prices and costs rose and fell like so many updrafts, it was hard to plan for a profitable mine.

Over a half decade the issue kindled, heated, and then simmered. Copper prices and production costs never seemed to match to favor Kennecott's bottom line. A shift in either prices or expenses, though, meant Miners Ridge was always under threat. In 1977, *Wild Cascades* reminded the North Cascades Conservation Council membership of Kennecott's continued presence and threat. Thankfully, no road slithered up the Suiattle Valley, but helicopters kept bringing prospectors to Miners Ridge, leaving "the Cascades' largest garbage dump—miles of plastic pipe, sheets of plywood, rusting oil drums, hardened sacks of cement, wire, lumber, and old clothing scattered everywhere throughout the meadows of this fragile alpine country." Kennecott remained a "sleeping giant" who, if roused to wake, could finally scrape out Plummer Mountain's shoulder. Be prepared, the *Wild Cascades* warned, to combat the stealth threat.[61]

There is no mine, and there never will be. Kennecott Copper Corporation sold its claim in 1986 to the Chelan County Public Utility District (PUD), which used the site to gather snowfall data. The Wild Sky Wilderness bill that passed in 2008 allowed for a land swap for the district and subsequently created a conservation easement between the PUD and the Forest Service. When implemented in 2010, the easement meant the long-contested mining claims were put to bed for good. When that happened, Gary Paull, the ranger who coordinated recreation for the forest, said, "The Kennecott mine was one of my greatest fears as a kid, and [I] have been following it ever since—nudging and prodding from the inside hoping to see this outcome." He was in good and long-standing company.[62]

On July 18, 1967, Brock Evans wrote to Kennecott's president, Frank R. Milliken. Evans was courteous and sought common ground. Like Milliken, Evans acknowledged the nation's mineral needs and searched for a balance in using land and other resources. But he drew a distinction. Wilderness and scenic beauty were also scarce and needed careful stewardship and protection. That is what Evans wrote to Milliken: "We do not believe that we have yet reached the point where *in this place*, the scenic and wilderness value is transcended by the mineral value. In other words, our view is that proper utilization of *this place* is for the other two of its three primary natural resources—the scenic beauty and the wilderness."[63] *In this place*—Miners Ridge—Evans pointed out that wilderness mattered more than minerals.

All this activity—the articles and the letters to editors, the speeches and protests, the hearings and meetings—showed the deep resonance of not just wild places but this wild place: Miners Ridge, Glacier Peak Wilderness Area, North Cascades. Perhaps Kennecott Copper Corporation was not stopped directly by a successful lawsuit or by mass direct action. Maybe the combination of copper prices, changing costs, and differing priorities tipped the balance. Yet the grassroots action made a difference to that place and that place made a difference to the grassroots growing out of university halls, doctors' offices, and suburban living rooms to convene along wild trailsides.

Notes

1. Miners Ridge is often referred to as Miner's Ridge. In quotations, I maintain the original spelling.

2. This scene is reconstructed from Brock Evans, "The Mining of Natural Beauty," *Cooperator: The Voice of the Puget Sound Cooperative League*, August 1966, p. C; Brock Evans, "Memo to Kennecott File," January 4, 1973, Brock Evans Papers (accession #1776–006), Box 22, folder 44, Special Collections, University of Washington, Seattle; Brock Evans, Seattle, WA, to Frank Milliken, New York, NY, March 3, 1967, Brock Evans Papers (accession #1776–006), Box 22, folder 40, Special Collections, University of Washington, Seattle.

3. An examination of any of the public hearings will reveal the range of occupations represented; for instance, *Hearings before the Subcommittee on Parks and Recreation of the United States Senate*, 90th Cong., 1st sess., on S. 1321, April 24–25, May 25, 27, 29, 1967. These proceedings recorded approximately 40 percent women and 67 percent men—the difference is that some letters included wives and husbands jointly.

4. It is not clear when the comparison to the Alps originated, but by the 1960s it had become the most common trope in the popular press. For instance, see "Our Wilderness Alps," *Sunset*, June 1965, n.p.; Paul Brooks, "The Fight for America's Alps," *Atlantic Monthly*, February 1967, 87–99.

5. Brock Evans, "Showdown for the Wilderness Alps of Washington's North Cascades," April 1968, n.p. It is unclear how this Sierra Club–produced pamphlet was distributed, but a copy is found in Sierra Club, Northwest Office Paper (accession #2678–009), Box 9, folder Speeches and Writing, "Showdown for the Wilderness Alps of Washington's North Cascades," Special Collections, University of Washington, Seattle.

6. A detailed chronology of various administrative moves is J. M. McCloskey, "Historical Chronology of Forest Service Action Regarding Glacier Peak Area," Sierra Club, Northwest Office Papers (accession #2678–005), Box 10, folder North Cascades Conservation Council 1964– (1962–68 retired), Special Collections, University of Washington, Seattle. Limited Area was a Region Six–specific classification that managed land as wilderness until further studies determined a more permanent classification. A brief journalistic account of creating Glacier Peak wilderness is in Michael Frome, *Battle for the Wilderness*, rev. ed. (Salt Lake City: University of Utah Press, 1997), 135–36. Descriptions from an activist involved in various campaigns can be found in Michael McCloskey, *In the Thick of It: My Life in the Sierra Club* (Washington, DC: Island, 2005), 41–46. The best scholarly account is Kevin

Marsh, *Drawing Lines in the Forest: Creating Wilderness Areas in the Pacific Northwest* (Seattle: University of Washington Press, 2007), 38–60.

7. The Wilderness Act is Public Law 88–577 and is reprinted in an appendix in Frome, *Battle for the Wilderness*, 214, 220. For Zahniser and the campaign for the bill, see Mark Harvey, *Wilderness Forever: Howard Zahniser and the Path to the Wilderness Act* (Seattle: University of Washington Press, 2005).

8. Harvey, *Wilderness Forever*, explores the compromises on 232.

9. Polly Dyer, Auburn, WA, to Grant [McConnell], June 6, 1956, Polly Dyer Papers (accession #3258–4), Box 5, folder Glacier Peak 2, Special Collections, University of Washington, Seattle. Dyer deserves scholarly attention. She appears most extensively in Dee Arntz, *Extraordinary Women Conservationists of Washington: Mothers of Nature* (Charleston, SC: History Press), 29–35, 37–44. Arntz's book is not always reliable on specific details, however. See Dyer's appearance in Marsh, *Drawing Lines in the Forest*, 42, 55, 84; Adam M. Sowards, *The Environmental Justice: William O. Douglas and American Conservation* (Corvallis: Oregon State University Press, 2009), 49–50, 54. Dyer's greatest claim to fame—although too few know this—is her use of the word *untrammeled* to describe wilderness, a descriptive word Howard Zahniser adopted in his drafting of the Wilderness Act. See Harvey, *Wilderness Forever*, 119, 202.

10. The anonymous letter is not available in N3C records, but for background, see Brock Evans, Seattle, WA, to Governor [Daniel J.] Evans, January 7, 1966, North Cascades Conservation Council Records (accession #1732–011), Box 8, folder Kennecott Mine General Correspondence 1966, Special Collections, University of Washington, Seattle.

11. Dwight to Harvey [Manning], August 18, 1966, North Cascades Conservation Council Records (accession #1732–011), Box 8, folder Kennecott Mine General Correspondence 1966, Special Collections, University of Washington, Seattle.

12. Brock Evans, Seattle, WA, to Bert Thomas, Columbus, OH, August 4, 1966, Brock Evans Papers (accession #1776–006), Box 22, folder 40, Special Collections, University of Washington, Seattle.

13. Handwritten notes apparently from Brock Evans to Pat[rick D.] Goldsworthy in North Cascades Conservation Council Records (accession #1732–011), Box 8, folder Kennecott Mine—Facts and Statistics 1967–1971, Special Collections, University of Washington, Seattle; see also "About the Mine: Rumors and Speculations and Miscellany," *Wild Cascades* (December 1966–January 1967): 11; Patrick D. Goldsworthy, Seattle, WA, to John B. Oakes, New York, NY, October 4, 1966, Brock Evans Papers (accession #1776–006), Box 22, folder 35, Special Collections, University of Washington, Seattle (quotation). Goldsworthy also let the paper know that conservationists might buy advertising space for publicity.

14. A photocopy of the *Mining Year Book, 1966*, page on Kennecott is found in North Cascades Conservation Council Records (accession #1732–011).

15. Brock Evans to Gov. Evans, January 7, 1966; "Big Mine Near Everett?" *Seattle Post-Intelligencer*, December 23, 1966; "Kennecott Copper Eyes N. Cascades," *Bellingham Herald*, December 22, 1966.

16. "GSA News Release," August 2, 1966, Wildernesses and Primitive Areas Glacier Peak Wilderness, folder no. 3a, Record Group 95, National Archives, Seattle, WA; Region 6, Division of Recreation and Lands Recreation Studies (095-74E0241), Box 8/147765, Brock Evans Papers (accession #1776-006, Box 22, folder 38, Special Collections, University of Washington, Seattle. An assistant secretary of defense informed Senator Henry "Scoop" Jackson that "the inevitable damage to the natural beauty of the wilderness area" made Miners Ridge a poor fit for the program; see Paul R. Ignatius, Washington, DC, to Henry M. Jackson, Washington, DC, April 7, 1967, Brock Evans Papers (accession #1776-006), Box 22, folder 38, Special Collections, University of Washington, Seattle.

17. The plan, as conservationists understood it, is outlined in Patrick D. Goldsworthy, Seattle, WA, to J. Herbert Stone, Portland, OR, July 26, 1966, North Cascades Conservation Council Records (accession #1732–011), Box 8, folder Kennecott Mine General Correspondence 1966, Special Collections, University of Washington, Seattle. For coverage, see "Big Mine Near Everett?"; "Kennecott Copper Eyes N. Cascades" (first quotation). For speculation about purchasing Kennecott's claims, see Philip H. Zalesky, Everett, WA, to N3C Board Member, July 14, 1958; David Brower, Berkeley, CA, to Northern Cascades cooperators and especially to fellow directors of the North Cascades Conservation Council, July 16, 1958 (final quotation); both in Polly Dyer Papers (accession #3258–4), Box 5, Unnamed Folders, Special Collections, University of Washington, Seattle. Also, "Open-Pit Mine in Cascades Draws Fire," *Skagit Valley Herald*, December 23, 1966; "Huge Open Copper Mine Considered for Cascades," *Bremerton Sun*, December 23, 1966; "Copper Mine Proposal Criticized," *Columbia Basin Herald*, December 23, 1966; "Cascades Mining Attacked," *Tri-City Herald*, December 23, 1966; "Copper Pit Proposed in N. Cascades," *Aberdeen World*, December 23, 1966; Walt Woodward, "Open-Pit Copper Mine Possible in Proposed Park," *Seattle Times*, December 22, 1966; Don Davis, "Tending to Business," *Everett Herald*, March 21, 1967.

18. Goldsworthy's notes from the meeting are contained in North Cascades Conservation Council Records (accession #1732–011), Box 8, folder Kennecott Mine—Minutes of Meetings with Kennecott Copper Corporation 1969, n.d., Special Collections, University of Washington, Seattle. These notes were closely formulated into an article that appeared as "Kennecott Meets with Conservation Leaders," *Wild Cascades* (December 1966–January 1967): 4, 21, and in *Mountaineer*,

April 1967, 11–12. The 1 percent figure comes from George Marshall, Los Angeles, CA, to Frank R. Milliken, New York, NY, February 14, 1967, North Cascades
Conservation Council Records (accession #1732–011), Box 8, folder Kennecott
Mine General Correspondence 1967, Special Collections, University of Washington,
Seattle. Brock Evans pointed out the difference between the stated plans from this
meeting and the public pronouncement about no decision in Brock Evans, Seattle, WA, to Thorton Thomas, Bellevue, WA, February 6, 1967, Brock Evans Papers
(accession #1776–006), Box 22, folder 40, Special Collections, University of Washington, Seattle.

19. Goldsworthy's notes.

20. Harvey, *Wilderness Forever*, 196–98, 209, 218–19.

21. Walt Woodward, "Open-Pit Copper Mine Possible in Proposed Park," *Seattle
Times*, December 22, 1966 (quotation). By summer of 1967, Chriswell took a more
public and critical role, leading the press and Seattle's mayor on a multiple-day
pack-trip through Glacier Peak country during which he announced likely restric-
tions on Kennecott's operation. Trip recounted in "Ride-in to Glacier Peak," *Seattle:
The Pacific Northwest Magazine* (October 1967): 23–27; "Restrictions Announced on
Open Copper Mine," *Seattle Post-Intelligencer*, August 27, 1967; "Kennecott Copper to
Be Asked to Go Underground," *Wenatchee Daily World*, August 31, 1967; Brock Evans,
Seattle, WA, to Gene Marine, San Francisco, CA, October 10, 1967, Brock Evans
Papers (accession #1776–006), Box 22, folder 40, Special Collections, University of
Washington, Seattle.

22. Arthur W. Greeley, Washington, DC, to Patrick D. Goldsworthy, Seattle,
WA, September 2, 1966, North Cascades Conservation Council Records (accession
#1732–011), Box 8, folder Kennecott Mine General Correspondence 1966, Special
Collections, University of Washington, Seattle.

23. This exchange can be reconstructed with "Wilderness Act Bars Pit Mine,"
Bellingham Herald, January 17, 1967; Brock Evans, Seattle, WA, to Herbert J. Stone,
Portland, OR, January 20, 1967 (Evans mistakenly reversed the J. and Herbert in
his name); Lloyd Meeds, Washington, DC, to Arthur W. Greeley, Washington, DC,
January 23, 1967; Arthur W. Greeley, Washington, DC, to Lloyd Meeds, February 10,
1967; J. Herbert Stone, Portland, OR, to Brock Evans, Seattle, WA, January 26, 1967;
all in North Cascades Conservation Council Records (accession #1732–011), Box 8,
folder Kennecott Mine General Correspondence 1967, Special Collections, University of Washington, Seattle.

24. Proceedings are available in Maxine E. McCloskey and James P. Gilligan, eds.,
Wilderness and the Quality of Life (San Francisco: Sierra Club, 1969), v.

25. Orville Freeman, "Address," in McCloskey and Gilligan, *Wilderness and the
Quality of Life*, quotations from 109–10.

26. Freeman, "Address," iii, 110. For reference to the news conference, see "Kennecott Is Asked to Leave Untouched Copper Claims in West," *Wall Street Journal*, April 10, 1967.

27. Freeman, "Address," 110, 115.

28. Brock Evans thanked Freeman in Brock Evans, Seattle, WA, to Orville H. Freeman, Washington, DC, April 21, 1967, Brock Evans Papers (accession #1776–006), Box 22, folder 40, Special Collections, University of Washington, Seattle. The president of the Sierra Club wrote to the president of Kennecott to inform him of the secretary's position in George Marshall, Los Angeles, CA, to Frank R. Milliken, New York, NY, April 28, 1967, Brock Evans Papers (accession #1776–006), Box 22, folder 39, Special Collections, University of Washington, Seattle. And the United Steelworkers of America issued a press release critical of Kennecott's position in "News from the USWA Press Release," April 7, 1967, Brock Evans Papers (accession #1776–006), Box 22, folder 45, Special Collections, University of Washington, Seattle.

29. Stan Dayton, "Behind the By-Lines," *Engineering and Mining Journal* (May 1967), Brock Evans Papers (accession #1776-006), Box 22, folder 46, Special Collections, University of Washington, Seattle.

30. F[red] T. Darvill, "Deplores Open Pit Mine Proposal in Wilderness," *Skagit Valley Herald*, December 28, 1966; Lloyd Meeds, Washington, DC, to Dr. F[red] T. Darvill, Mount Vernon, WA, December 29, 1966, North Cascades Conservation Council (accession #1732–011), Box 8, folder Kennecott Mine General Correspondence 1966, Special Collections, University of Washington, Seattle.

31. F[red] T. Darvill, Mount Vernon, WA, to Kennicott [*sic*] Copper Company, New York, NY, January 19, 1967, North Cascades Conservation Council (accession #1732–011), Box 8, folder Kennecott Mine General Correspondence 1967, Special Collections, University of Washington, Seattle; Frank R. Milliken, New York, NY, to Dr. F[red] T. Darvill, Mount Vernon, WA, February 6, 1967, Brock Evans Papers (accession #1776–006), Box 22, folder 38, Special Collections, University of Washington, Seattle; "Copper Firm Stockholder Hits Open-Pit Mine Plan," unsourced newspaper article in Brock Evans Papers (accession #1776–006), Box 22, folder 49, Special Collections, University of Washington, Seattle.

32. Malcolm R. Wilkey, New York, NY, to Fred T. Darvill Jr., MD, Mount Vernon, WA, January 23, 1967, North Cascades Conservation Council Papers (accession #1732–001), Box 8, folder Kennecott Mine General Correspondence 1967, Special Collections, University of Washington, Seattle; "Copper Firm Stockholder"; "Statement of Fred Darvill, MD, Kennecott Copper Corporation, Annual Stockholders' Meeting, Biltmore Hotel, May 2, 1967," North Cascades Conservation Council Papers (accession #1732–001), Box 8, folder Kennecott Mine—Speeches and

Writings, misc. 1960–1970, Special Collections, University of Washington, Seattle (quotations). A summary of the meeting is found in Robert A. Wright, "Copper Concerns Report Earnings," *New York Times*, May 2, 1967; "Kennecott Profit Showed Big Gain in First Quarter," *Wall Street Journal*, May 3, 1967.

33. Walt Woodward, "Copper Firm Warned against Cascades Mine," *Seattle Times*, undated clipping in North Cascades Conservation Council Records (accession #1732–011), Box 8, folder Kennecott Mine—Clippings 1966–1970, n.d., Special Collections, University of Washington, Seattle.

34. "Crisis at Miners Ridge," *Washington Post*, May 3, 1967. The day before the editorial, the *Post* included a news story summarizing the issue, focusing on Forest Service efforts to stall or stop Kennecott; see Eric Wentworth, "US Forest Service Strives to Prevent Big Open-Pit Mine," *Washington Post*, May 2, 1967.

35. "Stop Kennecott Group Organized," *Wenatchee Daily World*, April 30, 1967; Rob and Cindy Cole, "An Open Pit on Miner's Ridge Large Enough to Be Seen on the Moon," unsourced clipping in Brock Evans Papers (accession #1776–006), Box 22, folder 49, Special Collections, University of Washington, Seattle. In a personal conversation with the author, August 7, 2015, Robert Michael Pyle remembered the University of Washington's Conservation Education Action Council inviting Douglas, knowing he had led other protest hikes in the region.

36. William O. Douglas, *My Wilderness: The Pacific West* (Garden City, NY: Doubleday, 1960), 152–68, 165 (quotation). Douglas's contributions to American conservation, although not his role at Glacier Peak, have been treated extensively in Sowards, *Environmental Justice*; for Douglas in Northwest conservation, see 48–56, 83–91.

37. Maribeth Morris, "Protestors Crash Douglas Camp-In," *Seattle Post-Intelligencer*, August 6, 1967 (first quotation); Marjorie Jones, "Douglas Leads Glacier Peak Protest," *Seattle Times*, August 6, 1967 (second and third quotations); "Miner's Ridge Film: Notes to Editor-Producer," May 13, 1968, North Cascades Conservation Council Records (accession #1732–011), Box 8, folder Kennecott (Mine) Film 1968, Special Collections, University of Washington, Seattle; "Justice Douglas Leads Hikers to Glacier Peak," *Wenatchee Daily World*, August 7, 1967; Brock Evans, Seattle, Wa, to Dick Miller, Pittsburgh, PA, October 10, 1967, Brock Evans Papers (accession #1776–006), Box 22, folder 40, Special Collections, University of Washington, Seattle. Although Douglas's chapter in *My Wilderness* demonstrated that he knew of the potential for a copper mine, he was first alerted to the imminent threat when the president of the North Cascades Conservation Council wrote to the secretary of agriculture and copied Douglas; see Patrick D. Goldsworthy, Seattle, WA, to Orville L. Freeman, Washington, DC, March 9, 1967, N3C, folder Kennecott Mine General Correspondence 1967, Special Collections, University of Washington, Seattle.

38. Morris, "Protestors Crash," outsiders, Backstrom quotations; Jones, "Douglas Leads," sign, birdwatchers' quotations. In "Justice Douglas Leads Hikers," Backstrom admits that there would only be three or four years of work. Evans to Marine. Richard White explored the dynamic of knowing nature through work as opposed to leisure in his classic essay "'Are You an Environmentalist, or Do You Work for a Living?': Work and Nature," in *Uncommon Ground: Toward Reinventing Nature*, ed. William Cronon (New York: W. W. Norton, 1995), 171–85. The essay title came from a bumper sticker found in Northwest timber towns in the 1990s.

39. The North Cascades Conservation Council records contain two folders of materials related to the film; rather than cite the voluminous correspondence, readers are referred to those folders: North Cascades Conservation Council (accession #1732–001), Box 8, folder Kennecott (Mine) Film 1967–1968, Special Collections, University of Washington, Seattle; North Cascades Conservation Council (accession #1732–001), Box 8, folder Kennecott (Mine) Film 1968, Special Collections, University of Washington, Seattle. Benjamin A. Shaine, a student-activist who recorded Douglas along with Goldsworthy, described the taping in his thesis. Benjamin A. Shaine, "Kennecott on Miners Ridge: A Description and Analysis of the Controversy over the Proposal of the Kennecott Copper Corporation to Construct an Open-Pit Copper Mine in the Glacier Peak Wilderness Area of Washington," honors thesis, Oberlin College, Oberlin, OH, 1969, North Cascades Conservation Council (accession #1732–001), Box 8, folder Kennecott Mine—Speeches and Writings—"Kennecott on Miner's Ridge" by Benjamin Shaine, unpaginated, Special Collections, University of Washington, Seattle.

40. Quoted in Morris, "Protestors Crash."

41. "Remarks of Justice William O. Douglas Regarding Kennacott [*sic*] Copper Corp. Proposed Open-Pit Copper Mine on Miners Ridge, July 21, 1968," North Cascades Conservation Council (accession #1732–001), Box 8, folder Kennecott (Mine) Film 1967–1968, Special Collections, University of Washington, Seattle.

42. Benjamin A. Shaine, "The Proposed Open-Pit Copper Mine in the Glacier Peak Wilderness of Washington State: An Analysis," Oberlin College, Oberlin, OH, May 1968, Brock Evans Papers (accession #1776–006), Box 22, folder 46, Special Collections, University of Washington, Seattle, 5.

43. Benjamin [A.] Shaine, Oberlin, OH, to Brock Evans, Seattle, WA, May 15, 1968, Brock Evans Papers (accession #1776–006), Box 22, folder 36, Special Collections, University of Washington, Seattle.

44. Shaine to Evans, May 15, 1968; Ben[jamin A. Shaine], Aspen, CO, to Brock and Rachel [Evans], January 20, 1969; Ben[jamin A. Shaine], Oberlin, OH, to Brock Evans, Seattle, WA, March 4, 1969; all in Brock Evans Papers (accession #1776–006), Box 22, folder 36, Special Collections, University of Washington, Seattle.

45. A profile is found in Paul Sabin, *The Bet: Paul Ehrlich, Julian Simon, and Our Gamble over Earth's Future* (New Haven, CT: Yale University Press, 2013).

46. Ben[jamin A.] Shaine, "The Continuing Threat to Miners Ridge," *Wild Cascades* (February–March 1970): 2 (plush suite quotation); Benjamin [A.] Shaine, Oberlin, OH, to Frank R. Milliken, New York, NY, April 11, 1969, North Cascades Conservation Council Records (accession #1732–001), Box 8, folder Kennecott Mine General Correspondence 1968–73, Special Collections, University of Washington, Seattle (quotation on p. 2). This file also includes a press release distributed by Oberlin College on behalf of Shaine. The *Washington Post* seems to have referenced the petition in the editorial "Imperiled Wilderness," *Washington Post*, May 15, 1969.

47. Benjamin [A.] Shaine, "Notes on Meeting April 11, 1969 with Kennecott on Miners Ridge Operation," North Cascades Conservation Council Records (accession #1732–011), Box 8, folder Kennecott Mine—Minutes of Meetings with Kennecott Copper Corporation 1969, n.d., Special Collections, University of Washington, Seattle (quotations on 1, 2). Shaine's published summary of his meeting in the N3C newsletter is Ben[jamin A.] Shaine, "The Continuing Threat to Miners Ridge," *Wild Cascades* (February–March 1970): 2–6. See also the coverage in Walt Woodward, "Kennecott Adamant on Glacier Peak Mining, *Seattle Times*, May 16, 1969.

48. The North Cascades National Park story is told in many places, but the best scholarly accounts can be found in David Louter, *Windshield Wilderness: Cars, Roads, and Nature in Washington's National Parks* (Seattle: University of Washington Press, 2006), 105–63; Marsh, *Drawing Lines in the Forest*, 38–60.

49. Brock Evans, Seattle, WA, to Dick Miller, Pittsburgh, PA, October 10, 1967, Brock Evans Papers (accession #1776–006), Box 22, folder 40, Special Collections, University of Washington, Seattle.

50. Evans, "Memo to Kennecott File." This perspective seemed obvious to others; a letter from Tacoma declared it "glaringly obvious that the Forest Service has no jurisdiction to stop the operation." John C. Migdula, Tacoma, WA, to Henry M. Jackson, Washington, DC, May 25, 1967, Henry M. Jackson Papers (accession #3560–4), Box 209, folder 29, Special Collections, University of Washington, Seattle.

51. Robert M[ichael] Pyle, Seattle, WA, to Henry M. Jackson, Washington, DC, May 9, 1967, Henry M. Jackson Papers (accession #3560–04), Box 210, folder 1, Special Collections, University of Washington, Seattle. Kennecott frequently said they would begin working as soon as the snow melted. See numerous other letters in the same box for similar requests to speak at the hearings.

52. Brock Evans, "Memo to the North Cascades 1968 File," January 11, 1973, Sierra Club, Northwest Office (accession #2678–005), Box 10, folder North Cascades 1972, Special Collections, University of Washington, Seattle.

53. "Aspinall's Snit," *Seattle Post-Intelligencer*, April 23, 1968; Walt Woodward, "Many Barred from North Cascades Hearing," *Seattle Times*, April 19, 1968. Of course, his and Jackson's antipathy transcended the North Cascades, as the Colorado politician at the time eyed the Columbia River with hopes of rerouting its water to the Southwest, a prospect that more than riled Jackson.

54. During the campaign, the Sierra Club produced a document that highlighted legislation's insufficient protections, including for Miners Ridge, in Sierra Club, "A North Cascades National Park for America's Alps," Sierra Club, Northwest Office, 1967? (accession #2678–001), Box 2, folder Washington—North Cascades, Special Collections, University of Washington, Seattle. The club's publication was attached to the Park Service's pamphlet promoting the park.

55. Walt Woodward, Seattle, WA, to Brian Corcoran, Washington, DC, September 19, 1968, Henry M. Jackson Papers (accession #3560–04), Box 210, folder 7, Special Collections, University of Washington, Seattle.

56. Frank R. Milliken, New York, NY, to Clark H. Jones, San Bernardino, CA, June 12, 1967, North Cascades Conservation Council Records (accession #1732–011), Box 8, folder Kennecott Mine General Correspondence 1967, Special Collections, University of Washington, Seattle.

57. Copper workers actually worked two weeks beyond their contracts, during which consumers stockpiled even more copper. Robert Walker, "Copper Strike Is Taken Calmly," *New York Times*, August 13, 1967; Robert Walker, "Storm of Apathy Greets Copper Rise," *New York Times*, February 18, 1968. The *New York Times* article includes a chart comparing global and domestic prices.

58. "Kennecott vs. the North Cascades," *Steel Labor* (January1968): 7 (quotations). Brock Evans sent a detailed account of Kennecott's and conservationists' activities to the United Steelworkers; it is, in fact, one of the most thorough accounts available. See Brock Evans, Seattle, WA, to Dick Miller, Pittsburgh, PA, October 10, 1967, Brock Evans Papers (accession #1776–006), Box 22, folder 40, Special Collections, University of Washington, Seattle.

59. "Kennecott vs. the North Cascades," *Steel Labor* (January 1968): 7. The publisher shared a draft with Brock Evans; see Richard L. Miller, Pittsburgh, PA, to Brock Evans, Seattle, WA, December 21, 1967, Brock Evans Papers (accession #1776–006), Box 22, folder 39, Special Collections, University of Washington, Seattle; Brock Evans, Seattle, WA, to Richard Miller, Pittsburgh, PA, January 26, 1968, Brock Evans Papers (accession #1776–006), Box 22, folder 40, Special Collections, University of Washington, Seattle (quotations). United Steelworkers was not the only union that made its opposition known to Senator Jackson; see letters from the Amalgamated Transit Union registering its "strong opposition" and the Window Cleaners Union "stating strongly our disapproval," as well as Jackson's reply to the

Culinary Workers and Bartenders Union; August Antonino, Seattle, WA, to Henry [M.] Jackson, Washington, DC, April 19, 1968 (transit); Hugh Sugiura, Seattle, WA, to Henry M. Jackson, Washington, DC, April 15, 1968 (window cleaners); both in Henry M. Jackson Papers (accession #3560–04), Box 210, folder 1, Special Collections, University of Washington, Seattle; Henry M. Jackson, Washington, DC, to Hazel M. Leirdahl and Harold A. Dodson, Renton, WA, May 16, 1968, Henry M. Jackson Papers (accession #3560–04), Box 210, folder 5, Special Collections, University of Washington, Seattle (culinary).

60. Charles B. Camp, "Down with Copper," *Wall Street Journal*, August 24, 1966; Ray Vicker, "Four Major Copper-Producing Countries Meet Today on Price Levels, Cut in Output," *Wall Street Journal*, June 1, 1967; "Rise in Copper Output to Offset Higher Costs Urged by Anaconda Co.," *Wall Street Journal*, September 7, 1967; all in North Cascades Conservation Council Records (accession #1732–011), Box 8, folder Kennecott Mine—Clippings 1966–1970, n.d., Special Collections, University of Washington, Seattle; *Congressional Record—Extension of Remarks*, June 4, 1969, 4598–99, Brock Evans Papers (accession #1776–006), Box 22, folder 46, Special Collections, University of Washington, Seattle.

61. "Wilderness Mines: Cause for Concern," *Wild Cascades* (Spring 1977): 12.

62. Joel Connelly, "The Open Pit Is Finally Put Away," *Seattle Post-Intelligencer*, May 5, 2010, accessed August 14, 2015, https://blog.seattlepi.com/seattlepolitics/2010/05/05/the-open-pit-is-finally-put-away/ (quotation); Bill Sheets, "Swap Adds Miner's Ridge to Glacier Peak," May 7, 2010, accessed August 14, 2015, https://www.heraldnet.com/article/20100507/NEWS01/705079879. The Forest Service did not wish to acquire the lands outright because of concerns about liability and potentially having to pay for cleanup costs. Gary Paull, personal communication to the author, June 8, 2017.

63. Brock Evans, Seattle, WA, to Frank R. Millik[e]n, New York, NY, July 18, 1967, Brock Evans Papers (accession #1776-006), Box 22, folder 40, Special Collections, University of Washington, Seattle (original emphasis).

13

Oil and Water

Fracking Politics in South Texas

Hugh Fitzsimmons

These are the two liquids in my life. I am composed of one and tethered to the other. Paradoxically, both enrich me. As I write this chapter, the incessant vibrato of a multimillion-dollar, sixteen-stage "zipper frac" pulsates 8,000 feet beneath my feet. It shatters a stillness that can never be recaptured, telegraphing its message to a world obsessed with conquering nature to fuel a need that has no end in sight. Each "frack" consumes over 5.4 million gallons of that rarest of dwindling assets: freshwater. In Dimmit County, Texas, where I live, we have the ignominious distinction of being the county with the most freshwater extracted for use in hydrologic fracturing in the entire United States, just over 14.2 billion gallons as of 2016. This process is projected to repeat itself with tens of thousands of wells being drilled here in South Texas alone, swallowing and potentially polluting our groundwater.

For a rancher like me, this is a recipe for disaster. And while our state agriculture uses far more water than does unconventional oil and gas extraction, irrigation water stays in the hydrologic cycle and is used to produce sustenance for the people while providing longer-term jobs and stability for the

DOI: 10.5876/9781607328483.c013

citizens of our county. I believe our county needs to make the critical transition back to a restorative agriculturally based economy and move away from an extractive hydrocarbon-based economy.

Drilling of the Eagle Ford shale is continuing like there is no tomorrow, which should not be too far off given the frenetic pace of what the oil industry terms a "play." For the past fifty years, my family's ranch has gone through one conventional energy play after the next. What a curious word we have chosen for the unleashing of "industry" on what was once the natural world. In fact, this activity—a play—is an industrial mining operation complete with thousands of trucks and hundreds of multi-ton drilling rigs and engines, behemoths that dwarf the surrounding countryside. They tower like swollen steel giants above the canopy of green mesquite trees that blanket this land. They are here to do their bidding as quickly and efficiently as their 2,000-horsepower diesel engines will allow. At sunset, the lights on the rigs are almost beautiful, like a Christmas tree decorated for the holy days. They remind me of what the English and Irish landed gentry used to call a "folly," massive monuments the landlord built on his estate for the purpose of erecting a structure that would serve as a conversation piece. Perfect. Too bad that nowadays the conversation has shifted from how much oil and gas is produced to how much water is left. Drillers have served their purpose well and enriched the fortunate few while simultaneously draining our freshwater.

At its core, hydrologic fracturing is about using pressure to break open and release oil and gas that is reluctant to flow to the surface, held tight in the shale formations that are over a mile beneath where I sit. The process has been around since 1947, but the genie came out of the bottle down here in 2008 with the advent of what is known as the "super frack." This involves the high-pressure pumping of water, sand, and chemicals down the well bore and into the target shale formation. If done correctly and with an exactitude that the industry loves to tout, all is well. Existing fissures in the rock widen and are propped open by the sand that is carried by the water and chemical slurry. The pressure pumps force over 15,000 pounds per square inch of this mixture into the shale before the propent does its job and the process of flowback begins.

In this section of the Eagle Ford, the operator loses around 80 percent of the flowback water as it makes its way back to the surface. Flowback is the period when escaping chemicals can migrate into other formations' groundwater, be vented into the atmosphere, or wander into our stream beds and ponds with devastating consequences—especially after a heavy downpour or micro-burst, which have become common over the past few years. The best-case scenario is that it will channel into the formations below and become trapped by the overburden of higher rock, keeping it out of our groundwater. Worst case: given that geology is not an exact science, there can be and have been variables that upset the hydrocarbon roulette wheel.

The ranch my grandfather purchased in 1932 once lay between two great rivers, bound on its north by the slow, steady, and tree-shrouded Nueces and on the south by the shallow and wide-open Rio Grande. When I was a child, this ranch was my playground. I was always afield with horse, rod, dog, and gun. Carefree and running wild, a boy with a man's set of tools. What gave that boy the push, the juice to go and do as he pleased was knowing that he was never as big as the land itself. It served as a kind of yardstick that measured wonder, hiding a surprise behind every bush.

That same ranch is where I choose to raise my bison herd today. Some may see this as my folly. We are a grass-fed–only operation that depends entirely on rainfall and a limited supply of groundwater to sustain the native grasses and forbs the bison eat. This country was once known as the *desploblado*, a place Spanish explorers called "no man's land." Even then, it was less than desirable for sustaining anything other than the herds of wild mustangs and bison that had free rein in this sea of grass. It always lacked one crucial life-giving element: water.

When one of the first water wells on the ranch was drilled in 1927, the driller went to the one spot where he knew he would connect with what he was seeking. Down in the bottom of a white brush thicket surrounded by a stand of mesquites that are as thick as a horse's rear end was a long solid slab of Carrizo sandstone outcrop. This is not only the spot where the geology and hydrology unite to hold the water but the spot where the formation of brush, trees, and the surrounding slope of terrain converge to funnel the wind to the windmill.

In a light wind, when no other mill is turning on the ranch, the San Francisco windmill will be steadily spinning in what breeze there is. It is magic. Its creaky old wooden tower is held fast by four mammoth cedar posts that a man would serve jail time for today were he foolish enough to cut one. Its weathered pine superstructure has seen drought, flood, windstorm, and hurricane. An Aeromotor fan drives the sucker rods sixty-seven feet into this shallowest of reservoirs, what the water well drillers call the "Blue Sands." They are the first to gather what little recharge we have and the first to go dry. At the base of the well is a small square block of evenly poured cement, and incised with great precision and care into that cement is a reverse "Swastika," a symbol that predates the Nazi sign of death and domination. In its true form, it is a Navajo symbol for "fair winds and good luck." Its very presence always sustained me through times when I wondered what in the world I was doing and how much longer it would be until we got a good soaking rain. The San Francisco gave up the last hint of its moisture in early 2013.

I can still remember a time when that resource seemed inexhaustible to me. My first big water memory was in the early fall of 1964. My family was all under one roof. Even my grandparents from Wichita Falls were with us at our home on San Pedro Creek. The soil was saturated from an earlier August rain, so when that storm slowly wormed its way out of the Gulf of Mexico and stalled with us in its crosshairs, we were in for a meteorological event of thunderous proportions. I remember going to bed with the faint "pat, pat, pat" of rain on the roof. When morning came, the first thing I heard was the wind and rain working in violent rhythmic concert. Gusts of water blew sideways with gale force against the windows. Family lore has me going to the window and looking out past the wall toward the big live oak 100 yards distant from where I stood. "The River Nile has come to the San Pedro," is purportedly what I said. Indeed, there was now a river where once there had been a gentle creek. Cracked willows uprooted by a force of nature unknown for decades floated past me as I stared in astonishment and boyhood wonder at the transformation of a land I thought I knew, scouring sandstone and sweeping all that was not anchored before it. The fear of flood in a land of drought—what a delight to be surrounded by something beneficial you have no control over. As if we were in the path of an approaching tornado, we huddled together. The bond of danger glued us together.

At the time there were two somewhat aimless yet amiable brothers at the ranch who were the cook's boys, the sons of Mr. and Mrs. Hawkins. She cooked in the bunkhouse, up before daylight and feeding a dozen or so men at the long table where half-awake cowboys came to attention at the sight and smell of refried beans and Crisco oil popping on the butane stove. Her husband, as I remember, was known for getting up every morning and going down to the creek to hunt for arrowheads. As I was sitting on the front porch of the bunkhouse one day watching old man Hawkins go through a Hill's Brothers coffee can filled with broken pieces of flint and ancient scrapers, I asked him what his sons wanted to be when they grew up. He scowled and squinted his beady eyes before spitting into the yard: "All those boys are good for is braiding quirts. They just sit around all day and twist leather together." Perhaps so, but they did rise to the occasion on the morning of September 17, 1964.

After the initial shock of the flood had subsided, the grownups started to ponder an evacuation plan. The water was still rising and the rain was still falling. It came down in seemingly endless sheets, blowing sideways in sudden bursts against the windows. I recall a brief lull in the storm, at which point we all walked down to the creek.

On the other side of the bank stood the Hawkins boys. They were trying to yell, but the roar of the creek drowned out their words. Then they drove off and returned in ten minutes. They taped a message to an arrow and drew back the bow, and I watched the arrow arch over the creek and land a few feet from my father. The note read something to the effect of "drive out the back route through Faith Ranch and go to Laredo." By now, the rain had ceased, and we realized that our plight was not as dire as we had predicted. But it had been an episode of intense danger, and the thrill of it still lingers fifty years later. I can still see that white aluminum arrow with its red and blue fletching slice across the sky with an ageless grace and speed. It is what a ten-year-old remembers. My grandfather had a little witticism where rainwater is concerned. When asked what the annual rainfall was, he would reply, "We generally get around twenty-one inches a year, and it usually comes in two ten-inch rains, but we never get the other inch."

I paid scant attention to oil and gas operations on the ranch in my formative years there. I was outside with my own private thoughts of adventure and exploration in a land still untamed by road and drill bit. I made many trips down the rivers. But when the summer of 1980 came and gas and oil prices spiked, it set off a drilling frenzy on the ranch that caused me to sit up and take notice. What I remember more than anything was my father's reaction to a well that came in with an initial force and pressure that made everyone hop on the gravy train with glee. It was not long before visions of airplanes and new trucks clouded our thoughts. His glee became infectious and for the first time I thought, "My God, can this really be true?" I'm sure that financial gain fueled my thinking; there is something so innately joyous in observing hydrocarbons flowing from a well and into a pipeline. Like Jett Rink in the film *Giant*, there was an ecstatic overflow of giddiness from operators and mineral owners: your well has come in, and any consequences of its production take a back seat to the benefits of free money. It was not too different from getting that first rush of adrenaline when you are hunting, following a scent as old as time and feeling the presence of something greater than yourself. The hydrocarbon endorphin had been unleashed, and it suffused your very being. And just like that, before you could gain your footing and absorb the impact, there were hundreds of little pump jacks, tanks, separators, diesel compressors, and pipelines all working in a glorious harmonic convergence to extract and produce something that nature had kept secret since way before our time began. We had made our pact with industry, neglecting a truism that has come to haunt me: "there is always free cheese in the mousetrap."

We had a big wide-open ranch with plenty of everything. What difference did it make to sink a few wells into the pasture and soak up what we were lucky enough to be on the receiving end of? Who needs water when we have all this oil and gas? My excitement, as it turns out, was only exceeded by my naïveté. Pressures soon dropped and the well became so-so, just like all the others.

It seems that there is an inherent propensity for family discord when it comes to balancing individual desires and land use. Ranchers for the most part do not govern by consensus and committee. Our issues were seemingly settled in the late 1990s, and I received my section of the ranch with a mixture of elation infused with independent thinking that set me off on a distinctive path of discovery. I wanted to bring back the animal that had been here for 10,000 years. I turned back the clock and started the first commercial bison herd in South Texas. My work became my life and my life became my work. In the blink of an eye, I populated the ranch with the largest land mammal on the North American continent. I felt the need to surround myself with the presence of the past, a bulwark that would connect me to a time when freedom and natural selection set the kingdom of the buffalo apart. It is the oldest continuously harvested herbivore on the North American continent, and the sight of hundreds of these magnificent creatures roaming a land their species had not graced for two centuries thrilled me to my core.

In 2005, unbeknownst to me, the trust that controls the executive rights to execute leases on the ranch decided to lease our deep rights to a major independent oil company. My father and the rest of the family complied; the lure of unlocking vast reserves and the economic incentive were just too great.

A wise old rancher once told me, "Sunny, cash can make you careless." And the $100-a-barrel oil of 2014 covered up a lot of mistakes on the part of industry and landowners. This truism has been amplified exponentially, given the run-up in price and speed with which the Eagle Ford Play has accelerated since the most recent boom in 2008. Oil selling at $100 a barrel and the alacrity with which the industry has pursued it can displace your perspective and disorient you in relation to the natural world. It gives you a false sense of security and overrides what you know and, more important, have taken for granted until now. Just sign here.

Because the oil and gas industry in Texas is exempt from any restrictions regarding the extraction of underground water for use in fracturing, its representatives are free to take all they want, providing they have the permission of the landowner. Like a grandparent letting a four-year-old loose in a candy store, our state is allowing the unprecedented depletion of what the law asserts belongs to one owner but that by its nature belongs to us all. The desire is to create private property in a communal resource, a concept that is destined to fail as the resource becomes depleted over time. As a state, Texas has been operating a twenty-first-century highly complex and technical drilling, extraction, and production operation using water law from eleventh-century England.

In 1805, the rule of capture was first tested in Queens County, New York. It seems a Mr. Post had shot and wounded a fox that escaped and was then shot and killed by a Mr. Pierson. Post sued Pierson and won in the lower court, claiming the fox was his because he was the one who drew first blood and initiated the pursuit of the fox. The Supreme Court of the State of New York reversed that decision when Pierson countersued, claiming the fox was his because he captured (by killing) it and should therefore have possession. The court sided with Pierson, which is the basis for our water law in the state of Texas. The man who captures/kills it has possession.

This is also known as "the tragedy of the commons." Accurately named, it is the absolutely worst possible tragedy for the land, the landowner, and living organisms that need water. It panders to the most debased side of our nature, and it runs something like this. The rule of capture, which in our state was established in 1904, says that if you own the land, you own the water beneath it. You can pump with impunity until the well goes dry.

At the same time, you are most likely, especially in the case of small land-holdings, depleting the water from beneath your neighbor's land, hence the commons. The tragedy comes when a man with a conscience shows up and says, "I will not pump an excessive amount because I would not want my neighbor doing that to me." Well, too bad, too sad if your neighbor across the fence does not share the same ethical perspective. His view is probably simple: if it is legal and if I do not use it and or sell it, then someone else will. A precious resource held in common is headed for catastrophe.

Here is where oil and water really do not mix: we need this water to stay alive, and so does "industry." When a well is spudded, a term that makes the process seem almost bucolic, water is employed to lubricate the drill bit as it rotates through the various formations. Then once the drillers are past the water-bearing strata, they switch to a diesel-based fluid for the rest of the drilling. On balance, these operations use a minimal amount of freshwater, but when it is time to frack, they better have the water in place or the game is over. Conventional drilling requires much less water, but without the frack-ing you don't have a chance in shale, and to have a frack you must have a copious and readily abundant supply of water.

Ranchers in my neighborhood have had the good fortune to have a rela-tively clean and accessible underground water source. But is it worth risking that resource for the finite carbon entombed below? Yes, you say, if you own your mineral rights and can sell that precious water to an oil company for a dollar per barrel. But if you are a landowner with no such rights whose water is being drained by a neighbor's well that is pumping water day and night, taking in some cases three months to fill a frack pit, you are out of luck.

In a recent meeting with one of our operators, their water guy said it best when I asked him what he did. He replied, "I hunt water wherever I can find it. I hunt it down." That's right, I thought to myself. He hunts down water and he kills it. Down here, he hunts down something that should be on the endangered species list, for water is not only alive, but it also brings and sustains life. The industry blends a fracking carcinogenic cocktail of die-sel, water, various herbicides, benzene, toluene, xylene, and other chemicals it then injects at over 20,000 pounds per square inch and pumps down the borehole with sand to blast open the fissures that hold what the industry is after. Once the frack is complete, the fun really starts. Flowback. In our particular geologic location, we only get roughly 20 percent of the water back. The remainder is lost into God knows where, coursing through strata no one even knows about, never to be seen again. Lost to the ages unless we have a seismic event, which could send those carcinogens seeping into another adjacent formation and up an abandoned well. Dimmit County has had twenty-two "cluster earthquakes" since 2008. "Surprise," Mr. Benzene says as he pops up like a jack-in-the-box. "And you thought I was gone."

Now human nature, as far as I can tell, does not lend itself to either moderation or reasonable behavior when it comes to the extraction of anything. We pump, mine, and dig until it is gone. John Adams once said, "Facts are stubborn things." Nowhere is that more in my face than this stubborn fact: I would not have the ranch were it not for the extraction of hydrocarbons. Ranching is a marginal economic endeavor at best. High labor costs and variable commodity prices conspire all too often to deflate a rancher's best-laid plans. Yet through raising bison and selling the meat, by leasing the land at a premium for deer and quail hunting, I could squeak by. The rainbow of hydrocarbons on the horizon was just too tempting, though, and while there is no free lunch, there is always free cheese in the mousetrap.

When the most recent boom began, I got my first taste of both the greenback intoxicant and the accompanying environmental hangover the morning after. Money such as I had never seen the likes of was paid to landowners as damages, and I sold some of my water for fracking. The mad dash was on. Over 400 trucks a day raced down our little one-lane county road to drill that first well. White clouds of caliche dust powdered so fine you could not see out the windshield. It was like driving through a New England whiteout blizzard, only the temperature on the dashboard of my truck read 104 degrees. The road got so potholed and washboarded that when the school bus came down the road one afternoon, its steering wheel came off in the driver's hands.

Another well was soon to follow, accompanied by heaps of garbage on the side of the road, lost truckers who wandered all over the ranch, and an eighteen-wheeler jackknifing on the road and discharging its load of contaminated frack water into the pasture. The third well brought the issue to a head. They had to run a pipe from my two strongest water wells to the frack pit, and my well could not keep up with the demand. They were pumping away and all was going as planned until they drained the tank I was pumping into down to the muddy bottom. When I saw this, I asked them to stop pumping for a few days so my tank could recover and my bison would have the water they needed. In addition to not having water to drink, they could easily have waded into the mud for that last sip of water and gotten stuck there. A slow and painful death was sure to follow.

What is curious about that incident is that they granted my request. This was in the middle of the worst single-year drought in Texas history. During 2011, it did not rain. The drillers interpreted my asking them to suspend pumping for a few days as a refusal on my part to provide any more water to them. Not my intention at all. Their response was not to frack the next stage. Not one peep from them about "hey Mr. Sunny, how about turning the water back on?" Instead of offering to truck in a few eighteen-wheelers to refill my tank so the bison could have a drink, they just folded their tent and went away without so much as a "see you later." Subsequently, I learned that their inability to communicate with me cost them in the neighborhood of $250,000. The rush was on in 2011, so it was on to the next location.

I tried to turn my full attention to my bison, but the surrounding physics of fracking surmounted and suppressed what the San Francisco mill could never overcome. On a visit to the windmill, I peered over the side of the pila to see a drowned Harris hawk and a seven-foot Blue Indigo snake, both dead because they were lured to something they needed and were trapped when the water level fell. Another man's straw had drained my glass. That was the last straw, as it turned out, for me.

In June 2011, that record-breaking summer when even the dimwits started to believe in climate change, I drove west from I-35 to Carrizo and passed a dozen or more large white plastic banners flimsily attached to barbed-wire fences. Printed in bold black letters were the words "Fresh Water for Sale." When I looked down under the deceivingly green canopy of mesquites that lined the sides of the highway, I saw two things: prickly pear cactus and red dirt. The plant life was either gone or going dormant to survive. Drought and desiccation prevailed, with only isolated patches of green where irrigation systems using groundwater tried in vain to make up for no rain.

I went as a guest to my first Wintergarden Groundwater Conservation District monthly board meeting. This is usually not my style. Most days I blow through Carrizo as fast as I can to get to the ranch. This time I had an idea that I asked the board to put on the agenda. Our district's hydrologist, a learned and thoughtful individual as well as a great teacher, was making a presentation to the board. My proposal was to have this same presentation given at a later date and to heavily publicize the event to inform the public. Yet just as my agenda item was set to be opened for discussion and a vote, one of the board members, a lawyer, said he had to go meet a client. Suddenly, there was no quorum and no vote. I was disappointed but left it at that. No action on that agenda item meant no information to the public, which meant business could continue unimpeded and industry could have all the water it wanted.

It was time for me to stop complaining and start campaigning; I became a candidate for a seat on the board of the Wintergarden Groundwater Conservation District. My strategy, if you can call it that, was to motivate the Hispanic community to vote for me because it is the predominant voting bloc in the county. I went to the political and social "godfather" of the county, a man who knew the community better than anyone, and he told me who I should contact and where I should campaign. Let's just say it was an unconventional approach. What is even stranger is that my opponent, the lawyer who had to leave that meeting, is my lawyer. No hard feelings, we go to the same church, and I beat him by thirty-seven votes for the open seat on the water board.

I began by just listening and reading about water law, hydrology, and recharge and in general trying to educate myself on a subject matter that I knew was critical but that I had also taken for granted. The "boom" had graced us with two water-based conundrums from which we could not escape. The first and most obvious was the drawdown in our aquifer. Fracking consumed one-third to one-half of our annual recharge every year, and unless we received sixteen inches or more of rain a year, there would be no recharge. In effect, our water was being mined. The second was the even harsher reality of what must be done with the contaminated wastewater from the frack. The depletion of the aquifer is the one most people understand, but according to groundwater hydrologist Ronald Green, it is the injection wells that are truly the "ticking time bombs of the Eagle Ford," along with every other shale formation from Pennsylvania to North Dakota and beyond. And if a frack breaks out of the driller's target formation, the fluid can find a migration pathway that could contaminate groundwater. In most peoples' minds, when it comes to water levels, if you turn the tap on the faucet and a stream of water comes forth, then all is well in the water world. Unless, of course, you drop a line down the borehole of your well and see that it now rests at 179 feet below sea level when last month it was 160 feet below sea level. Information avoidance is something of a psychological narcotic when it comes to water-level reality. If the trough is full, how could there be a problem?

I knew that ranchers in our groundwater conservation district had reported drops of up to 300 feet in their static water levels where fracking had been intense. Submersible pumps kept pumping even when the water dropped below the intake. They overheated, burned through the casing, and then dropped to the bottom of the well. Not a pretty picture, but one that was becoming common.

At my first official meeting of the water board, I found out about an incident that had taken place on April 11, 2011. The water board general manager had received a call from Larry Mogford, a local attorney and rancher. He had just come in from the pasture and seen something that was as revolting as it was terrifying. A plugged and abandoned oil well from the 1940s that was on his property was oozing a black and brownish sludge the consistency of month-old chocolate pudding. It was a breakout. Injected frack water from a disposal well that was just over a quarter of a mile away had migrated to Larry's abandoned well, and the pressure from the injection well had pushed the fluid up the casing and onto the ground. Had Larry not discovered the breakout, the toxic sludge containing known carcinogens would have eventually percolated down into the aquifer. The sight of those photographs, toxic sludge on bare drought-stricken earth, will be with me until the day I die. If this breakout had not been discovered, it would have been the end of the story for Dimmit County and the Carrizo aquifer.

The Mogford breakout prompted the board to establish a policy of protesting each and every disposal well permit application in our district. I attended another board meeting where the agenda included a disposal well company's intention to inject into the Glen Rose formation. When I was a young boy, my father told me about the Glen Rose and how it held a massive amount of freshwater at extreme depths and temperatures. How, I thought, could we as a water board allow the disposal of carcinogenic waste into a freshwater source? I had found my fight.

The visual impact of those photographs at the Mogford breakout was still with me when our general manager said the name "Glen Rose." There was now a disposal well destined for this formation. The power of remembrance infused me with a passion that had been smoldering since childhood, ignited with those words. It was my trigger, and it was a hair trigger at that. I decided to appear before the Railroad Commission of Texas, which has regulatory authority over disposal wells. My aim was to oppose the company that wanted to inject into an aquifer that in some areas of the district could be a source of drinking water.

On the day of that protest hearing before the Railroad Commission, I felt like a man who had little more than truth on his side. I had no lawyer, no hydrologist, and no petroleum engineer at the table with me. The other table had two of each, as well as maps, engineering reports, and seismic logs of corresponding wells. What I had was history. So when it was my turn to speak, I told the story of a little boy going with his father to see the drilling rig that was boring down over 13,000 feet into the Sligo formation. It turned out to be a dry hole, but on its way down it encountered the Glen Rose horizon, an oil and gas strata that in certain areas can contain vast quantities of water. The driller took my father into his trailer and handed him a mason jar filled to the brim with clear, clean water. He explained, "It comes out at over 200 degrees, but if you let it cool it's good enough to drink, and there is a lot of it." This childhood remembrance came tumbling from my lips with a force as powerful to me as it was alien to my nature. I felt like Patrick Henry standing before these learned lawyers and scientists. A compromise was reached with the opposition, which agreed to dispose into another formation and leave the Glen Rose just where it has been for the past 7 million years.

Naturally, hubris took its toll. When I tried the Patrick Henry speech again on my next visit before the Railroad Commission examiners, the opposition pummeled me with maps, pressure gradients, and all manner of scientific and engineering statistics. With my tail tucked firmly between my legs, I limped back down I-35 and reported to the water district. Perhaps we needed counsel; what a novel idea. After retaining a water lawyer, we managed to negotiate and cajole injection well companies into resolutions that have been much more balanced and favorable for us. Today, it remains our single most critical issue; we might recover our recharge and the depletion our aquifer has suffered if extraction is moderated. But a breakout and contamination of the aquifer from an injection well means game over.

As a regulatory body charged with protecting our state's natural resources, the Railroad Commission seems more concerned with granting permits for hydrologic fracturing than with the role of environmental watchdog. In fact, when a new well is presented for permitting, the surrounding existing wells are only taken into account as they relate to each other on the surface. What is ignored entirely is how they could affect each other on a subterranean level. In the mid-1980s, the Austin Chalk formation was the "big play" in South Texas. Over time, most of those earlier wells petered out and a good number were plugged down to the freshwater aquifer before being converted into water wells. If the integrity of the casing and cement is good, there is no problem. But the Austin Chalk lies directly above the Eagle Ford, so if your newly converted water well is next to an Eagle Ford frack, then your water well could start pumping frack fluid rather than water.

I have always been a fan of the quotations of Benjamin Franklin. My favorite is on my calling card for the water district: "You will know the value of water when the well runs dry." But there is another he proffered during the turbulent days of the revolution that speaks to our continuing predicament in Dimmit County. When describing the necessity for a unified colonial front against the crown he said, "We can hang together or we can hang separately." Our natural resources are what should unify us as landowners. But a fire hose of money has been turned on the counties in the Eagle Ford, and telling someone not to take money from the sale of a resource that is legally theirs is a tough sell. Truckers at the height of the boom in 2013 were taking home $100,000 a year. Unless, of course, they were sleep-deprived, hopped up on Red Bull at two in the morning, and are now remembered by the floral wreaths and crosses that dot the farm-to-market roads they drove.

I once heard fracking described as "the last gasp of a dying industry." That seems accurate enough to me. I just hope that last gasp does not suck all the oxygen out of the room or the water out of the ground. So to understand how best to change hearts and minds, I need to remember what speaks to us as a society. We are rational Western thinkers, aren't we? Science and education is where I will put my energy in the future. Good, hard, irrefutable science that is presented in an educational format to inform and educate the public is how I believe we need to proceed. Knowledge is power, and if absolute power in the form of industry has been corrupting absolutely, then we need absolute knowledge as a counterbalance.

When the Eagle Ford, which has now become the Eagle Edsel, first arrived, there was great celebration and fanfare over how fantastic and magnificent the technology was that brought this about. Finally, everyone thought, with the power of sand, water, diesel horsepower, and chemicals, we could achieve energy independence. Driving down the Dentonio Road four years ago, staring at the rear end of an eighteen-wheeler full of frack sand imported from Wisconsin, and straining for visibility as I inched along enveloped in a cloud of dust, I caught a glimpse of Old Glory. There at my neighbor's entrance fluttered the tiny tattered remains of one of those dime-store American flags. Wired to the fence, it waved resolutely at every passing welder and roughneck who sped with unbridled enthusiasm toward the future.

Remember how much fun it used to be when you were a kid and you had a balloon? You would huff and puff until that rubber balloon was just about to explode, squeeze the neck tight, then let her rip just to see what wayward trajectory your dirigible would take. That is what the Eagle Ford experience has been like. The balloon expanded all the way to $110.12, but the edge of the cliff was there and the rock began to crumble. The only problem is that in our neighborhood it takes $75-a-barrel oil to make the fracking process pay. This morning we are at $48.17. How quickly fortunes can change. Now we are left with half-completed motels and quarter-inch sheetrock flapping in the breeze. The man camps have emptied out. Even the Chinese donut man in Big Wells folded his tent and moved on.

The bison are still here.

14

New Dawn for Energy Justice in North Carolina

MONICA MARIKO EMBREY

"We need everyone to change everything" was the rally cry of the People's Climate March in New York City in 2014.[1] People from all walks of life—students and seniors, northerners and southerners, people of diverse racial and socioeconomic backgrounds—marched side by side demanding climate justice. This pivotal rally, as big as the civil rights marches of the 1960s, marked a significant turning point in the climate movement. After years of negotiations to overcome division, the more mainstream, predominantly white, "environmental" movement and the people-of-color–led "environmental-justice" (EJ) movement successfully united around a common demand: bold action on climate change to protect people and the planet.[2] Rooted in the Jemez Principles for Democratic Organizing, mainstream environmental and environmental justice leaders solidified a powerful alliance at the People's Climate March in hopes of advancing energy justice for all.[3]

The effort to address climate injustice by reducing greenhouse gas emissions has been growing for years. Communities are organizing against fossil fuels at every step in the process, from extraction to transportation to

DOI: 10.5876/9781607328483.c014

exportation to combustion. Grassroots campaigns across the country have formed against mountaintop-removal coal mining, hydraulic fracturing, oil drilling, oil and gas pipelines and compressor stations, terminals to export fossil fuels overseas, and coal-fired, gas-fired, and nuclear power plants. Environmental and environmental-justice advocates have led this opposition to climate pollution, unprecedented in scope and scale.

Simultaneously, there have been efforts to reimagine how to replace the currently damaging energy systems with sustainable and just practices of energy production and distribution.[4] Energy efficiency and clean, renewable energy sources like solar and wind have gained widespread popularity. A March 2015 Gallup Poll showed that 79 percent of Americans support more emphasis on solar and 70 percent are in favor of more wind, compared to only 28 percent who support more coal and 35 percent more nuclear energy.[5] The dramatic drop in renewables costs, coupled with growing consumer demand, has led to more clean sources powering the electrical grid, with solar growing fourfold from 2010 to 2014[6] and wind growing tenfold from 2005 to 2014.[7] Demands for accessible and affordable renewable energy options are also rising in hopes that the new green economy will address the economic needs of those who have been exploited by the fossil-fuel industry. Clean energy cooperatives, community-owned solar gardens, and green-jobs training centers are spreading nationwide, simultaneously restructuring unjust electricity infrastructure and social power relations.[8]

The stakes for reducing fossil fuel emissions and building the renewable energy economy have never been higher. How these efforts are organized matters as much as what is demanded. In this chapter I will explore examples of how activists in North Carolina have successfully aligned diverse communities using the Jemez Principles to organize against an incredibly powerful electric utility. Their examples demonstrate how a strong collaboration between the historically divided environmental and environmental-justice movements is necessary to avert the worst climate catastrophes' disproportionate impact on poor and marginalized people and simultaneously build a more just and sustainable world.

Contemporary Environmental-Justice Movements and Principles

The movements addressing environmental concerns have been divided for decades. One branch developed primarily with a focus on wilderness conservation, while the other sought to redress the inequitable impact of pollution. Efforts of the contemporary, mainstream environmental movement have been led by national organizations focused on preserving pristine natural places. Their campaigns often ignored how environmental pollution disproportionately impacted low-income communities and communities of color. In the 1970s and 1980s, toxic pollution poisoned low-income families in Love Canal, New York, Cancer Alley, Louisiana, and Warren County, North Carolina. The contemporary environmental-justice movement grew out of the response to this epidemic.[9]

One of the environmental-justice movement's critiques was that mainstream environmental organizations, which have succeeded in protecting forests, oceans, and wildlife habitat, often adopted solutions that disregarded human communities impacted by these new policies, regulations, or laws. By ignoring how race and socioeconomic class influenced who benefited and who was harmed, many mainstream organizations unintentionally upheld racist and classist power dynamics. As EJ advocates accused national environmental leaders in a "Letter to the Group of Ten" in 1990, "Racism is a root cause of your inaction around addressing environmental problems in our communities."[10] The injustice, whether accidental or intentional, was pervasive.[11]

As two preeminent scholars on environmental movements, Ronald Sandler and Phaedra Pezzullo, explain in their co-edited volume *Environmental Justice and Environmentalism*: "Although the environmental movement and the environmental justice movement would seem to be natural allies, their relationship over the years has often been characterized by conflict and division. The environmental justice movement has charged the dominant environmental movement with racism and elitism and has criticized its activist agenda on the grounds that it values wilderness over people."[12] The ongoing tension has complicated efforts to develop a genuine collaboration.

To address the lack of alignment, communities of color whose interests were not prioritized by national nongovernmental organizations (NGOs) developed guiding principles and working agreements. In December 1996, a gathering of environmental- and economic-justice leaders drafted "the Jemez Principles" with the "intention of hammering out common understanding between participants from different cultures, politics, and organizations."[13] The six overarching concepts are:

1. Be inclusive
2. Emphasize bottom-up organizing
3. Let people speak for themselves
4. Work together in solidarity and mutuality
5. Build just relationships among ourselves
6. Commit to self-transformation.

Since the 1990s, some progress has been made to align the work of environ-mental and EJ movements more closely.[14] Increased dialogue spurred by the "Letter to the Group of Ten," Green 2.0—which is pressing for an increase in racial diversity across mainstream environmental NGOs, foundations, and government agencies—and other efforts have promoted collaboration. Several national organizations have adopted principles or developed their own guidelines to improve their internal cultures, hiring practices, lobbying agendas, and political platforms to address concerns of the EJ movement. For example, the Jemez Principles guided the planning and execution of the People's Climate March in 2014, bringing together hundreds of communities from across the country to allow for deeper solidarity among environmental and EJ advocates. While collaboration poses significant challenges, historical tensions must be overcome, as Sandler and Pezzullo argue, so that "the goals of both movements might be achieved together effectively."[15]

This effort was not about combining environmental and environmental justice into one movement but instead about identifying key opportunities for collaboration. While neither the environmental nor the environmental-justice movement is monolithic in its approach to defining the problems of or the solutions to energy justice, there are distinct differences between the two movements. As Sandler and Pezzullo explain, "Evidence of undeni-able and irreconcilable differences between the environmental justice and environmental movements challeng[es] the prospects or even the desirabil-ity of . . . merging the two movements into one single, unified movement." Despite challenges, there are opportunities for groups to form alliances that can enhance each other's effectiveness. Recognizing the importance of the respective approaches while acknowledging the differences between them is critical for collaboration. Sandler and Pezzullo conclude, "In other words, for these two movements to work well together, they must also come to terms with the ways they must work apart."[16]

North Carolina: History of Environmental Injustice and Resistance

One of the places where communities are organizing around the critical lessons from past environmental-justice fights is North Carolina; in fact, the state
is widely considered a birthplace of the modern EJ movement.[17] In 1982, residents of Warren County, North Carolina, resisted the state's effort to build a
hazardous waste facility in their backyard.[18] The state government planned to
dump over 6,000 truckloads of soil poisoned with polychlorinated biphenyls
(PCBs) in this rural, predominantly African American community. The plan
sparked massive protest by residents, who were joined by civil rights activists
in six weeks of civil disobedience with hundreds of arrests. Their resistance attracted national attention and brought to light the racism inherent
in the efforts to dump toxins in Warren County. This moment marked one
of the first times the social crisis of racism and the environmental crisis of
pollution were inextricably linked in a protest. It sparked academic reports to
document the trend, including *Toxic Wastes and Race in the United States* (1987)
by the United Church of Christ, the first report of its kind that identified
environmental racism as a national crisis.[19]

Unfortunately, Warren County is not the only example of environmental
injustice in North Carolina. Duke Energy, one of the largest electric power
companies in the world, has a long legacy of polluting the state's air, water, and
land ever since its founding in 1904. Environmental and labor organizations have
repeatedly targeted the company for its unjust practices. The Oscar-winning
film *Harlan County, USA* documented Duke's 1973 labor dispute with Kentucky
coal miners striking for safer working conditions and decent wages.[20] In that
same decade many protested Duke's growing use of nuclear power. Protests
continued in the early 2000s against the company's reliance on coal combustion. That said, the company's overwhelming economic, political, and social
power makes the utility a formidable giant in a David-and-Goliath struggle. By
the twenty-first century, Duke Energy had become a massive utility, serving
7.4 million customers in six states across the Southeast and the Midwest.[21]

Despite long odds or perhaps because of them, community members from
different backgrounds and interests have come together—with considerable
success—to hold Duke Energy accountable. What follows are stories of how
ordinary people became activists and stood up to Duke Energy to demand
climate justice in North Carolina. Their leadership provides insight on how

to bridge the divide between environmental and environmental-justice movements. The application of the Jemez Principles has enabled deep, transformational victories. While the work is far from over, community members, together with environmental, EJ, and other allied organizations, have built a solid foundation for addressing North Carolina's energy crisis.

Principle 1: Building Inclusive People-Powered Campaigns (2007–2011)

Be Inclusive: If we hope to achieve just societies that include all people in decision-making and assure that all people have an equitable share of the wealth and the work of this world, then we must work to build that kind of inclusiveness into our own movement.[22]

It was hard to believe that many of the guests in Beth Henry's kitchen, chatting over shared casseroles and curries, were meeting face to face for the first time. The lively conversation felt more like a family reunion than a protest planning meeting. After introductions to match names and faces, the discussion focused on plans for the next morning. For several months in 2011, these grassroots activists and representatives from environmental and environmental-justice organizations had held regular conference calls to plan what would become the first annual protest outside Duke Energy's shareholder meeting.

In the years leading up to that evening, Beth Henry, a retired lawyer, mother, and native North Carolinian, had spent countless hours volunteering for efforts to reduce greenhouse gas emissions. After witnessing firsthand the impacts of warmer weather on her native plant garden, Beth started reading extensively about the climate crisis. She learned about plans by Duke Energy to construct new coal-fired power plants an hour from her home. In 2009, Duke Energy was one of the last utilities in the country investing in new coal, the largest source of carbon dioxide.[23] Beth got to work organizing to stop the proposed plants.

Joined by others concerned about local pollution and global climate impacts, Beth submitted testimony to regulators and engaged in civil disobedience against the proposal. Despite massive public outcry, state regulators approved construction permits for one of the two proposed 800-megawatt coal-fired units at Cliffside.[24] The mainstream environmental grassroots opposition was no match against Duke Energy's political capital. The company had spent millions of dollars to influence politicians and regulators, both directly with campaign contributions and lobbying[25] and indirectly by supporting industry front-groups.[26]

The lessons from Cliffside stayed with activists like Beth Henry. In the following years, she organized to build inclusive people power so their opposition would not be narrowly dismissed as upper-middle class, white, environmental concerns. The group applied this practice of inclusivity in three distinct areas: issue framing, grassroots outreach, and leadership roles. In spring of 2011, after an intentionally inclusive planning process, activists decided to direct their demands in a new way. With a hand-painted banner that read "Quit Coal! Quit Nuclear! Clean, Safe Energy Now!" Beth and her allies re-launched their efforts directly to Duke Energy's executives at their annual shareholder meeting.[27]

The group expanded its focus beyond a single facility to challenge the company's business plan, a strategy that created an opportunity to incorporate different tactics. Outside the shareholder meeting, activists gathered with bullhorns and handmade signs, while inside the meeting a delegation dressed in business suits asked pointed questions of Duke Energy's CEO and board of directors. Beth and her friends made sure Duke Energy executives heard diverse voices connecting a wide variety of issues.[28]

By challenging Duke Energy's entire business model, the group more easily diversified. Beth and her allies invited social-justice advocates to attend the rally, leading to racial diversity better representative of Charlotte's demographics. Activists chanting in unison outside Duke Energy's corporate headquarters included African Americans, Latinos, whites, and Asian Americans from different socioeconomic backgrounds and geographic regions. Immediately following the protests, the group reconvened with social and environmental-justice leaders to plan next steps. The new faces of environmental activism in North Carolina stemmed from an intentional focus to be inclusive.

Principle 2: Organizing Coal Communities from the Bottom Up (2012)

Emphasize bottom-up organizing: To succeed, it is important to reach out into new constituencies, and to reach within all levels of leadership and membership base of the organizations that are already involved in our networks.[29]

From her living room window, Sara Behnke could see white steam billowing out of smokestacks across Mountain Island Lake. Neighborhood kids had named the facility the "cloud machine," but Sara had never paid much attention until she heard a lecture about how pollution impacts reproductive health. She learned that the facility was a Duke Energy coal-fired power plant named Riverbend.[30] In 2012, coal powered over half of North Carolina's electricity demand.[31] Riverbend was eighty-three years old, one of the oldest of fourteen coal plants in the state.[32] The facility pumped thousands of tons of mercury, lead, arsenic, soot, sulfur dioxide, nitrogen oxides, and carbon dioxide into the air and water over its lifetime.[33] Its smokestacks lacked modern pollution controls, so the steam billowing in Sara's backyard was especially toxic.

Sara had recently beaten back a rare cancer and, with her husband, David, was raising two young children, Anna and Cade, in their lakefront home. Her growing concern about the impact of pollution on her and her children's health was personal. Sara reached out to environmental advocates and was connected to Beth Henry. Over coffee, they agreed to work together to shut down the old polluting coal plant. A proposal to relocate her children's elementary school directly beside Riverbend's high-hazard coal ash dumps made the threat even more urgent. Sara started hosting meetings with other neighborhood parents in her living room to explain the problem and plan their response. Parents became engaged, driven by the need to protect their children. They decided to circulate petitions at neighborhood swim meets while kids attended practice.

Within months, Sara organized hundreds of parents to speak up against moving the school and to demand the coal plant's retirement. Top leaders in the group attended zoning and planning meetings and spoke with emergency responders about the catastrophic threat if the ash dumps were to breach. The proposal for the school had one access road that, if blocked, meant all of the school's children, teachers, and staff would be directly in harm's way. Their campaigning successfully prevented the school relocation, an important first victory that showed the power of bottom-up organizing. The residents on Mountain Island Lake continued to increase pressure on Duke Energy to retire Riverbend. In May 2012, Sara and her eleven-year-old daughter, Anna, attended the Duke Energy shareholder meeting to ask Duke Energy CEO Jim Rogers to immediately retire the Riverbend coal plant. Despite their impassioned pleas, CEO Rogers refused.[34]

Determined to build people power and make their voices heard, Sara aligned her group with environmental and health organizations. They hosted a movie screening in their suburban community to raise awareness that Riverbend was not a "cloud machine" but a dangerous coal plant. Hundreds attended and collectively raised their voice for energy justice. By the following February, less than a year after Sara's initial meeting with CEO Rogers, Duke Energy officials had publicly committed to shut down Riverbend coal plant within two months.[35] The community's success was rooted in neighbors organizing neighbors to build grassroots power from the bottom up.[36] Within a few years, over half of the state's coal-fired power plants—eight of the fourteen—were set to retire.

Principle 3: People Speak against Rate Hikes for Dirty Energy (2013)

Let people speak for themselves: We must be sure that relevant voices of people directly affected are heard.[37]

There was not an empty seat in the courthouse as hundreds of people crowded into the hearing room, armed with signs and stickers that exclaimed "No Rate Hikes for Dirty Energy."[38] People gathered to share their personal stories with North Carolina regulators about the impact Duke Energy's request to significantly raise electricity rates for polluting facilities would have on their lives. The testimonies continued for eight hours straight, with about 100 stories as different as the audience members telling them.

A growing group of advocates, who saw strength in aligning across issues, recruited and trained speakers for the hearings. Bill Gupton, an avid hiker and chair of the local Sierra Club chapter, joined Hector Vaca, a tenant and immigrant rights organizer with Action NC, as two of the main conveners. Bill was driven by his passion to fight climate change and protect the natural beauty of the planet. Hector had fought for years to prevent low-income community members from being evicted from their homes, often because of expensive utility bills. Bill and Hector partnered with community leaders to form the "No Rate Hikes for Dirty Energy" coalition, an effort to hold Duke Energy accountable by strategically aligning diverse organizations. The coalition would unite constituencies with seemingly different interests to break down typical racial and socioeconomic barriers under the banner of energy justice.

Advocates focused on public hearings as the venue to make the voices of their communities heard. Bill Gupton developed a communications plan that encouraged everyone to speak from their own experiences: "green" messages addressing climate and pollution issues, "blue" messages for health concerns, and "red" messages for economic impacts. Hector Vaca would work to host these trainings in Spanish to make them accessible to Latino immigrant communities. The umbrella "No Rate Hikes for Dirty Energy" successfully built off the intentional focus on inclusivity and organizing from the bottom up to bring people together and let them speak for themselves.[39]

At the Charlotte hearing, Phyllis Jones, a retired teacher on a fixed income, testified against Duke Energy for raising rates on those most vulnerable, including African Americans and seniors. Mother-daughter duo Heidi and Kayla Martinez testified about how their love for the outdoors was threatened by climate-change pollution from Duke Energy's coal plants. Silvia Sanchez testified in Spanish about coal pollution's impact on hers and her daughter's health as people living with asthma. Annie Vereen, a dance studio owner, testified about how the compounding increases in residential and commercial electricity bills hurt small businesses. Shequan Forte, a college student at Johnson C. Smith University, a historically black college, testified about how she, an expectant mother, worried about pollution in the drinking water.[40]

Ultimately, the coalition won real environmental and economic victories by building on its members' different strengths. Community opposition successfully reduced three rate hike requests made by Duke Energy to pay for coal, gas, and nuclear plant construction.[41] In 2011, Duke had requested a 17 percent residential rate increase,[42] but regulators only approved a 7.2 percent increase.[43] In 2013, two rate hike requests were cut in half, from 12 percent to 5.1 percent[44] and from 14 percent to 7.5 percent,[45] respectively, because of vocalized resistance. These efforts further expedited coal plant retirements. After the 2013 proceedings, regulators also imposed a limit on how soon Duke Energy could request another rate hike. The campaign turned the daily anger many felt in isolation into a vibrant movement of unified voices.

Principle 4: Solidarity to Address the Coal Ash Crisis (2014)

Work together in solidarity and mutuality: Groups working on similar issues with compatible visions should consciously act in solidarity [and] mutuality and support each other's work.[46]

As she sat down to dinner, Kate Fulbright got a call that a pipe had burst at one of Duke Energy's facilities, causing tens of thousands of tons of toxic coal ash to spill into the Dan River.[47] Over the next few hours, she called her group of friends to share the news. Years of insufficient regulation enabled the slurry of carcinogens and neurotoxins found in coal ash, including mercury, lead, arsenic, hexavalent chromium, and other heavy metals, to contaminate the neighboring waterway.[48] Her dinner quickly transformed into an organizing meeting to gather information and develop an action plan.

Kate Fulbright, a recent college graduate who worked waiting tables at a diner, joined the grassroots group Charlotte Environmental Action, an offshoot of Occupy Charlotte, because of her concerns about energy justice. The group targeted Duke Energy as the largest contributor of greenhouse gas emissions in the United States and the main polluter in the region.[49] Despite months of submitting petitions and organizing actions to pressure the company to protect downstream communities from potential coal ash catastrophes, their efforts had not received a response.[50] With no laws requiring coal ash cleanup, it had been a long and hard effort to protect waterways across the state.

Duke Energy stored coal ash in thirty-six active dumps at its fourteen coal plants in North Carolina and had more dumps than any other state rated "high hazard," a ranking associated with the potential for loss of human life.[51] The group learned that the crisis at the Dan River was the third largest coal ash spill in US history. Huddled around her small wood fireplace, Kate and her friends quickly decided to reach out to allies for solidarity to organize around a crisis of this scale.[52] Over the following weeks, community leaders who had never previously met were organizing rallies together in front of Duke Energy headquarters in a massive public outcry. Local, regional, and national groups representing a range of issues found common interests and came together to support one another, including such organizations as Action NC, Appalachian Voices, Center for Community Change, Charlotte Environmental Action, Clean Air Carolina, Greenpeace USA, NC Conservation Network, NC NAACP, NC Riverkeepers, NC WARN, Progress NC, Sierra Club, Southern Environmental Law Center, and Waterkeeper Alliance. The silence from Duke Energy executives in the days following the spill[53] was conspicuous compared to the protest chants that filled the air and TV coverage that filled the airways.[54] In February 2014, many people in North Carolina and around the country were talking about coal ash.

The crisis of the Dan River spill helped activists consolidate an unprecedented broad alliance of environmental, environmental-justice, health, racial, economic, and social-justice organizations that had been evolving over several years. Partners who first worked together in the "No Rate Hikes for Dirty Energy" coalition joined national leaders including the Reverend William Barber, president of the NC NAACP and founder of the Moral Monday movement, and grassroots community members who lived beside coal ash dumps to lead a protest outside Duke Energy's annual shareholder meeting later that year.[55] This new alliance brought together people who had previously never imagined protesting against Duke Energy with seasoned activists outside corporate headquarters.[56]

By standing in solidarity, the groups elevated the need for coal ash regulation and were heard loud and clear by Duke Energy executives in Charlotte and politicians in Raleigh. Charlotte Environmental Action's efforts were finally getting a response. That summer, the Coal Ash Management Act of 2014 passed, the first law in the country to oversee cleanup efforts.[57] While only four of the fourteen coal ash sites would be guaranteed to be excavated, the remaining ten would be evaluated by state regulators.[58] Notably, these four locations were the same places where the most active fights to retire coal-fired power plants took place, demonstrating the continued success of those bottom-up grassroots campaigns. While this policy did not meet all of the coalition's demands, the collaboration successfully formed new relationships and alliances critical for the multi-year evaluation process.

Principle 5: Just Relationships Lead to Energy Democracy for All (2014)

Build just relationships among ourselves: We need to treat each other with justice and respect, both on an individual and an organizational level, in this country and across borders.[59]

Sitting in a circle of folding chairs, a group of community leaders met to discuss their long-term strategy for energy justice. It was just a few weeks after the large rallies against Duke Energy's coal ash pollution. While the protests were necessary to demonstrate the public outrage over mismanagement, the seasoned activists knew they would need to unify their demands to continue to make progress. Old friends and new allies attended the gathering.

The Reverend Rodney Sadler, a professor at Union Presbyterian Seminary, was a longtime social-justice advocate representing the NC NAACP and the Moral Monday movement. Luis Rodriguez started his activist career as a main convener of Occupy Charlotte and was an organizer with Action NC. Danielle Hilton was on the board of Clean Air Carolina and an organizer with Charlotte Environmental Action. They established norms on how they would collaborate by sharing their individual and organizational visions for the future.

The conversation centered on how this group could advance a triple bottom line—economic justice, social equity, and environmental protection—in its calls for energy justice. Renewable energy surfaced as a solution to the intersecting challenges North Carolinians were facing by providing new employment opportunities, more affordable utility bills, and a reduction in dependence on polluting power plants. Their interests aligned with the growing trend; recent breakthroughs in pricing and existing state incentives[60] had caused solar power to take off.[61] In 2014, North Carolina ranked fourth nationally for overall installed solar capacity and second for new installations.[62] With more than 166 solar companies employing over 5,600 people, the booming solar economy offered exciting organizing possibilities to energy-justice advocates.[63]

Activists were not the only ones noticing this trend. The popularity and accessibility of solar posed a risk to Duke Energy's business model. As a regulated monopoly, Duke had a captive customer base in the Carolinas that solar power threatened, a trend some analysts hyperbolically coined "the utility death spiral."[64] Furthermore, the steady demand for grid-tied electricity was the company's justification to regulators for investing in gas to replace its retiring coal fleet. Duke Energy's long-term business plan included proposals to construct nine new gas power plants and hundreds of miles of gas pipelines.[65] The combination of an economic recession, increased energy efficiency measures, and more customers turning to solar meant demand for electricity was down and expensive infrastructure construction would be more difficult to explain. The monopoly business model relied on large projects to secure shareholder profits, as expenses were passed along to captive ratepayers. That led Duke Energy, like many utilities across the country, to oppose solar policies.[66]

Duke Energy's first attempt to "block the sun" was an attack on net metering. One of the most critical state policies for residential systems, net metering allows owners of rooftop solar to be credited for the electricity they deliver to the grid. North Carolina law guaranteed customers would be compensated at the same rate they were charged to purchase power. But in a private meeting with state lawmakers, representatives from Duke Energy shared a plan to reduce the net metering credit by half, cutting the amount customers would receive from eleven cents down to about six cents per kilowatt hour.[67] They claimed this would reduce the burden on low-income customers, especially communities of color, who were typically not installing solar themselves.

The deep trust community leaders from environmental, racial, and social-justice organizations had established after years of intentional collaboration allowed them to act quickly. Only five days after the announcement, local representatives from Action NC, Greenpeace USA, NC NAACP, and a city council member joined together in a press conference to denounce the credit reduction. The announcement exposed Duke Energy's proposal as an attack on rooftop solar, part of a scheme designed by the right-wing corporate bill mill group the American Legislative Exchange Council (ALEC).[68] The organizers effectively countered the utility's argument by having community leaders who represented low-income customers speak alongside environmentalists. The classic divide-and-conquer tactic the utility attempted to separate advocates along class lines failed, and Duke Energy dropped the proposal. Rodney, Luis, and Danielle continued to collaborate and build stronger connections. Ultimately, the long-term relationships based on mutual respect were the foundation necessary to protect the net metering program.

Principle 6: Transforming Ourselves with Rooftop Solar (2014 and beyond)

Commit to self-transformation: As we change societies, we must change from operating on the mode of individualism to community-centeredness. We must "walk our talk."[69]

Nearly every hand in the auditorium was raised as the crowd pledged to talk to friends and neighbors about rooftop solar assessments. Hanna and Michael looked at each other and smiled. They had been organizing this event for months, calling volunteers to help with outreach, arranging childcare to make it accessible to parents, and ordering enough pizza to feed the crowd. The energy in the room marked a significant moment; people frustrated by Duke Energy's refusal to provide safe, healthy, and affordable electricity started turning to rooftop solar to power their own communities.

Hanna Mitchell, a recent college graduate, moved to Charlotte to organize grassroots community members to support solar, as she had previously done in California. Michael Zytkow, a former leader of Occupy Charlotte and the first independent candidate on the city council ballot in Charlotte's history, was excited by the opportunity to bring energy democracy to his community. Both were employed by Greenpeace USA, one of the twenty-one organizations that came together to form Solarize Charlotte. Solarize, a model promoted by the US Department of Energy, connected homeowners with a certified solar installer offering discounted rates.[70] Community members who had long fought against dirty fossil-fuel pollution were happy to embrace clean energy solutions that put power back in their hands.

Years of deep collaborations with diverse communities informed the energy-justice advocates' decision that it was not enough for solar to be available only for white middle-class homeowners. Solarize Charlotte intentionally focused its outreach efforts to reach diverse communities. Hanna attended fifty street festivals and neighborhood meetings to spread the word, including presenting to the Muslim American Society, Líderes en Acción, and the Charlotte NAACP. Michael led a team of canvassers who knocked on doors in historically African American and Latino neighborhoods to meet community members at their homes. Outreach efforts were completed in English, Spanish, Hindi, and Gujarati, allowing communities to live their values and "walk their talk" in multiple languages.

Solarize Charlotte was remarkably successful at allowing people to take power back into their own hands, with over 600 households enrolling to receive assessments. Inspired by the response, energy-justice advocates across North Carolina promoted their own Solarize efforts.[71] By the next year, nineteen Solarize programs had launched, adding hundreds of new rooftop systems to the grid. While Solarize helped reduce many barriers, significant obstacles remained to bring solar power to all communities.[72] In North Carolina, residential solar installations required ownership of one's roof and an average $21,000 upfront investment, which made solar accessible only to wealthier households. Many rooftops were unsuitable for solar because they were shaded by trees or faced a poor direction for sunlight.[73] Michael and Hanna learned that to overcome these barriers, other states had enacted policies like creating community solar gardens to make solar accessible to renters and third-party sales financing mechanisms to make it more affordable for homeowners.

Compelled by its business model to oppose the democratic pursuit of solar power, Duke Energy actively blocked proposals to expand solar access.[74] Confronted with Duke Energy's opposition, North Carolinians started demanding affordable solar for all at the 2015 Duke Energy annual shareholder meeting. In addition to the annual protest, a group representing renters and homeowners interrupted CEO Lynn Good's briefing during the meeting, chanting "stop blocking rooftop solar" until they were escorted out of the meeting.[75] Their escalatory action spoke to a growing desire to transform their communities.

Creating Everybody's Movement

The North Carolina experience demonstrates that deep collaboration between environmental and environmental-justice movements can be incredibly successful. In five years, activists have leveraged their grassroots power and organizational alliances to achieve significant victories favoring people and the environment over the powerful monopoly utility Duke Energy. In the coming years, activists will continue to organize to open solar access to all North Carolinians and prevent polluting natural gas infrastructure from replacing the retiring coal-fired power plants. This movement will be guided, in the future as now, by an inclusive set of organizing principles that has built a broad-based coalition committed to achieving environmental justice and advancing participatory democracy. Its enduring commitments reflect the chant heard at the 2014 People's Climate March: "We need everybody to change everything." These commitments will also make the success of the solar energy revolution in North Carolina not a matter of if but when.

Building alignment between the historically diverging environmental and environmental-justice movements is critical to address the growing climate crisis. Angela Park, a researcher specializing in environmental justice, explains: "Currently, climate change is not everybody's movement in the United States. New thinking and action will be necessary for these two movements to work together. Everyone will have to take risks or suffer a shared fate of failure."[76] By continuing to collaborate and build a more diverse, inclusive, and equitable organizing approach, energy-justice activists can tackle the most formidable fossil-fuel industry and utility adversaries.

Notes

1. "People's Climate March," September 21, 2014, accessed August 8, 2016, https://peoplesclimate.org/.

2. The terms *environmental* and *environmental justice* are used to describe differences within the contemporary movements, but these are simplifications; neither grouping is monolithic, and each is often composed of a diversity of opinions and participants.

3. Hanna Kozlowska, "The Climate Movement Is about Much More Than Just Climate," *New York Times*, September 23, 2015, accessed August 8, 2016, https://op-talk.blogs.nytimes.com/2014/09/23/the-climate-movement-is-about-much-more-than-just-climate/?_r=1.

4. Paul Davidson, "Off the Grid or On, Solar and Wind Power Gain," *USA Today*, April 13, 2006, accessed August 8, 2016, http://usatoday30.usatoday.com/tech/news/techinnovations/2006-04-12-off-the-grid_x.htm.

5. Rebecca Riffin, "US Support for Nuclear at 51%," *Gallup*, March 30, 2105, accessed August 8, 2016, http://www.gallup.com/poll/182180/support-nuclear-energy.aspx.

6. According to Environmental Impact Assessment (EIA) data, the amount of solar grew from 2,326 MW in 2010 to 12,057 MW in 2014. See also, Silvio Marcacci, "US Solar Energy Capacity Grew an Astounding 418% from 2010–2014," *Clean Technica*, April 24, 2014, accessed August 8, 2016, https://cleantechnica.com/2014/04/24/us-solar-energy-capacity-grew-an-astounding-418-from-2010-2014/.

7. According to EIA data, from 2005 to 2014, wind generation increased from 6,456 MW to 60,661 MW. Claire Cameron, "US Solar Generation Grew 418% in Last Four Years," *Utility Dive*, April 24, 2014, accessed August 8, 2016, https://www.utilitydive.com/news/us-solar-generation-grew-418-in-last-four-years/255100/.

8. Laurie Guevara-Stone, "The Rise of Solar Co-Ops," *Renewable Energy World*, June 19, 2014, accessed August 8, 2016, https://www.renewableenergyworld.com/articles/2014/06/the-rise-of-solar-co-ops.html.

9. David Pellow, *Power, Justice, and the Environment: A Critical Appraisal of the Environmental Justice Movement* (Cambridge, MA: MIT Press, 2005).

10. Richard Moore et al., "Letter to the Group of Ten," *Southwest Organizing Project*, March 16, 1990, accessed August 8, 2016, www.ejnet.org/ej/swop.pdf.

11. Ronald Sandler and Phaedra Pezzullo, *Environmental Justice and Environmentalism: The Social Justice Challenge to the Environmental Movement* (Cambridge, MA: MIT Press, January 2007), 11–14.

12. Sandler and Pezzullo, *Environmental Justice and Environmentalism*, 1.

13. "Jemez Principles for Democratic Organizing," Southwest Network for Environmental and Environmental Justice, December 1996, accessed August 8, 2016, http://www.ejnet.org/ej/jemez.pdf.

14. Sandler and Pezzullo, *Environmental Justice and Environmentalism*, 311.

15. Sandler and Pezzullo, *Environmental Justice and Environmentalism*, 2.

16. Sandler and Pezzullo, *Environmental Justice and Environmentalism*, 310.

17. Cheryl Katz, "Birth of the Movement: People Have to Stand Up for What's Right: A Q&A with Two Environmental Justice Pioneers," *Environmental Health News*, June 20, 2012, accessed August 14, 2018, http://www.climatecentral.org/news /birth-of-the-movement-a-qa-with-two-environmental-justice-pioneers.

18. Eileen McGurty, *Transforming Environmentalism: Warren County, PCBs, and the Origins of Environmental Justice* (New Brunswick, NJ: Rutgers University Press, 2007).

19. Benjamin Chavis and Charles Lee, *Toxics Wastes and Race in the United States: A National Report on the Racial and Socio-Economic Characteristics of Communities with Hazardous Waste Sites*, United Church of Christ, Commission for Racial Justice, 1987, accessed August 14, 2018, http://www.ucc.org/environmental-ministries_toxic -waste-20.

20. *Harlan County, USA 1976*, Cinema 5, producer and director Barbara Kopple, 1976.

21. "About Us: Our History," Duke Energy, n.d., accessed August 14, 2018, https://www.duke-energy.com/about-us/history.asp.

22. "Jemez Principles for Democratic Organizing."

23. "Proposed Coal Plant Map," Sierra Club, 2016, accessed August 8, 2016, https://content.sierraclub.org/coal/environmentallaw/plant-map.

24. "Cliffside," Sierra Club, December 2012, accessed August 8, 2016, https:// content.sierraclub.org/Coal/environmentallaw/plant/cliffside.

25. "Duke Energy's Political Spending," Common Cause, 2015, accessed August 8, 2016, https://www.commoncause.org/fact-sheets/duke-energy-political-spending.pdf.

26. Gabe Elsner, "Coalition Sends Letter to Duke Energy CEO: Drop ALEC," Energy Policy Institute, August 29, 2012, accessed August 8, 2016, http://www .energyandpolicy.org/coalition_sends_letter_to_duke_energy_ceo_drop_alec/.

27. Mitch Weiss, "Green Activists, Tea Party Target Duke Meeting," *Asheville Citizen-Times*, May 6, 2011, A9.

28. "Environmental Groups Protest outside Duke Energy Meeting," WSOC TV, May 5, 2011, accessed August 8, 2016, https://www.wsoctv.com/news/news /environmental-groups-protest-outside-duke-meeting/nGQRc/.

29. "Jemez Principles for Democratic Organizing."

30. "Riverbend Steam Station," Duke Energy, accessed August 14, 2018, https:// www.duke-energy.com/our-company/about-us/power-plants/riverbend-steam -station.

31. "North Carolina Electricity Profile 2013," US Energy Information Administration, March 24, 2016, accessed August 8, 2016, https://www.eia.gov/electricity/state/NorthCarolina/.

32. "Riverbend Steam Station."

33. "Environmental Impacts of Coal Power: Air Pollution," Union of Concerned Scientists, May 22, 2015, accessed August 8, 2016, https://www.ucsusa.org/clean_energy/coalvswind/co2c.html#.VrFiIkbvvMs.

34. Jason Stoogenke, "Cancer Patient Questions Duke Energy CEO about Local Coal Plant," May 3, 2012, accessed August 8, 2016, https://www.wsoctv.com/news/news/local/cancer-patient-questions-duke-ceo-about-local-coal/nNQnq/.

35. John Downey, "Duke Energy Shuttering Buck and Riverbend Coal Plants," *Charlotte Business Journal*, February 1, 2013, accessed August 8, 2016, https://www.bizjournals.com/charlotte/blog/power_city/2013/02/duke-energy-shuttering-buck-and.html.

36. Michael Grunwald, "Inside the War on Coal," *Politico*, May 26, 2015, accessed August 8, 2016, https://www.politico.com/agenda/story/2015/05/inside-war-on-coal-000002.

37. "Jemez Principles for Democratic Organizing."

38. Ratepayers in Telling Duke Energy No Rate Hikes for Dirty Energy," Charlotte Sierra Club, June 2013, accessed August 8, 2016, https://charlottesierraclub.files.wordpress.com/2013/06/sierra-club-cpg-duke-rate-hike-fact-sheet.pdf.

39. "Groups Unite to Oppose Annual Rate Hikes," Consumers against Rate Hikes, NC WARN press release, February 3, 2011, accessed August 19, 2018, http://www.ncwarn.org/2011/02/consumers-against-rate-hikes/.

40. "Tell Duke Energy: No Rate Hikes for Dirty Energy," Greenpeace USA, June 21, 2013, accessed August 8, 2016, https://www.youtube.com/watch?v=ZjAZpUmxQjo.

41. Paige Sheehan, "Duke Energy Carolinas Reaches Proposed Settlement in Its Request to Raise Base Rates in North Carolina," Duke Energy, October 20, 2009, accessed August 8, 2016, https://www.duke-energy.com/news/releases/2009102002.asp.

42. Jason Walls, "Duke Energy Carolinas Requests Approval from the North Carolina Utilities Commission to Increase Electric Rates," Duke Energy, July 11, 2011, accessed August 19, 2018, https://www.prnewswire.com/news-releases/duke-energy-carolinas-requests-approval-from-the-north-carolina-utilities-commission-to-increase-electric-rates-124853919.html.

43. Betsy Conway, "Duke Energy Carolinas Reaches an Agreement with North Carolina Public Staff in the Company's Request to Raise Customer Rates," Duke Energy, November 23, 2011, accessed August 19, 2018, https://www.prnewswire.com/news-releases/duke-energy-signs-6-billion-credit-agreement-134584593.html.

44. Lisa Parrish, "Duke Energy Carolinas Files NC Rate Increase Request," Duke Energy, February 4, 2013, accessed August 14, 2018, https://www.prnewswire.com /news-releases/duke-energy-carolinas-files-nc-rate-increase-request-189665591.html.

45. Eddie Fitzgerald, "Progress Seeks Rate Hikes: New Bern Electric Costs Would Be Unaffected," *Sun Journal* (New Bern, NC), February 20, 2013, accessed August 14, 2018, http://www.newbernsj.com/article/20130220/News/302209885.

46. "Jemez Principles for Democratic Organizing."

47. Bruce Henderson, "Timeline: Dan River Coal Ash Spill," *News and Observer* (Raleigh, NC), February 20, 2015, accessed August 8, 2016, http://www.newsobserver .com/news/local/article10883951.html.

48. Rhiannon Fionn, "Some Background on NC Coal Ash Regulations and Issues," *Coal Ash Chronicles*, February 6, 2014, accessed August 14, 2018, https://clclt .com/theclog/archives/2013/07/23/a-coal-ash-history-lesson-from-the-queen-of -coal-ash; "Coal and Water Pollution," Union of Concerned Scientists, December 26, 2017, accessed August 14, 2018, https://www.ucsusa.org/clean-energy/coal-and -other-fossil-fuels/coal-water-pollution#.W3McK7gnaUk

49. "The Greenhouse 100," Political Economy Research Institute, January 2016, accessed August 8, 2016, https://www.peri.umass.edu/greenhouse/.

50. Lisa Evans, Michael Becher, and Bridget Lee, "State of Failure: How States Fail to Protect Our Health and Drinking Water from Coal Ash," *Earth Justice*, April 2011, accessed August 8, 2016, http://earthjustice.org/sites/default/files/State ofFailure_2013-04-05.pdf.

51. "Southeast Coal Ash," Southern Alliance for Clean Energy, n.d., accessed August 14, 2018, http://www.southeastcoalash.org/about-coal-ash/.

52. Bob Geary, "A Movement Emerges against the Duke Energy–Progress Monopoly," *IndyWeek*, March 26, 2014, accessed August 8, 2016, https://www .indyweek.com/indyweek/a-movement-emerges-against-the-duke-energy-progress -monopoly/Content?oid=3981303.

53. Gerry Broome, "Duke Energy Apologizes for Nation's Third-Largest Coal-Ash Spill," *Associated Press*, February 8, 2014, accessed August 8, 2016, https://www .cbsnews.com/news/duke-energy-apologizes-for-nations-third-largest-coal-ash-spill/.

54. "Media Coverage of Coal Ash and Dan River Spill," Southern Alliance for Clean Energy, February 2, 2014–February 2, 2015, accessed August 8, 2016, http:// www.southeastcoalash.org/?p=12943.

55. Martha Waggoner, "NAACP Leader: Coal Ash Spill Is Disaster, Sin," *Associated Press*, March 5, 2014, accessed August 8, 2016, http://www.greensboro.com /business/naacp-leader-coal-ash-spill-is-disaster-sin/article_a7bba9d4-a4cb-11e3-8a86 -0017a43b2370.html.

56. Mitch Weiss, "Hundreds Protest during Duke Shareholder Meeting," *Associated Press*, May 1, 2014, accessed August 8, 2016, https://www.citizen-times.com /story/news/local/2014/05/01/hundreds-protest-duke-shareholder-meeting /8576351/.

57. Bruce Henderson, "NC Legislators Reach Compromise on Coal-Ash Bill," *Charlotte Observer*, August 19, 2014, accessed August 8, 2016, http://www .charlotteobserver.com/news/local/article9153350.html.

58. "NC Senate Unanimously Passes Coal Ash Cleanup Bill That May Not Go Far Enough," *Think Progress*, June 30, 2014, accessed August 8, 2016, https:// thinkprogress.org/climate/2014/06/30/3454808/nc-coal-ash-bill-passes-senate/.

59. "Jemez Principles for Democratic Organizing."

60. Christina Nunez, "Solar Energy Sees Eye-Popping Price Drops," *National Geographic*, October 2, 2015, accessed August 8, 2016, https://news.nationalgeographic .com/energy/2015/10/151002-solar-energy-sees-eye-popping-price-drops/.

61. Steve Devane and Paul Woolverton, "Future Is Bright for Solar in NC," *Fayetteville Observer*, January 9, 2016, accessed August 14, 2018, http://www.fayobserver .com/article/20160109/news/301099886.

62. "State Solar Policy: North Carolina Solar," Solar Energy Industry Association, June 2018, accessed August 14, 2018, https://www.seia.org/state-solar-policy/north -carolina.

63. "State Solar Policy: North Carolina Solar."

64. Christopher Helman, "Will Solar Cause a 'Death Spiral' for Utilities?" *Forbes*, January 30, 2015, accessed August 8, 2016, https://www.forbes.com/sites/energy source/2015/01/30/will-solar-cause-a-death-spiral-for-utilities/#778271603b05.

65. John Downey, "Duke Energy's Long-Term Plans Can Prove Dicey in a Rapidly Changing Industry," *Charlotte Business Journal*, October 23, 2015, accessed August 8, 2016, https://www.bizjournals.com/charlotte/blog/energy/2015/10 /duke-energy-s-long-term-plans-can-prove-dicey-in-a.html.

66. Joby Warrick, "Utilities Wage Campaign against Rooftop Solar," *Washington Post*, March 7, 2015, accessed August 14, 2018, https://www.washingtonpost.com /national/health-science/utilities-sensing-threat-put-squeeze-on-booming-solar -roof-industry/2015/03/07/2d916f88-c1c9-11e4-ad5c-3b8ce89f1b89_story.html?utm _term=.3ad187701964.

67. Gabe Elsner, "Duke Energy's Plans to Attack Solar in North Carolina," Energy and Policy Institute, February 14, 2014, accessed August 14, 2018, http:// www.energyandpolicy.org/net_metering_2014_north_carolina_s_duke_energy _plans_attack_on_solar.

68. John Downey, "Groups Accuse Duke Energy of Blocking NC Solar Development," *Charlotte Business Journal*, January 27, 2014, accessed August 8, 2016, https://

www.bizjournals.com/charlotte/blog/power_city/2014/01/groups-accuse-duke
-energy-of-blocking-nc-solar.html.

69. "Jemez Principles for Democratic Organizing."

70. "About Solarize: Solarize Programs," Solar Outreach Partnership, n.d.,
accessed August 14, 2018, https://www.energy.gov/eere/about-office-energy
-efficiency-and-renewable-energy.

71. Devane and Woolverton, "Future Is Bright for Solar in NC."

72. Alex Kotch, "Battle over Solar Energy's Future in North Carolina Heats Up
as Bipartisan Bills and Civil Protests Mount against Duke Energy's Obstructionism,"
DeSmog, March 6, 2016, accessed August 8, 2016, https://desmogblog.com/2016/03
/06/battle-over-solar-energy-s-future-north-carolina-heats-bipartisan-bills-and-civil
-protests-mount-against-duke-energy.

73. Herman Trabish, "Note to Utilities: Here's Why 2015 Is the 'Tipping Point'
for Community Solar," Utility Dive, August 11, 2015, accessed August 8, 2016,
https://www.utilitydive.com/news/note-to-utilities-heres-why-2015-is-the-tipping
-point-for-community-sol/403284/.

74. Kotch, "Battle over Solar Energy's Future in North Carolina Heats Up."

75. Monica Embrey, "Activists Demand Duke Energy Stop Blocking Rooftop Solar," Greenpeace Blog, May 5, 2015, accessed August 8, 2016, http://www
.greenpeace.org/usa/duke-energy-stop-blocking-sun/.

76. Angela Park, "Everybody's Movement: Environmental Justice and Climate
Change," Environmental Support Center, Washington, DC, December 2009, 5.

15

The Dakota Access Pipeline, Environmental Injustice, and US Settler Colonialism

KYLE POWYS WHYTE

We must remember we are part of a larger story. We are still here. We are still fighting for our lives, 153 years after my great-great-grandmother Mary watched as our people were senselessly murdered. We should not have to fight so hard to survive in our own lands.[1]

—*LaDonna Brave Bull Allard, Standing Rock Sioux Tribe*

"Standing Side by Side in Peaceful Prayer"

Starting in April 2016, thousands of people, led by Standing Rock Sioux tribal members, gathered at camps near the crossing of the Missouri and Cannon Ball Rivers to stop the construction of the Dakota Access Pipeline (DAPL) there—creating the #NoDAPL movement. DAPL is a 1,172-mile pipeline for transporting crude oil from North Dakota to refineries and terminals in Illinois. As a business venture, DAPL's investors seek to profit by offering a cheaper transportation alternative to rail. DAPL's advocates claim the pipeline will meet the highest environmental safety standards. They also claim the venture will produce greater US energy independence and jobs while it

DOI: 10.5876/9781607328483.c015

lessens the environmental risks of oil trains,[2] although it is unclear how the new pipeline could increase oil production, oil consumption, employment, and state tax revenues.[3]

The #NoDAPL movement sees the pipeline as posing risks to the water quality and cultural heritage of the Dakota and Lakota peoples of the Standing Rock Sioux Tribe. Part of DAPL's construction is occurring on lands and through waters the tribe never ceded consensually to the United States and that remain environmentally and culturally significant for tribal members' safety and wellness. The construction has already destroyed culturally significant places, including ancestral burial sites.[4] In September 2016, US District judge James Boasberg opined against the tribe's request for a preliminary injunction against construction. His opinion states that the permitting agency for that segment of DAPL, the Army Corps of Engineers (ACE), in coordination with the builder, Energy Transfer Partners (ETP), adequately consulted the tribe about any risks to cultural heritage.[5]

A close review of the information in the judge's opinion and knowledge of how US and corporate consultation processes work reveals another perspective: ACE and ETP did not allow sufficient time, resources, or attention to evaluate the environmental or cultural risks of the pipeline. They relied on assessment processes, modes of communication, and external consultants that—taken together—are known to lack sensitivity and accountability to Indigenous peoples' concerns, rights, and capacities to participate on genuinely equal footing with powerful private and government parties.[6]

The tribe's DAPL ordeal started before 2016. In 2012, the tribe made a resolution against future pipelines in relation to the movement to block the Keystone XL Pipeline;[7] since 2014, the tribe has rejected DAPL in a meeting with ETP and expressed concerns and objections to ACE.[8] Following the judge's September 2016 opinion, ACE temporarily halted construction and in November stated that "additional discussion and analysis are warranted in light of the history of the Great Sioux Nation's dispossessions of lands, the importance of Lake Oahe to the Tribe, our government-to-government relationship, and the statute governing easements through government property."[9] In December, ACE denied the easement for ETP to complete DAPL. ACE's decision by no means ended DAPL, however, as US president Donald Trump signed an order in January 2017 to support the pipeline, and shortly thereafter ACE reversed its decision, permitting DAPL's completion.[10]

While appearing as direct action or a standoff, many Indigenous persons whose work created the #NoDAPL movement say it is really about ceremony, prayer, and water protection. The meanings of English-language expressions such as "ceremony" and "water is life" arise from time-tested Indigenous knowledge that prescribe respectful moral relations with water and other non-human beings and entities as vital for securing human safety and well-ness. Robin Wall Kimmerer and Kathleen Dean Moore describe #NoDAPL as "a story that is so ancient it seems revolutionary."[11] Protectors know that "the land is sacred, a living breathing entity, for whom we must care, as she cares for us. And so it is possible to love land and water so fiercely you will live in a tent in a North Dakota winter to protect them."[12]

At the camps, the protectors endured violence at the hands of law enforce-ment and DAPL's private security, including being pepper sprayed, shot with rubber bullets, attacked by dogs, denied nourishment and supplies, threat-ened by lawsuits, and drenched with cold water during the onset of winter temperatures.[13] Many protectors have sacrificed fulfilling some of their per-sonal obligations at home, raising money to support theirs and others' par-ticipation.[14] Moreover, protectors withstood the frustrating realization that the #NoDAPL movement inevitably attracted some disingenuous allies who did not respect Indigenous knowledge, cultural protocols, and the wisdom of tribal elders.[15]

Away from the camps, many people have advanced #NoDAPL. Indigenous and allied academics created the free online Standing Rock Syllabus for edu-cators.[16] The American Friends Service Committee's report, *We Are Our Own Medicine*, demanded US interventions regarding violence against pro-tectors and the defective consultation process.[17] The United Nations Special Rapporteur on the Rights of Indigenous Peoples, Victoria Tauli-Corpuz, has called for the United States to halt construction of the pipeline and to honor the tribe's right to free, prior, and informed consent.[18]

Many more solidarity-building actions have been taken by diverse people everywhere. According to tribal chair David Archambault II, "Thousands of people—from members of the Standing Rock Sioux Tribe, tribes across the nation and First Nations in Canada, to non-Native supporters in the United States and around the world—have stood in solidarity against the harm and destruction caused by the Dakota Access Pipeline; we have stood side by side in peaceful prayer."[19]

The Injustice of DAPL

As a Potawatomi scholar-activist, I am concerned with how critics of #NoDAPL often focus on defending the pipeline's safety precautions, the many attempts ACE made at consultation, and US "rule of law." Many such critics even claim that it is tragic that US and corporate relations with the tribe broke down, given all the precautions and accommodations made by ETP and ACE.[20] Yet critics rarely engage what LaDonna Brave Bull Allard, in the epigraph to this chapter, calls "the larger story." To me, as an Indigenous supporter of #NoDAPL, part of the larger story concerns how DAPL is an injustice against the tribe. The type of injustice is one with which many other Indigenous peoples can identify—US settler colonialism.

I write this chapter from my own perspective to show at least some of the relevant reasons why DAPL is an injustice of a certain settler colonial type. I am against the view that the tribe's ordeal with DAPL is merely about a breakdown in consultative relations or an isolated disagreement over safety. Nick Estes discusses how the Mni Wiconi and #NoDAPL movements arose in the context of two centuries of the tribe's resistance to oppression.[21] I seek to show how there are many layers to the settler colonial injustice behind DAPL that will take me, by the end of this chapter, from US disrespect of treaty promises in the nineteenth century to environmental sustainability and climate change in the twenty-first century. Before addressing these inter-related issues, I begin with some more abstract definitions.

An *injustice* occurs when one or more groups of people seek to achieve their own perceived economic, cultural, and political aspirations by system-atically inflicting harm and risks on one or more other groups of people. Infliction is *systematic* when the perpetrators gains come at the expense of others under the conscious or tacit belief that doing so is acceptable because the others are of certain skin colors, cultures, genders, disabilities, and other social identities. Perpetrators often create and impose these social identities on people they perceive to be instrumental to or to standing in the way of the achievement of their aspirations. Racism is a type of injustice, then, as are sexism, able-ism, ethnocentrism, and settler colonialism.

Settler colonialism refers to complex social processes in which at least one society seeks to move permanently onto the terrestrial, aquatic, and aerial places lived in by one or more other societies who derive economic vitality, cultural flourishing, and political self-determination from the relationships they have established with the plants, animals, physical entities, and ecosystems of those places. When the process of settler colonialism takes place or has already occurred in a region, the societies moving in or who have already done so can be called "settlers"; the societies already living there at the beginning of settlement, "Indigenous peoples."

The settlers' aspirations are to transform Indigenous homelands into settler homelands. Settlers create moralizing narratives about why it is (or was) necessary to destroy other peoples (e.g., military or cultural inferiority), or they take great pains to forget or cover up the inevitable violence of settlement. Settlement is deeply harmful and risk-laden for Indigenous peoples because settlers are literally seeking to erase Indigenous economies, cultures, and political organizations for the sake of establishing their own. Settler colonialism, then, is a type of injustice driven by settlers' desire, conscious and tacit, to erase Indigenous peoples.[22]

The concept of settler colonialism highlights one type of injustice that has occurred widely throughout the world, with the United States a major example. The concept helps shed light on some key reasons why the tribe and many Indigenous peoples everywhere are justified in opposing DAPL. I am not using the concept to accurately represent or stereotype the motivations and histories of every non-Indigenous arrivant or immigrant to North America as only "settler." Neither am I suggesting that all oppression in the US context boils down to some struggle between settler and Indigenous populations, although a strong case can be made that in that context, it is more than just "white" people who are perpetrators in different ways of settler colonial injustice. I also do not use the concept to suggest that colonialism is exclusive from or more fundamental than other injustices, such as global imperialism, capitalism, racism, or patriarchy. An analysis more detailed than what I offer here would certainly attempt to intertwine them all, where appropriate.

Those qualifications aside, US settler colonialism emerges in the experiences of Indigenous peoples as a recent, highly disruptive type of injustice amid an exponentially longer history of our peoples' lives in North America. Indeed, Indigenous peoples everywhere in North America have long-standing traditions of comprehensive governance systems designed to relate to places with particular ecological conditions for the sake of ensuring cultural integrity, economic vitality, and political self-determination for current and future generations. In my own work, I look at how Indigenous governance systems operate quite differently from those of the US federal government, in operations ranging from selection processes for leadership to the construction of gender and gender fluidity to environmental ethics.

Indeed, the ceremonies at the #NoDAPL camps, expressions such as "water is life," the sacredness of the Black Hills, the leadership of women, and the many other moral claims about plants, animals, and ecosystems protectors are making arise from the time-tested knowledge of Dakota and Lakota governance systems that predate US settlement. From what I have learned through personal experiences with friends and colleagues and the writings of protectors cited earlier, Dakota and Lakota governance systems were organized to operate flexibly throughout the year to ensure that they were attuned to the dynamics of local ecosystems, especially seasonality. Lakota and Dakota peoples developed complex spiritual relationships with the places they still inhabit or live near that furnish highly practical knowledge of how to steward bison and grasslands and keep water clean. They developed ceremonies, such as giveaways, that reaffirm norms in which sharing, not hoarding, is incentivized, which some Indigenous studies scholars have shown to be integral to environmental sustainability.[23] Dakota and Lakota peoples' origin and other stories connect them intimately to places, such as the Black Hills and the place of sacred stones, in ways that are intrinsically valuable to their cultural flourishing and spiritual health. The water protectors' morality flows, then, from Indigenous governance systems that support cultural integrity, economic vitality, and political self-determination and the capacity to shift and adjust to the dynamics of ecosystems.

In the nineteenth century, US settlers sought to move to the places in which the Dakota and Lakota ancestors of the Standing Rock tribal members already had complex cultural, economic, and political relationships. US settlers had diverse motivations, such as fur trading, gold mining, farming, and establishing settlements beyond the so-called frontier. While peoples have had to adapt to different changes in different historic periods, such as the Indigenous adoption of the horse in North America, US settler colonialism viciously imposed harm and risks on the ancestors of the Standing Rock Sioux Tribe that have continued through the DAPL ordeal.

It is precisely this social process of settler colonialism that explains why it is no accident that ETP sought to build a key segment of DAPL through tribally significant lands and water systems. Many public resources document this history of settler colonialism, including the tribe's website, the Standing Rock Syllabus, the North Dakota studies portal, and conventional academic research.[24] In what follows, I briefly describe some of that history of settler colonialism to express my limited version of the "larger story" of the #NoDAPL movement, drawing widely from many public sources given that this information is, ironically, highly accessible to anyone but little known.

The Colonial Déjà Vu of Indigenous Erasure

Dakota and Lakota peoples historically maintained peaceful and conflictive diplomatic and trade relations with many other Indigenous peoples in the plains and woodland regions of North America and beyond. A different challenge emerged in the middle of the nineteenth century. Enter US settlers, who began overharvesting bison for furs to ship to distant markets without concern for the relationship between bison and bison habitat and the Dakota and Lakota peoples. When gold was discovered in California in the late 1840s, many more settlers arrived. In 1851 the federal government negotiated the first Treaty of Fort Laramie, with a limited number of Sioux leaders, to define territories in which each particular tribal group ranged according to its own governance system, which amounted to about 134 million acres in what are now the states of North Dakota, South Dakota, Montana, Wyoming, and Nebraska.

However, the United States refused to engage in a treaty-making process that would allow Indigenous leaders to reach consensus among themselves according to the protocols of their Indigenous governance systems. Settlers ended up violating the treaty repeatedly by entering the territory, and many tribal groups did not ultimately respect its non-consensus status. As a result of further settler immigration; military intervention; the construction of railroads, wagon roads, and mail stations; and the desire to explore for gold, the United States negotiated the 1868 Treaty of Fort Laramie. This treaty reduced the Indigenous land base to 25 million acres contained within what is now the state of South Dakota, forming the Great Sioux Reservation.

Despite the 1851 and 1868 treaties, settlers continued to enter Sioux lands illegally, disrupting Dakota and Lakota peoples. Analogous to the armed guards for DAPL builders who engage in constant surveillance of the protectors, the US military set up strategic positions, such as forts, to ensure that settlers could pursue their business ventures without encountering resistance. Again, instead of honoring the original treaty agreements, the United States forced the ancestors of the present-day Standing Rock Sioux Tribe to sever more of their relationships to the places that mattered to their cultures, economies, and political self-determination. The United States instantiated the 1877 Starve or Sell Bill, in which it self-authorized access to the Black Hills for gold mining.

With the passage of the Sioux Bill in 1889, the United States, wanting control over additional Indigenous places, liquidated the Great Sioux Reservation into six smaller reservations, with the Standing Rock one about 2 million acres. The lack of Indigenous consent to these actions led the US Supreme Court to claim in 1980 that a "more ripe and rank case of dishonorable dealings will never, in all probability, be found in our history."[25] The Sioux Bill, as the local instantiation of the Dawes Allotment Act (1887), further broke up the Standing Rock Reservation into private property (often 160-acre parcels) for tribal members, an effort intended to force Indigenous peoples to adopt farming lifestyles that would pose less resistance to settlement. Settlers took the rest of the parcels—usually the most arable lands.

The United States eventually made it impossible for immediate or extended family groups to manage allotments cooperatively. Tribal members could not sell their allotments for twenty-five years unless the United States deemed them "competent." The federal government developed many schemes to divest Indigenous persons of their allotments before the twenty-five years elapsed. Indigenous persons, who typically had to farm arid land and received inadequate support from the United States to transition to farming, were often considered so incompetent that government agents leased their land to settlers.

The United States required that Indigenous allotments be divided equally among the heirs, creating land that had too many owners to make use of the land. US agents also exercised tax codes corruptly, so that even Indigenous persons who were "declared competent" owed more in taxes than they could afford to pay. The large region of diverse and dynamic ecosystems from which Dakota and Lakota governance systems arose had been reduced in size exponentially; its ecological conditions were transformed as a result of mining, farming, grazing, and settler infrastructure.

Well into the twentieth century, the government and churches sent many Dakota and Lakota children to boarding schools, some as far away as Virginia and Pennsylvania. The schools divested students of their language, cultures, and knowledge, replacing them with technical skills for settler occupations. The children were sometimes physically abused or even murdered. Back in their homelands, the United States made Dakota and Lakota cultures "illegal" in 1883, including imposing a ban on giveaways and many other ceremonies that were vital for reaffirming land- and water-based ethics and knowledge of Indigenous governance systems. During this entire narrative, the US military frequently attacked Indigenous communities that continued to live according to their own governance systems, including the Massacre of Whitestone Hill (1863) referenced in the epigraph.[26]

Because of the economic pressures of the 1930s, which were felt nationally but were even more severe within tribes—a direct result of land dispossession from allotment—the United States sought to create new laws and programs on reservations. The Bureau of Indian Affairs (BIA), however, exercised control over economic development programs, such as community ranching and other land leasing, which often meant that tribal members got less money than they deserved through actions such as the BIA underselling to settler buyers.

The United States also created incentives for loan programs for tribes to consolidate lands and promote economic development, yet to access the money, tribes had to yield aspects of their political self-determination by organizing their governments according to US standards for corporate charters and elected tribal councils under the Indian Reorganization Act (1934). The BIA held authority over these councils' decisions, making tribes face the dilemma of choosing between certain immediate economic incentives and maintaining political self-determination. The Standing Rock Tribe initially rejected the act. In the late 1940s, ACE created a major dam as part of the Pick-Sloan Missouri River Basin Program, seeking to improve irrigation and other forms of water control to improve settlers' business ventures and living conditions. While many settlers benefited from the Lake Oahe Dam, its reservoir shrunk the tribes' land base, displacing many tribal members and destroying quality timberlands and soils for cultivation and wildlife habitats. From the beginning, Standing Rock leaders were adamantly opposed to the construction of the dam.[27]

As would any community that had faced these conditions for over 100 years, the people living on the tribe's reservation today endure high unemployment and heightened health risks that historically were not problems of comparable severity for their ancestors. US settlement sought to erase Dakota and Lakota peoples to make way for the business ventures and other aspirations of settlers.[28] It erased political self-determination by disrespecting treaties and pressuring for the adoption of BIA-controlled constitutions, erased economic vitality by transforming ecosystems and dividing Indigenous lands, and erased cultural integrity by stripping Indigenous peoples of their languages and ceremonies. Today, many settler Americans in North Dakota and South Dakota actually believe moralizing narratives which purport that Dakota and Lakota peoples are pathologically dependent on the United States for bare survival.[29] Public education in those states does not attend equally to Indigenous and settler histories, being complicit in covering up the violence of settlement. Acts of anti-Indigenous discrimination against many persons occur daily.[30]

Now imagine what it felt like for tribal members most immediately, but also for Indigenous peoples everywhere, when it became known that DAPL, a settler business venture, was rerouted from a location farther away from the tribe because of threats to the water quality of the settler city of Bismarck, North Dakota. Imagine how they felt when they learned that law enforcement was willing to step in to block protectors from expressing themselves through prayer, ceremony, and thanksgiving. Colonial déjà vu!

Environmental Injustice or the Ecology of US Settler Colonial Erasure

The women of the Brave Heart Society, White Buffalo Calf Woman Society, and Stone Boy Society describe DAPL as literally contributing to the physical erasure of Indigenous peoples—an ultimate outcome they will not allow.[31] Again, settler colonialism refers to complex social processes in which at least one society seeks to move permanently onto the terrestrial, aquatic, and aerial places lived in by one or more other societies who derive economic vitality, cultural flourishing, and political self-determination from the relationships they have established with the plants, animals, physical entities, and ecosystems of those places. Settler colonialism is an "environmental" injustice, for the US settlement process aims directly to undermine the ecological conditions required for Indigenous peoples to exercise their cultures, economies, and political self-determination. Ecological conditions refer to the complex relationships with place that are the substance of Indigenous governance systems.[32]

Settler-colonial tactics, expressed through their treaty making or allotment policies, and settler colonial technologies—from dams to mines to farming implements—literally change hydrological flows, soil nutrients, and many other ecological conditions. Changes in ecological conditions alter the way settlers perceive terrestrial, aquatic, and aerial places, which aids settlers' moralizing narratives and forgetfulness. Settlers perceive ecosystems, for example, simply as open lands and waters that belong to them so they can route a pipeline as long as it is safe or the tribe is consulted according to settler laws. They do not perceive ecosystems that continue to participate in relationships with Indigenous peoples—relationships that ultimately support Indigenous cultural integrity, economic vitality, and political self-determination.

If we unravel the settler colonial layers of DAPL even further, a more ecologically insidious dimension of US settler colonial environmental injustice becomes apparent. For numerous reasons—including settlers' lack of long-term knowledge of the environments they inhabit even years after settlement—they have transformed ecological conditions in ways that are not sustainable for themselves, Indigenous peoples, or anyone else. They have created ecological conditions that are key factors in crises relating to dangerous climate change, excessive pollution, and the decline of certain ecological processes and services (e.g., pollination, vegetation barriers, shade). In the US context, militarization and the agricultural, transportation, and extractive industries that were facilitated by broken treaty agreements, allotment, and boarding schools are the ones polluting and overusing lands and waters. Climate scientists have shown that the military and these industries play roles in contributing to increasing concentrations of greenhouse gas emissions in the atmosphere, a major cause of dangerous climate change.[33]

The destabilization of the climate system, or human-caused (anthropogenic) climate change, produces ecological conditions that disrupt human societies through impacts such as rising sea levels, more severe droughts, warming freshwater, and faster-melting glaciers. While all humanity should be concerned about climate change, many Indigenous peoples are among the populations whose safety and wellness are most immediately in peril. Indigenous peoples are among the first people to have to resettled, having to decide to relocate as a result of sea-level rise in the Arctic and the Gulf of Mexico. Warming reduces Indigenous access to culturally and economically significant plants and animals, such as moose (Great Lakes), salmon (Pacific Northwest), and many berries and traditional crops such as Timpsila (Great Plains).[34]

Thinking about its geographic and cultural proximity to Standing Rock, the Oglala Lakota Nation's climate-change program is concerned about drought in the region, leading to water scarcity as well as stress on tribal agriculture, ranching, and wildlife habitats. More severe storms may affect crop timing and forage production; extremely hot weather may create risks for elders and community members who practice seasonal ceremonies during hot months. Some plants, including ones used ceremonially, may disappear in certain areas.[35]

Moreover, we find that disproportionate Indigenous suffering is produced by changing environmental conditions and, once again, the machinations of US settler colonialism. Most relocating tribes, for example, are vulnerable precisely because they have been forced to live permanently on tiny areas of land with limited adaptive options. Members of the United Houma Nation and the Isle de Jean Charles Band of Biloxi-Chitimacha-Choctaw Indians in the Gulf of Mexico have been repeatedly confined by European and US settlers to small areas of land. The Isle de Jean Charles is one such location, an island that over time has shrunk, from 5 miles by 12 miles to ¼ mile by 2 miles, and faces continuing stresses from coastal erosion and saltwater intrusion associated with climate change.[36] Of course, the shrinking occurred initially before climate change because of US settler oil and gas companies dredging canals and cutting pipelines, public water-control infrastructure and flood-control measures, and industrial agriculture development. The United States continues to complicate the relocation process by failing to recognize both tribes as sovereign self-determining peoples, cutting both tribes out of resources and opportunities to take leadership in decisions about their own responses to the shrinking island and climate change.[37]

Tribes' loss of cultural and economic relationships with species such as moose and salmon occurs largely because their reservations are too small or fragmented to allow Indigenous communities to follow the species' movements, the species habitat moves into Canada, or the United States fails to honor treaties that are supposed to guarantee continued tribal access to the species despite changing ecological conditions. The Oglala Lakota Nation, in its description of its climate-change program, references land dispossession and jurisdictional limits as the reason why north-moving wildlife ranges and changes in berry and crop habitats will be problematic for it, as well as the reality that it has fewer resources to use for adaptation planning because of the legacies of US settler colonialism.[38] For the Standing Rock Sioux Tribe, as climate change becomes more apparent in its homelands, the shifting plant and animal habitats tied to agriculture, wildlife, and ceremonial species, as well as the loss of territory and resources as a result of US settler colonialism, will make it harder to adjust.

Climate change also opens up more Indigenous territories, such as in the Arctic, to pressure from colonial exploitation, as thawing snow and ice create access to resources—such as oil and other hydrocarbons—that were previously hard to access. This further oil exploration will likely lead to the same detrimental effects seen with past extractive industries. The workers' camps, or "man camps," created to support drilling and mining in regions like the Bakken intensify sexual and gender violence through increases in the trafficking of Indigenous women and girls.[39] Some of the sites of violence are the same North Dakota fields that seek to send oil down the DAPL.

Today, maps of the oil and gas pipelines attest to the sheer ecological disruption of US settler colonialism.[40] Even abandoned coal mines still leak carbon into the atmosphere.[41] Many of the "solutions" to human-caused climate change will affect Indigenous peoples adversely, as we see globally with the reemergence of hydropower in Asia as a clean energy solution and forest conservation programs in Africa—both of which often displace Indigenous peoples in those regions.[42] Dam development was one of the phases of settler colonial injustice against the Standing Rock Sioux Tribe through the Lake Oahe Dam.

Taking Up the Larger Story

Settler colonial injustice is environmental injustice. In this expansive sense, the tribe's ordeal with DAPL is far from over when we consider the larger story—a story that, depending on who tells it and how, can start in many places, such as the US settler disruption of time-tested Dakota and Lakota governance systems, and continue on through global climate change and environmental sustainability. US settler colonialism continues to work to erase Indigenous peoples culturally, economically, and politically. It is hard to distinguish US protection of gold miners from similar protections of DAPL workers and investors.

The #NoDAPL movement's significance extends beyond debates about the adequacy of the ETP's safety standards or ACE's discharge of its consultative duties. I believe the movement, together with Indigenous movements globally, has the power to motivate people to address the myriad forms of erasure that contribute to the operations of settler colonial injustice in sectors ranging from education and philanthropy to people's everyday comportment. LaDonna Brave Bull Allard's words are again deeply insightful: "We must remember we are part of a larger story. We are still here. We are still fighting for our lives on our own land."[43]

Notes

An earlier version of this chapter appeared in Red Ink: An International Journal of Indigenous Literature, Arts, & Humanities, Issue 19.1, Spring 2017 and we are grateful to the editor for permission to republish.

1. LaDonna Brave Bull Allard, "Why the Founder of Standing Rock Sioux Camp Can't Forget the Whitestone Massacre," September 3, 2016, accessed August 17, 2018, Yesmagazine.org.

2. "Dakota Access Pipeline," 2015, daplpipelinefacts.com; Scott Montgomery, "Victory at Standing Rock Reflects a Failure of US Energy and Climate Policy," December 5, 2016, accessed August 17, 2018, TheConversation.com.

3. Jonathan Thompson, "The Twisted Economics of the Dakota Access Pipeline," *High Country News*, November 29, 2016.

4. Standing Rock Sioux Tribe, "Standing Rock Sioux Tribe Condemns Destruction and Desecration of Burial Grounds by Energy Transfer Partners," *Indian Country Today Media Network*, September 4, 2016, accessed August 17, 2018, https://newsmaven.io/indiancountrytoday/archive/standing-rock-sioux-tribe-condemns-destruction-and-desecration-of-burial-grounds-tbGDUq4PWoaOVUZEiVIweA/; Chip Colwell, "How the Archaeological Review behind the Dakota Access Pipeline Went Wrong," November 20, 2016, accessed August 17, 2018, TheConversation.com/how-the-archaeological-review-behind-the-dakota-access-pipelne-went-wrong-67815.

5. James Boasberg, United States District Judge, *Standing Rock Sioux Tribe v. US Army Corps of Engineers*, Civil Action no. 16-1534 (JEB), 2016.

6. Colwell, "How the Archaeological Review behind the Dakota Access Pipeline Went Wrong"; James Grijalva, "Resistance, Resilience, and Reconciliation: Indigenous Human Rights to Environmental Protection in a Fossil Fuel Frenzy," *The Jurist*,

April 11, 2017, accessed August 17, 2018, http://jurist.org/forum/2017/4/James
-Grijalva-resistance-resilience-and-reconciliation-indigenous-human-rights-to
-environmental-protection-in-afrenzy.php.

7. Talli Nauman, "Sioux Nation Takes Stand on Keystone XL," *Native Sun News*,
February 24, 2012.

8. Amy Dalrymple, "Audio: Tribe Objected to Pipeline Nearly 2 Years before
Lawsuit," *Bismarck Tribune*, November 30, 2016; see also Boasberg, *Standing Rock
Sioux Tribe*, for details on instances when the tribe expressed objections to DAPL.

9. US Army Corps of Engineers, "Statement Regarding the Dakota Access
Pipeline," November 14, 2016, accessed August 17, 2018, https://www.usace.army
.mil/media/news-releases/news-release-article-view/article/1003593/statement
-regarding-the-dakota-access-pipeline/.

10. Steve Holland and Valerie Volcovici, "Trump Clears Way for Controversial
Oil Pipelines," *Reuters*, January 24, 2017.

11. Robin Wall Kimmerer and Kathleen Dean Moore, "The White Horse and
the Humvees—Standing Rock Is Offering Us a Choice," *Yes! Magazine*, November 5,
2016, accessed August 17, 2018, https://www.yesmagazine.org/people-power/the
-humvees-and-the-white-horse2014two-futures-20161105.

12. Kimmerer and Moore, "The White Horse and the Humvees."

13. "Dakota Access Pipeline Company Attacks Native American Protestors
with Dogs and Pepper Spray," *Democracy Now*, September 4, 2016; Derek Hawkins,
"Police Defend Use of Water Cannons on Dakota Access Protestors in Freezing
Weather," *Washington Post*, November 21, 2016; Eyder Peralta, "Dakota Access
Pipeline Protests in North Dakota Turn Violent," NPR, September 4, 2016; Mike
Nowatzki, "State Pulls Relief Resources from Swelling Dakota Access Pipeline
Protest Camp," *Bismarck Tribune*, August 22, 2016; Max Blau, Kalt Richmond, and
Marisa Russell, "North Dakota Pipeline: Protestors Vow to Stand Ground," CNN,
November 30, 2016; James MacPherson, "Dakota Access Pipeline Owners Sue
North Dakota Protestors," [Minneapolis] *Star Tribune*, August 16, 2016.

14. Joe Whittle, "'We Opened Eyes': At Standing Rock, My Fellow Native Americans Make History," *The Guardian*, November 30, 2016.

15. Valerie Richardson, "Complaints Grow over Whites Turning Dakota Access
Protest into Hippie Festival," *Washington Times*, November 28, 2016.

16. NYC Stands for Standing Rock Collective, "#StandingRockSyllabus," 2016,
accessed August 17, 2018, https://nycstandswithstandingrock.files.wordpress.com
/2016/10/standingrocksyllabus7.pdf.

17. Sharon Goens Bradley, Arlo Iron Cloud, Richard Iron Cloud, Margaret Jackson,
Jamie Bissonette Lewey, and Jeff Smith, *We Are Our Own Medicine*, American Friends

Service Committee, 2016, accessed August 17, 2018, https://www.afsc.org/sites/afsc
.civicactions.net/files/documents/We%20Are%20Our%20Own%20Medicine_1.pdf.

18. "United Nation Experts Validate Standing Rock Sioux Opposition to Dakota
Access Pipeline," *Indigenous Environmental Network*, September 23, 2016, accessed
August 17, 2018, http://www.ienearth.org/united-nation-experts-validate-standing
-rock-sioux-opposition-to-dakota-access-pipeline/.

19. Bradley et al., *We Are Our Own Medicine*, 2.

20. Patrick Springer, "ND Governor Says Pipeline Company 'Abdicated' Role
in Defending Project," *Grand Forks Herald*, December 8, 2016; Associated Press,
"Dakota Access CEO Vows to Truck on with Oil Pipeline Despite Violent Protests,"
Fox News, September 14, 2016; Montgomery, "Victory at Standing Rock"; Kevin
Cramer, "What the Dakota Access Pipeline Is Really About," *Wall Street Journal*,
December 6, 2016; Boasberg, *Standing Rock Sioux Tribe*.

21. Nick Estes, Our History Is the Future: Standing Rock versus the Dakota
Access Pipeline, and the Long Tradition of Indigenous Resistance (New York:
Penguin/Random House, forthcoming).

22. A reference featuring diverse scholarship on settler colonialism, including
from Indigenous studies and by Indigenous scholars, is Tate Lefevre, "Settler Colonialism," in *Oxford Bibliographies in Anthropology*, ed. John Jackson (Oxford: Oxford
University Press, 2015), 1–26, accessed August 17, 2018, http://oxfordindex.oup.com
/view/10.1093/obo/9780199766567.016.0125#fullTextLinks.

23. For example, Ronald L. Trosper, "Northwest Coast Indigenous Institutions
That Supported Resilience and Sustainability," *Ecological Economies* 41, no. 2 (2002):
329–44; Nick Estes, "Lakota Giving and Justice," *Old Wars*, November 16, 2015,
accessed August 17, 2018, https://therednation.org/2016/09/18/fighting-for-our
-lives-nodapl-in-context/.

24. Nick Estes's "Fighting for Our Lives: #NoDAPL in Historical Context," *Red
Nation*, September 9, 2016 (https://therednation.org/2016/09/18/fighting-for-our
-lives-nodapl-in-context/), provides a comprehensive account.

25. *United States v. Sioux Nation of Indians*, 448 US 371 (1980).

26. Allard, "Why the Founder of Standing Rock Sioux Camp Can't Forget the
Whitestone Massacre."

27. Robert Kelley Schneiders, "Flooding the Missouri Valley: The Politics of
Dam Site Selection and Design," *Great Plains Quarterly* 17 (1997): 3–4, 237–49.

28. Standing Rock Sioux Tribe, "Statistics," n.d., StandingRock.org; North
Dakota Department of Health, "North Dakota American Indian Health Profile,"
n.d., accessed August 17, 2018, https://www.ndhealth.gov/HealthData/Commun
ityHealthProfiles/American%20Indian%20Community%20Profile.pdf.

29. Jenni Monet, "Climate Justice Meets Racism: This Moment at Standing Rock Was Decades in the Making," September 16, 2016, accessed August 17, 2018, *Yesmagazine.org*, September 16, 2016, accessed August 17, 2018, https://www.yesmagazine.org/people-power/this-moment-at-standing-rock-was-decades-in-the-making-20160916.

30. Monet, "Climate Justice Meets Racism."

31. Women of the Brave Heart, White Buffalo Calf Woman, and Stone Boy Societies, "Lakota Women Call on President Obama to Stop Violence by Dakota Access Pipeline," *San Francisco Bay View*, September 12, 2016.

32. Indigenous studies offers a range of important accounts on what I call the ecology of settler colonialism. See, for example, Eve Tuck and K. Wayne Yang, "Decolonization Is Not a Metaphor," *Decolonization: Indigeneity, Education, and Society* 1, no. 1 (2012): 1–40.

33. The website of the Intergovernmental Panel on Climate Change can be found at https://www.ipcc.ch/.

34. Institute for Tribal Environmental Professionals, "Tribal Profiles," 2009?, can be found at http://www7.nau.edu/itep/main/tcc/Tribes/, accessed August 17, 2018; Kathryn Norton-Smith, Kathy Lynn, Karletta Chief, Karen Cozzetto, Jamie Donatuto, Margaret Hiza Redsteer, Linda E. Kruger, Julie Maldonado, Carson Viles, and Kyle P. Whyte, "Climate Change and Indigenous Peoples: A Synthesis of Current Impacts and Experiences," *Tech. Rep. PNW-GTR-944* (Portland: US Department of Agriculture, 2009), accessed August 17, 2018, https://www.fs.fed.us/pnw/pubs/pnw_gtr944.pdf?.

35. Institute for Tribal Environmental Professionals, "Prairies Region, Oglala Lakota Nation," 2009?, accessed August 17, 2018, http://www7.nau.edu/itep/main/tcc/Tribes/plns_oglala.

36. Julie Koppel Maldonado, "The Impact of Climate Change on Tribal Communities in the US: Displacement, Relocation, and Human Rights," *Climate Change* 120, no. 3 (2013): 601–14; Adam Crepelle, "Adam Crepelle (MPP '15) on the Struggle for Federal Recognition of Louisiana's Indian Tribes," Pepperdine Newsroom, December 12, 2016, accessed August 17, 2018, https://newsroom.pepperdine.edu/publicpolicy/2016/12/adam-crepelle-mpp-15-struggle-federal-recognition-louisiana%E2%80%99s-indian-tribes.

37. Maldonado, "Impact of Climate Change."

38. Oglala Lakota Nation, "Oyate Omniciyé: Oglala Lakota Plan," 2011, accessed August 17, 2018, http://www7.nau.edu/itep/main/tcc/docs/tribes/tribes_OglalaLakota.pdf.

39. Victoria Sweet, "Extracting More Than Resources: Human Security and Arctic Indigenous Women," *Seattle University Law Review* 37, no. 4 (2015): 1157–78; Sarah

Deer, *The Beginning and End of Rape* (Minneapolis: University of Minnesota Press, 2015).

40. American Petroleum Institute, "Pipelines," November 2016, accessed August 17, 2018, API.org.

41. "Abandoned Coal Mines Emit as Much CO_2 as a Small Power Plant," *Yale Environment 360*, June 27, 2016, accessed August 17, 2018, https://e360.yale.edu/digest/abandoned_coal_mines_co2_small_power_plant.

42. "Cambodia: Joint Indigenous Statement on Hydropower Dam Project," 2014, accessed August 17, 2018, https://iphrdefenders.net/joint-call-cambodias-indigenous-peoples-forced-evictions-indigenous-communities-kbal-romeas-village-lower-sesan-2-dam/; Richard Hendriks, Philip Raphals, Karen Bakker, and Gordon Christie. 2017. "First Nations and Hydropower: The Case of British Columbia's Site C Dam Project," *Items* (November 21, 2017), https://items.ssrc.org/first-nations-and-hydropower-the-case-of-british-columbias-site-c-dam-project/; Betsy Beymer-Farris and T. J. Basset, "The REDD Menace: Resurgent Protectionism in Tanzania's Mangrove Forests," *Global Environmental Change* 22 (2012): 332–41.

43. Allard, "Why the Founder of Standing Rock Sioux Camp Can't Forget the Whitestone Massacre."

About the Authors

Sophia Cheng is policy and research coordinator with the Restaurant Opportunities Center of Los Angeles (ROC-LA).

Jeff Crane is dean of the College of Arts and Sciences, Saint Martin's University. His recent books include *The Environment in American History* and *Finding the River: An Environmental History of the Elwha*.

Michael Egan teaches environmental history at McMaster University and is the author of Barry Commoner and the *Science of Survival: The Remaking of American Environmentalism* and, with Jeff Crane, editor of *Natural Protest: Essays on the History of American Environmentalism*.

Monica Mariko Embrey is senior campaign representative for the Sierra Club and formerly served as a climate and energy campaigner for Greenpeace USA, based in Charlotte, North Carolina.

Cody Ferguson is an assistant professor in the history department at Fort Lewis College and author of *This Is Our Land: Grassroots Environmentalism in the Late Twentieth Century*.

Hugh Fitzsimmons is a rancher who raises bison, along with a bevy of bees, on a 13,000-acre ranch in Dimmit County in south Texas. His memoir, *A Rock between Two Rivers: The Fracturing of a Texas Family Ranch*, appeared in 2018.

Paul Hirt is Senior Sustainability Scholar at the Julie Ann Wrigley Global Institute of Sustainability and professor of history at Arizona State University. His books include *The Wired Northwest, A Conspiracy of Optimism*, and the anthologies *Terra Pacifica* and *Northwest Lands, Northwest Peoples*.

Jill M. Holslin is a writer, photographer, and border activist who lives in Tijuana, Baja California, Mexico. Her work focuses on two issues: the US-Mexico border wall and urban art and culture in Tijuana.

Anna J. Kim is on the faculty of the School of Public Affairs at San Diego State University and winner of the 2018 William R. and June Dale Prize for Excellence in Urban and Regional Planning. Her articles have appeared in the *Journal of Applied Geography, Public Health Reports*, and the *Journal of Planning Literature*, among others.

Charles Laurier is the librarian of Lakeland Colleges–Japan Campus. He holds degrees from the University of Washington, the University of Iowa, and the School of the Art Institute of Chicago.

Bill McKibben is an author and environmentalist, founder of 350.org, and the Schumann Distinguished Scholar in Environmental Studies at Middlebury College. His many books include *Radio Free Vermont, Oil and Honey, Global Warming Reader*, and *Eaarth*.

Char Miller is the W. M. Keck Professor of Environmental Analysis and History at Pomona College. He is the author most recently of *San Antonio: A Tricentennial History, Not So Golden State: Sustainability vs. the California Dream, On the Edge: Water, Immigration, and Politics in the Southwest*, and *Seeking the Greatest Good: The Conservation Legacy of Gifford Pinchot*.

Jeffrey C. Sanders teaches in the history department at Washington State University. Among his publications are *Childhood and Environment in the Postwar American West* and *Seattle and the Roots of Urban Sustainability: Inventing Ecotopia*.

Brinda Sarathy is professor of environmental analysis and director of the Robert Redford Conservancy for Southern California Sustainability at Pitzer College. Her recent scholarship includes *Pineros: Latino Labour and the Changing Face of Forestry in the Pacific Northwest*.

Adam M. Sowards is professor of history at the University of Idaho and author of *Idaho's Place: A New History of the Gem State* (2014) and *The Environmental Justice: William O. Douglas and American Conservation* (2009).

Ellen Stroud is associate professor of history at Penn State University and author of *Nature Next Door: Cities and Trees in the American Northeast*, as well as numerous articles and chapters on environmental history.

Adam Tompkins is assistant professor of history at Lakeland College Japan in Shinjuku, Tokyo. His first book is *Ghostworkers and Greens: The Cooperative Campaigns of Farmworkers and Environmentalists for Pesticide Reform*, and he has had essays in *Natural Protest: Essays on the History of American Environmentalism* and the *Journal of the West*.

Kyle Powys Whyte holds the Timnick Chair in the Humanities and is associate professor of philosophy and community sustainability at Michigan State University. He is an enrolled member of the Citizen Powtawatomi Nation. His articles have appeared in journals such as *Climatic Change, Sustainability Science, Environmental Justice, Hypatia*, and *Ecological Processes*.

Index

Note: Page numbers in *italics* indicate illustrative material.